Employee Development Practice

We work with leading authors to develop the
strongest educational materials in Business,
bringing cutting-edge thinking and best learning
practice to a global market.

Under a range of well-known imprints, including
Financial Times Prentice Hall, we craft high
quality print and electronic publications which
help readers to understand and apply their
content, whether studying or at work.

To find out more about the complete range of our
publishing please visit us on the World Wide Web at:
www.pearsoneduc.com

Employee Development Practice

JIM STEWART

Reader in Human Resource Development
Department of Human Resource Management
at Nottingham Business School

FINANCIAL TIMES
Prentice Hall

An imprint of **Pearson Education**

Harlow, England · London · New York · Reading, Massachusetts · San Francisco · Toronto · Don Mills, Ontario · Sydney
Tokyo · Singapore · Hong Kong · Seoul · Taipei · Cape Town · Madrid · Mexico City · Amsterdam · Munich · Paris · Milan

For Pat, with love and gratitude

Pearson Education Limited
Edinburgh Gate
Harlow
Essex CM20 2JE
England

and Associated Companies throughout the world

Visit us on the World Wide Web at:
http://www.pearsoneduc.com

First published in Great Britain in 1999

ISBN 0 273 62811 9

British Library Cataloguing in Publication Data
A CIP catalogue record for this book can be obtained from the British Library.

10 9 8 7 6 5 4 3 2
04 03 02 01 00

Typeset by Land & Unwin (Data Sciences) Ltd.
Printed and bound in Great Britain by Redwood Books, Trowbridge, Wiltshire

CONTENTS

Foreword   vii

Acknowledgements   ix

1 Introduction   1
Purpose, aims and objectives · Readership · Structure and content

Part 1 THE CONTEXT OF EMPLOYEE DEVELOPMENT   7

2 Organisation, management and employee development   9
Introduction · Definitions · Summary and conclusion · Case study 2 · Suggested reading

3 The national context *by Bob Hamlin*   22
Introduction · A broad overview of national VET systems · Foundation VET for young
people · Continuing and further VET for adults · An international comparison of national
VET systems · Broad occupational VET systems: France · The general education system:
USA · Mixed system: Greece · The national VET system in the UK · An historical
perspective of the UK's national training system · The UK's national VET system:
1889–1979 · The UK's national VET system 1980–1998 · Industry training organisations
and lead bodies · Training and enterprise councils/local enterprise companies · Investors in
people (IIP) · National targets · A critical review of the UK's current national VET systems
· Observations and comments · A possible way forward · Summary and conclusion · Case
study 3 · Suggested reading

4 The organisation context   62
Introduction · The external context · The internal context · Summary and conclusion ·
Case study 4 · Suggested reading

5 The role and contribution of employee development   78
Introduction · The concept of role · The employee development function · Employee
development roles · Recent research · Applying the concept of role · Summary and
conclusion · Case study 5 · Suggested reading

Part 2 THE EMPLOYEE DEVELOPMENT PROCESS   97

6 Individual and organisation learning   99
Introduction · The science of psychology · Individual learning · Organisation learning ·
Summary and conclusion · Case study 6 · Suggested reading

Contents

7 Employee development: models and approaches   121

Introduction · The nature of a model · The Megginson model · The Ashridge research ·
The problem/solution model · Continuous development · The systems approach ·
Summary and conclusion · Case study 7 · Suggested reading

8 Establishing training needs   143

Introduction · Social and management research · The nature of training needs ·
Identifying training needs · Summary and conclusion · Case study 8 · Suggested reading

9 Design and implementation of employee development   163

Introduction · Use of objectives · Designing ED activities · Implementing development
activities · Summary and conclusion · Case study 9 · Suggested reading

10 Evaluating employee development contributions   178

Introduction · Evaluation – a central problem · Purposes of evaluation · The process
of evaluation · Problems with evaluation · Summary and conclusion · Case study 10 ·
Suggested reading

Part 3 MANAGING EMPLOYEE DEVELOPMENT   199

11 Employee development strategies   201

Introduction · Internationalisation of employee development · Action learning ·
The concept of the learning organisation · Summary and conclusion · Case study 11 ·
Suggested reading

12 Management development   219

Introduction · Management development – an overview · Management development –
definitions and meanings · Management development – approaches and methods ·
Management development practice · Summary and conclusion · Case study 12 ·
Suggested reading

13 Policy and ethics in employee development   240

Introduction · Employee development policy · The ethics of employee development ·
Ethics and ED policy · Summary and conclusion · Case study 13 · Suggested reading

14 Resourcing the ED function   261

Introduction · Costing and budgeting employee development · Physical resources ·
Specialist ED staff · Summary and conclusion · Case study 14 · Suggested reading

15 Conclusion   280

Introduction · Some significant themes · Success in IPD examinations · Summary and
conclusion

Bibliography   289

Index   301

FOREWORD

This book is a timely and welcome new addition to the emerging literature of the subject of Human Resource Development. It makes an important contribution in particular to the understanding of employee development within what can sometimes be a bewildering array of theories and concepts associated with the effective management of organisations. The context in which the book is written is a dynamic and fast-changing one; the business of human resources now is truly global because business itself is a globalised process.

At the recent world conference of the International Federation of Training and Development Organisations (IFTDO) there was serious discussion and a proposal that IFTDO should promote the idea of a World Summit of nations on training and development. The aim is to put development and learning on a par with the World Summit on Climate Change and the Environment as being fundamental to human development of the world as a whole. The IFTDO proposal for the need for such a World Summit is based on their prediction of fundamental shifts in the advanced economies of the world towards knowledge-based business while at the same time there is the growing dispersal of manufacturing capability to emerging economies. Whether such a Summit Meeting takes place is, of course, debatable but it indicates the scale of the significance now being attached to training and development.

In the United States the American Society for Training and Development (ASTD) has estimated the business value of training and development itself as a branch of business at some $6 billion per year and growing. Similarly, the future of HR in general is currently being widely debated and the significance of HR for business performance has been brought to the fore at a recent conference in the United States, where the prediction was made that within the next five years the movement between companies of HR executives will have as much influence on share values and prices as does currently the movement of chief executives. Indeed, there is at least one example in the UK whereby a prominent HR director moved in a deal like a football transfer to become chief executive of another company. When criticised over the move, his justification of the 'transfer fee' for his services was that it had been paid for instantly because on his appointment the share price of the company he joined had improved by 10p.

The sceptical reader may be musing on the old adage that 'one swallow does not make a summer' but there is clear empirical evidence from both the USA and the UK that the contribution of HR to business performance really does count and is growing in significance.

In a special issue of the US journal *Human Resource Management* (Volume 36, No 1), Dave Ulrich and Michael Losey considered the issue of the contribution to business of HR in the late 1990s. For some time it has been acknowledged in the literature of HRM that there is a need for the people management issues to be seen to play a strategic role in enhancing business performance. Thus it is not uncommon now for programmes in human resource development to contain substantial elements of business strategy. If HR is to prosper in the future, Dave Ulrich suggests, a number of key challenges face HR professionals that are very germane to these introductory remarks. In particular he argues that there is a clear and pressing need for better theorising on human resources, and for a stronger conceptual development that takes human resource development beyond what he calls 'mindless benchmarking', which we may equate with the time-honoured trainers' checklist approach. In addition to advancing theory that supports HR, he also argues eloquently on the challenge of developing a new range of HR tools – not the familiar trainer's toolkit, but rather the tools needed for 'the mastery of practice which is not yet defined'. Clearly, in both of these challenges, he is addressing the intellectual resources of HR. The third of his challenges to note is the need for continuing investment in the intellectual capital of HR. In its own particular way this book addresses aspects of these challenges laid down by Ulrich.

Elsewhere, Jim Stewart and I have strongly argued (Stewart and McGoldrick, 1996) the case for the development of new perspectives on HRD, for the intellectual space in which HRD can grow, and for the need to develop a new business vocabulary for HRD that allows human resource professionals to become a powerful influence on the strategic direction of organisations. In this new book, Jim Stewart has taken some of the issues on which we speculated much further, but has grounded them in a framework which is about the development of the next generation of professionals who will inhabit the world of human resource development.

The book makes no apology for building strong intellectual foundations for HRD. It develops a critical perspective that is always challenging in promoting the conceptual foundations of employee development in the bodies of knowledge from which we draw. It is also concerned to link theory and practice, and to ensure a bridging process between academic and professional perspectives.

The target audience for the book, as I mentioned above, is the group that we may define as the next generation of HRD professionals. Importantly, however, the book is not aimed at a closed market of training and development specialists but also addresses a broader community of interest among more mainstream business programmes.

The organisation of the text itself is both clear and concise, which is a characteristic of Jim Stewart's writing style. The narrative, tone and style enable some very difficult concepts and theories to be analysed and discussed in a clear way, without either baffling students with a complex jargon or over-simplifying difficult concepts. While it is in the nature of a written text to encourage learning that is based on reading and reflecting, the book also sets out a more interactive approach where the text is broken up by a number of exercises which, if done in the spirit in which they are written, are genuinely developmental. There are a number of mini case studies within the text overall and these are drawn from original and current research rather than 'made up' to illustrate a specific point the author wishes to make.

The timing of the publication of this book is fortunate. There is a sea change in public policy aimed at promoting the learning society, with initiatives in lifelong learning, social inclusion and ratcheting up of the nation's productive capability over a long-term perspective. The body of professionals using this book in their own career development will make a crucial contribution to these broader national developments and will have the benefit, it is hoped, of working in a society where individual, organisational and societal learning is at the heart of what we do.

Jim McGoldrick

ACKNOWLEDGEMENTS

There are a number of people I want to thank and acknowledge for their contribution in bringing this book to fruition. First, the reviewers of the original proposal and draft chapters. They steered the book in new and unplanned directions and, while I do not claim to have incorporated all of their comments, they certainly caused some heart-searching reflection. Second, my colleagues at Nottingham Business School for granting and covering my absence on a semester-long sabbatical which allowed the bulk of the book to be written. I want to thank Sally Sambrook, in particular, for allowing me to utilise some of her creative ideas in the book. I owe a debt of gratitude to Penelope Woolf, Sadie McClelland, her successor, and Liz Tarrant at Financial Times Management, for their support, encouragement and, above all, their patience. A fourth and enormous thank you to Jenny Fairbrother for her patience, skills and fortitude in turning my handwriting into excellent and readable printed text. Finally and, as always, thank you to Pat and Paul. Without your support, nothing is possible.

CHAPTER 1

Introduction

There are many reasons for writing this book. First, revisions by the Institute of Personnel and Development (IPD) to its syllabus related to the introduction of its Professional Qualification Scheme have provided an opportunity to address the subject of employee development afresh. I am, of course, not the first or only author to be attracted by that opportunity. The second reason is therefore more personal. As a Reader in Human Resource Development, I am paid to research and think deeply (hopefully!) about the subject. Being of the view that 'a fair day's pay deserves a fair day's work', I have done just that for more than two years. The book therefore reflects the results of my thinking and research, and has been written to share those results with a wider audience. I should, however, say at the outset that the content reflects my thinking more than my empirical research, since although the latter informs and influences the former, much of my research remains uncodified and unarticulated in the book. The ten or so case studies are the exception to this. A final reason for writing the book arises from my perception that the professional practice of employee development is in a state of flux. It may be that the fluidity associated with that state either is or will become established as normal in terms of the experiences of professional practitioners. Whatever the case may be, a state of flux provides opportunities to 'nudge' and 'push' in particular directions rather than others. This perhaps is the most important reason for the book. I hope and intend to have an impact on shaping the future of employee development, both as professional practice and as a field of academic enquiry and endeavour. This may seem rather arrogant, and it is certainly ambitious. However, with more than 20 years' experience as a professional practitioner, 12 of those within an academic environment focused on both researching the subject and educating future practitioners, I believe I have something worthwhile to contribute. This book is a medium to provide that contribution. In addition, and at the risk of being too 'open', I care about the subject, about those who practise it and about those, individually and collectively, who benefit or otherwise from employee development. This book is a means of putting that caring into practice.

Purpose, aims and objectives

I have opened the book by declaring my reasons for writing it. These give some indication of the purpose of the book. However, I think it is useful to devote particular attention to aims and objectives. Doing so reflects what is considered good practice in employee development and, therefore, declaring my purpose in specific detail will follow that practice. In addition, it will provide some means for readers to judge both the relevance and success of the book. The overall aims of the book are as follows:

- to introduce and explore concepts associated with and relevant to the syllabus of the IPD Employee Development module;
- to provide a practical and accessible exposition of key theories informing the professional practice of employee development;
- to provide a useful and useable resource to support the teaching and learning of employee development as an academic subject;
- to facilitate and support a critically informed examination of the theory and practice of employee development.

It will be worth expanding on these aims. They suggest a clear connection with the IPD syllabus, and this is deliberate. The book is intended to cover the ground indicated in the IPD specification. However, this does not mean that the syllabus has determined the content, or that I have provided either *all* the information or *only* information relevant to that syllabus. The book has an openly-declared purpose of preparing students for either IPD national examinations in employee development, or internally set and assessed examinations in universities which provide IPD accredited modules. This purpose is achieved, however, by my interpretation of the syllabus in terms of which are the *key* or *critical* concepts, and in terms of the understanding required to utilise and apply those concepts in professional practice.

This raises a second important point about the aims of the book. While the final aim explicitly assumes a separation between theory and practice, I am not at all certain that such a separation is either valid or useful. I share the IPD philosophy that professional certification must mean the ability to practise in the profession. Therefore my purpose in the book is to help equip individuals successfully to meet the expectations placed upon those performing specialist roles in employee development. This 'practice' orientation and purpose is reflected in the title of the book.

A final point on the IPD connection is to recognise that the book is intended to have relevance to and application in the study of employee development as a subject. This means that its content is not restricted to the IPD Employee Development Module but is intended to have value in the full range of employee development-related modules in the IPD qualification scheme. Particular chapters will, of course, have greater or lesser relevance to particular modules. However, as indicated above, the book is intended to support the teaching and learning of employee development as a subject rather than being restricted to one specific syllabus.

Two more points are worth articulating. First, I have attempted to create a resource which will be valuable both to those teaching and to those learning employee development. Although the book is written for those learning to practise employee development, I believe and hope that the content will include some insights and perspectives which will give pause for thought on the part of experienced teachers of the subject. I will not achieve my grand purpose of developing the subject unless this is the case. So my intention is that the book will provide a resource of interest and value to both teachers and learners in their joint examination and exploration of the subject.

The final point I wish to make about the aims of the book is that I wish to encourage alternative paradigms and perspectives to be applied to support critical thinking about the subject. I do not believe we can go very far with this at this moment, at least not in a book with an overt aim of supporting entry to professional practice through meeting the standards and requirements of a professional body. However, the subject will not progress and develop unless it is exposed to critical evaluation, and neither will professional practice. Therefore, I have deliberately introduced concepts and theories from outside mainstream treatments of employee development, and equally deliberately encourage their use in evaluating the validity and utility of mainstream treatments.

This statement and discussion of the aims of the book allows me to articulate my objectives. Again reflecting what is considered good practice in employee development, and indeed in teaching and learning practices in higher education, these are expressed in terms of what readers can expect to have achieved through using the book:

- to explain and analyse the national and organisational context of employee development;
- to describe, compare and critically evaluate a range of theories and concepts related to individual and organisational learning;
- to describe, compare and critically evaluate a range of approaches to and methods of applying employee development in practice;
- to identify, explain and critically evaluate the assumed functions and activities associated with managing employee development in the context of professional practice.

Readership

A primary readership for the book will be anyone studying employee development as part of their IPD qualification programme. This will include those studying in universities which provide their own postgraduate diploma or Masters degree courses approved by the IPD, as well as those preparing for the IPD national examinations. However, the book has not been written exclusively for this audience and other readers are envisaged and expected. In fact, all those who 'study' employee development, including academics, constitute the intended readership. It is, however, possible to identify some specific audiences.

It seems to be an increasing trend to include employee development in undergraduate studies, partly to seek accreditation for such programmes from the IPD. I have had in mind potential readers at undergraduate level, although I have assumed they will be final-year students who have either recent or current exposure to and experience of employment and/or management practices in work organisations. As already stated, the book is concerned with application. Therefore, its value to undergraduate studies will be limited to the extent that students can relate personal experience of work organisations to the content. This experience does not have to be in practitioner roles. However, the book has not been written to consider the subject at a purely or exclusively conceptual level, and achievement of its aims and objectives assumes and requires regular interaction between reader and text based on personal experience. The book is relevant then only to the extent that such interaction can be achieved.

There are a number of other postgraduate programmes where the book will be relevant. Perhaps the most obvious of these will be Diploma in Management Studies and MBA programmes which include human resource and/or employee development content, either as mandatory or elective modules. The book assumes no prior specialist knowledge or experience and therefore will be appropriate for and relevant to non-specialist readers. In addition, many universities offer well-established Masters degrees in the professional areas of human resource management and human resource development. Many of these specialist programmes require IPD membership at the point of entry, and the book is aimed primarily at those studying for such membership.

However, the book will be valuable for specialist and post-IPD Masters programmes, for two reasons. First, some students on such programmes will not be specialist employee development practitioners and may not have studied the subject at IPD level. Second, even those who are specialists are likely to have been exposed to traditional or mainstream treatments. The inclusion of alternative perspectives and encouragement of critical evaluation will provide a fresh look at the subject, and one which may lead to a questioning of established beliefs and practices. Therefore, the book will have value in advanced studies of the subject.

A final group of intended and expected readers is that of professional practitioners not involved in a course of formal study. The points made in the previous paragraph on a fresh look at the subject, and the practice orientation of the book already emphasised, provide sound reasons for the book's relevance to practitioners. It is not assumed that all readers will be students, and the content and design of the book does not require that to be the case. It can be read and used by practitioners who are not also, formally at least, students, and it is hoped it reaches such a readership.

Structure and content

There are two levels of structure to be aware of: the overall organisation of the content and the common structure of each of the substantive chapters. Each will be dealt with in turn.

The book is organised into three parts. This reflects a personal view of how the subject of employee development can be usefully categorised. The categorisation also reflects a personal view on how the various elements of the IPD syllabus relate to each other. In the sense of 'a personal view', the categorisation is purely arbitrary, and other possibilities are recognised and acknowledged. However, the categorisation does have a logic which, from experience, seems to work. The three parts to the book are as follows:

- Part 1 The context of employee development
- Part 2 The employee development process
- Part 3 Managing employee development.

Part 1 is concerned with factors, issues, concepts and theories which *affect* the professional practice of employee development. The book is premised on a view that employee development is subject to many influences, whether it is viewed as an academic subject or as an area of professional practice.

Chapter 2 sets the subject in the context of organisation and management theory, and provides some working definitions. Governments have policies related to vocational education and training (VET) which can and do influence professional practice. Similarly, while organisations provide unique contexts, there are common factors associated with processes of organising and managing which create potentials and limit the possibilities of and for employee development. Each of these contexts – the nature of organisation and management theory, government policies and initiatives, and organisational conditions – have an impact upon and influence the roles adopted by professional practitioners. A chapter is devoted to each set of influencing factors and Part 1 closes with a chapter examining the potential and actual roles and contributions of employee development.

Part 2 is concerned with the 'what' and 'how' of employee development. It is therefore concerned with the *processes* of professional practice. A sound understanding of learning lies at the heart of professional practice and so Part 2 begins with an examination of learning theories in Chapter 6. Chapters 7–10 form the rest of Part 2. Individual chapters are devoted to a consideration of the specialist activities in which practitioners engage as part of their professional role. How these activities are undertaken will be influenced to some extent by particular models of employee development, and these are explored and analysed in Chapter 7. The activities of identifying training needs, designing and implementing interventions and evaluating employee development are examined in Chapters 8, 9 and 10.

Part 3 focuses on those activities that might be associated with managing employee development. Thus, design and implementation of development strategies are explored in Chapters 11 and 12. The two critical activities of formulating policy and resourcing the function form the subject of Chapters 13 and 14. The former includes an examination of 'ethics' and how that concept relates to policy, while the latter considers resources under the traditional headings of physical and human. The book's concluding chapter, as well as attempting to draw together some threads, speculates about future directions for the subject and the profession.

Each substantive chapter (that is all except this one and the conclusion) follows a common structure. This includes the following features:

- Introduction
- Objectives
- Main content
- Activities
- Summary and conclusion
- Case study
- Suggested reading.

The introduction sets the scene for the chapter and outlines its main purpose. This is then translated into a set of specific objectives. Readers are encouraged to check and assess whether these are achieved as they work through the chapters. The main content of each chapter is interspersed with 'activities'. These are designed and intended to encourage exploration and application of the concepts discussed in the main content. They are also, in many cases, sequential and cumulative; that is, in any given chapter, Activity 3, for example, will assume that Activities 1 and 2 have been completed. However, they are not sequential and cumulative in terms of the book, although the main content is intended to have that feature.

Completing the activities within each chapter is essential if the chapter objectives are to be achieved. It is possible to read the main content and ignore the activities. However, this will not serve any of the purposes of the book. Most activities refer to 'your organisation'. This can be taken to mean any organisation with which you are familiar. Most also refer to 'a colleague', sometimes with an instruction that this means a work colleague. In the absence of this instruction, 'a colleague' is meant to indicate someone with whom you are studying and who also carries out the activity. If either of these presents a problem (that is, you are not a student and/or you do not have work colleagues) then any other person can and will serve a valuable purpose. The important and critical requirement is that you *discuss* your responses to activities with some other person who will have views on the topic.

Each chapter closes with a summary of the main arguments and an application case study. All case studies have two features in common. First, they are based on recent or current research and therefore present actual scenarios experienced by professional practitioners. Second, they are written from the perspective of the practitioner involved. The intention is to encourage identification with the problems and issues encountered in professional practice. The purpose of the case studies is to facilitate discussion at least of applying the concepts examined in the chapter. They also serve the purpose of illustrating the practical implications of theoretical concepts.

Given the points made about activities and case studies, it will be clear that they are an essential and integral component of the book. They are certainly important in achieving the objectives of the book and individual chapters. The book as a whole has a logical structure and sequence. My expectation and advice, therefore, is that the book should be read and worked through from start to finish. However, it is recognised that alternative categorisations are possible, and so a different order might be chosen. In addition, particular parts and/or combinations of chapters may have specific relevance for particular modules or courses of study or issues being faced in practice.

This book is concerned with the professional practice of employee development, and definitions are addressed in Chapter 2. However, it should be made clear as a final introductory point that the book is not concerned with employee development schemes such as those researched and promoted by the Department for Education and Employment (DfEE, 1995b, 1996). That work, in my view, suggests a narrow definition of the concept of employee development. This book addresses a much wider and more eclectic conceptualisation of employee development.

As part of this eclecticism, Chapter 2 examines potential and possible meanings of the concepts of *organising* and *managing*, as well as of employee development. In doing so, it introduces a variety of paradigms which lead to differing perspectives on the meaning of the concepts and therefore plays an important role in setting the scene for the rest of the book.

PART 1

The context of employee development

Organisation, management and employee development

Introduction

What exactly is employee development (ED) and why does it matter? Seeking to answer these questions will help us gain an understanding of the nature and scope of employee development, and what it is that development professionals are trying to achieve through their practice. However, it is important to recognise that right answers do not exist. As we will see later in this chapter, varying perspectives on the nature and purpose of organising and managing influence views on the professional practice of employee development. The existence of varying perspectives, as well as denying the possibility of single, correct answers, also means that the questions are much more complex than they might appear. So too, therefore, will be the process and outcome of answering them. One consequence of this complexity is that, in the end, professionals have to examine the arguments for themselves, make their own judgements and reach a personal understanding. It is important to remember these points as the arguments and analysis presented in this chapter unfold. These points also determine the following learning objectives which the chapter is intended to achieve.

CHAPTER OBJECTIVES

- Explain varying perspectives on the nature of organisations and the purpose of management.

- Analyse and critically evaluate a range of understandings of the meaning of employee development.

- Articulate and justify a personal position on the nature and purpose of employee development.

Definitions

The examination of the professional practice of ED cannot proceed without a shared understanding of the meaning of some relevant and important concepts being established. However, remembering the points made in the introduction, it is important first to establish the status of the definitions which will be used in the rest of the book. These definitions will be decided on the basis of their **utility**; that is, they will be useful in serving the purpose of the book. They are not the only, nor necessarily the best, descriptions of the concepts being applied; rather, they are the author's preferred definitions.

The professional practice of ED occurs primarily, though not exclusively, in the context of organisations. The concept of 'organisation' itself is bound up with other, related concepts such as 'management' and, by association, with ideas to do with 'goals', 'strategy' and 'functions'. We will examine some of these in more detail in Chapter 4. However, they are important here too since definitions of 'organisation', for example, influence and shape definitions of employee development.

Organisation

One of the most interesting ways of conceptualising the meaning of 'organisation', or thinking about the term, is through the use of metaphor. The value of doing this has been clearly demonstrated by Gareth Morgan (1997) in his seminal work *Images of Organization*. Morgan suggests that, among others, four metaphors have been, both in the past and currently, particularly powerful. These are organisations as machines, as living organisms, as brains and as cultures. And because these metaphors are so powerful they have been influential in approaches to the design and management of organisations. This influence derives from the fact that metaphors are used only to not **describe** organisation but also to **define** the concept. In other words, the power of metaphor leads to the belief that organisations *are* machines, or brains or organisms. Once the metaphor becomes the defining characteristic of the meaning of the concept, it also determines beliefs about the purpose of organisations and how best to manage them.

Activity 2.1

Think about the implications of defining organisations as machines.

1 What might this lead to in terms of beliefs about the overall purpose of organisations?

2 How will the metaphor influence the design of organisations?

3 What effect will the metaphor have on the way managers approach their job and the way they relate to and interact with their staff?

4 Given the responses to these questions, what are the implications for the practice of employee development?

We can perhaps illustrate the powerful influence of metaphor by briefly examining the implications of conceiving organisations as 'brains'. Applying this metaphor leads to an emphasis on information processing and thus a concern with ensuring efficient and effective communication systems and processes. The focus of these systems and processes, as with a brain, will be both external (i.e. the environment in which the organisation operates) and internal (i.e. the functioning, health and performance of the organisation itself). This internal focus is related to a further consequence of the brain metaphor, in that decision making and decision-making processes are seen as important functions within organisations because the quality of decisions (again as with a brain and its host organism) will affect the immediate and long-term survival of the organisation.

Application of the brain metaphor, deliberate or otherwise, can be seen in analyses of organisations as decision-making systems such as those provided by Simon (1960) or Weick (1979). The former introduced the concept of 'bounded rationality' and the latter the idea of 'enacted environment', both of which in different ways argued limits to the rationality of organisation decision making. Weick in particular draws on the psychology of individual decision making, thus, implicitly at least, applying the brain metaphor to the analysis of organisations.

Perhaps the latest application of the metaphor, certainly of interest to this book, is the developing idea of 'learning organisations'. This will be examined in more detail in a later chapter. What can be said for now is that the idea itself is utilised by Morgan (1997) as an example of the brain metaphor being used. In his support, two illustrations are suggested. The first is the direct application by Garratt (1988) in his work on the learning organisation, in which he labels directors collectively as the 'business brain'. The second comes from Pedler, Boydell and Burgoyne (1991) who include the role of 'boundary workers' as 'environmental scanners' in their specification of the characteristics of a learning company. This seems to directly reflect the arguments made earlier of organisations as information-processing systems and the importance attached to internal communication about external factors.

Working with Gibson Burrell, Morgan has produced an additional and complementary way of categorising varying perspectives on organisation (Morgan, 1995). This categorisation utilises the concept of paradigms, which can have multiple meanings, some simple and some complex. For Morgan, the term is used in the sense of denoting a particular and specific view of the world and reality. It is important to understand, however, that any particular world view can be, and usually is, implicit because paradigms are associated with and derived from assumptions which are taken for granted. In other words, individuals are commonly unaware that they adopt a paradigm at all, or of the nature and characteristics of the particular paradigm to which they hold, because they are unaware of their assumptions. The fact that such assumptions are taken for granted means that they are rarely, if ever, brought into conscious awareness, and are, therefore, rarely questioned, tested or challenged. Because paradigms are associated with and derived from such assumptions, the same is therefore true of paradigms. Thus, each of us unconsciously brings our particular paradigm to our understanding and analysis of the concept of organisation.

Activity 2.2

In his work on organisation culture, Edgar Schein (*see* Brown, 1998) proposes the notion of 'basic assumptions' which individuals hold in relation to five critical dimensions or factors. While recognising that basic assumptions are by definition difficult to access and articulate, you will find it useful to attempt to identify your own by answering the questions overleaf.

▶

1 To what extent are human beings in control of their environment and vice versa?

2 What is the nature of 'truth' and 'reality' and how, if at all, can each be established?

3 To what extent is human behaviour governed by material motives, and how variable is this?

4 What is the purpose and value of formal work activity *vis-à-vis* alternative activities?

5 How should individuals relate to and interact with each other? To what extent, if at all, should this vary according to context, e.g. work, family, friends, neighbours?

Burrell and Morgan (Morgan, 1995) propose a categorisation of four broad world views, or paradigms, which have and do influence social analysis and the development of social theory. Since organisation is a social phenomenon, the same is obviously true of organisation theory and analysis. The basis of the categorisation, or typology, is the application of two dimensions. The first concerns assumptions about the nature of science and the establishment of truth, while the second focuses on the nature of society and other social systems. Assumptions about science can vary according to the degree to which science is held to be objective or subjective. Assumptions about society can vary according to the degree to which society is held to be concerned with regulation and stability or with radical change. Application of these two dimensions gives rise to formulation of four paradigms, described below.

The functionalist paradigm

This paradigm assumes an objective, social reality which can be empirically analysed and understood through application of scientific methods. Social systems are seen as inherently concerned with stability and continuity and therefore as developing institutions which serve regulatory purposes.

The interpretive paradigm

By contrast, the interpretive paradigm assumes that social reality has no concrete or objective existence. Rather, it is the case that social reality is created subjectively by individuals and their interactions. Through this process, multiple social realities are created, maintained and changed. Therefore, in organisational terms, there is no single, objective entity to be analysed and understood. However, in common with the functionalist paradigm, the interpretive paradigm assumes an underlying pattern and order in the social world and therefore is nearer the regulation pole rather than the radical change pole of the 'nature of society' dimension.

The radical humanist paradigm

The third paradigm shares with the interpretive paradigm assumptions about science and the nature of truth. This paradigm, too, assumes reality is socially and subjectively created and is therefore not capable of objective analysis. However, the radical humanist paradigm views social institutions as negative in the sense of constraining and controlling human thought, action and potential. These negative attributes lead to alienation rather than positive outcomes. Therefore, there is a concern in this paradigm with radical change rather than with regulation.

The radical structuralist paradigm

We have seen so far a paradigm associated with objective science and regulation (functionalist), one associated with subjective science and regulation (interpretive) and one associated with subjective science and radical change (radical humanist). It will come as no surprise, therefore, that the final paradigm, radical structuralist, lies at the objective science and radical change poles of the two dimensions. This paradigm shares with the radical humanist paradigm a set of assumptions that social systems so far developed by human beings are oppressive and alienating. The paradigm further assumes an inherent drive for radical change in society (and organisations). However, this paradigm also assumes that social systems have independent, concrete and objective existence and are therefore capable of scientific analysis.

It should be clear, as Morgan argues, that these different and varying paradigms will and do have important implications for the study and analysis of organisations. Given that, adoption and application of a particular paradigm will have consequences for prescriptions on organisation design and how to manage them. For example, it is probably true that the vast majority of textbooks on management (that is, books which seek to provide prescriptive advice on how to manage organisations) adopt a functionalist perspective. What is also probably true is that writers of such books rarely declare that they are in fact applying the functionalist paradigm, largely because in most cases they are unaware of doing so. However, it is important for serious study of organising and managing to be aware of the existence of varying perspectives and to be able to recognise which paradigm is being applied in any particular piece of writing.

There are two additional perspectives which need to be mentioned before coming to a declaration of the paradigm and associated definition to be applied in this book. The first is a resurgence of interest within organisation studies and analysis in using the concepts and perspectives of what is termed 'critical studies'. Using the Burrell and Morgan typology, this would probably fall into the radical humanist paradigm. An excellent description, exposition and analysis of this perspective can be found in Alvesson and Wilmott (1996). The second is the more recent but increasingly significant line of academic enquiry and writing known as postmodernism. This 'world view' questions and challenges most, if not all, of the assumptions informing most, if not all, of the established paradigms, perspectives and traditions in research and writing on organisations and management. If pressed to categorise postmodernism in terms of the Burrell and Morgan typology, the radical humanist would seem to come closest, which probably reflects the areas of commonality between the two perspectives (Alvesson and Deetz, 1996). Two fairly recent books by Tony Watson (1994) and Karen Legge (1995) provide clear expositions of postmodernist ideas in organisation analysis in ways which have particular relevance for the study of employee development. A more generic though detailed exposition can be found in Chia (1996), although the treatment offered there will be perhaps too academic for some.

Activity 2.3

Think about the implications of adopting and applying the interpretive paradigm of Burrell and Morgan and, in particular, its assumptions concerning social reality.

1 What will this mean in terms of the purpose or purposes of organisations?

2 How will application of the paradigm influence organisation design?

3 What might be the consequences of **1** and **2** for the practice of employee development?

The rather lengthy examination of the concept 'organisation' is important because it allows us to reach two significant conclusions. First, that all analyses of and prescriptions for organising and managing are provisional and contested. To illustrate the meaning of this assertion, we can say that there are very few educated people who would argue that the world is flat. We can be (fairly) certain therefore of two things: that the world is in fact round, and that if we say so we will not be argued with. Neither, though, is true of organisation and management theory. There are competing perspectives and paradigms and therefore there is scope for disagreement and argument. Since there are legitimate grounds for argument, we cannot be **certain** that any particular perspective is right, and therefore we must treat each as provisional.

The second conclusion is a particularly significant and important example of where disagreement exists. It concerns the nature of existence that we can and do attribute to organisations. Common sense and everyday use of the concept is built on an assumption that organisations have independent, objective existence. Thus, we talk and write of '*the* organisation' and '*organisation* goals and strategies'. Our use of language creates the idea of an organisation as an 'it', i.e. an objective entity. I believe however, that any application of intelligent thought would tend to support a view that organisations do not have the same existence as material objects in the world, even though our language use does not differentiate between them. This view can be contradicted and argued against if, for example, a functionalist paradigm is adopted. Thus we can conclude that a critical area of dispute in the study of organisations and management is whether organisations are conceptualised as objective or subjective entities.

I have begun to indicate my views already. It seems important to me to accept the fact of everyday speech. I also believe that conceptualising organisations as objective entities has value. This means that it is easier to think about, analyse and decide upon action in relation to organisations if we treat them **as if** they have independent existence. All of this is in the context of a firm persuasion that work organisations, in common with other forms of social organisation such as the family or society, are the subjective creation of subjective human beings. This leads to the following definition of organisation which will be the one to be generally applied in the rest of the book.

Organisations are collections of individuals arranged into a regular and recognisable system of relations for the purpose of producing and/or providing some economic goods or services. The system of relations normally reflects two characteristics: application of the concepts of employer and employee, and institutions to govern the distribution and use of power and authority.

This definition is, primarily, within the functionalist paradigm. It does, however, allow for the application of alternative perspectives. While the major part of the book, following the definition, will be in the functionalist tradition, alternatives will be used regularly to critically evaluate the validity and utility of functionalist analyses.

Management

It will be obvious by now that the concept of management, or more accurately **managing**, is inextricably bound up with ideas about organising and organisations. The connections between the two have been argued to be central to the development of modern societies (Drucker, 1977). That being the case, we can limit the examination of the concept since much of the previous section has relevance and application here.

My own definition is as follows.

Management, or managing, is essentially a process of agreeing and achieving organisation objectives.

(Stewart, 1996, p. 8)

There are two points to be made about this definition. The first is a simple one in that the application of the concept of organisation as objective entity is clearly evident. The second is a little more complex.

In most textbooks, managing is assumed to be a technical, impartial, instrumental and neutral process and set of activities (Alvesson and Wilmott, 1996). Analyses produced on managing therefore tend to focus on providing technical prescriptions and solutions to what are defined as purely technical problems, for example, to do with overcoming resistance to change (Burnes, 1996). Such analyses are concerned with only and exclusively the second part of my definition, i.e. the efficient and effective *achievement* of organisation objectives. The first part of the definition recognises that objectives initially have to be formulated and *agreed*.

Much writing on management starts from a point that objectives can be assumed. For example, industrial and commercial organisations will, it is assumed, seek to survive, grow and prosper. These objectives will be measured in economic and financial terms, for example, turnover, profit levels, return on investment, market share and shareholder value. In public service and voluntary organisations the measures may be different, although perhaps still expressed in the language of economics and finance, but the basic objectives of survival and growth are still assumed. My definition is intended to indicate that organisation objectives need not be, and often in practice are not, taken for granted. Managing can and does involve the engagement of competing interests in a political process out of which organisation objectives emerge (Watson, 1994). In addition, human beings can, individually and collectively, decide to value and pursue any objectives they wish, including non-economic purposes. Therefore, as Alvesson and Wilmott (1996) argue, the formulation and agreement of objectives calls into question established and prevalent conceptions of managing as being a professional activity solely concerned with means rather than ends. Focusing on questions to do with objectives (i.e. ends), as well as techniques (i.e. means), makes clear that managing is more problematic than many texts assume.

A related point arises out of these arguments. It is simply that they suggest that there is no need to assume a necessity for *managers* or *management* (as a collective noun) in organisations. *Managing* as a process of agreeing and achieving objectives, according to my definition, has to occur. However, this does not logically imply that particular positions or formalised roles have to exist or be created, or that particular individuals have to be designated to perform such roles. Alternative arrangements are possible. To close this discussion of the concept of management, reference can be made to recent and more populist analyses of organisations and their role in society which have also called into question the assumptions concerning the primacy of economic goals (Handy, 1994) – which were until recently taken for granted.

Education, training and development

We now come to examining and defining concepts which are more central to the professional domain with which this book is concerned. We begin with what might be termed standard definitions.

Activity 2.4

1 Produce your own definition of the following words:

(a) education

(b) training

(c) development.

2 Examine your definitions and identify what is similar and what is different when each is compared to the others.

3 Using the results of **2**, specify the critical, defining characteristics of each word which differentiate it from the others.

4 Assess the importance or significance of the defining characteristics in terms of their implications for the practice of employee development.

Education

Education is defined as activities which aim to develop the knowledge, skills, moral values and understanding required in all aspects of life rather than a knowledge and skill relating to only a limited field of activity.

(MSC, 1981, quoted in Reid and Barrington, 1997, p. 7)

Training

Training is a planned process to modify attitude, knowledge or skill behaviour through learning experience to achieve effective performance in an activity or range of activities. Its purpose, in the work situation, is to develop the abilities of the individual and to satisfy the current and future needs of the organisation.

(MSC, 1981, quoted in Reid and Barrington, 1997, p. 7)

Development

> Developing people as part of an overall human resource strategy means the skilful provision and organisation of learning experiences, primarily but not exclusively in the workplace, in order that business goals and organisational growth can be achieved.
>
> Such development must be aligned with the organisation's vision and longer term goals in order that, through enhancing the skills, knowledge, learning and innovative capability of people at every level, the organisation as well as the individual can prosper.
>
> (Harrison, 1997, p. 7)

A cursory examination and comparison of these definitions reveals many similarities. All focus on concepts such as knowledge, skills and understanding. Two directly refer to learning, while the third, education, could be said to imply learning since the activities referred to are intended to develop knowledge and skills, among other characteristics. The definitions of training and development share a focus on and concern with the needs of organisation and work. Perhaps the only difference of significance between the three definitions is the reference to 'all aspects of life' in the MSC definition of education. Comparing the two MSC definitions also makes clear that this wider focus is seen by those authors at least as the critical differentiating feature between education and training. However, relying on this feature as a defining characteristic can have problems. Consider, for example, the apparently ceaseless emphasis on ensuring that compulsory education is relevant to the needs of employers and employment, and the associated developments in higher education which similarly emphasise vocational relevance and preparation for the 'world of work' in undergraduate studies. Relatedly, in the field of business and management at least, there are reported increases in the use of formal, qualification-based programmes for management development and an increasing number of partnerships between education providers (business schools in universities) and employing organisations to tailor content and delivery of such programmes (Thomson et al., 1997). In addition, if we look at what might be considered to fall in the domain of development rather than education, we can find examples which question the distinction. Perhaps the best illustration of this is the following quotation.

> WARNING: participating in a self-development programme might change your life . . . We hope it will.
>
> (Megginson and Whitaker, 1996, p. 28)

Of course it may be argued that self-development programmes are not necessarily associated with employing organisations. However, such programmes are argued to be both increasingly relevant and common (Stewart, 1996) and the context from which the quote is taken is employer-sponsored and organisation-based programmes. So, we can conclude that to think uncritically about the meaning of important concepts can lead to definitions and claimed or assumed differentiating characteristics which do not hold up to scrutiny. As Rosemary Harrison (1997) argues, finding or establishing either accurate or acceptable definitions is no easy matter.

A further complicating factor is the growing interest in and use of the term Human Resource Development (Stewart and McGoldrick, 1996a). Harrison (1997) almost abandons the use of the term 'employee development', apart from the title of her book, in favour of HRD. One of her reasons for doing so is the argued growing importance of non-employee development (Walton, 1996), i.e. those individuals and groups important to the organisation but who are not included in the standard employer-employee relationship, for example, self-employed subcontractors, suppliers, agents and distributors. For this and other reasons I am in agreement with Harrison that HRD is a more useful term. Making that statement creates a dilemma, however. It is that, as well as education, training and development, I now have to define and differentiate employee development and HRD. I do, however, have a very simple solution.

I have argued elsewhere that debate over the meaning of and differences between education, training and development is futile and unproductive (Stewart, 1992). What is more significant and important is what they have in common, which is a focus on influencing the learning processes of individuals and organisations. In the same work I proposed a tentative model of HRD which, among other purposes, allows education, training and development to be encompassed within the concept of HRD. The model is reproduced in Fig. 2.1. It provides a graphic representation of the following definition.

Human resource development encompasses activities and processes which are *intended* to have impact on organisational and individual learning. The term assumes that organisations can be constructively conceived of as learning entities, and that the learning processes of both organisa-

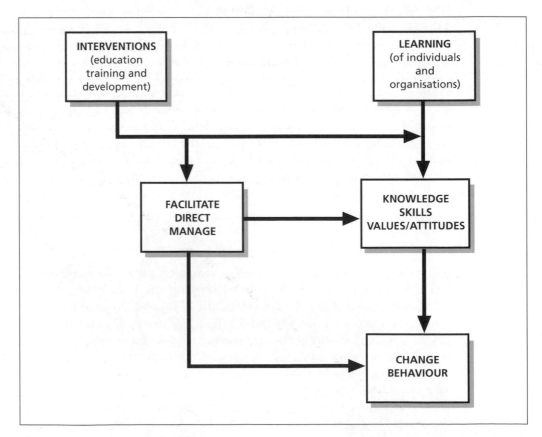

Fig. 2.1 Towards a model of HRD

tions and individuals are capable of influence and direction through deliberate and planned interventions. Thus, HRD is constituted by planned interventions in organisational and individual learning processes.

(Stewart and McGoldrick, 1996b, p. 1)

The final sentence in the quote precisely summarises the model and therefore is probably the most significant in the whole paragraph. It is significant, too, in that it captures in a few words my own beliefs about the nature and scope of HRD. We will therefore return to the sentence, together with the rest of the paragraph and the model, as we proceed through the book. However, I am left with my dilemma over employee development *vis-à-vis* HRD. Rather than abandon the term, I intend to use employee development and HRD as synonyms throughout the text, *unless otherwise stated*. So, unless I indicate otherwise, for employee development read HRD and vice versa.

How do my definition and model relate to and connect with what I have written on the concepts of organisation and management? It should be clear in relation to organisation that while alternative paradigms are accepted as potentially valid, the functionalist paradigm is applied in conceiving of organisations as learning entities. This is because doing so is useful in thinking about and deciding upon employee development practice.

In relation to managing, it may appear that HRD is concerned primarily, if not exclusively, with *achievement* of organisation objectives. However, this is not the case. Unlike other writers (for example, Harrison, 1997, Reid and Barrington, 1997, Moorby, 1996) I do not assume that HRD is necessarily bound up with achieving organisation objectives which are either pre-determined by the economic system or which are determined solely by specified groups such as boards of directors or senior management teams. The model emphasises that the purpose of HRD is to change individual and collective behaviour. There are, of course, large questions about what behaviour is desired or required on the part of whom, and how that is to be determined. Achievement of organisation objectives, as we shall see in later chapters, is the usual starting point in addressing those questions. However, behaviour directed towards formulating and agreeing objectives can and does change, and the direction of change can be influenced through interventions in learning processes. HRD therefore does not have to be exclusively focused on supporting achievement of a set of given objectives. It can also have the purpose of changing established objectives and objective-setting processes.

Summary and conclusion

We have established in this chapter that employee development is situated in a conceptual and theoretical context which is characterised by debate, disagreement and division. Despite the picture painted by many textbooks, the study of organisation and management is contested terrain, with few, if any, certainties. We have also seen that concepts central to the practice of employee development are problematic and not amenable to final and comprehensive definition. However, working definitions have been given which provide a context for the rest of the book. The main conclusions to be drawn are first that the definitions we will use have value in their utility in thinking about and practising HRD, and second that, since universal agreement does not exist, individual professionals have to work out a position for themselves to inform their practice. Activity 2.5, which closes this chapter, will support that process.

Activity 2.5

The process of organising and managing can serve either oppressive or emancipatory purposes (Alvesson and Wilmott, 1996). In simple terms, working in organisations can be experienced as denying individual identity, expression and value, which leads to alienation and lack of attachment, or it can be experienced as fulfilling, meaningful and as developing and releasing potential which leads to satisfaction and a sense of community. Consider this dichotomy in addressing the following questions.

1 How would you characterise the experience of the majority of employees in your organisation?

2 How does this experience compare with your own? What are the reasons for any similarities or differences?

3 What impact and influence does employee development practice have on creating the experience of the majority?

4 Should employee development policy and practice serve emancipatory purposes? What are the reasons for your answer?

5 How can employee development serve achievement of emancipatory purposes? (*Note*: Irrespective of your answer to **4**.)

Case study 2

Chris is a newly appointed training officer working in a regional brewery which operates in a national market. Industry analysts, including those employed by the large brewing companies, all agree that there is surplus capacity in UK brewing, which is also coming under increasing pressure from companies based in mainland Europe. However, Chris is very enthusiastic about her new role and is keen to apply the techniques she has learned on the range of short courses she has attended, and through gaining her Certificate in Training Practice at a local college. The company has provided sponsorship for these activities and Chris is very clear that her role is to apply her skills to enable employees to perform their jobs well which, in turn, will help ensure continued success for the company and employment for staff. In particular, meeting the demands placed on employees by the company's commitment to the Total Quality Management Programme is, in Chris's view, a significant part of her job.

Chris is successful in her role and within three years is promoted to training and development manager. This brings her into contact much more with senior managers and other functional heads. As a result, Chris is more aware of conflicts between different functions and disputes over matters of policy and resources. In fact, she now sees this as the most important part of her job. As a general approach, Chris finds going for small but high-profile and demonstrable successes can lever influence and credibility when negotiating larger resources. Although the approach works well and Chris finds herself enjoying the political games, she is not always successful.

Chris is good enough to achieve a further promotion. Responsibility for management development across both brewing and retail operations, and across all head-office functions, falls within her remit. This brings about a change in her relationships with other managers. Chris begins to lose patience with the 'political games' as she no longer views other managers as competitors. Her closer working relationships lead to a greater understanding of and sympathy with their problems and frustrations. Chris begins to believe that a lot of the 'organisation politics' is caused by lack of clear communication and resulting misunderstandings. Her 'mission' is to devise and implement training and development processes for all staff, but especially managers, which will produce and support high levels of commitment to common objectives. Her attendance at a course leading to membership of the IPD has provided her with lots of ideas on how this can be achieved.

A further five years on and Chris is director of employee development. She is proud of the fact that she is the first person in the company's history to hold a director-level appointment with responsibility for training and development. She has moved on professionally and personally. Chris no longer believes in the possibility of 'perfect' communication or understanding, or of every employee holding the same values or agreeing with the same objectives. She believes her success in her career has come, in part, from developing a 'managerial maturity', helped by completing an MSc in HRD at a local university. Chris understands the need for a high tolerance of ambiguity and to not expect simple or universal answers to managerial problems. She approaches her work on the basis of trying out small initiatives, building on them if they work and abandoning them if they do not. Chris accepts that managing is full of uncertainties and that organisations are rarely, if ever, unitary entities. Her role now, as she sees it, is to reconcile the demands of different stakeholders as best she can while maintaining her professional and personal integrity. And to do this in a way which at least helps to ensure the continued survival of the company, even if the value of that help cannot ever be really known or demonstrated.

Discussion questions

1 In what ways has Chris's paradigm changed over her career?

2 To what extent can the framework proposed by Burrell and Morgan be used to categorise Chris's developing paradigm?

3 What evidence in the case can be used to assess the validity or otherwise of the Burrell and Morgan framework?

4 How do Chris's varying views of her role compare to the view you hold of your role?

Note: This case is based on and derived from the work of Colin Fisher (1996). I am grateful for his permission to amend his original.

Suggested reading

Alvesson, M. and Wilmott, H. (1996) *Making Sense of Management*. London: Sage.

Harrison, R. (1997) *Employee Development*. London: IPD.

Morgan, G. (1997) *Images of Organization*. London: Sage.

Stewart, J. and McGoldrick, J. (eds) (1996) *Human Resource Development: Perspectives, Strategies and Practice*. London: Financial Times Pitman Publishing.

CHAPTER 3

The national context

by Bob Hamlin

Introduction

National vocational education and training systems form a significant part of the economic environment of most nation states, particularly advanced industrial countries (AICs). Hence, as in the UK, vocational education and training (VET) is near the top of national political agendas and at the centre of public policy in most countries. As Lundy and Cowling (1996) point out, VET is a political issue because of its relationship to levels of unemployment, national productivity and industry competencies. To secure competitive advantage in international and national markets, a country's labour market must, in terms of its size and skill composition, be capable of meeting the needs of the country's business organisations.

To help demonstrate the extent to which a country links its VET system to the business economy, Harrison (1997), drawing on the work of van der Klink and Mulder (1995), refers to 'a market labour matrix' comprising on the one side 'primary' and 'secondary' segments, and on the other the 'external' and 'internal' aspects. Essentially, entry to the primary segment requires people to have professional and specific vocational qualifications, whereas the secondary segment relates to low-skill jobs involving routine physical work requiring comparatively little training.

The external aspect of the labour market refers to unemployed people, including school-leavers, whereas the internal aspect relates to employees inside organisations. Different countries adopt different routes to achieving competitive advantage. Focusing primarily on comparatively low added-value and low-quality products, UK manufacturing has tended historically to compete predominantly on grounds of efficiency and low cost, and has sufficed with a comparatively low-skilled workforce. This explains to a large extent why the secondary segment of the labour market in the UK is much larger than the primary segment, and also why in part vocational training in most sectors of industrial Britain has been comparatively weak and unsuccessful.

In contrast, German manufacturing has, in the main, followed a 'quality' route to international competitiveness focusing on high-added value products requiring high levels of skill. It is undoubtedly the case that for more than four decades VET in Germany has been strong and successful. More than 70 per cent of its workforce is now in the primary segment of its national labour market. With increasing competition from developing countries around the world, including China, AICs will need increasingly to adopt 'high added-value' and 'quality' routes for securing any form of sustained competitive advantage. Furthermore, with the increasing impact of information technology, significant growth will occur in technical, administrative, managerial and professional occupations which require high-level skills. In the case of the UK, Australia, Japan and the USA it is projected the growth in these occupations in the ten years from 1990 to the end of the century is likely to range between 20–40 per cent (Jagger *et al.*, 1996). This calls for a high-skills strategy, one requiring a strong, sound and successful national VET system capable of ensuring each country generates the high-level skills needed to compete successfully in the world. For the past decade or so the vision of successive UK governments for the country's national VET system has been that 'everyone has the opportunity and incentive to continue learning throughout life, and that the economy has the skills it needs to meet and beat the best in the world' (Employment Dept Group, 1991:28). This vision, as Harrison (1997) observes, is essentially the same as the European Commission's vision for VET within the EU. Although the vision adopted by most AICs is similar, the ways in which their VET policies have been formulated and implemented are very different.

The aim of this chapter is to enable the reader to appreciate these differences, and in particular to obtain a sound understanding of the UK national VET system. Furthermore, to compare it with those of other major AICs and assess its likely effectiveness in achieving the government's goal of 'providing world-class vocational education and training' and 'producing the best-trained workforce in Europe'.

First, an overview of the national VET systems of various AICs will be described, highlighting the three main approaches to the initial training of young people, namely the dual, state-led and mixed systems. The various types of continuing and further education and training strategies for adults will also be described. A more detailed description of the particular approach adopted by one of the countries representative of those subscribing to each of the three systems respectively will then be given, from which comparisons can be made. The UK national VET system will be explained in greater detail, first with an historical perspective to provide understanding of the cultural roots that have informed, shaped and to a large extent 'dictated' the approaches of successive governments. This will be followed by a critical examination of various features of the UK's latest national VET system highlighting its strengths and weaknesses in light of informed comment. The chapter will close with a number of concluding observations and comments. This will lead to achievement of the following objectives.

CHAPTER OBJECTIVES

- Define and explain various approaches to VET.

- Describe policies and practices adopted in relation to VET in three European countries.

- Compare and contrast the key features and characteristics of differing approaches to VET policy.

- Describe and explain recent and current VET policies in the UK.

- Critically assess and evaluate current VET policies in the UK.

A broad overview of national VET systems

The state plays a major role in the vocational education and training of all advanced industrial countries, but in varying ways and to differing extents. These differences have resulted from deep historical and cultural roots, often going back to the earliest phases of industrialisation, as Hamlin (1995) demonstrates in relation to the UK. Finegold and Crouch (1994) claim the main actors, decision makers and social partners who influence how a national VET system operates and who, therefore, are the principal stakeholders, include:

- *The employers,* who play any or all of three distinct roles either separately or co-operatively through employer organisations, namely providing training, funding VET and/or employing people after completion of the training;
- *The state,* or institutions it controls, which can also play the three roles mentioned above;
- *The trade unions,* which can act either separately or collectively at national, sectoral, company or plant level, and thereby exercise a major influence on the functioning of the national VET system;
- *The providers* of VET including teachers, trainers, educators, schools, colleges and universities which affect the nature of VET at the point of delivery and influence the development of national VET policies as members of representative organisations;
- *The individual,* who invests in the development of his/her skills directly through paying course fees as well as investing time and effort, and indirectly through deferred earnings. It should be noted that it is only through individuals being willing to engage in VET that the other 'actors' can help raise the skills level of the nation. Once the skills have been created they remain the sole property of the individual.

There are two broad types of vocational education and training, namely foundation VET for young people and continuing and further VET for adults.

Foundation VET for young people

In order to create a successful high-skills economy it is generally agreed by all countries that the vast majority of 16 to19-year-olds must remain in education and training beyond the first phase of secondary education. This is in order to ensure a sufficient supply of individuals with the foundation of general/transferable knowledge and skills from which they can build advanced skills. Finegold and Crouch (1994) argue that if education and training at this stage is left solely to the market, there is likely to be an under-investment in foundation skills. One answer to this market failure can be compulsion, which many countries have used and/or are using. However, it is a high-cost option, with the state normally obliged to supply the resources necessary to fulfil education and training requirements. This can lead to high numbers of unwilling students or trainees, who may cause problems for the VET providers.

The institutional arrangements made by various countries for foundation education and training are of two main types, dual systems and state-led systems, although some countries adopt mixed systems which fall between the two.

Dual system (e.g. Germany, Switzerland, Austria and Denmark)

In the dual system, which is strongly identified with Germany, the responsibility and provision of VET for 16 to 19-year-olds is shared between employers and the state. The majority of young people enter an apprenticeship with a firm which includes mandatory release for general education and vocational preparation conducted in schools or colleges.

In Germany, the dual system is maintained through a supportive network of national and regional institutions. The network comprises the Federal Institute of Vocational Education which works with various 'social partners' to define the content of training for the 380 officially recognised occupations. These include the regional states (Länder) which require all firms with apprentices to employ at least one qualified trainer (a 'Meister' who must possess the 'Meister' certificate), and local Chambers of Commerce and Industry which have the responsibility for registering the training contracts of apprentices, administering the examinations, and ensuring that the specific on-the-job training provided by employers accords with the state-wide general training plan.

State-led system

In the state-led system the state is the main regulator and provider of education for 16 to 19-year-olds. State-led systems can be sub-divided, based on whether the dominant mode of provision is 'broad occupational education and training' or 'general education'.

Broad occupational VET system (e.g. Sweden, Belgium, Holland, Norway and latterly France)

In this system, which is most strongly identified with Sweden, there is a very dominant vocational track. However, it is the state institutions rather than employers which provide, in some form or other, the vocational or technical education for the majority of 15 to 18-year-olds.

General education system (e.g. in the USA and Japan)

This system focuses almost exclusively on laying a broad, non-specialised, non-vocational foundation of general knowledge upon which employers can build organisation-specific training and development. In the USA the system consists of general education in comprehensive state high schools until the age of 17 or 18, followed by VET in either public or private post-18 institutions and/or training on the job in companies. One problem in the USA is that while this system encourages individuals to remain in school, it provides few incentives for the majority to work hard. This has resulted in low levels of educational attainment.

In sharp contrast, the Japanese education system, which institutionally resembles that of the USA but is culturally driven, sets high educational standards and creates powerful incentives for individuals of all abilities to invest their time and effort in full-time education. In practice it achieves very high levels of educational attainment. However, this heavily centralised, rigidly structured education system based on a test-centred national curriculum is being questioned as Japan fights to retain its international competitiveness. It fosters rote learning rather than creative thinking and is thought likely to be less appropriate for the future. Concerns are being expressed about an education system that induces severe stress and is geared to developing disciplined workers.

Mixed system (e.g. in the UK, Greece, Spain and Australia)

In countries which have a mixed system, such as the UK, academic education generally enjoys high prestige. However, unlike Germany where a similar academic elite exists, there has been no clearly defined, high-status, technical or vocational routes for the majority of the population. Throughout the 1960s the UK national VET system had some resemblance to the dual system of Germany, but the sharp decline in traditional and standards-based apprenticeships during the 1970s and 1980s left the UK with a 'jungle' of full and part-time VET routes and qualifications at the post-16 stage. However, the framework of National Vocational Qualifications (NVQs) and Scottish Vocational Qualifications (SVQs) now in place is bringing a greater degree of coherence into the provision of VET, as we shall see later.

Activity 3.1

1 What role do employers in your industry/economic sector emphasise most in relation to VET?

2 To what extent do you think this is appropriate?

3 What are the relative strengths and weaknesses of the three systems of foundation VET?

4 What features/characteristics of the dual and state systems could the UK usefully adopt?

5 What would be the implications of this for the role adopted by employers in your industry/sector?

Continuing and further VET for adults

Various AICs have developed different institutional strategies for dealing with market failure problems associated with poor voluntary investment by employers in continuing and further VET for adults.

State intervention

State intervention has either been direct through state funding and/or the provision of training, or indirect through legislation that compels or encourages employers to invest in the vocational education and training of adults. In France since 1971 there has been a statutory obligation on firms to spend a percentage of their annual wage bill (in 1998 set at 1.5 per cent) on VET activities, either in the direct training of their employees or in the form of a training levy which contributes to the State Training Fund. Other countries also operate a training levy scheme, at least for some sectors of their economies. These include Sweden, Australia and Germany (construction industry). As we shall see, most companies in most industrial sectors of the UK were at one time subject to paying an annual statutory training levy, but as in Germany this now applies only to the construction industry.

State-led employer co-operation

In Italy and Japan the public authorities tend to take a leading role in facilitating the formulation of co-operative organisations. They also provide tax incentives and investment subsidies to help companies overcome market failure problems through investment in VET and through the aggressive pursuit of high-skill strategies.

Employer-led corporatism

In Germany the state has not had to play such an active role in further or continuing training because of the deep-rooted strength of employer and trade union organisations. While not exercising the statutory responsibilities as they do over apprentices, Chambers of Commerce in Germany play a strong informal role in encouraging the delivery of continuous training within companies by publicly discrediting those firms which poach skilled labour. Furthermore, the powerful trade unions negotiate wage settlements for the whole sector based on what the most profitable firms are able to afford, thereby forcing weaker companies continuously to improve performance and productivity in order to survive.

Market-based systems

The long history of state non-intervention in the internal operations of firms, particularly in the UK (where it is known as 'voluntarism') and in the USA, has meant that training of the adult workforce has been left largely to individuals and their companies acting in a market environment. Although companies have invested quite heavily in training, this has been targeted to very specific organisational needs. Investment in general skills has tended to be discouraged because of the high rates of turnover and labour mobility this creates in the workforce.

An initial comparison

Historically, The UK has lagged behind most AICs in producing overall a highly skilled and educated workforce. Taking participation rates of 16 to 19-year-olds in post-compulsory education as an indicator, in the early 1990s only 36 per cent of young people in the UK were in education compared to 83 per cent in Belgium, 80 per cent in Germany and 72 per cent in France (Shackleton *et al.*, 1995). The comparison has been much more favourable at the higher skills level. For example, by 1995, 23 per cent of employed people in the UK had vocational qualifications at levels equivalent to the UK NVQ Level 4 or above, compared to 21 per cent in Germany and 19 per cent in France, though this fell short of the 28 per cent in Japan and 30 per cent in the USA (Jagger *et al.*, 1996).

However, it is generally agreed that the UK has a long way to go to catch up on its main competitors in terms of creating a high-skills economy capable of competing with the best rather than the average. It is to be hoped that the new national VET system now in place in the UK will be capable of achieving this vision. However, as we shall see later, many commentators have serious reservations about the UK's approach to its national VET system, with some believing it to be flawed and incapable of achieving the desired goals and vision. Hence, although each competitor country is different in terms of its history, culture and economic structure, which have influenced the shape of its national VET system, the question needs to be asked whether lessons can be learned from making international comparisons. To help answer this question a more detailed examination of the different national VET systems of particular competitor countries is provided in the following section.

An international comparison of national VET systems

So far only the briefest outline of the differences between the three broad types of national VET systems to which AICs subscribe has been given. For comparison purposes we focus here in some detail on the VET arrangements of one of several countries subscribing to each of the three types of systems. Attention is drawn to the particular strengths of each system, but also to some of the weaknesses that give cause for concern. However, for an in-depth comparison readers should refer particularly to Burgess (1997), O'Dwyer (1995), Shackleton *et al.* (1995) and Layard *et al.* (1994) whose works have largely informed much of what follows in this section.

Dual systems: Germany

The dual system in Germany is based on a 'corporatist' approach and involves at national level a tripartite Federal Institute of Vocational Training comprising employers, trade unionists, educationalists and government representatives who operate under the regulations of the Federal Vocational Training Act of 1969. Each component of the dual system is the responsibility of a different political authority and is tightly regulated at federal and state level. On-the-job training is the responsibility of central government acting on the advice of the Federal Institute. Off-the-job training in vocational schools falls under the authority of each constituent state within the German Federation of States, with co-ordination between the *Länder* achieved through the Ministry of Education. Within each *Land* at regional level a major role of the local Chamber of Industry and Commerce is to oversee training at company level, register training agreements, advise on the operation of the system, organise examinations and validate the vocational training qualifications.

Initial vocational training system for young people

The dual system, with its implied commitment to broad-based skills for all young people from the age of 16 across the full range of academic ability, is seen as the foundation of the country's acknowledged high-skills economy. Germany succeeds in getting roughly 90 per cent of its young people to obtain a well-recognised, high-status qualification by the age of 18. Almost 20 per cent of 16-year-olds remain in full-time schooling, culminating in the *Abitur* examination which provides entrance to higher education. About 70 per cent enter apprenticeships under the dual system, which last from two to three years with the requirement of one or two days a week off-the-job general and vocational education in local schools (*Berufsschulen*) but linked to on-the-job training received inside companies. A high proportion of 18-year-olds with the *Abitur* qualification choose not to go to university but to undertake an accelerated apprenticeship which has high status. The remaining 10 per cent who are unable to obtain or drop out from apprenticeships are offered places on government-run VET schemes.

The system has been deeply rooted in the strong traditions of particular trade guilds and professions and in local self-regulation, as well as in a dense network of tripartite institutions at national, regional and local level. Through this system, on-the-job training under the supervision of qualified instructors (*Meisters* who are accredited as 'master craftsmen/craftswomen'), paid for by employers, is combined with off-the-job training conducted in special vocational schools financed out of the public purse. Attendance at these schools is obligatory for all young people aged between 16 and 18 not otherwise in full-time education.

The provision of training places is entirely the responsibility of employers, but there is no obligation to train and no formal right to vocational training. However, accreditation as a training firm offers advantages to an employer as it gives access to a home-grown pool of skilled workers and a competitive advantage.

Firms may not employ young people in any of the nationally accredited and recognised occupations, of which there are about 380, unless they offer training on terms specified under the Vocational Training Act. Employers who want and need to recruit good quality young people must offer training opportunities based on well-developed training programmes. For approval as a training company they must employ craftspeople who have passed the appropriate *Meister* examinations.

Within apprenticeships the basis of the training relationship is the training agreement (contract) between the employer and the trainee, which must be in writing. The pay of trainees (apprentices) is customarily set by collective agreement but is substantially below the full-time adult rates for the duration of the apprenticeship.

Under the dual system the vocational training schools, paid for and administered by the respective *Land* governments, provide the theoretical element of vocational training as well as offering basic preparatory courses for school-leavers entering the labour market who lack basic educational attainment. Craft training schools can supplement or replace company training and train young people for qualifications awarded by the Chamber of Commerce.

The dual system provides clear incentives for all the social partners in the German national VET system to invest in general and transferable skills provided through foundation vocational education and training. Individuals realise that access to a good job is contingent upon obtaining at least a craft qualification, and that an apprenticeship is the first step towards higher level qualifications. Employers support the system because the cost of apprenticeship is relatively low. The state benefits from the dual system because it provides the means of getting most citizens to a high level of skill at a lower cost per person to the government than would be possible through full-time education.

Continuing training for adults

Works councils and employers are statutorily required to co-operate and promote training for adult workers, with works councils having the right of co-determination in some areas. Paid educational leave has been legislated for in the majority of *Länder*, entailing five days leave a year for participation in vocational training and education at recognised institutions. The vocational training need not be confined to the employee's immediate workplace, and may include the acquisition of key skills. There are no mandatory requirements on levels of training expenditure. However, mandatory requirements exist in certain trades where only 'time-served' apprentices may be employed. On average, companies spend about 0.8 per cent of payroll costs on training which in the pharmaceutical industry is closer to 2 per cent.

Some concerns

The major strength of the German VET system is the underlying institutional structures which ensure the effective involvement of private companies in the initial training of young people. In manufacturing this has led to the development of a highly skilled and co-operative workforce that has been well trained over relatively long periods in deep company-specific skills. This has enabled German companies to engage in and develop incremental product and process innovations which have given them a significant competitive edge in international markets. However, as Soskice (1994) points out, such well-trained, well-paid and job-secure skilled workers have little incentive to leave their companies to join small, emergent businesses. Furthermore, they are less well equipped with the particular skills necessary for working in rapidly changing environments and coping with successive waves of radical technological innovations that characterise, for example, high-tech companies. Hence the dual system is increasingly being criticised for being rigid, for the long period needed to acquire basic skills, for too much theoretical training and for general inflexibility.

There are also concerns that growing sectors which have no nationally recognised occupations (e.g. the media) find the dual system of diminishing relevance, and that service industries in need of flexible and capable people look instead to graduates and those with higher vocational qualifications. The dual system is predominantly weighted to traditional industry and commerce and is in danger of focusing too much on potentially obsolete technical knowledge. Furthermore, the system has had the effect of producing a highly segmented labour market, sharply divided between skilled and unskilled workers, with many employees not using the skills for which they have been trained.

Harrison (1997) points out that the German VET system is, overall, bureaucratic and expensive, with hourly labour costs at double the UK levels. In addition, 16-year-olds are increasingly opting for an academic education at universities rather than for craft or technician education through apprenticeship arrangements. This is causing Germany to suffer from a general skills shortage, particularly in some sectors of the economy. Hence the appropriateness of the dual system is beginning to be questioned and there are pressures for it to be reformed in order to make it more responsive to market needs.

Broad occupational VET systems: France

As Harrison (1997) explains, in the 1960s France had more acute problems of skills shortages and poor educational attainment levels than the UK faced at the end of the 1980s. There was also widespread reluctance by employers to invest in the vocational training of young people. Yet by the 1980s France had managed to equip its workforce to cope effectively with the pace of technological change by adopting a state-interventionist approach and converting to a broad occupational VET system.

The French system of national VET is now one of the most highly regulated and centralised with its emphasis on general academic education at all levels, including vocational qualifications and the heavy reliance on school-based VET.

Initial vocational training system for young people

Initial vocational training takes place primarily through the state education system with apprenticeships accounting for only a small proportion of trainees, primarily in craft occupations in small enterprises outside the mainstream industrial and technical sectors. Training is subject to a number of statutory requirements, including compulsory employer funding, the requirement to establish a company training plan and time-off rights for employees.

Most initial vocational training follows the end of compulsory education at the age of 16. The principal initial vocational qualification for craft occupations is a vocational training certificate called the *certificat d'aptitude professionnelle* (CAP), which takes three years to acquire and entails practical and theoretical training.

A less specialised vocational studies certificate, the *brevet d'études professionnelles* (BEP), which is available for skilled and semi-skilled workers, takes two years to complete. A higher degree of technical education is provided in specialised schools leading to the *baccalaureat* or a technician certificate called the *brevet de technicien* (BT). This qualification is roughly equivalent to the UK BTEC National Certificate and National Diploma. Vocational education in France is largely funded by a training tax on companies employing more than ten employees, which in 1998 was set at the statutory minimum of 1.5 per cent of the annual wage bill.

Apprenticeship training is part of the education system and is financed by an Apprenticeship Training Tax. This totals 0.5 per cent of the wage bill and is payable by all employers. Of this, 0.2 per cent directly finances apprenticeships which, in 1977, amounted to the equivalent of £3 000 to £5 500 paid for each apprentice over a period of two years depending on age and the kind of training received. The remaining 0.3 per cent revenue raised from the Apprenticeship Training Tax goes to finance other training and educational institutions, including higher education.

Apprentices must be aged between 16 and 25 at the beginning of the contract which customarily is of one to three years' duration, must be in writing and registered with the relevant labour authorities. Such contracts generally lead to recognised vocational qualifications such as the CAP, BEP and BT or to higher level technical qualifications. An employer who takes on trainees under an apprenticeship contract must register them with an Apprentice Training Centre, ensure they receive appropriate practical experience within the company and ensure their practical experience progresses in line with the theoretical training. Training must be carried out jointly at the workplace and at the training centre.

Apprentices are paid a percentage of the national minimum wage which starts at 25 per cent for a 16 to 17-year-old and rises to 78 per cent for those aged 21 or over in the third year of the apprenticeship. For people not in employment a range of training courses are provided which are usually governed by a fixed-term contract. In the public sector people have access to training in two main ways – through training plans devised by the employer or by taking training leave in accordance with their legal time-off rights. This is administered and financed on a national level. Recent training framework agreements in the civil service signed by the respective 'social partners' provide for a minimum investment equivalent to 3.2 per cent of the wage bill. This is spent on in-house training and external minimum training entitlements which vary depending on the employee category.

Under the Labour Code there are obligations placed on employers, both at the sectoral level through collective agreements, and at company level, to prepare annual training plans in consultation with works committees and works councils. It is obligatory for negotiations to take place every five years at the industry level between the relevant trade unions and employer organisations. Companies are bound by sectoral collective agreements to arrange several discussions a year with the social partners (e.g. the trade unions) for the purpose of outlining the kind of training being made available by the company and the way in which it is being used.

Continuing training for adults

By law, continuing vocational training is made available to all employees. This is aimed at helping them to adapt their skills to technological change and to maintain or improve their existing skills. It is regulated by legislation, with all firms required to meet minimum levels of training expenditure or pay a levy to the national training fund. The levy in 1998 was set at 1.5 per cent of the wage bill, although average expenditure is about 3 per cent. Banking and insurance lead the field with about 8 per cent of the wage bill being invested in training, excluding introductory on-the-job training.

Adult training is governed by the Labour Code, the provisions of which may be improved by collective or company agreement. One of the most common forms chosen by employees is 'individual training leave' which is paid absence of up to one year for full-time training, or of 1200 hours for part-time training outside the company. Employees who have already been on individual training leave may not request a further period of training within certain time limits, depending on the length of leave already taken. Remuneration on vocational training leave is fixed at 80–90 per cent of previous salary if less than one year full time, or 1200 hours part time. In excess of this, remuneration is fixed at 60 per cent of salary. The proportion of annual training tax allocated to financing training leave is 0.2 per cent of the wages bill.

France has maintained a rigid division between education and training, with initial vocational education being conducted in schools and seen as the sole responsibility of the state. Training, on the other hand, being specifically related to the firm, is seen as the prime responsibility of the employer. Essentially the state treats compulsory education and initial vocational education as pure public goods; it provides the system and charges society via levies and taxes. Recent changes in the system provide a much broader range of academic and vocational options and this has resulted in an increasing proportion of young people entering the labour market with formal qualifications.

Some concerns

Because virtually all initial training is school based, and employers are given only a limited role, there is much criticism that what is provided may be limited in relevance to work situations and to the overall requirements of the economy. For all its logical structure, the French VET system has some problem areas. For example, the lower level CAP and BEP qualifications are not always recognised by collective agreements when workers join companies. The contraction of traditional industries and restructuring of markets and organisations means there are fewer promotion opportunities for people who have invested heavily in high-level technical qualifications which are no longer required. Furthermore, the strictly defined and regulated system tends to prevent both re-entry into the system and the accreditation of informal learning because officially training does not include informal on-the-job learning. Additionally, because of the bias which the training levy system gives to formal off-the-job training, the tendency to concentrate continuing training on the already well qualified is accentuated.

The general education system: USA

Initial vocational training 'system' for young people

In the USA there is no national VET system as such, but rather a 'patchwork' of vocational education programmes which are mostly undertaken in educational institutions. These differ in purpose, design, target, provision and funding from state to state and between institutions. Initial vocational training is mainly the responsibility of employers, with little regulation and no reliance on formal qualifications. Most training is conducted informally on the job. Formal company training is not a significant source of vocational training in the USA. However, the traditional craft apprenticeship system inherited from Britain still survives, albeit on a very small scale covering only a limited number of occupations in construction and manufacturing. The survival of the formal apprenticeship has been attributed mainly to the influence of the respective labour unions rather than the employers, but less than 2 per cent of school leavers enter formal apprenticeships or training schemes.

Regarding vocational education as part of compulsory high-school education, each state is legally required to prepare a five-year plan and supervise a system of vocational education in all high schools. However, as in the UK and elsewhere, vocational education has traditionally been accorded lower status than academic study, and consequently is often criticised for providing poor preparation for work.

Continuing training for adults

The proportion of high-school leavers remaining in full-time post-compulsory education has traditionally been much higher in the USA than in other countries, and in 1998 stood at 45 per cent. Although universities play a major role in preparing people for work, there are two types of higher education institutions that provide specific vocational education programmes: community colleges and private vocational colleges. These provide 'open' courses of study for adults requiring basic and continuing vocational education, as well as customised 'closed' courses for local industry and businesses, and off-the-job training programmes designed to provide the vocational education element of formal apprenticeship schemes.

The USA is significantly different from other countries in that the proportion of young people leaving school and moving into formal vocational training provided by employers is very small (12 per cent). This is because most school leavers receive general or job-related vocational training/education in a full-time education institution, thereby reducing the need for employers to provide entry-level training. However, employer-provided training is on the increase, although some critics maintain it is still inadequate.

Some concerns

A major advantage of the US vocational education 'system' is its flexibility and high participation rates of 18-year-old school leavers and adults. However, there are major concerns, particularly regarding the associate degrees and vocational certificates awarded by community colleges and private vocational colleges. These have been criticised for the wide variation in quality and lack of transferability between states and institutions. These problems are associated with a lack of national curricula for these awards, and the general lack of common national standards and certification for vocational education and training.

Despite these concerns about the perceived weaknesses of the US training and educational system, it has been highly successful in ways which the VET systems of other countries, including the UK, have not (Soskice, 1994). The USA most clearly has the highest average productivity level in the world, ahead of Germany, Japan and France and greatly ahead of the UK. As Soskice points out, the USA is overwhelmingly the world leader in radical innovation, particularly in the newly emergent high-tech 'sun-rise' industries. This success is largely attributed to what is perceived as a major advantage of the US 'general education' system: its capability in equipping young people and adults with the problem-solving, customer-oriented, computing and social communication skills demanded not only by the new high-tech industries, but also by service-sector organisations where new patterns of work and customer interaction have emerged.

Although there is no national vocational training system as such in the USA, the state does play a significant role at a national level by funding and providing training and retraining for various disadvantaged groups in society.

Mixed system: Greece

In Greece, education is a basic mission of the state. Its aim is to provide moral, intellectual, vocational and physical instruction for all Greeks, to promote national and religious awareness, and to develop free, responsible citizens. Greeks have the right to free education at all educational levels which is provided in education institutions funded by the state. Vocational education and training for young people between the age of 15 and 18, which is part of compulsory education, is a joint responsibility of the Ministry of National Education and Religious Affairs (MNERA) and the Ministry of Labour. The MNERA is also responsible for the provision of vocational education in post-compulsory secondary education, while the Organisation for Vocational Education and Training (OEEK) has total responsibility for vocational training.

Initial vocational training system for young people

The Greek national system of VET was established in 1992 with the passing by parliament of Law 2009. It embraces the organisation, development and provision of vocational training, the formal certification of vocational training, the integration of secondary school leavers into training, and the implementation of all kinds of national or local community VET programmes.

Young people leave lower secondary level school (*Gymnasio*) at the age of 15. All those not entering employment at this stage have the opportunity, subject to ability, to progress to upper secondary level education in colleges (*Lykeia*) which specialise either in general education or technical-vocational education (or a combination of both) in preparation for and leading to access to university entrance examinations. Alternatively, young people can undertake two years of technical-vocational education at upper secondary level in a Technical-Vocational School (TES) designed to lead to employment. As part of the national VET system, a body called the Organisation for Manpower Employment (OAED), jointly supported administratively by the Ministry of Labour, the General Confederation of Workers of Greece (GSEE) and the Association of Greek Industries (SEU), runs an 'apprenticeship system' primarily for those aged between 15 and 18, although in exceptional cases up to the age of 23. The apprenticeship lasts three years and comprises a mixture of off-the-job technical and vocational training in OAED apprenticeship schools, and practical work on the job in public or private firms. In the first year apprentices attend classes at school every day, but this is reduced to only one day a week in the second and third years. At the end of the apprenticeship they are awarded an OAED Diploma (*Ptychia*) which is equivalent to the certificates awarded by the TES.

Continuing training for adults

In parallel with the *Lykeia*, the TESs and the OAED apprenticeship schools, the national VET system also comprises Institutes of Vocational Training (IEK). These aim to deliver every type of vocational training, whether initial or continuing, across the full range of scientific, technical, vocational and practical subjects. The training takes place both in state and private education institutions, and in firms and industries local to these institutions. Courses comprise both theoretical and practical work, with students being placed in firms towards the end of their course wherever possible. The IEK admit adults of all ages and levels of educational attainment, as well as apprentices attending or leaving OAED courses. Additionally, they admit school leavers from all types of *Lykeia* and TESs. This means leavers from general *Lykeia* not going to university are provided with initial vocational training, while leavers from non-general *Lykeia* are given the opportunity to supplement their technical vocational knowledge. Upon successful completion of an IEK course, trainees are awarded an appropriate Certificate of Vocational Training (*Vevaiosi epagelmatikis katartisis*) which gives them the right to progress towards the award of a Diploma. It should be noted that the IEK provision of vocational training is free to all students.

Activity 3.2

1 Describe the role adopted by employers in Germany, France, USA and Greece.

2 How do each of these roles compare to the three possible roles described earlier in the chapter?

3 Review your responses to Activity 3.1 and consider the following questions:

(a) how could or should the role of employers in your industry/sector change?

(b) what are the relative strengths and weaknesses of approaches to VET in Germany, France, USA and Greece?

(c) what lessons could the UK learn and apply from any of these countries?

The national VET system in the UK

For decades the national vocational education and training system of the UK has failed to deliver the skills base which the country has required for competitive advantage. Writing in 1994, Layard, Mayhew and Owen drew attention to the fact that there was not enough vocational education and training in the UK, that it was less than in most other Western Europe countries, and that the UK's national training system could not be relied upon to provide what was needed.

Since the turn of the century institutional weaknesses in vocational training have been seen as contributory factors in the progressive and relative economic decline of the UK. Layard *et al* (1994) argue that for far too long the 'basic' problem with VET in the UK has been the fact that too few 16 to 18-year-olds have received adequate education and training. As already mentioned, comparisons conducted in 1992 revealed the UK near the bottom of international league tables. Until recent times roughly two-thirds of the national workforce had no vocational or professional qualifications compared with only a quarter in Germany and a half in France.

The main weakness exists at the lower technician, craft and skilled worker level rather than at degree or higher technician levels where the comparisons have been more favourable. The situation appears particularly serious in engineering and technology, areas in which France and Germany have been producing roughly twice as many qualified people than the UK. For Germany in particular, its VET system has made possible quite different systems of work within industry, resulting in much greater productivity and a higher economic return from investment in sophisticated capital equipment. Conversely, too much of UK industry has been trapped in a low-skills and increasingly low-tech equilibrium from which the only escape would be if the nation could dramatically increase the skills and competence of its human capital.

However, despite many attempts to do so, including the latest version of the national VET system introduced and developed by successive Conservative governments, and endorsed by the new Labour government, doubts remain whether the system can deliver the high skills economy that is required. A skills revolution remains a pressing economic and social imperative for the UK, as reflected in the government's Green Paper 'The Learning Age' (DfEE, 1998). The country's weakness still lies predominantly in basic and intermediate skills, with almost 30 per cent of young people failing to reach a basic level of skill by the age of 19, 7 million adults having no formal qualifications, 21 million adults out of a population of approximately 58 million not reaching even an intermediate level of skill, and more than one in five adults having poor literacy and numeracy skills which put the UK ninth in a ranked list of 12 AICs.

Hence the need for another attempt at relaunching the national VET system with additional improvements. However, even if all the refinements proposed in the 'Learning Age' Green Paper are fully implemented, it is still open to question whether the refined system can succeed, particularly bearing in mind the range of factors that have historically thwarted all previous attempts by successive governments to rectify the UK's skill deficits. These factors still apply to a greater or lesser extent within the national culture, and include:

(a) attitudes rooted in the nineteenth-century notions of apprenticeship and voluntarism.
(b) youth and apprentice pay in the UK being unusually high relative to the pay of adults, thus encouraging many young people to leave school early and discouraging employers from training.
(c) the under-valuation of skill which has resulted in skill differentials in the UK being substantially lower than in continental countries.
(d) the national training policy constantly changing because of short-term responses by successive governments to what persists as a long-running problem.
(e) 'short-termism', where managers tend to think of skill training as a short-term cost to be avoided, rather than an essential long-term investment.

To understand more fully the significance of these 'cultural' factors, it is useful to view the national VET system from the perspective of its historical past.

An historical perspective of the UK's national training system

For almost 100 years, from the late 1880s to the mid-1980s, the history of training in the UK has been one of chronic under investment, persistent failure and recurrent periods of acute skills shortage. Whenever comparisons have been made between the UK's training practices and those of its Western European competitors, the conclusion has been that countries such as Germany and France have had better national VET systems, more capable of quickly responding to technological change and economic growth. In contrast, the UK training system, which until recent years changed little despite numerous attempts by successive governments spanning most of the twentieth century, failed to produce the quantity or quality of skilled labour required to meet national needs.

The two deeply rooted nineteenth-century traditions of apprenticeship and voluntarism, which had been strongly upheld by employer associations and trade unions alike until the late 1980s and early 1990s, had a strong influence on the thinking of governments of all political persuasions. This largely determined the degree and type of state intervention in the nation's training system. Entry to the traditional apprenticeship in most industries, which was invariably confined to school leavers who then had to 'serve their time', was the predominant system for supplying skilled workers into the national labour market. Essentially, apprenticeships were the responsibility of employers, but were always strongly influenced by the trade unions and, in some industries, 'controlled' by them. The tradition of voluntarism in state–industry relationships stemmed from the belief that matters such as labour relations, and therefore vocational training, were for industry alone. Governments should not interfere or be involved. Hence an apprenticeship was seen not as a concern of government but rather a matter solely for industry. This 'voluntarist' approach contrasts sharply with the 'corporatist' approach that applies in Germany and the 'state-interventionist' approach in France.

Another factor characterising the UK training system for many decades, and contributing to its failure, has been that of short-termism. Operating with very near time horizons, UK managers, unlike their counterparts in other AICs, have tended not to invest in long-term vocational training. This has been because of uncertainty about recovering the costs of developing skills, plus the inhibiting effects of short-term investment evaluation criteria applied by company bankers and financial institutions. Reluctance to invest in training has also been accentuated by the comparative high cost of apprenticeships in the UK which has been virtually double that in some AICs such as Germany.

In light of these factors successive governments have left the responsibility for vocational education and training largely in the hands of employers although, as we shall see, the state has intervened at times through legislation.

The UK's national VET system: 1889–1979

At the latter end of the nineteenth century the UK was perceived as failing to provide proper industrial (vocational) training for sufficient numbers of workers compared to other industrialised nations such as Germany. This led to the Technical Instruction Act of 1889, which was the first significant government intervention to have an impact on industrial training in the UK. It resulted in the setting up of technical schools and colleges throughout the country, some modelled on the technical institutes in Germany.

The next major government intervention came during the First World War with the setting up of training courses in technical schools, instructional factories and instructional bays situated in certain private firms. However, after the war government-sponsored industrial training was focused on disabled ex-servicemen only, leaving the traditional apprenticeship system to provide skilled able-bodied workers for the labour market. During the depression years the government intervened with the creation of an 'interrupted apprenticeship' scheme. This was aimed at helping able-bodied ex-servicemen, whose apprenticeship had been interrupted by the war, to finish their training and thereby compensate for the very low numbers of apprentices recruited by industry. To offset the worst effects of mass unemployment the government set up and funded training schemes for the unemployed. Most of these were run in Government Training Centres (GTCs) which were vastly expanded in size and number during the Second World War.

In the immediate post-Second World War period, industrial training slipped from the political agenda. However, skill shortages again gave cause for concern in the 1950s when the national training system came under widespread criticism. By the early 1960s it was widely recognised in governmental and educational circles that the UK lagged behind its main European competitors in terms of skill levels and technical education qualifications, and that the voluntarist approach to national VET was failing.

In 1962 the Conservative government published a White Paper entitled 'Industrial Training: Government Proposal' which highlighted the link between skills shortages and national economic performance. The paper had the widespread support of all the opposition parties and led to the passing in Parliament of the 1964 Industrial Training Act by the newly elected Labour Government. It had three main aims:

- to ensure an adequate supply of properly trained men and women at all levels in industry;
- to ensure an improvement in the quality and efficiency of industrial training;
- to share the cost of training more evenly among firms.

The primary means of achieving these aims was through a network of tripartite Industrial Training Boards (ITBs) covering all the main industries, with board membership being made up of employers, trade unionists and educationalists. Each ITB had statutory powers to raise annual training levies from employers within scope, and to disburse monies back in the form of grants depending on the quantity and quality of training provided by the company. Some training levies were set as high as 2.5 per cent of the wages bill, as was the case in the engineering industry. The government's intention was to administer a national VET system comprising a stick-and-carrot mechanism, with the stick (the levy) compelling employers to train their employees, both young and adult workers, and the potential carrot (the grant) spreading the costs of training across companies. It was hoped the tripartite composition of the ITBs would help break down the strength of trade unions over the form, structure and working of apprenticeships and would bridge the schism (the 'great divide') that still existed between education and training.

More than 25 ITBs were established as statutory organisations under the 1964 Act, together with a number of voluntary boards such as the Local Government Training Board. The impact of ITBs varied greatly from industry to industry and from skill category to skill category. Outside the formal apprenticeship schemes they achieved only marginal increases in vocational training for skilled and semi-skilled workers. By the end of the 1960s the traditional UK apprenticeship system, operating under the umbrella of the respective ITBs, was still being criticised for perpetuating the unofficial age–entry restrictions to skilled trades, the use of 'time serving' as the main form of becoming qualified as a skilled worker, and the general lack of standardised training programmes and formal qualifications.

Contrary to intention, ITBs tended to concentrate more on increasing the volume of what industry had already been doing, rather than on cultivating major reforms of the process of training skilled workers. ITBs were increasingly criticised for not questioning sufficiently the way industry deployed and utilised its skilled labour, for not effectively challenging the appropriateness of the traditional apprenticeship system, and for failing to address the question of unemployment which had increased to a level that posed both social and political problems for the government. ITBs were also criticised for favouring large firms, for being unrealistic in the expectations of small firms, for becoming too bureaucratic, and for demanding too much paperwork.

Employers became uneasy over what they perceived to be escalating state interventionism with too much power residing in the hands of government officials. This led to a review of the 1964 Act and the consequent introduction of the 1973 Employment and Training Act. This was a compromise response to the conflicting demands within industry, and to trade union opinion that had shifted away from voluntarism towards more state intervention in training. On the assumption that through the levy-grant mechanism ITBs had brought about an irreversible shift in training, the 1973 Act drastically reduced the powers of the ITBs. It set an upper limit of 1 per cent for the training levy that ITBs could raise, required them to introduce a levy abatement and exemption system, and transferred the financing of ITB operating costs to a newly created central government co-ordinating body called the Manpower Services Commission (MSC). The MSC went on to become the leading national voice on vocational training matters and the primary mechanism for implementing national policies.

Two downturns in the economy during the 1970s saw manufacturing industry dramatically cutting back on the number of apprenticeships, and a shift towards service industries where there was no tradition of apprenticeship. This led to increased pressure on the government to take a more active and direct role in vocational training which resulted in a variety of *ad hoc* funded measures being introduced by the MSC to counter growing unemployment. These ranged from support for training places in industry (e.g. 'special measures') to job creation programmes (e.g. the Youth Opportunities Programme [YOP]).

By the end of the decade the MSC was focusing its efforts mainly on the YOP initiatives which were aimed at encouraging employers to provide training and work experience for unemployed young people. However, YOPs induced fears that the state might be subsidising in-company vocational training that would have happened anyway, and that the 'special measures' scheme might be leading to an actual reduction in the training effort of industry (Sheldrake and Vickerstaff, 1987).

The UK's national VET system 1980–1998

Despite the abundance of schemes developed by the MSC throughout the 1970s, the number of apprenticeships continued to decline, adult retraining remained neglected, and high youth unemployment persisted. Moreover, little progress had been made in persuading industry to adopt any radical new approaches to skills training which would lead to an increase in the supply of skilled workers into the labour market. Detailed reviews of the working of the 1973 Act followed which led to the 1981 Employment and Training Act passed by Parliament under the newly elected Conservative government. Of the 24 statutory ITBs, 16 were abolished and replaced by more than 200 voluntary Industry Training Organisations (ITOs). The 1981 Act was quickly followed by the government publishing in December 1981 its White Paper entitled 'New Training Initiative – A Programme for Action' which set out three primary objectives:

- to reform the apprenticeship system and enable all young people to enter training at different ages and acquire agreed standards of skill and qualifications;
- to enable all young people under 18 years either to continue in full-time education or to benefit from planned work experience combined with vocational training and education;
- to enable adults to acquire, increase or update their knowledge and skills during their working lives.

Unlike earlier attempts to reform the UK training system, the National Training Initiative (NTI) focused upon the content and process of training, not just the quantity. It was seen initially as a partial return to a voluntarist national training system. But in the event, through its heavy focus on a Youth Training Scheme (YTS) put in place to achieve NTI Objective 2, the initiative was to mark 'an unparalleled extension of intervention by the state in the nation's training system' (Sheldrake and Vickerstaff, 1987). As with the YOPs scheme, YTS became the butt of much criticism and disillusionment.

It took another five years before any real progress was made towards achieving the other primary NTI objectives. These developments were triggered following calls for training standards (and vocational qualifications) of a new kind to overcome the nation's skills deficits, and repeated calls for the elimination of the cultural divide between education and training that was still in evidence. The aims were set out in the government's White Paper entitled 'Working Together – Education and Training' (ED and DES, 1983) which resulted in the setting up in 1986 of the National Council for Vocational Qualifications (NCVQ), a landmark development in the creation of the present national VET system. The vision was to develop a coherent and comprehensive system of vocational qualifications that enabled a clear understanding of the level of any course and its equivalent. The outcome was the development of National Vocational Qualifications (NVQs) in England and Wales and Scottish Vocational Qualifications (SVQs) in Scotland. Since SVQs are named to reflect minor differences in administrative arrangements in Scotland, while the two qualifications are actually the same, the term SNVQ is used to refer to both.

The SNVQs for particular occupations were based on national standards designed to convey levels of competence and skill and the ability of individuals to perform activities in employment. The work of establishing the national occupational standards was carried out by Lead Bodies (LBs) which were set up progressively for each respective occupation. For those that were industry-specific the respective ITO took on the role as the LB. However, for occupations that crossed sectors, non-industry-specific LBs were set up. All LBs were required to use a common approach for identifying occupational standards, namely functional analysis (*see* Jessup, 1991, Mansfield and Mitchell, 1996). Through this means the functions of a particular occupation were broken down into areas of competence, each of which comprised units and elements of competence expressed in terms of outcomes, range statements, and associated performance criteria. Hence SNVQs related to the outcome of courses or programmes of learning, not the input.

A tier system of SNVQs covering different areas of work within a given occupation was established with five levels. SNVQ Level 1 corresponded to 'basic skills and competence in routine repetitive tasks', whereas SNVQ Level 5 covered 'professional and higher and middle management' occupations. Awards were still given by bodies such as BTEC, RSA, City and Guilds and the professional institutes, but their training standards had to be assessed, approved and accredited by the NCVQ. In addition, the NCVQ pioneered approaches to assessing pre-existing competences; people who had acquired skills informally through work or other experience could have them certified through the SNVQ system. The development of SNVQs was aimed not only at accrediting individuals' skills according to common standards, regardless as to how acquired, but also to remove the stigma from vocational qualifications, giving them equivalent esteem to academic qualifications and thereby encouraging more people to pursue them and raise the overall attainment level of the workforce.

The 1987 Employment Act introduced substantial changes in the nation's training infrastructure. The tripartite MSC was abolished, thereby breaking all links with the corporatist training arrangements of the past. This was replaced with a Training Commission which was given specific responsibility for training and nothing else, thus marking 'a watershed in UK training history because training and unemployment were no longer linked together!' (Lundy and Cowling, 1996). In 1986 the government published its White Paper entitled 'Training for employment'. This led to the launching later that year of a New Adult Training Programme, subsequently called Employment Training (ET), which replaced all adult training schemes. It was similar to YTS in design and delivery and, like YTS, required great commitment and employer involvement to be successful. When, however, the Trades Union Council announced its intention to boycott ET programmes, the government used its 1988 Employment Act to abolish the Training Commission and replace it with a Training Agency reporting to the Department of Employment.

Towards the end of the 1980s it became evident that NTI had been only partially successful in changing the UK training system. In its White Paper entitled 'Employment for the 1990s' (December 1988) the government identified lack of skills as the most significant barrier to jobs growth, and proposed establishing a 'training and enterprise framework that would meet Britain's key employment needs and increase its international competitiveness'. In developing the national VET system further it provided a major role for employers, though not just at national level. More importantly, it involved them more at the industry level through existing and newly created ITOs, and at the local level by setting up a national network of Training & Enterprise Councils (TECs) throughout England and Wales, and an equivalent network of Local Enterprise Companies (LECs) in Scotland. The respective purposes of ITOs, TECs and LECs were, and still are, to develop policies for the promotion of training, the setting of occupational standards as necessary, and ensuring that training meets the needs of particular sectors and local labour markets.

Industry training organisations and lead bodies

Since their creation, Industry Training Organisations have been voluntarist strategic bodies responsible for defining the current and future skill requirements and training needs of their respective industry sectors, as well as ensuring that these needs are met. As already mentioned, many ITOs were formed from the network of Industrial Training Boards which had been in existence since the 1964 Industrial Training Act. ITOs have been independent, employer-led bodies dedicated to improving company performance and individual career prospects through systematic training and development. Depending upon the industrial sector, ITOs have either been fully independent bodies, separate recognisable bodies that have been subsidiaries of or closely associated with a trade or employer organisation, trade or employer organisations acting as ITOs, or bodies supported by a single, large employer. ITOs have obtained their funds mainly through subscriptions from member companies and organisations, and from the sale of publications and services.

Lead Bodies were set up to establish the occupational standards upon which NVQs* and SVQs* could be based in particular occupational areas. As already mentioned, for those occupations that were industry/sector-specific, the respective ITOs became the lead body, whereas for occupations common to all industries or sectors, independent lead bodies were set up, for example, the Management Charter Initiative (MCI) and the Training and Development Lead Body (TDLB).

(*Note: For ease of reading, from here on the term NVQ will be used to refer to both the Scottish SVQ and the English and Welsh NVQ.)

Training and enterprise councils/local enterprise companies

By 1992 the government had established 83 Training and Enterprise Councils throughout England and Wales and 22 equivalent Local Enterprise Companies in Scotland. These business-led, locally based organisations, headed by employers, were responsible for promoting training throughout industry and the community to eliminate the UK's skills deficiency. They were modelled on the Private Industry Councils (PICs) developed in the USA and, like PICs, were intended to attract more and more private investment over a number of years to reduce the level of central government funding of training.

The main aims of TECs and LECs were to encourage more effective employer investment in training, to encourage more individuals to take responsibility for their training needs, to administer government programmes, and to act as intermediaries between government and training providers. They also aimed to ensure the provision of minimum standards of training for those on government training schemes, and for specific groups in the community. In short, TECs and LECs exist to ensure training closely matches and meets the skills needs of the local labour market, and to promote the development of small businesses at the local level.

At the outset, TECs and LECs were responsible not only for the delivery of the Employment Training Scheme, but also for running the Youth Training Scheme, subsequently called Youth Training (YT), the Business Growth through Training (BGT) programmes, and a newly launched Investors in People (IIP) initiative. The other major initiative around this time for which TECs/LECs had administrative responsibility was the government's Training Credit (TC) scheme, subsequently called the Youth Credit (YC) Scheme. This entitled school leavers between 16 and 17 to 'buy' approved training relevant to their employment and career aspirations.

Investors in people (IIP)

IIP is a national standard which provides a framework for establishing corporate goals and targets, communicating with employees, and training them to meet those goals and targets. It broadly guides an organisation to address such issues as planning, communications, performance review, people management, and management effectiveness, plus training and development processes. There are four principles within the IIP framework:

- Principle 1 – *commitment* from top management to develop all employees to achieve its business objective;
- Principle 2 – *planning*, involving regular reviews of training needs and plans for the training and development of all employees;
- Principle 3 – *action* to ensure training takes place from recruitment and induction, and ongoing throughout employment;
- Principle 4 – *evaluation* of the investment in training and development to assess achievement and improve future effectiveness.

IIP provides a framework tool for bringing about organisational change and development and for benchmarking against other organisations. Implemented correctly, it can prove a powerful mechanism for embedding principles and practices of total quality management (TQM) into an organisation.

National targets

In 1993 the government established a set of National Education and Training Targets to be achieved by the year 2000. As a means to achieve these targets it established the business-led National Advisory Council on Education and Training Targets (NACETT), which was given the task of accelerating the take-up of NVQs by increasing their profile and acceptability with employers. In its drive to improve the country's international competitiveness the government again reasserted in its White Paper 'Helping Businesses to Win' (1994) the importance of securing a high-skills economy, and the need for further improvements in vocational education and training. This led in 1995 to the National Education and Training Targets being revised and set at the target levels illustrated in Fig. 3.1. These targets are subject to a further revision yet to be finalised.

NATIONAL TARGETS FOR EDUCATION AND TRAINING

Foundation learning

By age 19

- 85 per cent of young people to achieve NVQ Level 2 or equivalent.
- 75 per cent to achieve NVQ Level 2 competence in the key skills of communication, numeracy and information technology.

By age 21

- 35 per cent to achieve NVQ Level 3 competence in these key skills.
- 60 per cent to achieve NVQ Level 3 or equivalent.

Lifetime learning

- 60 per cent of the workforce to be qualified to NVQ Level 3 or equivalent.
- 30 per cent of the workforce to have a vocational, professional, management or academic qualification at NVQ Level 4 or above.
- 70 per cent of all organisations with 200 or more employees, and 35 per cent of those employing 50 or more, to be recognised as Investors in People.

Fig. 3.1.

Source: Based on the Review of the National Targets for Education and Training, NACETT, 1995.

Just as the national training system had been transformed during the ten years from 1984 to 1994, the national education system was also reformed through a series of Acts. The aim was not only to raise educational standards and levels of achievement, which fell far behind those of Germany, France and Japan (National Commission on Education, 1993), but also to contribute more effectively to the national training policy objective of developing a permanent bridge between school and work for all young people under 18, as set out in the 1981 New Training Initiative.

Until the late 1980s vocational education in secondary schools was a neglected area, being treated as less important than the study of traditional academic subjects. Whatever vocational education comprehensive schools provided, it was concentrated on academic low-achievers. In an attempt to rectify what business people regarded as major shortcomings, namely the poor attitudes to work and discipline of school leavers and their poor basic education and limited understanding of the work environment, the government launched the Technical and Vocational Education Initiative (TVEI). This initiative, in part, encouraged increasing numbers of young people to remain in education until they were 18 years old, even if they did not wish to enter higher education.

The Education Reform Act of 1988 led to the introduction of a common National Curriculum which shared many features with the NVQ model, particularly the specification of outcomes linked to statements of attainment. A further development was the introduction of a General National Vocational Qualification (GNVQ), designed to have a parity of esteem and equivalence to two grade-D GCSE A-levels. GNVQs, which were piloted during the early 1990s and have become well embedded as part of secondary education provision in the UK, attempted to bridge the divide between vocational and academic qualifications by offering alternatives to academic studies. Despite the government's impetus behind them, there remains some concern that GNVQs may still be seen as inferior to their academic equivalents, and may not be fully accepted by employers and higher education (HE) institutions, although there are signs that such reservations about GNVQs and the barriers to them are being eroded.

A further important development in the national VET system triggered by the 1991 White Paper 'Higher Education: a new framework' was the rapid expansion of the HE sector following the conversion of polytechnics into universities. These operate within a single framework of HE under the auspices of the Higher Education Funding Councils, with an equality of status and standards accredited to both academic and vocational awards. The proportion of school leavers entering universities and colleges of HE has since risen from around 10–15 per cent to 30 per cent. This is expected to rise to 35 per cent or more as we move into the twenty-first century. As part of this development there has been a proliferation of vocationally oriented degree programmes on offer from HE institutions.

In 1996 the government merged the Department of Employment and the Department of Education into a single Department for Education and Employment (DfEE). The impact of this on the national VET system has led to the merging of the National Council for Vocational Qualifications and the Schools Curriculum Assessment Authority to form the Qualifications and Curriculum Authority (QCA). The merging of the employment and education departments should help to eliminate the deleterious 'schism' between education and training which, as argued in this chapter, has been deeply embedded within the UK cultural consciousness for the best part of the twentieth century.

In 1998 the new Labour government appeared to be adopting the national VET system inherited from the outgoing administration without significant change. However, in its Green Paper 'The Learning Age', the government set out a number of key principles and plans of action that presaged a further refinement of the system. A summary of these principles and actions is given in Fig. 3.2.

Activity 3.3

1 Identify the main trends and developments of the UK's VET policy over the course of the century.

2 What have been the main strengths and weaknesses of each period?

3 How do these strengths and weaknesses compare to those evident in alternative approaches adopted in other countries?

4 What are your views on the current approach to VET policy in the UK?

THE LEARNING AGE: A RENAISSANCE OF A NEW BRITAIN

Principles and action plan – a summary

- Sharing responsibility (for learning) with employers, employees and the community by promoting new partnerships between firms, employers and trade unions and providing advice to businesses and small firms in particular so that they address their skills needs through becoming Investors in People.
- Achieving world class standards and value for money by better management, target setting and improved quality assurance; and making sure that teaching meets the highest professional standards.
- Working together as the key to success through all the main bodies locally agreeing a strategy for improving access to learning; more coherent planning and advice for young people at 16 and beyond; and working with our European partners so that we make the most of European programmes.

The main steps proposed for helping move people to benefit from world-class education and training include:

- expansion of FE and HE to provide for an extra 5 million young people and adults by 2002;
- creating the University of Industry (Ufi) to make it easier for individuals to learn and firms to meet their skills needs;
- setting up individual learning accounts to encourage people to save to learn;
- investing in young people so that more continue to study beyond the age of 16;
- giving all 16 and 17-year-olds a legal right to undertake education and training to NVQ Level 2;
- including national traineeships as high-quality, work-based routes to NVQ Level 2;
- expanding modern apprenticeships;
- tackling skills shortages with a new National Skills Task Force;
- looking to TECs/LECs for integrated plans for local workforce development;
- raising quality and standards across teaching and learning after the age of 16 through a new Training Standards Council based on proposals by Sir Ron Dearing's National Committee of Inquiry into HE;
- building a qualification system which is easily understood, values both academic and vocational learning, meets employer and industry needs and promotes the highest standards.

Fig. 3.2

Source: Government Green Paper (1998) 'The Learning Age: A Renaissance of a New Britain'.

A critical review of the UK's current national VET system

As in the USA, but in marked contrast to Germany and France, vocational education and training in the UK has been and still remains largely unregulated. Employers are not normally obliged to provide training for any employees and such training as is provided need not lead to formal qualifications. Why this is so is firmly rooted in history, as we have seen. However, the current national VET system has revolutionised the training landscape in the UK. For the first time the country has in place a clear, coherent and comprehensive system of VET which Reid and Barrington (1997) suggest, 'is worthy of comparison with those of its two main "competitors" – France and Germany', and is attracting much interest from other countries around the globe. However, there have been and continue to be many commentators and critics who doubt whether the new system is capable of delivering a high-skills economy. On the other hand, there is evidence of considerable support for the new system, particularly in those occupational areas where there has been no tradition of VET. While it is too soon to assess whether the new VET system will be a success, a review of some of the evidence to date will provide a few pointers.

Since the creation of the NCVQ in 1986 government has paraded the 'significant advances' and 'success stories' of the new VET system. However, in the early years, take-up of NVQs was very slow and patchy. By early 1993 fewer than 350 000 or so NVQ certificates had been awarded, with more than 80 per cent of these relating to just three of the 11 NCVQ listed occupational areas, and most at NVQ Levels 1 and 2. By June 1997, 1 621 563 NVQ certificates had been awarded, covering all occupational areas, though mostly at levels 1, 2 and 3. Few level 4 certificates had been awarded, except in the occupational area of Business Services (48 253), the next highest being in Engineering (3 330). At NVQ Level 5, only 4 090 certificates across all occupational areas had been awarded, with most of these in Business Services. Hence to date it appears that NVQs are popular and widespread in some industries, such as retail, which have had no previous system of vocational qualifications, but much less popular in engineering, manufacturing and construction, which have had a long history of traditional apprenticeships.

A number of reasons have been put forward for the sluggish take-up in most sectors, and the overall 'low' take-up at NVQ Levels 4 and 5 in particular. For example, Drowley (1996) argues that the rigidity of the NVQ structure is the cause and suggests future take-up of Level 3 and 4 NVQs in supervision and management is likely to slow down dramatically. This echoes some of the criticisms of Smithers (1993) who suggested there were deep flaws in the detail of NVQs. At the root of the problem is the NCVQ insistence that candidates should be assessed on what they could do, rather than including what they know and understand. This has meant that underpinning knowledge and understanding has had to be inferred from observed competent performance only, the assumption being that if candidates for an NVQ show themselves capable of carrying out specified tasks, the necessary knowledge and theory must have been acquired also, and therefore requires no separate assessment.

Also, the approach dictated by the NCVQ precludes the effective and efficient use of conventional paper and pencil assessment and test procedures. By implication this means all existing vocational qualifications involving both practical and written examinations, including the BTEC Higher National Certificates and Diplomas and the City and Guilds craft and technician certificates, should be replaced. This aspect of the new VET system has been sharply challenged, particularly by Smithers. Focusing on the plumbing and electrical trades, the Smithers Report concluded it was difficult to see how the NVQs would match the qualifications being phased out, or how they would improve or maintain the quality of craft level work. Furthermore, the report presented evidence that unlike much of the traditional vocational education and training in the UK, the new

NVQs did not match the standards of VET found in Germany and Holland. Hence, Smithers concluded, it was difficult to see how NVQs would improve the inadequate skills of the national workforce and even more difficult to see how the NVQ pathway would raise educational attainment.

In the engineering industry, Senker (1996) found that any contribution of NVQs in training workers to cope with organisational and technological change is likely to be slight. Echoing the concerns of Smithers, he argued that the whole question of assessing knowledge and understanding in the NVQ system is deeply controversial, particularly the extent to which knowledge and understanding can be inferred from a limited range of practical demonstrations.

More recently, serious concerns regarding workplace assessment versus written test and examinations have been expressed in other occupational areas. For example, the National Council for the Training of Journalists (NCTJ), while very supportive of the new Modern Apprenticeship and Level 4 NVQs in journalism, points out that many (if not most) newspaper editors 'believe the subject of law and public affairs in particular require a thorough understanding and unless adequately tested by examination, serious problems could arise from simple ignorance'. For this reason many newspaper companies refuse to take up NVQs and instead are sticking with the traditional vocational qualification for journalists, which culminates in the NCTJ National Certificate Examination. However, arguing the need for a single skills qualification for the newspaper industry, the NCTJ has called for NVQs to become the basic skills assessment for journalists, but with the necessary underpinning knowledge and understanding being tested by examination (Bennett-England, 1997).

Some commentators believe the whole NVQ system is flawed. Senker (1996) claims there are fundamental defects which trace their origins to the narrow terms of reference of the Review of Vocational Qualifications, which recommended the establishment of the NCVQ and the subsequent imposition by the NCVQ of an inflexible interpretation of its brief. At the time this was characterised by the 'dogma' and 'ideology driven' approaches of the government.

Much criticism has centred around the NCVQ's adoption of top-down 'functional analysis' as the sole methodology for deriving the occupational standards at all NVQ levels in all occupational areas. Stewart and Hamlin (1992) argued a case against the drive towards competence-based qualifications using only functional analysis. They claimed this could lead to mechanistic and reductionist specifications which would be so far from the reality of how work is actually done as to be positively unhelpful. These concerns about functional analysis were further elaborated by Stewart and Sambrook (1995). Senker (1996) goes further and argues that there is good evidence that the methodological basis of the NCVQ system is totally unsound. Drawing on the work of Eraut (1994) and Kelley (1989), he argues that serious problems arise when attempts are made to apply functional analysis across a whole industry or occupation. Under conditions where there are no firm rules about working practices in different companies, either in principle or in practice, Senker concludes the process of functional analysis as a whole must inherently be largely arbitrary. Furthermore, as there is no clear basis on which the allocation of functions between occupations and workers (within engineering) can be determined, competence as defined by functional analysis often relates to arbitrarily defined roles.

Senker (1996) also claims the level of competence achieved and attested by the NVQ Level 3 occupational standards and qualifications in engineering is often significantly lower than that which engineering companies require their craftsmen and craftswomen to achieve. Typically, craft trainees are awarded their NVQ qualifications approximately two-thirds of the way through the engineering craft apprenticeship, which is based on the higher standards demanded by companies rather than on externally imposed standards. Moreover, NVQ Level 3 qualifications in engineering are deemed in the industry to be not very demanding in terms of underpinning knowledge. Consequently, many employers continue to send their apprentices on day release at colleges of further education to attend traditional courses of vocational education designed to impart sufficient requisite theoretical knowledge and understanding.

As mentioned already, the take-up of NVQs at Levels 4 and 5 has been very small in all but one occupational area. A major factor has been the burden not only on candidates in terms of the time and effort required to build a portfolio of evidence sufficient to demonstrate mastery in all the NVQ units and elements of competence, but also on employers in terms of the time, effort and costs of the assessment process and the associated administration. The original NCVQ idea of 'mastery learning' also led to problems with the assessment of GNVQs, for which students had to build 'massive' records of achievement against long lists of learning outcomes, placing intolerable burdens not only on students but also on teachers (*see* Smithers, 1993).

The appropriateness of NVQs at Levels 4 and 5 has also been questioned, particularly at Level 5 relating to the occupational standards for management as devised by the Management Charter Initiative. Many commentators have expressed doubts about the appropriateness, desirability and practicability of applying the competency approach as 'idealogically' and 'dogmatically' advocated by NCVQ (*see* Jacobs, 1989, Burgoyne, 1990, Stewart and Hamlin, 1992 and 1993, and Mumford, 1997). Their criticisms have centred not only around what Burgoyne argues are the limitations, narrowness and inappropriateness of the MCI universal mechanisms, or the significance of 'situation-specific' criteria of managerial effectiveness as revealed by Stewart and Hamlin (1990), but also around concerns regarding the soundness and sufficiency of the research and research methods used to derive the competences (*see* Bates, 1995, Tate, 1995, Mumford, 1997, and Woodall and Winstanley, 1998). (*See also* Chapter 12.)

In a critique of the competency movement and NVQ framework in Britain, Bates (1995) argues for a widening of the parameters of research in order to address other major issues of concern, such as the perceived relevance of NVQs to individuals and company needs, and the soundness of the fundamental precepts of competence-based education and training. Tate (1995), expressing reservations about the competence model, especially the MCI framework, claims it is based on insufficient research evidence, which is a view echoed by Mumford (1997). He claims that while some aspects of management are common to all management jobs, the areas in which managers need to be competent are more likely to be specific to the particularities of the organisation. This view is supported by Woodall and Winstanley (1998) who highlight the fact that in general most companies adopting the MCI competency approach find they have to adapt the generic MCI descriptions of competence and invest in a process of defining organisation-specific competences. The concerns about the MCI approach to identifying and developing management competences to which Mumford and Woodall and Winstanley refer are similar in substance to those voiced by Eraut (1994) and Senker (1996) concerning the development of the Levels 3 and 4 NVQs in engineering.

Another concern regarding the UK's national VET system is how to stimulate enough employees and employers to invest in vocational training (and vocational education) for the purpose of enabling individuals to become sufficiently competent to achieve an NVQ as assessed against occupational standards. There has been a widely held view, supported by past and present government ministers, that because industry as a whole gains from training, each firm should pay for the vocational education and training of its employees. However, Layard *et al.* (1994) argue that this is a fallacy. Vocational education and training which leads to nationally recognised qualifications inevitably raises an individual's value to many employers. Hence, having trained someone, the firm then has to pay the individual for the full value of the qualification, otherwise they could be poached. However, in many cases the firm does not need the individual to exercise all the skills associated with the qualifications. Hence the firm has no incentive to pay for training, except for that which is specific to the needs of the firm.

Individuals are unlikely to invest enough in their own training for a number of reasons. These include, as Layard *et al.* suggest, the possible underestimation of the expected or calculated return on the investment, the overestimation of the risk accruing to individuals when training, and the premium people place on their current earnings over future rewards, which leads them to discount training. They go on to argue that for these reasons a 'free market' in training without state subsidies is likely to lead to too little training. Hence there is a strong case for at least partial state finance for VET (e.g. free course tuition, as in Greece) as has been the case historically in the UK for academic education. Until 1998 nearly all UK students were able to get free academic education, but in the case of non-degree level VET the national practice has been to charge fees. Yet none of the UK's main continental competitors, including France, Germany and Italy, charges fees for the regular VET provided in their public colleges.

Late in 1996 the credibility of NVQs came under attack in a major government-initiated study carried out by the Centre for Economic Performance. Its report roundly condemned the whole NVQ system, not only for achieving little, but also for adding complexity and obscurity to the national structure of vocational qualifications (the opposite of what was intended), and displacing some valued traditional vocational qualifications (*see* Clare, 1996).

Bearing in mind the range of criticisms already illustrated, it is difficult to see how the NVQ framework can survive as a completely coherent and fully comprehensive national VET system without some modifications.

Just as NCVQ and NVQs have been criticised and their efficacy brought into question, so too have ITOs, LBs, TECs and LECs, but to a lesser extent. Harrison (1997) argues that the success of ITOs has been questionable, although other evidence suggests that some ITOs have been particularly effective. However, the sectoral framework of the national VET system has been perceived generally to have become overly complex, and government proposals initiated by the outgoing administration of John Major to rationalise the framework by forcing more mergers between ITOs, LBs and Occupational Standards Councils (OSCs) has been widely welcomed.

The Report and Proceedings of the House of Commons Employment Committee on the Work of TEC's (Employment Committee, 1996), which used evidence from the

Scottish Affairs Committee of Inquiry into the Work of LECs in Scotland, concluded that TECs/LECs 'had made a modest contribution only to the improvement of the national training system for the unemployed and to the promotion of economic regeneration and enterprise, and their impact had not been as dramatic as was hoped'. Concerns were also expressed about the structure of the TEC system, about the central government faults of bureaucracy and resistance inherited by TECs from their predecessor organisations, and about the need for more accountability and openness. However, on balance, the picture was positive and favourable towards the TECs. Harrison (1997) concludes that despite a mixed record, the TEC system appears likely to survive, although several TECs have merged with their respective local chambers of commerce to form dual-role unitary organisations.

In light of the mounting groundswell of hard-hitting criticisms of the newly created competence-based national VET system, the government commissioned for completion by early 1996 three independent reviews focusing on GNVQ assessment (The Capey Report), the top 100 NVQs (The Beaumont Report) and qualifications for 16 to 19-year-olds (The Dearing Report) respectively. Capey (1995) concluded that 'the qualification is clearly meeting important demands . . . students are being motivated by the independent approach to learning that the GNVQ offers'. However, the review identified the need for simplification of the assessment and recording requirements and recommended, among other things, improvements to increase rigour, quality, manageability and cost-effectiveness, and to reduce the assessment burden. These improvements were planned to be introduced from September 1998.

Beaumont (1995) concluded that there was widespread support for the SNVQ concept, with 77 per cent of employers (87 per cent in Scotland) indicating that the benefits of SNVQs outweighed the costs. However, the review also reported significant criticisms of the implementation of SNVQs. Assessment was seen as a major area of concern, with many perceiving 'a lack of rigour and consistency, and standards marred by complex, jargon-ridden language' resulting from functional analysis. Consequently, the NCVQ (and by inference the QCA, its successor organisation) embarked upon a programme of intensive activity to improve the NVQ system, including giving consideration to the possible introduction into NVQs of a significant element of external assessment. At the time of writing the outcome of these considerations had not been revealed.

Dearing (1996) proposed 198 recommendations for improving the provision of qualifications for 16 to 19-year-olds, the major implementation of which was planned for the autumn of 1998. Besides endorsing the Capey and Beaumont proposals, the key Dearing recommendations which would have an impact on the national VET system were:

- a national framework of qualifications at four levels (entry, foundation, intermediate and advanced), with three pathways (GCSE/A-levels, GNVQs and NVQs);
- combinations of these awards leading to National Certificates and Diplomas;
- a relaunch of Youth Training as National Traineeships;
- bringing existing traditional vocational qualifications within the national framework of qualifications;
- the merger of NCVQ with the Schools Curriculum and Assessment Authority (SCAA) to form the Qualifications Curriculum Authority.

At the time of writing it is too soon to comment on the impact of these three national reviews other than to observe that some of the recommendations have been acted upon.

1 Identify the main strengths and weaknesses as you see them of competence-based NVQs.

2 What are the implications of these for national VET policy?

3 How would you rate the degree of coherence in the various policies and initiatives, e.g. TECs, IIP, NVQs, currently being adopted in VET policy?

4 How would you describe or characterise the UK's current approach to VET policy?

Observations and comments

It is undoubtedly a fact that the introduction and development of the NVQ system over the past ten years or so has revolutionised the UK's national VET system. NVQs appear to be here to stay, at least at Levels 1, 2 and 3, and most probably at Level 4. However, evidence suggests a complete, coherent, comprehensive and fully credible NVQ system, including Level 5 NVQs, is still a compelling yet unrealised goal. Even if all the recommendations of the Capey, Beaumont and Dearing reports were to be fully and effectively implemented, it is difficult to see how the forward momentum of NVQs at the higher levels will be achieved. For this to come about it is suggested that NVQs at all levels across all occupational areas need to be recognised and demanded by employers as the required 'passports to practice' in place of other VET qualifications. Additionally, GNVQs, whether complementing or replacing traditional vocational education qualifications, must, by whatever means necessary, secure the same level of esteem and acceptability, both nationally and internationally.

Mutual recognition and transferability of VET qualifications within the European Union (EU) will become increasingly desirable, yet there are doubts as to whether the UK's GNVQs will compare favourably with equivalent qualifications in other EU countries (*see* Smithers, 1993, Senker, 1996). This is unlikely if, as appears to be the case in the engineering industry, employers have to educate and train their apprentices far beyond the 'minimum' Level 3 NVQ standards of a Modern Apprenticeship, especially if employers refuse to recognise the NVQ as an entry qualification (passport to practice) for employment in particular trades or occupations. Moreover, if, as in the newspaper industry, the majority of employers firmly believe competence cannot be safely inferred or demonstrated at NVQ Level 4 without the testing of key areas of underpinning knowledge and understanding through conventional examinations, and the outcome of such testing continues not to be a required component of the NVQ portfolio of evidence, then these higher level NVQs will continue to lack credibility in the eyes of top management. Consequently, they will continue not to be accepted as alternative entry qualifications to the professions.

The government's vision of an all-embracing, clear, coherent and comprehensive national VET system, with all NVQs at all levels achieving their full potential, will come about only if the MCI Level 5 qualifications, and other Level 5 NVQs, ultimately become acceptable replacements for, or alternatives to, existing professional qualifications. They need to become recognised as passports to practice for professional positions as well as the lower level occupations. However, the critical stumbling block is the problem of credibility and confidence, particularly in the testing of requisite theoretical knowledge and understanding at this level, and the gathering of sufficient reliable evidence that truly does attest to 'mastery competence' across the full range of occupational standards.

A possible way forward

It is believed that these problems can be overcome if, as Stewart and Hamlin (1993) suggest, greater flexibility and variability can be allowed in the way the NVQ system and criteria are interpreted and implemented in practice. They have identified five key principles that should inform and guide the design and operation of any national system of education and training, whether based on competency approaches or traditional methodologies. For example, national VET systems should be capable of (a) removing barriers to access to development opportunities and qualifications; (b) recognising current ability achieved through means other than formal vocational education and training; (c) being flexible in practice in terms both of development and assessment; (d) responding to the different needs of different occupations at different levels, from foundation to professional; and (e) being relevant to vocational practice.

Although, as a generalisation, the UK NVQ system appears to meet these five principles, there are clearly two where the interpretation and implementation of NCVQ (now QCA) policy has created problems, as suggested in this chapter. These are the two principles of 'being flexible' and 'responding to the needs of different occupations' which in practice still do not seem to be translated into recognition of variation in qualifications or sufficient flexibility in assessment at the professional levels in particular.

Stewart and Hamlin put forward two suggestions for making clear more overtly, and more publicly, that flexibility and variation to meet the needs of particular occupations are recognised and valued within NVQs. One relates to a proposed slight modification to the definition and meaning attached to the concept of competence. As currently defined, competence is taken to mean in practice that a person is fully competent in virtually all aspects of the occupation or job in a recognised employment context. This implies that mastery in performing to defined standards in real work settings has been achieved and demonstrated. Stewart and Hamlin suggest it would be helpful if the definition and meaning of competence for the purpose of NVQs encompassed a notion of 'threshold competence' or 'potential competence'. They see this notion as indicating that a person, while not yet fully competent at a 'mastery' standard, has in fact demonstrated the capacity and capability of becoming so as a result of proven basic ability and potential within the occupational field. It could be argued that this notion of 'threshold' or 'potential' competence reflects more accurately what has in fact been attested to by many NVQs awarded to date at all levels of the NVQ framework, particularly those delivered predominantly in colleges and schools alongside, or as integral parts of, vocational education and training programmes.

Stewart and Hamlin suggest that the point of qualification for some NVQs, or parts of NVQs, should be permissible at the 'threshold' or 'potential' competence level to meet the differing needs of different types and levels of occupations, although care would need to be taken not to exclude or play down important components of competence. This slight change would obviate the requirement, at NVQ Level 5 in particular, for candidates to build 'massive' portfolios of evidence comprising 'appropriate observed performance' and 'assessed in real-time work-related activities' from which full competence at the mastery standard can be safely and credibly inferred. However, this means the NVQ could not be claimed to be a 'passport to practice at mastery level' qualification, as can apply with lower level NVQs where the gap between 'mastery' and 'threshold' competence is very close or negligible.

Should it be the case that employers and the government wished jointly for NVQs to become essential vocational qualifications that must be obtained for a person to be recognised as qualified in any occupation and at every level, then this would preclude the use of the notion of 'threshold' competence. In this case another way would need to be found to maintain forward momentum of the NVQ system. Here, the second suggestion put forward by Stewart and Hamlin (1993) might prove helpful. They proposed that greater flexibility and variability in the balance of the different types of evidence used for assessment at different levels of the NVQ framework should be allowed. Whereas at Levels 1 and 2 virtually most, if not all, of the evidence could be inferred from direct observation in the workplace, at Level 5 the majority of the required evidence might be made up essentially of a combination of 'inferred competence from assessed real-time work-related activities' and 'demonstrated skills and underpinning knowledge and understanding through simulation and tests', with the latter comprising the major proportion of the portfolio. However, picking up on concerns about the lack of rigour of NVQs, and insufficient testing of essential theoretical underpinning that employers and others want to see at the higher levels of the NVQ framework, a further development of the Stewart and Hamlin proposal might be to make some form of certificated vocational education a mandatory component of an NVQ portfolio of evidence. This would mean specifying for inclusion established FE or HE-delivered vocational education or professionally related academic qualifications, either complete or in part, or other tailored replacement educational qualifications specifically aligned to NVQ occupational standards.

Candidates not able to produce the requisite VE-certificated evidence, but who believed they already possessed all the essential 'theoretical' underpinning, would need to demonstrate this aspect of their competence. This could be done by submitting themselves to the formal procedures for securing Accreditation of Prior Learning or Achievement (APL/APA), a service that many universities and colleges offer as part of their 'open access' policies. This process would be greatly helped by achieving convergence and close alignment between the learning outcomes of all vocational education and professional qualification programmes and the relevant NVQ occupational standards, although not at the expense or exclusion of leading edge advancements in the relevant field of knowledge. Furthermore, there would need to be closer collaboration between providers of NVQs and GNVQs and institutions of higher education. How the balance of the three types of portfolio evidence (including certificates of vocational education) for a given

NVQ might be variably and differently determined would depend on the depth, breadth and complexity of the skills, underpinning knowledge and understanding required for full competence at mastery level. This is illustrated in Fig. 3.3, which is a refinement of an earlier model first suggested by Stewart and Hamlin (1993).

The three dimensions of the model can be considered as representing the varying breadth, depth and complexity of the occupations contained within each of the five NVQ levels. It is suggested that this model has potential for resolving some of the problems beyond those that might be solved following implementation of the Beaumont and Dearing recommendations. The particular problems in mind include not only those already highlighted, but also the following:

(a) the mismatch between general and specific roles, and the related controversy over 'generic' versus 'situation-specific' competences.
(b) the question of affordability of NVQs both in terms of the amount of time required to gather sufficient evidence to demonstrate full mastery competence and of the comparatively high financial costs of workplace assessment.

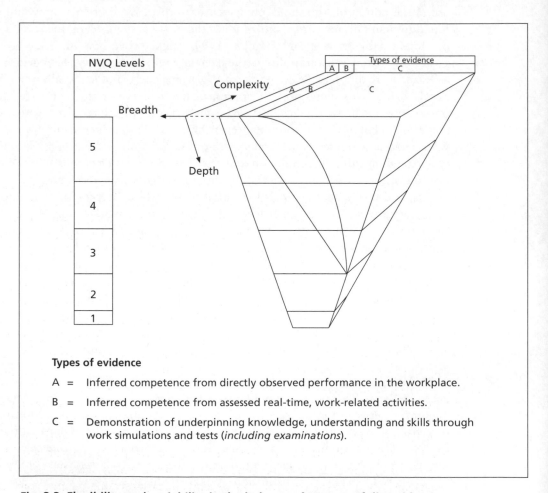

Types of evidence

A = Inferred competence from directly observed performance in the workplace.

B = Inferred competence from assessed real-time, work-related activities.

C = Demonstration of underpinning knowledge, understanding and skills through work simulations and tests (*including examinations*).

Fig. 3.3 Flexibility and variability in the balance of NVQ portfolio evidence

(c) the continued perceived lack of recognition given to the importance of assessing sufficiently the underpinning knowledge and understanding upon which credible competence depends.

(d) the lack of naturally occurring evidence in the workplace, particularly where employers deny opportunities for employees to develop and demonstrate competence outside the boundaries of their existing jobs.

(e) the heavy reliance on testimonial evidence, particularly at NVQ Level 5 where observed performance is either inappropriate or impossible to gather within realistic timescales, which is open to potential abuse and the subsequent disrepute of the qualification.

It is believed the model has potential for resolving some of the practical problems of implementing the competence philosophy, particularly at the higher levels of the NVQ framework, and could help maintain the forward momentum of NVQs.

Activity 3.5

1 What are the advantages and disadvantages from an employer's perspective of the current NVQ system?

2 How could the system be changed to improve its benefits for employers?

3 What would this mean for the role of employers in national VET policy?

Summary and conclusion

The competence approach has already brought about significant and beneficial change in the UK national VET system. The system has the potential to deliver the high-skill, high-performance, high-productivity economy the country needs, subject to the Capey, Beaumont and Dearing recommendations being implemented, but also subject to further modification on the lines suggested above. However, the historical factors mentioned earlier which thwarted various attempts by previous governments to create an effective national training system still persist to a greater or lesser extent. Although the nineteenth-century notion of apprenticeship has been replaced, the new Labour government's vision of the Modern Apprenticeship to be delivered through the current national VET system essentially adopts the same voluntarist approach as that of the outgoing Conservative administration. The government has turned away from the previous Labour Party and current Liberal Democratic Party ideas of adopting a predominantly state-interventionist approach in the form of a training tax on employers as in France.

However, in its Green Paper: The Learning Age, the government does suggest introducing a modest degree of interventionism into the national VET system by giving all 16 and 17-year-olds in jobs a legal right to undertake education and training to NVQ Level 2. This bears similarities to the system in Greece and Germany and would place some degree of compulsion on employers, but only those which actually employ 16 and 17-year-olds. To avoid the costs of training and educating young people, some companies –

especially small and medium-sized enterprises (SMEs) – may adopt policies of recruiting adults only, particularly if youth and apprentice pay remains high compared to that in other AICs. (This will be less likely if the Low Pay Commission principle of a reduced statutory minimum wage for young workers, with the under-18s exempted, as reported by Jones (1998), is accepted and implemented by the government.) Furthermore, if skilled status remains undervalued in the UK, as in the past, with narrow pay differentials between unskilled, semi-skilled, skilled, craft and technical jobs, then there will be little incentive for workers to aspire to the acquisition of higher level skills and NVQs. Moreover, even though unemployed young people will also have the legal right to undertake education and training, and will be encouraged 'to save to learn' through 'individual learning accounts', as Layard *et al.* (1994) suggest, many will choose not to invest time and money in vocational education and training without some degree of certainty that a job will be there at the end of their investment.

A further concern is that unless those aspects of the UK culture inducing short-termism into the running of businesses can be reduced or eliminated, it is unlikely, under the current voluntarist national VET system, that a great enough number of employers will invest sufficiently in educating and training the nation's workforce.

Soskice (1994) goes so far as to argue that 'the UK should hold no serious hope of emergence from its low-skills equilibrium (and low-skills economy) via the route of company-based initial vocational training for young people' because of 'the lack of appropriate basic underlying institutions within the British private sector, namely long-term financial institutions, co-operative industrial relations systems and powerful collectively organised employers'. The cost to the UK of these weaknesses and deficiencies has been high. As McKinsey, the firm of management consultants, revealed in its preliminary report to the government in May 1998, the UK's average company performance remains far below that of its main trading partners – in both manufacturing and services. In terms of corporate productivity and international competitiveness, the country still appears to be lagging behind France and Germany by 25–30 per cent, and as much as 40 per cent behind the USA (Jamieson, 1998).

With these facts in mind, perhaps it should be no surprise that some commentators such as Soskice argue that the UK should adopt a 'general education' route for its national VET system along American lines, and that national VET policies should be focused on mass post-16 education and mass higher education. Empirical evidence in the USA and the UK suggests that higher education can and does provide the key social, organisational, computing and learning skills demanded by companies in an increasingly service and client-dominated economy. Via a general education route, the top two-thirds of school leavers would enter higher education and the bottom one-third would enter vocational training. However, Soskice argues that a national training system for the bottom third of each post-compulsory schooling age group should not depend upon private sector companies because of the institutional deficiencies. Rather, a system should be based more around public sector initial training schemes linked to state-funded vocational education, as in France.

Finally, unless NVQs secure the same level of credibility and esteem as existing alternative vocational qualifications, particularly at the higher levels of the national framework, and become recognised and demanded by employers as passports to practice, the government's goal of producing the best trained workforce in Europe through 'world-class education and training' delivered through a clear, coherent, comprehensive national VET system is unlikely to materialise. The government may need to go beyond its present principles and action plans for building the Learning Age. This may mean incorporating a more state-interventionist approach into the national VET system and doing more to change those aspects of the UK culture that deter employers, employees and the unemployed from investing in learning. Alternatively, it may mean abandoning the competence-based NVQ approach as the predominant route to a high-skill, high-performance, high-productivity economy, and instead converting to an American-style general education approach with NVQs confined to low-skill occupations.

Activity 3.6

Review the results of all the previous activities in this chapter and discuss with a colleague the following questions.

1 Is the current UK VET policy framework appropriate to employers, individuals and the nation?

2 What are the implications of current and planned initiatives for employers?

3 What problem and opportunities does current policy create for the practice of employee development and the role of development practitioners?

4 What recommendations would/can you make to your organisation on the best response to current and planned initiatives?

Acknowledgement
This chapter was contributed by Bob Hamlin, Divisional Manager, Wolverhampton Business School.

Case study 3

Smithers and Jones is a long-established, family-owned, small chain of department stores. The company owns and operates six stores in city centre locations across East Anglia and the south-east of England. Products are aimed at middle income families and include the whole range of household goods, including furniture, 'white' and 'brown' goods, haberdashery and kitchenware. Other departments provide clothing for all members of the family, of all ages, as well as mother and baby products, beauty products and sports and leisure goods. Some departments include in-house concessions where space is rented to manufacturers who are responsible for merchandising and staff. The company stands or falls on its reputation for high-quality goods, fair pricing and excellent customer service. While there have been many changes during the 75 years or so of the company's existence, recent history has shown that these qualities are still valued by customers. Despite the intensification of competition, a general drift to specialist retailers situated in out-of-town retail parks, and the growth of giant shopping centres, Smithers and Jones continues to prosper. The previous five years have achieved steady growth in sales turnover and profits, and the current year is certain to continue that trend.

Although there is a head office with the usual functions, located in the first and still the largest store, each store operates relatively independently, although they all adopt a similar structure. Each one is headed by a general manager, with department and functional heads responsible for the operations and performance of the store. Functional heads include a personnel manager who reports to the general manager, with a 'dotted line' responsibility to a services director on the main board who is ultimately responsible for group personnel policies and practice, among other things. Each store also employs a training and development officer who reports directly to the personnel manager, but also has a 'dotted line' responsibility to the head of group management development in head office, who reports directly to the services director.

This apparently confusing structure is perfectly clear to Jenny Roberts. Jenny has worked for Smithers and Jones since leaving school 12 years ago with two A-levels. Jenny began as a management trainee and therefore has direct experience of most of the stores' operations. Her career to date has included more than six years as department manager in two different departments. Three years ago, Jenny accepted the position of training and development officer in the head office store as a move into personnel and away from store management. Having recently completed her Institute of Personnel and Development (IPD) qualification, Jenny expects a promotion soon into a more generalist personnel role, either in the head office function or in another store. She has no real desire to leave Smithers and Jones, but would consider doing so if her ambitions cannot be satisfied.

Jenny's current concern is with rising labour turnover and absence figures among sales staff. Her analysis indicates that these are particularly marked among junior, and younger, staff across all departments. Apart from these figures, Jenny has been receiving increasing numbers of complaints from senior sales staff, supervisors and department managers about the behaviour and performance of junior staff. While recruitment is undertaken by line managers with support from personnel staff, Jenny is involved in induction and initial training of new employees. This consists of four half-day induction sessions delivered off the job over the first two weeks of employment, and a structured series of five one-day courses and on-the-job modules delivered by Jenny and department supervisors over six months. With more than 800 staff, and the traditional high labour turnover in retail, induction and initial training form a significant part of Jenny's job. She has made improvements to this training during her three years, but has considered for some time that a major rethink and redesign is required. Although she is not certain of the reasons for the problems with junior staff, Jenny senses an opportunity to persuade others of her view. In particular, the store personnel manager will need to provide support.

Jenny recently met an adviser from the local TEC at an IPD branch meeting and followed this up with some discussions on the potential use of NVQs at Levels 2 and 3 in the store. The former would be potentially relevant to induction and initial training, while the latter could be applied to existing sales staff and recruits as they progress with the company. The TEC staff have also been promoting the benefits of Investors in People accreditation to Jenny, as well as wider use of NVQs, especially those in management, for other staff in the store. Decisions on training for sales staff are within the remit of the store. However, use of management NVQs would need the support and involvement of the head of group management development. Jenny is confident that the financial support available from the TEC will be attractive to her colleagues. However, she is not yet certain that adopting NVQs will be appropriate, although IIP seems to be a worthwhile target for the store.

Discussion questions

1 What advice would you give Jenny to help her continue her investigations and assessment of the potential of retail NVQs?

2 What might be the advantages and disadvantages for the store seeking to gain IIP accreditation?

3 What relevance and contribution, if any, might NVQs in retail have to the problems with junior staff in the store?

4 What relevance and contribution, if any, might NVQs in management have to Smithers and Jones as a company?

Suggested reading

Harrison, R. (1997) *Employee Development*. London: IPD.

Reid, M. and Barrington, H. (1997) *Training Interventions (5th edn)*. London: IPD.

Truelove, S. (1995) *The Handbook of Training and Development (2nd edn)*. Oxford: Blackwell Business.

CHAPTER 4

The organisation context

Introduction

The professional practice of employee development (ED) occurs primarily in work organisations. As we saw in Chapter 2, it is concerned with organisational and individual learning processes. It is therefore important that professionals have an understanding of the nature of organisations and are able to apply that understanding to analyse the particular circumstances of a specific organisation. Providing that understanding and developing that ability is the purpose of this chapter. However, it needs to be recognised that a single chapter can provide only a brief overview of the vast amount of research and writing devoted to developing organisation theory. This chapter will therefore concentrate on examining the most important concepts, and will do so, primarily, from the single perspective of the functionalist paradigm.

Organisations are social phenomena which occur within a wider social context. As part of our examination we need also to identify the processes occurring in that wider context to understand some of the critical influences on organisations. The conventional way of expressing the location of these processes is to refer to the external, or 'operating environment', of the organisation (Stewart, 1996). In other words, processes which occur within an organisation are referred to as 'internal' and those which occur outside are referred to as 'external'. This distinction has been questioned, both in its validity and utility, by application of the concept of 'autopoiesis' (Morgan, 1997). The idea of autopoiesis was developed in biology and therefore its use in the study of organisations relies on the metaphor of organisations as living organisms. It is also a rather complex concept and it is not entirely relevant to our purpose. However, autopoiesis does support a very important and significant argument: that organisations are not passive and reactive entities shaped unconditionally by external and independent forces. The idea of autopoiesis suggests that the environment within which an organisation operates, and the organisation itself, are part of the same system and therefore mutually interactive and sustaining. So, the distinction which we will apply and follow between external and internal processes should be seen as a useful analytical device rather than a necessarily true or accurate representation of actual relationships.

CHAPTER OBJECTIVES

- Explain and evaluate arguments concerning the process of globalisation.

- Specify and describe critical organisation processes, especially political dimensions.

- Analyse a specific organisation context.

- Formulate approaches to accessing and increasing the power and influence of the ED function.

The external context

There are two important concepts to consider before examining external processes in any depth. These are the ideas of 'bounded rationality' and 'enacted environment' briefly introduced in Chapter 2. As was suggested, these ideas argue limitations on the extent to which external factors can be known, understood or analysed with any degree of accuracy. They do therefore raise questions about the validity of any environmental analysis.

Limiting factors

The idea of bounded rationality was devised by Herbert Simon (1960) to express his argument that decision making in organisations was limited by the constrained information-processing abilities of organisation members. Individuals have limited capacity in terms of the amount of information they can deal with at any one time. Related to this, they are able to formulate and assess only a limited number of options or alternatives when considering what action to take. Finally, irrespective of the information-processing capabilities of individuals, it is always the case that not all relevant information can be known. This argument has two related points. First, the world is far too complex for all potentially relevant information to be identified and accessed. Second, the outcomes or results of alternative actions can only be anticipated or predicted. Since they occur in the future, they cannot by definition be known. Simon further argued that these limitations, which affect individual decision making, become institutionalised in organisation processes and therefore also constrain the rationality of organisation decisions.

The focus of Simon's work and his idea of bounded rationality is organisation decision making. However, to the extent that it is valid, it has obvious implications for analysing and understanding the operating environment. If Simon's arguments are accepted, it must be the case that we can never fully understand the range, nature and effects of external factors and processes having impact on the performance and functioning of organisations. All attempts to produce such an understanding will be limited by the operation of bounded rationality.

Activity 4.1

1 Select a recent example where you made a significant decision. Examples might include a major purchase such as a new car or house, or accepting a new job. Consider and answer the following questions:

(a) what factors did you take into account?

(b) how much information did you have on each of the factors?

(c) what alternatives did you consider?

(d) how did you estimate the relative value of each of the alternatives?

2 Select a significant factor in your organisation's operating environment. Examples might include competitor activity, trends in customer demands or recent/impending government legislation. Consider and answer the following questions:

(a) what do you know about the factor?

(b) what else do you need to know and how can you find out?

(c) what alternatives are open to your organisation in response to this factor?

3 Use the results of 1 and 2 to assess the validity of bounded rationality.

The work of Karl Weick and his concept of 'enacted environment' (Weick, 1979) is perhaps more directly applicable to attempts to analyse the operating environment. However, this concept contains an even more significant implication: that what we understand to be the reality of the environment is in fact socially constructed. In other words, the environments in which we live and work are those that we shape, create and construct in the shared meanings and beliefs we have in common with those with whom we live and work. What this means in practice is that individually and collectively we *select* only certain factors to pay attention to, then *interpret* the significance and relevance of those factors to our situation and then *give meaning* to the factors in a way which creates shared understanding. The result is a socially constructed, or collectively created, environment which then becomes for us **the environment**. Thus, according to Weick's analysis, the environments which organisations seek to influence and survive in are not those which may or may not have objective existence, but are those that we enact, or create, for ourselves.

The detail of Weick's argument, and the analysis of the concept of autopoiesis, have much in common and, as Morgan (1997) recognises, can be seen to lend support to each other. This raises the point that Weick's arguments do not necessarily support a view that environmental factors have no objective existence. His analysis focuses on the social and psychological processes which have the effect of creating a mutually accepted understanding of the environment, irrespective of any correspondence between that understanding and any actual or real environment. The important point is that, for members of a particular organisation, the enacted environment *is* the real environment since it is that to which they respond. It is important, too, to understand that the use of the word 'environment' in the concept does not have to be thought of exclusively in terms of external factors, in the sense of outside the organisation. The concept has equally important application to internal factors and indeed shared understandings of organisation as an abstract concept and how it applies to a particular organisation. This application is illustrated by Morgan's (1997) use of the concept of enacted environment when examining the metaphor of culture in analysing organisations. For our purposes here, though, the concept of enacted environment provides a sound reason for treating with some caution the following analysis of what is claimed to be a critical external trend.

Globalisation

It need hardly be said that the world is argued to be experiencing fundamental and significant change (Stewart, 1996, Burnes, 1996, Dawson, 1994), or that this change has significant implications for employee development (Harrison, 1997, Moorby, 1996, Torrington, 1994). One major change process that perhaps captures many of the significant changes said to be affecting organisations is that known as 'globalisation'. This process is argued to be changing the very conditions which gave rise to work organisations as we currently experience and understand them (Dicken, 1992) and, relatedly, necessitating the creation of new approaches to organising and managing (Hamel and Prahalad, 1994). Thus, it is important to examine the meaning of the concept, and the arguments on its significance or otherwise, as part of reaching an understanding of the organisational context of employee development. We will begin with a brief look at definitions.

Use of the term 'globalisation' is relatively recent (Waters, 1995), especially in relation to academic analyses of social change (Robertson, 1992). Perhaps this is due to earlier analyses being framed in terms of what is known as the 'convergence thesis' (Kerr, 1983). The academic debates over the similarities or differences of meaning between these two concepts need not concern us too much here. What both have in common is analyses which examine the extent to which the world is becoming *similar* – that is, social arrangements sharing the same characteristics across the world irrespective of national or societal cultures – and the extent to which the world is becoming *unified* – that is, the significance of national identities expressed through the creation and independence of nation-states is declining.

Robertson (1992) rather neatly overcomes the latter debate by arguing that development of the nation-state is an aspect of globalisation in that it is a form of social organisation that has spread across the globe. Notwithstanding that point, Giddens (1989) provides a useful definition of globalisation as the phenomenon of increasing interdependence of world society. This definition, while accepting the utility of viewing the world as a society, does not necessarily imply unity or integration. The world, according to this definition, is to be seen not as a single social system but as a collection of separate yet increasingly interdependent social systems. Much analysis of this interdependence from an organisation or business perspective emphasises economic factors and relationships (Dicken, 1992). However, political and cultural factors are also argued to be of importance (Ritzer, 1993, Waters, 1995, Fukuyama, 1995) and therefore of relevance from an organisation perspective.

Explanations seeking to account for globalisation tend to differ according to whether the analysis is from an economic or sociological perspective. The following definition of the process also indicates possible causes which have wide support among various theorists.

> The compression of the world as a whole and the intensification of consciousness of the world as a whole . . . both concrete global interdependence and consciousness of the global whole in the twentieth century.
>
> (Robertson, 1992, p. 8)

The first of these conditions, 'compression of the world as a whole', refers to the re-ordering of time and distance in everyday lives, perhaps most famously expressed by the idea of 'the global village' (McLuhan, 1964). To illustrate this argument, think about the typical life experience of a person born in the UK, an 'advanced' and industrialised country, as recently as the early part of this century. In all probability, such a person was born, lived and died in the same town or village, with no direct contact outside that town or village, and little, if any, awareness of or interest in places and events elsewhere. Contrast that experience with your own. Communication of information across the world is commonplace through the internet and live television broadcast by satellite, as is overseas travel for both business and pleasure. Robertson's (1992) second condition in some ways follows from this since 'consciousness of the world as a whole' is related to awareness, knowledge and understanding of places and events outside our direct experience. The condition finds some support in the work of Waters (1995), although his analysis goes further in arguing that people are becoming increasingly aware of the globalisation process, in terms of social and cultural arrangements at least.

There are three additional factors which are argued to be significant in supporting the process of globalisation (Giddens, 1989). These are:

- *The role of global institutions*. These can be of two types. The first is known as 'non-state actors' and includes organisations such as the United Nations and International Monetary Fund. The second is defined as 'trading networks', for example, the EU and OPEC. A significant distinguishing feature of global institutions is that they are not controlled or bound by any individual, participating government.
- *Global issues*. This factor refers to those issues confronting the world which have implications for all countries but which cannot be solved or resolved by the independent action of any single country. Perhaps the most obvious example is global warming, itself an example of the broad spread of concerns falling under the collective title of the environment or green issues. Other examples include natural disasters and famine.
- *Cultural influences*. This factor reflects the growth and spread of cultural influences, styles and tastes from across the globe. The spread of such influences is obviously facilitated and supported by the compression of time and space through development and application of communications and information technology in particular.

Activity 4.2

1 Identify and describe some of the global cultural influences which are evident in UK society.

2 What implications might arise from these for the design and management of work organisations?

Additional arguments

There are theorists and writers who argue a different perspective and analysis. One of the more academic, though of particular interest to the study of the management of work organisations, is that produced by Goldthorpe (1985). Although the focus of Goldthorpe's work was the earlier convergence thesis, rather than globalisation as defined and discussed here, it remains relevant since his analysis argues against a trend of social arrangements becoming the same or similar. Concentrating specifically on structural characteristics related to dealing with the operation of a capitalist economy, Goldthorpe argued that societies still have choices open to them and therefore are not impelled to adopt a single approach.

A number of writers have focused on the influence of national or societal culture, especially as culture operates to shape approaches to organising and managing (Adler, 1986, Lane, 1989, Child and Keiser, 1979). The analyses arising from these primarily empirical studies suggest that cultural differences are significant in producing different managerial approaches. A particularly influential study produced by Hofstede (1980) supports the argument that, whatever the nature and effects of globalisation, the process does not imply a trend towards similarity or commonality in organising and managing. Hofstede identified four significant dimensions on which managerial beliefs, attitudes and behaviour can and do differ according to national characteristics. We do need to recognise the location of most of these analyses in the 'convergence' rather than 'globalisation' debate. However, a more recent and influential work appears to cross this conceptual divide. George Ritzer (1993), an American sociologist, has devised the concept of 'McDonaldization'. This refers to Ritzer's argument that McDonald's, the chain of fast-food restaurants, represents the paradigm case of what he sees as a wider process producing similarities and commonalities in all aspects of life, similarities and commonalities which cross and transcend national borders. Ritzer's work therefore supports a view of globalisation producing convergence in, among other things, approaches to organising and managing. The critical characteristics of the process of McDonaldization according to Ritzer are as follows:

- *Efficiency*: a concern with and value attached to reducing the time and effort required to satisfy a need or want. These are not exclusively material needs and wants, though McDonald's is focused on the material need to satisfy hunger.
- *Calculability*: importance and significance attached to only that which can be measured in a standardised manner. The effect of this is to associate quality with quantity, for example, ratings being used to judge television programmes, box-office takings in the case of films, or best-seller lists for books. League tables used in health care or education are other examples.
- *Predictability*: a concern with reducing uncertainty illustrated by the standardisation of products and services. McDonald's epitomises this characteristic, with consumers being certain of receiving the same product and service experience whenever they eat at a McDonald's restaurant, wherever it may be.
- *Control*: the control effects of technology and bureaucracy on the behaviour of individuals, whether as employees, consumers or citizens. Ritzer suggests, for example, that the McDonaldization process can and does replace the 'sovereign consumer' with docile conformists who comply with the demands of producers and providers of goods and services.

1 Think about and produce some examples/evidence which would support a view that societies and countries around the world retain particular and unique cultural characteristics.

2 Think about and produce some examples/evidence which would support a view that cultural differences are becoming less evident and/or significant and, therefore, that countries are becoming more similar or the same as each other.

3 Consider the weight of these two sets of examples/evidence and produce an argument either in support of or against the position adopted by Ritzer.

Ritzer's argument on the *fact* of increasing similarity, if not the nature of particular characteristics, finds support in the work of Marceau (1992) and Waters (1995). The former suggests specifically that adoption of organisation and managerial principles from Japan – in other words, the Japanisation of organisation behaviour – is now a global phenomenon. The latter uses a similar argument to illustrate how globalisation impacts on and influences similar approaches to organising and managing.

The analyses considered in this section illustrate and support an argument that globalisation is a significant feature of the external environment. The process can and does create opportunities for organisations, both in terms of product markets and in terms of ideas on new approaches to and forms of organising and managing. The process may also consist of, and support operation of, forces which shape the conditions in which organisations operate, and therefore which demand internal organisation responses. We now consider this internal context in more detail.

The internal context

We discussed in Chapter 2 some of the problems in defining the term 'organisation', and its close association with the concept of 'managing'. In this section we will treat both concepts as unproblematic in the main and therefore adopt what might be termed a traditional or established perspective. This perspective will be recognised as falling within the functionalist paradigm (Burrell and Morgan, 1979). It is important to bear in mind, therefore, that alternative paradigms and interpretations are possible.

Organisations have been defined as sets of relationships in which people co-operate to achieve tasks (Watson, 1994). What this definition does not specify, although perhaps implies, is that task achievement is normally associated with some overall purpose. So, we can say that organisations exist to achieve some goal or purpose. The pursuit of some purpose is therefore a defining characteristic of an organisation. The definition offered by Watson indicates a further defining characteristic in that it uses the word 'people'. So, organisations consist, again normally, of two or more individuals. A third characteristic, following from the second, is competition for power and resources. While Watson seems to emphasise co-operation in his definition, his research clearly indicates the existence of conflict over the allocation of power and resources (Watson, 1994).

Arrangements are required in organisations, first to ensure control and co-ordination of effort in carrying out tasks relevant to purpose, and second to resolve and mediate conflicts over power (for instance, to decide purpose and/or relevance of tasks) and allocation of resources. Such arrangements are what we refer to as 'organisation structure'. The concept of structure is central to the internal context and has as its main focus authority relations – in managerial language, the organisation hierarchy – which have the effect of defining limits in terms of decision making about purpose and resources (Fredericks and Stewart, 1996). Structure is also concerned with specification and co-ordination of tasks. Thus, organisations have to secure and account for their resources, utilise these resources in producing some goods or services, and ensure that goods and services remain relevant to the needs and wants of consumers or clients. They need also to promote the maximum co-operation between members of the organisation in achieving purpose (Watson, 1994). Thus, organisations commonly group tasks associated with meeting these needs into organisation functions (Huczynski and Buchanan, 1992, Mullins, 1993). The functions listed in the earlier sentences translate into accountancy and finance, production or operations, marketing and people management. Separation of specialist functions is then a common feature of organisation.

Separation brings problems of co-ordination, however, and intensifies the potential for conflict over power and resources. This situation of problems over co-ordination and those arising from conflict is probably in most people's experience of organisations. Many readers could recount examples of how different functions pursue tasks which, to outsiders at least, seem to support functional objectives to the detriment of the organisation's purpose. This situation provides the major rationale for and purpose of management. We can, therefore, say that the functions of management are to control resource allocation and utilisation, and to ensure that pursuit and achievement of tasks is in support of organisation purpose. We will return to this point as we examine the internal context in more detail.

Purpose

Organisation purpose can be, and is conceived of, as operating at different levels (Moorby, 1996). These different levels are characterised by varying usage of the concepts of vision, mission, aims and objectives (Harrison, 1997, Mullins, 1993, Burnes, 1996). Given this varying usage, it is useful to examine the most important terms.

- *Vision*. The concept of vision, certainly as applied in organisation and management theory, is rather abstract and nebulous. Essentially, it is concerned with a 'picture that people hold in their minds' (Harrison, 1997, p. 19). Since it is held in the mind, vision is usually aspirational rather than representing something having current existence. It needs to be both challenging and possible. Moorby (1996, p. 37) quotes the following, attributed to John F. Kennedy, as an example: 'To put a man on the moon.'
- *Mission*. The concepts of vision and mission are closely related and can be easily confused (Moorby, 1996). However, Moorby is in agreement with Harrison (1997) in suggesting that mission is concerned with articulation of commitment to achievement of the vision. Harrison further suggests that a mission statement gives more concrete form to the vision. In some formulations, mission relates to the organisation's key

purpose through indicating factors such as products and markets (Cummings and Huse, 1989). An example of this is Parker Pens, an organisation which experienced a transformation when it came to understand that its market and products were concerned with valued gifts rather than with writing instruments.

- *Goals and objectives*. The terms 'goals' and 'objectives' are often used as synonyms (Moorby, 1996). Both refer to what an organisation wishes and intends to achieve expressed in *specific* and *measurable* terms. In some ways it is useful to think of goals and objectives as providing the answer to two questions. First, what will be different about the organisation and/or the world if we achieve our mission? Second, how will we know if we have achieved our mission? Both questions demand answers which are measurable. As well as being measurable, objectives are usually set within defined timescales. Thus, it is usual to have long-term – say 5–10 years – medium-term – say 3–5 years – and short-term – say 1–3 years – objectives. Such formulations also begin to provide the measures against which performance and success can be assessed.

The concepts considered so far address, in part, the question of *why* in relation to an organisation. They provide a rationale and justification for the organisation's continued existence. In doing so, they also help to answer the question *what* in terms of what the organisation wishes or intends to achieve. In simple terms, what is the organisation there to do? The remaining key question is *how* will those ambitions be achieved? This question is answered by examining a further concept.

- *Strategy*. This is a complex concept which, according to one leading writer on the topic (Mintzberg, 1990) can lay claim to ten different perspectives. Watson (1994) provides a useful description in arguing that strategy is concerned with managing relations with the environment in order to ensure the long-term survival of the organisation. So, strategy has an external and long-term focus. That statement is likely to find broad agreement in the academic literature. However, a point of disagreement and debate is the extent to which strategy is deliberate or emergent. The former views strategy as the result of rational processes of analysis out of which plans are formulated and implemented which provide and detail the means by which an organisation will achieve its mission. The latter questions the argued rationality and linearity of the former, and argues instead that strategy emerges from sometimes unrelated and *ad hoc* decisions, themselves the result of compromises and resolutions of competing interests.

Accepting strategy formulation as deliberate, the process can be said to involve three stages. These are strategic analysis, planning and implementation (Johnson and Scholes, 1997). These stages can be and are applied at three levels to produce a corporate strategy concerned with the organisation as a whole, a business strategy focused on significant elements or units within the organisation, and a functional strategy for each of the specialist functions. These three levels have a linear relationship in that functional strategies are derived from and contribute to business strategies, and business strategies are derived from and contribute to corporate strategy. All strategies in turn, at whatever level, derive from and enable achievement of the organisation's mission. This set of relationships is represented in Fig. 4.1.

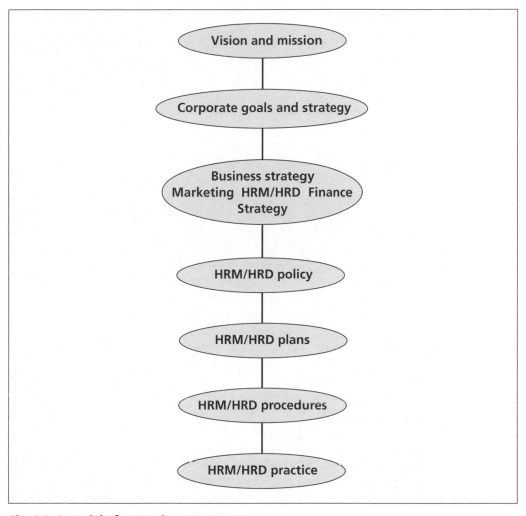

Fig. 4.1 A model of strategic management
Source: Stewart, J. and McGoldrick, J. (1996) *Human Resource Development: Perspectives, Strategies and Practice*. London: Financial Times Pitman Publishing.

Activity 4.4

1 (a) imagine you are the top manager or chief executive and write a mission statement for your organisation.

   (b) compare what you have written with the official statement if one exists. If not, ask the top manager, or some other senior manager, what they believe the organisation's mission to be and then compare.

   (c) analyse similarities and differences and think about reasons for them.

2 (a) access or formulate a description of your organisation's business strategy.

   (b) evaluate the connections and degree of 'fit' between the mission and strategy.

The political dimension

The description of the internal context so far has indicated potential conflict. Conflict can arise for at least three reasons. First, because different groups in organisations have their own material interests and pursue these (Fox, 1974, Watson, 1995). An example, perhaps oversimplified, would be between senior managers and other employees over the distribution of surplus resources. Second, and relatedly, because there can be disagreement over the 'what', i.e. the purpose, mission and objectives of the organisation. For example, individual values differ and some may wish to give greater emphasis to serving the interests of customers or clients while others believe shareholders or other sources of funding should be given priority. Third, because there can be disagreement over the 'how': the means, or strategy, by which the organisation achieves its purpose. An example, again perhaps oversimplified, would be between an operations department which believes emphasising the features and quality of the product will achieve success, and a finance department which believes lowering costs is necessary. The latter two reasons can usefully be considered in more detail.

In a seminal contribution to organisation theory, Etzioni (1961) suggested that organisations pursue three sets of goals. These are order, economic returns and cultural unity. Depending on the nature of specific organisations, goals within these different types will be more or less emphasised. For example, prisons will particularly value order, commercial companies will particularly value economic returns, and religious or charity organisations will particularly value cultural unity. To emphasise the point, most or all organisations will have purposes associated with each type of goal, but will vary in the value they attach to each. Etzioni's analysis went on to identify different sources or types of power which can be and are used to achieve these different sets of goals, and to relate these different types of power to a classification of types, or levels, of involvement on the part of organisation members. In summary, achievement of order implies use of coercive power and leads to alienative involvement; economic goals require use of remunerative power leading to calculative involvement; and cultural goals rely on use of normative power for their achievement which results in moral involvement. In more simple terms, achievement of order relies on potential and actual use of punishment, on the basis of which organisation members merely comply with organisational requirements; economic goals rely on the potential and actual provision of rewards, and organisation members expend effort on the achievement of those goals to the extent that they expect and value the associated rewards; and cultural unity depends on genuinely shared beliefs and values on the basis of which individuals give freely of their commitment to the organisation.

This analysis suggests two key points. First, any organisation has to and will decide to give emphasis and priority to one or two of these potentially competing goals. For example, individuals cannot be both compliant and committed. Second, individuals are likely to vary in the value they attach to the different types of goals. Thus, there is likely to be disagreement and conflict over what the organisation's purpose(s) should be.

Turning to the issue of 'how', i.e. strategy, further areas of potential disagreement are revealed. To take a broad example, the work of Michael Porter (1980, 1985) has been highly influential on thinking and writing on strategic management. Porter (1985) suggests the idea of three broad, or generic, strategies which are available to commercial organisations as a means of gaining advantage over competitors. These are 'cost leadership', which relies on becoming the lowest cost producer; 'differentiation', which requires some unique and distinct characteristic to be offered to a wide market; and 'focus', which can be based on either cost or quality in a tightly specified market segment. According to Porter, all business strategies can be incorporated under one of these three headings, and organisations need to decide which they are going to apply and pursue.

It should be easy to identify how such a decision is likely to produce conflict since each of the generic strategies will lead to different distributions of power and influence among specialist functions. For example, any strategy with cost as a focus is likely to lead to a heavy emphasis on cost and management accounting within the organisation and thus raise the status and profile of those working in that function to the relative detriment of other functions. Therefore, decisions about what strategy to adopt are likely to generate disagreement and conflict.

Formally, the existence of structural arrangements such as a managerial hierarchy and specifications of roles and responsibilities exist to deal with and resolve disagreements and conflict. As Harrison (1997) argues, understanding and operating within the structure and culture of a particular organisation is essential for ED practitioners. However, structure is concerned primarily with Politics with a capital P, that is, the official processes for dealing with conflict. In focusing also on culture, Harrison (1997) raises the significance of unofficial and more informal processes for gaining and exercising power and thus influencing decisions. This is confirmed by Moorby (1996), who highlights the role of individual personalities and relationships in organisational politics. So, all organisation members at whatever level can and do engage in a political process.

The need for development practitioners to develop and apply political skills is well documented (Harrison, 1997, Moorby, 1996, Johnston, 1996). Johnston (1996) provides a particularly useful analysis of why and how power is important to the HRD function. Her use of the framework developed by French and Raven demonstrates that professionals do not have to rely exclusively on formal authority. This is perhaps fortunate since most evidence suggests that HRD and those employed in the function rarely have high status in organisational hierarchies (Harrison, 1997). The sources of power available are as follows (French and Raven, 1959):

- *Reward.* This power base relies on the ability to award valued incentives, both material (e.g. salary and other financial rewards) and non-material (e.g. status and/or the indicators of status such as titles).
- *Coercive.* In French and Raven's framework, this power arises from the ability to withhold valued incentives and rewards.
- *Legitimate.* This power is associated with formal authority derived from position in organisational structure.
- *Expert.* As a source of power, this base relies on specialist knowledge and ability which is recognised and accepted by others. As Johnston (1996) points out, the strength of this power is related to the scarcity or otherwise of the expert ability.
- *Referent.* The final power base derives from personal characteristics which are usually associated with the notion of 'charisma'.

Implications for practice

There are some similarities and commonalities between these sources of power and the types of power identified by Etzioni and other writers (Johnston, 1996). This tends to support the argument advanced by Garaven and his colleagues, for example, that HRD specialists can and do rely more on their individual and collective networks than on their formal position to achieve their personal and functional objectives (Garaven *et al.*, 1993). In other words, development practitioners rarely find themselves in positions of strong, formal power and therefore need to cultivate and exercise alternative sources of power.

The cultivation and exercise of power raises questions about its purpose. Such questions have an ethical dimension which will be examined in a later chapter. The point to be made here is that organisations are political arenas in which specialist functions compete for resources and influence. The HRD function, if it is to survive and provide a full and proper contribution, needs to be adequately resourced and to be able to exercise influence throughout the rest of the organisation. So, the rationale for securing and exercising power is to create and sustain influence in order to, in turn, ensure a continuing HRD contribution to the long-term success of the organisation. The focus of influence will be, in general terms, the decision on purposes, i.e. 'what', and strategies, i.e. 'how', discussed earlier in the chapter. The question that now arises concerns what practitioners can do to ensure they have sufficient power to contribute to and influence those decisions.

A commonly suggested starting point seems to be to assess current and potential sources of power (Johnston, 1996, Moorby, 1996, Harrison, 1997). An informed understanding of the nature and sources of power obviously supports that process. This understanding has to be applied in the circumstances of a particular organisation context. For example, it could be argued that in a long-established financial services company such as one of the high street banks, formal or legitimate power will be of much more significance than in a young, small software consultancy firm. This organisational assessment can be usefully supplemented by an individual and team assessment of personal influencing styles and skills (Johnston, 1996, Harrison, 1997). These assessments will identify areas for developing future strategies for improving actual and potential influence.

Some of these strategies will be focused on professional development for practitioners. Indeed, Johnston (1996) argues that development of political and influencing skills should and will be a focus of continuous professional development (CPD) for development practitioners. Harrison (1997) places great emphasis on dealing with failure, perceived and actual. She argues a need for professionals to have worked out in advance clear strategies, approaches and responses for managing failure in order to minimise negative, and maximise positive, effects on power and influence. Moorby (1996) takes a perhaps more optimistic approach. Among other ideas, he suggests the following strategies and tactics:

- identify key players, that is those with most power and influence. These are likely to be chief executives and other senior managers;
- ensure the HRD function and contribution is compatible with what is important to key players;
- involve key players and other managers in all HRD activities and all stages in the process;

- produce evidence of success from HRD activities in terms which make sense and are important to key players and other managers;
- be aware of changing priorities in the organisation and be prepared to adopt and change HRD products and services.

Activity 4.5

1 (a) identify the key players in your organisation and determine what is important to them.

(b) assess the relevance of HRD activities and services to the priorities of key players.

(c) consider how HRD activities could be changed to increase relevance.

2 (a) consider and assess the success of the HRD function in your organisation in identifying and promoting its successes.

(b) create some ideas and approaches for promoting the function.

3 Discuss your responses to 1 and 2 with colleagues inside and outside your organisation.

Summary and conclusion

This chapter has been concerned with examining in broad terms the context of employee development. An established and widely applied distinction between the *external* and *internal* context has been applied in doing so. To return to the chapter's starting point, however, it is important to bear in mind that alternative paradigms and perspectives are possible and that some would question the validity of this distinction.

In considering the external context, particular attention has been given to the process of globalisation. We will return to this in a later chapter to examine potential organisation responses and related HRD implications. In terms of the internal context, organisations as political arenas have been argued to be an important consideration for HRD practitioners. Strategies for dealing with the political dimension have also been briefly described. The whole analysis in this chapter has been within the functionalist tradition. Before moving on, it is useful and instructive to consider the validity of the arguments presented here from the perspective of alternative paradigms. Activity 4.6 will help achieve this.

Activity 4.6

1 What would a radical-humanist paradigm analysis of the external and internal contexts focus on as key factors?

2 How do those factors differ from those presented in this chapter?

3 What are the implications of this for the practice of HRD?

Case study 4

Derek works for a well-known high street retailer. Although a long established and widely recognised 'brand', the company experienced a long period of falling turnover and declining profits. Partly as a result of this declining performance, ownership of the company changed twice in five years. Amendments instituted by new managers brought in following the last change of ownership resulted in a reduction from 1 200 to 800 branches and a reduction in the product range. The latter also brought about a restructuring of 'business areas', with all remaining products being located in five ranges. At the time of Derek's appointment, these changes were beginning to bring improvements in economic performance. However, Derek found clear differences between staff in retail operations and those working in head office in terms of understanding of and support for the company's intended strategy. This is based on a combination of Porter's differentiation and focused generic strategies. The intent is to identify and target precisely defined market segments and to provide an excellent and unique customer experience. While changes to enable adoption of this strategy in the stores are evident, little is happening in head office functions to devise and apply new processes and systems.

Derek's role is to act as management development manager for head office personnel. These are structured in six functions: IT operations, property management, human resources, marketing and public relations, logistics, and security. Historically and tradition-ally, head office functions have been perceived by those working in retail operations as 'controlling' rather than 'supporting'. In addition, each function has operated with little reference to others. This can be illustrated by the experience of store managers receiving contradictory information, advice or instructions from different functions in the same post delivery, or unannounced visits from staff from two functions on the same day. Derek quickly discovered high levels of resistance from some functional heads and members of their staff to both the new strategy of the organisation and the need to change established processes and methods of working.

As a new appointment with a brief to bring about change in head office functions, Derek enjoys the visible and personal support of the HR director, who sits on the main board. The director of retail operations is also keen to see changes in the way in which head office functions operate. To begin his task, Derek decides to organise and facilitate a series of 'open-frame' workshops with diagonal slices of staff across head office departments. The workshops will last one day and will have a maximum of 12 participants, with no more than four from any one function. Derek's covert agenda is to be able to observe at first hand how individuals from the different functions relate to and work with each other. The overt agenda is set by the title of the workshops: 'The implications of company strategy for head office functions.' Derek anticipates that this will begin to produce useful and useable data, and to reduce resistance to change by involving those affected.

Derek is confident that his first step is an appropriate one from the point of view of pro-fessional practice. He intends to build on the workshops, when completed, by working with functional heads and their senior staff, to help them produce functional strategies. However, he is concerned about the level of real support and participation he can expect and will receive from some heads and staff.

Discussion questions

1 What are the critical external and internal factors which will have impact on Derek's work?

2 What conception of 'strategy' is informing decisions in the organisation?

3 What are the 'political' factors which Derek will have to take into account in carrying out his role?

4 What bases and sources of power can Derek draw on in achieving his initial objectives?

5 What advice would you give Derek in announcing and preparing for his planned workshops?

Suggested reading

Dicken, P. (1992) *Global Shift: The Internationalization of Economic Activity*. London: Paul Chapman Publishing.

Johnson, G. and Scholes, K. (1997) *Exploring Corporate Strategy (4th edn)*. Hemel Hempstead: Prentice-Hall.

Mintzberg, H., Quinn, J.B., and Ghosal, S. (1998) *The Strategy Process*. Hemel Hempstead: Prentice-Hall Europe.

Moorby, E. (1996) *How to Succeed in Employee Development (2nd edn)*. Maidenhead: McGraw-Hill.

Ritzer, G. (1993) *The McDonaldization of Society*. California: Sage.

CHAPTER 5

The role and contribution of employee development

Introduction

Chapter 2 provided some definitions of key concepts associated with employee development. Chapters 3 and 4 described the national and organisational contexts within which those concepts are operationalised and applied. To close this part of the book, this chapter is intended to give more detailed and specific meaning to the concepts and, in doing so, to examine how they can be and are applied in practice. The approach adopted is to analyse the *role* and *contribution* of employee development. This approach therefore introduces two new concepts which are, perhaps fortunately, closely related. The idea of contribution immediately raises the question 'to what?'. The simple and obvious answer is contribution to achievement of agreed aims and objectives. The same can be said of role. Rules of grammar require a slightly different formulation of the question and answer to 'role in' rather than 'contribution to'. However, the essential meaning is similar. We are therefore concerned in this chapter with analysing how employee development aids and supports the achievement of agreed objectives.

One difference between the concepts of contribution and role is that the latter leads to a focus on relationships with other functions, rather than treating the contribution of ED in isolation. This is a significant distinction and an important feature. We will therefore be relying more on the concept of 'role' in our analysis, while remembering that 'contribution' is also part of our concern. Our concern and focus in this chapter can be applied at three levels at least. These are national, organisational and individual levels. In other words, we could examine the role of education, training and development *institutions* in society, the role of the employee development *function* in organisations, or the role of individual *development specialists* in their professional practice. There are similarities, relationships and connections between each of these. For example, we saw in Chapter 2 the assumed importance of economic and financial indicators in organisations, and in Chapter 3 the argued macro-economic benefits of state investment in education and training. Individual professionals will also use financial indicators to judge their performance, and will have them applied by others (*see* Harrison, 1997, Moorby, 1996). There can be assumed or argued linear, causal relationships between the three levels: that is, that individual practitioners contribute to the economic success of organisations, the success of which contributes to national prosperity. So, analysis at any one level has relevance and application at the remaining levels.

We will concentrate on the organisation and, in particular, individual levels, with the understanding that similar arguments could be used at a national level. In summary, this chapter is intended to achieve the following objectives. These objectives will require some understanding of the concept of role, and the ability to apply that understanding in conducting a role analysis.

CHAPTER OBJECTIVES

- Describe, apply and evaluate the concept of 'role analysis'.

- Compare, contrast and assess a range of models describing roles adopted by development specialists.

- Establish the primary focus of current personal role and potential for change.

The concept of role

The concept of role has been developed within both sociological theory (Taylor *et al.,* 1995) and social psychology (Myers, 1995). What this immediately tells us is that the concept is applied at a level of analysis greater than a single individual, and that it is concerned with *interactions* experienced by two or more people. We can say, therefore, that a role does not exist in isolation but is defined by its relationships with and connections to other, perhaps complementary, roles. In other words, role is a social concept and a way of examining and analysing social action and behaviour. Our everyday understanding and use of the word also provides a useful introductory point. The concept of role is often associated with performance of a part in a play or film or some other form of dramatic enterprise. This everyday use of the word is central to one aspect of its use in sociological theory. Erving Goffman (1959, 1968) explicitly uses a dramaturgical analogy in his work and, in doing so, views society as a drama and individuals as social 'actors' performing roles. A question that arises from this analogy is the extent to which any given or particular role is 'scripted'; that is, the degree of freedom individuals have in interpreting, shaping and defining their roles for themselves. The analogy helps to illustrate the question in that we can and do debate the differences in performances of, for example, Hamlet when played by, say, Lord Olivier or Mel Gibson. The fact that such debates occur suggests that dramatic actors are not tightly and inflexibly bound by the script provided by the author. They bring themselves to the role and therefore adopt an active involvement in creating and defining the character.

How true is this of social roles? Different perspectives within sociology will provide different answers (Taylor *et al.,* 1995, Giddens, 1989). Goffman suggests that, within socially defined, though not immutable, constraints, individuals can and do take an active part in constructing their social roles. This view finds support in the work of Strauss *et al.* (1963), who developed an analysis of organisations as 'negotiated orders'. Based on his studies of two psychiatric hospitals, Strauss argued that all members of the organisations examined, including patients, were engaged in continuous processes of negotiation over the goals, policies and procedures adopted and applied. Thus, different groups such as patients, doctors, nurses and non-medical staff, and individual members of each group, were actively involved in negotiating the role each should and would adopt in relation to the others. We can conclude, therefore, that individuals do have scope for interpreting, shaping and defining their roles. However, this scope occurs within limits and constraints, although some of these can be self-imposed.

The argument that constraints can be self-imposed comes from the work of George Mead (1934), a highly influential figure on the theories of both sociology and social psychology. Mead's analysis suggests that the idea of 'self' is both a social construct and is socially constructed. This is explained by his argument that the 'self' consists of two elements which he labels the 'I' and the 'me'. The 'I' is the part of the personality concerned largely with spontaneous impulses, desires and wants which are to do with selfish gratification. The 'me' element of the personality monitors and, to an extent, censures the 'I' by imagining and anticipating the consequences for and responses of other individuals. The 'me' element is developed by seeing one's behaviour from the point of view of others, in other words, by putting oneself in the place of others. Mead referred to this as 'role taking'. So, the 'me' element represents the internalised points of view of other people and, in that sense, constitutes an important part of individual personality. It is easy to see how some constraints at least are self-imposed since they arise from judgements of what others expect.

An important conclusion arising from the work of Mead and others is that the nature of social roles adopted, and how they are performed, results from social interaction. Mead's work on the concept of 'self' also provides a further important argument. The idea of 'others' suggests that defining a role, indeed defining 'self', relies on people other than individuals themselves. We need to identify who these 'others' are. Mead provides two related answers. First are those he labels 'significant others'. These are specific people with whom an individual interacts on a more or less regular basis. Second are those Mead labels as 'generalised others'. This term refers to expectations of a society in general, and particular groups or categories of individuals recognised within a society, for instance, men and women. Thus, we internalise a sense of self, and in our context here, a sense of role, from the points of view of people we know directly and from the point of view of generalised expectations of the society in which we live.

As an example, I have developed a sense of self from my parents, siblings, extended family members, friends and colleagues, all of whom are, for me, 'significant others'; and also, as a male academic, from my understanding of what our society expects from men, as opposed to women, and expects from academics, as opposed to other occupations. Thus, other men, and indeed women, can expect me to behave in certain ways towards them, as can students, whether men or women, since they all constitute for me 'generalised others' and we all share the same norms of social roles and associated behaviour.

Based on this discussion and analysis, we can formulate a definition of 'role'. This definition will need to incorporate the idea of expectations held by both significant and generalised others, as well as allowing for the active involvement of the individual in creating their role. The following meets these conditions.

A role is constituted by patterns of behaviour which arise from negotiated expectations of role holders and significant others within the constraints of institutionalised and generalised limitations.

The reference to 'institutionalised and generalised limitations' recognises and acknowledges the influence of structural factors (Giddens, 1989) within society as a whole which affect, if not determine, the amount of freedom any individual has over their decisions and action. The definition points the way to how the concept can be applied through role analysis as a way of understanding what constitutes a particular role, how it comes to be as it is and, perhaps most importantly, how roles can change. An understanding of the latter provides scope for individual practitioners to take a lead in determining the role of employee development in work organisations. We will return to this point later in the chapter.

Activity 5.1

1 Produce a list of common social roles in our society, e.g. mother or father. Aim for a minimum of five.

(a) identify the expectations of 'generalised others' for each of the roles on your list.

(b) assess how each of the roles has changed over your lifetime, and how these changes may have come about. Does the idea of 'negotiated order' help in understanding processes of change?

2 Discuss the results of **1** with a colleague who has also completed the activity and determine reasons for any similarities and differences.

Discussion

Our analysis of the concept of role has drawn heavily on the work of sociologists who are associated with 'symbolic interactionism' (Giddens, 1989, Taylor *et al.*, 1995). This is a particular school of thought within sociology which emphasises the importance of subjectivity in human experience and, related to this, the effects of human 'agency' in creating meaning and reality. Symbolic interactionism is thus identified by Morgan (1995) as an example of a mode of enquiry which falls within the interpretive paradigm (*see* Chapter 2). As such, the concept of role as discussed here rejects the scientific and objectivist assumptions of the functionalist paradigm. However, symbolic interactionism does share with functionalism a belief in underlying patterns of social order (Morgan, 1995) which roles, as sets of shared expectations, contribute to creating and maintaining. We can argue that the idea of contribution is closer to a functionalist paradigm in that it tends more to objectify organisations, and to analyse the role of different groups (professions, departments, functions) in terms of their purpose in achieving predetermined organisation goals, rather than as the outcomes of negotiated expectations. We will consider such an analysis of employee development before returning to an interactionist conception of role.

The employee development function

The use of the term 'function' perhaps indicates an identification with a functionalist paradigm. A possible contrast with the interactionist conception of role is the emphasis on 'generalised' rather than 'significant' others, in that the focus of analysis is system-wide – i.e. society or, in the case here, organisation – rather than on interactions between specific individuals. This also leads to an emphasis on relationships between elements in a system – e.g. occupations and/or specialist departments – rather than on interpersonal relationships between particular individuals (but see below). The following definition of the training function based on that provided by the former Manpower Services Commission's 'Glossary of training terms', and quoted in Reid and Barrington (1997), reflects these points.

> The purposes, structure and specialised activity of training and its relationships with other activities within a work organisation.
>
> (Reid and Barrington 1997, p. 178)

What this definition signals is that when we refer to the training function we are concerned with the structural relationships of development specialists *vis-à-vis* other specialists in work organisations. This may be assumed to operationalise into concern with the work of training departments and how it relates to that of other departments. However, in theory at least, there is no requirement for organisations to gather specialists together in one department, and such a situation is also common in practice. The definition highlights, however, that locating development specialists in an organisation structure is an issue which requires attention. Examining the purpose and the nature of the specialised activity can be a useful starting point. The model introduced as Fig. 2.1 in Chapter 2 provides some guidance.

The nature of the specialised activity of employee development is constituted by interventions in individual and organisational learning (Stewart and McGoldrick, 1996b). The purpose of such interventions, according to the model, is to change behaviour. This is achieved by acquiring new knowledge, skills and attitudes for individuals, and through developing core competence (Prahalad and Hamel, 1990) and shifts in culture at the level of organisations. The rationale for changing behaviour is to ensure survival and advancement (Harrison, 1997) of the organisation. So, we can say that the overall purpose of employee development is to develop individuals, groups and organisations to perform more effectively, and that this is achieved by providing and facilitating opportunities for individual and organisational learning.

All of this clearly emphasises the 'people focus' of employee development. We can contrast this with the focus on assets and money of accountants, the focus on plant and machinery of engineers, the focus on buildings and property of estate managers, and the focus on hardware and software of information specialists. The implication is that, as a people-focused function, employee development sits naturally with the other people functions bundled together as personnel, or human resource, management. The following potential advantages may accrue from such structural relationships:

- human resource planning feeds into forecasting development requirements;
- recruitment and training are planned together;

- selection is improved by feedback on trainees' performance;
- performance appraisal results in staff development;
- succession and promotion feeds into training and development plans;
- personnel records are not wastefully duplicated.

However, there can be reasons for separating personnel and employee development. The following are indicative:

- personnel has no or little influence;
- the chief executive assumes personal and direct responsibility for training;
- training is limited to one category of employee and training staff therefore report to the appropriate functional manager, e.g. production or sales;
- the function is decentralised to operational and functional departments.

Reid and Barrington (1997) examine eight different forms of structural relationships to illustrate the variety of arrangements found in practice. An additional and significant factor influencing decisions on structure, perhaps implicit in the final item on the above list, is the relationship between development specialists and managers. The latter term can be applied to top, senior, middle or line managers. Utilising the concept of 'staff' and 'line' from classical management (Mullins, 1993), employee development is a staff, or support, function which provides a service to line, or operational, managers. For example, manufacturing, production, sales, health and social care, call centre services can all be labelled as line, or operational, functions because they are concerned with the actual 'business' of the organisation. Personnel and employee development, in common with management accounting, for instance, are staff, or support, functions because they help and facilitate the effective execution of operational functions, but do not contribute directly to them. However, the managers of those operational functions are responsible and accountable for the performance of the employees within these functions because that performance is inextricably linked to the performance of the function. Therefore, line managers at all levels are responsible for the development, or otherwise, of their employees.

The conclusion, therefore, is that employee development is a management responsibility (Reid and Barrington, 1997). That being the case, establishing separate training departments with development specialists will have implications for how line managers respond to and exercise their responsibility for employee development, and for how the specialist and line functions relate to each other. This factor may argue for development specialists being structurally located in line departments, rather than in centralised personnel departments. Whatever the case in structural terms, it is a critical factor in terms of roles adopted by development specialists.

This section can be summarised by saying that the contribution of the development function is to support achievement of organisation objectives through ensuring appropriate and effective learning. We now move on to applying the concept of role.

Activity 5.2

1 Produce an organisation chart showing the location of the employee development function in your organisation and answer the following questions:

(a) how does the function relate structurally to other HR/personnel functions?

(b) what are the advantages/disadvantages of this relationship?

(c) what is the rationale for the current relationship?

(d) what are the implications/consequences of the current structure for relations between employee development and line functions?

2 Look at what alternative arrangements might be considered and whether any benefits could be achieved by change.

3 Share the results of **1** and **2** with work colleagues and gain their views on your analysis.

Employee development roles

There have been a number of studies which have resulted in formulations of various categories of potential and actual roles adopted by employee development specialists (Harrison, 1997, Reid and Barrington, 1997). This section is concerned with describing some of these. Before doing so, we will identify some of the factors which can and do have impact on shaping particular roles adopted in particular organisations at particular points in time. Recall that, from an interactionist perspective, roles emerge from expectations that are open to negotiation. Therefore, a given role is not likely to be static and unchanging, but rather will have a fluid and constantly evolving meaning. It is important, therefore, to understand that any suggested relationship between the influencing factors and role adopted cannot be viewed as permanent or deterministic.

Both Harrison (1997) and Reid and Barrington (1997) examine a range of factors which are argued to influence the role of employee development. The following list is indicative of the key factors.

- Top management support for and interest in employee development.
- Size of organisation in terms of numbers employed.
- Nature of operations and 'business' of the organisation, e.g. degree of complexity, range of occupational groupings.
- Need/demand for training and development, e.g. make-up of internal and external labour markets.
- Location and hierarchical position of person with ultimate responsibility for employee development.
- Culture of the organisation.
- External factors, e.g. degree of legislative regulation.
- Expertise, professionalism and credibility of development specialists.
- Personalities.

Some of these factors highlight the structural influences on the *function*, while others emphasise the influence of interpersonal relationships and interactions on *individual roles*. You may wish to categorise them according to that distinction. Both sets of factors are interrelated and act to shape particular roles adopted. The range of possibilities in terms of role varies according to alternative classifications. We begin our examination with a particularly influential typology (Harrison, 1997).

The work of Pettigrew *et al.*

Pettigrew, Jones and Reason (1982) produced a typology of trainer roles based on empirical research. The typology reflects labelling and definition of roles derived from actual practice rather than conceptual theorising, although the labels are a mix of actual and possible job titles, and the authors' ways of conceptualising what they found in their research. Their typology consists of the following five roles:

- *The provider.* This role is perhaps most closely associated with traditional, perhaps still common, conceptions of employee development. It is primarily concerned with delivering training services focused on operational, as opposed to strategic, issues, with the aim of maintaining or bringing about incremental improvements in organisation performance. It is probably most closely associated with job titles such as training officer.
- *The passive provider.* The basic distinction here is based on the level of proactivity on the part of the role holder. Passive providers do not seek to promote their services, probably because of a lack of expertise, especially in terms of political skills (Harrison, 1997). Their work is limited to low levels of minor importance to the organisation, and brings little power or influence.
- *The training manager.* This role most closely corresponds with actual job titles. As will be clear from the label, the role is managerial, with responsibilities for planning and allocating resources, including perhaps specialist development staff. The role encompasses co-ordination of training operations, and ensuring administration of the function runs efficiently and effectively.
- *The change agent.* A clear, defining characteristic of this role is the focus on changing, rather than maintaining, the organisation. The role is associated with the practice of organisation development (*see* Chapter 7) and has a focus on organisational problem solving through learning and development, rather than on delivery of standard training courses. Individuals adopting this role therefore act more like internal consultants than training providers.
- *Role in transition.* Pettigrew and his colleagues suggested a fifth role which represented those practitioners who were moving from 'provider' to 'change agent'. The role in transition therefore includes elements of both.

Development practitioners who adopt each of these roles will experience different kinds of relationships with line and operational managers. The first two, perhaps especially the passive provider, are likely to have 'distant' relationships with line managers. They will not be perceived as central or essential to operational requirements, and expectations of their contribution are likely to be low. Because of the managerial content of the role, training managers are likely to have closer relationships with other managers. This is probably associated with higher levels of expertise and credibility, higher levels of interaction through hierarchical position, and similarities of problems and concerns over resources and performance. The final two roles share a focus on working with and through line managers and therefore require, and rely on building, constructive relationships. Because of the focus on problem solving, they can be perceived as more credible, and their contribution as more relevant and valuable. As Reid and Barrington (1997) point out, there can be difficulties and dangers in adopting these roles, but, as Harrison (1997) argues, the change agent role most closely represents that adopted by significant numbers of senior HRD professionals.

The original research producing this typology does have limitations, especially the small and narrow sample, and the reliance on perceptions of development specialists (Reid and Barrington, 1997). However, the study lends support to the points made in Chapter 4 concerning the political context of organisations, and the need for professional practitioners to develop and apply political skills to secure power, resources and influence. According to the work of Pettigrew and his colleagues, this is an essential component in negotiating an appropriate and effective role.

The contract model

At about the same time as Pettigrew *et al.* produced their analysis, Jones (1981) put forward an alternative conception of trainer roles. This approach is known as the 'contract model'. It focuses on the relationships which development practitioners adopt in respect of their clients. Within this model, there are two potential clients: the organisation, and the individuals who receive and benefit from employee development services. There are, therefore, three parties to potential 'contracts': the development practitioner, the organisation and the individual employee.

Two broad contracts are possible. The first is termed the 'educational' or 'basic' (Jones, 1986) version of contractual relationships. Here, the practitioner's primary contract, and therefore commitment, is with and to individual employees. This represents what might be termed a traditional role for ED where there are loose connections between specialist practitioner services and organisation goals, and the main beneficiaries of investment in ED are seen to be employees as individuals. Where this model is applied, employees are nominated for courses without there being any necessary connections with their current or expected future job roles. The second version is termed the 'business' contract. Here, both employees and development practitioners have a primary contract with the organisation. The relationship between practitioners and employees is on the basis of a 'secondary' contract. Therefore, investment in ED, and ED activities, have strong connections with organisation goals and needs. Employee development is seen to support the primary contract between employees and the organisation by being focused on delivering services that directly enable individual employees to meet the requirements of the organisation.

The idea of a 'contract' supports the view that roles adopted are open to some negotiation. The two broad versions of potential contracts suggested by Jones (1981, 1986) indicate who constitutes significant others for development practitioners. Senior managers represent the organisation and they will hold expectations of the ED function and specialist staff. Managers of employees who constitute actual or potential trainees also hold expectations. As sponsors of those being developed, they will place demands on practitioners. Employees themselves, again as actual or potential trainees, hold and apply their own expectations. So, using Jones's model, we can argue that the version applied will be the outcome of a role negotiated by these parties to the contract.

Activity 5.3

1 Compare and contrast the work of Pettigrew *et al.* and that of Jones. In doing so, identify any similarities and differences in their analyses of trainer roles.

2 Consider the employee development function in your organisation and answer the following questions:

   (a) how would you categorise the function in terms of the Pettigrew *et al.* typology?

   (b) do different individual ED staff adopt different roles? If so, how and why?

   (c) how would you categorise the function in terms of the Jones contract model?

   (d) how do you account for the educational version or business version being applied?

3 Consider whether the role of ED could or should change, and how this might be brought about. Apply either the Pettigrew typology or the contract model in considering the direction of any change.

The work of Bennett and Leduchowicz

A further model of trainer roles from the early 1980s provides another perspective on the range of possibilities. Bennett and Leduchowicz (1983) posed two critical questions. The first was simply why invest in employee development? This obviously addresses the purpose and contribution of ED, to which two broad answers are possible. First, to maintain the organisation. This means that employee development is focused primarily on 'replacement' training and development, and on enabling employees to keep abreast of changing technology and legislative requirements, for example. This latter focus is summarised by 'updating' training and development. The second possible answer is to change the organisation. In this case, employee development is focused on enabling employees to do new and different things in new and different ways. It may imply a concern with management style, organisation culture and power relations within the organisation. The purpose and contribution here is to support creation of a new organisation form.

The second question posed by Bennett and Leduchowicz is how? In other words, the focus is on approaches, methods and techniques to be adopted. Again, there are two broad answers. The first is labelled an 'educational orientation'. This is constituted by traditional approaches such as standard courses which rely on didactic methods and techniques. The second broad answer is labelled 'intervention orientation'. This is constituted by a broader and more diverse range of approaches and methods which are selected, and tailored, to be appropriate and responsive to learners' work environments and roles. The range of methods adopted is likely to include a number of work and job-focused techniques such as action learning, coaching and mentoring.

It is important to understand that these two questions, and the possible answers, are independent. Development practitioners can pose each question, and adopt one of the broad answers, without reference to the other question or answers. This argument of Bennett and Leduchowicz (1983) leads them to propose four possible roles which are derived from combinations of each of the two possible answers to each of the two questions. The roles are as follows:

- *Caretaker role.* This combines the purpose of organisational maintenance with an educational orientation. Systems and procedures are the main focus, with menu-driven and standardised off-the-job courses being the primary development method.
- *Educator role.* A focus on organisational change combines with an educational-orientation to produce this role. A practitioner adopting the role sees a need for changing organisational form and uses traditional, education-orientated approaches and methods to achieve this.
- *Evangelist role.* While focusing on organisational maintenance rather than change, practitioners adopting this role are 'evangelical' about new development methods and approaches. In contrast to the educator, who is essentially trainer-centred in approach, evangelists are more learner-centred in their professional practice.
- *Innovator role.* The final role of innovator combines a concern with organisational change with an 'interventions' orientation in relation to approaches and methods. The role therefore supports and encourages organisation-wide changes through adoption of work-focused and learner-centred methods. More senior practitioners are more likely to adopt this role, although this need not be exclusive in practice.

Discussion

The models of trainer roles described so far have a number of points in common. None would claim to cover every possible role variation to be found in practice. Based on that, each provides analyses which represent ideal types. Therefore, it is unlikely that any particular individual practitioner could be labelled only as change agent or educator, or be argued to adopt a pure business version of the contract model. All roles will be a combination. However, as a matter of emphasis, all will be capable of classification as one of the types suggested in each of the models. Each of the models can be applied at the level of the function or at the level of individual practitioners. That is to say that we can categorise the role adopted by the whole employee development department, or that adopted by each professional practitioner within departments. In many cases, different individuals will adopt different roles within the same department. Finally, each of the models explicitly or implicitly applies the concept of 'role' as developed in social theory and to varying extents uses the ideas of significant others and role negotiation as a way of understanding how and why particular roles rather than others come to be adopted.

There are points of similarity, too, in the nature of the roles suggested in each of the models. The educator and caretaker roles in the Bennett and Leduchowicz typology can be argued to be similar to provider and passive provider in the work of Pettigrew and his colleagues. Both sets are resonant with the education version of the contract model produced by Jones. The business version of the contract model is more likely to operate when the change agent role is adopted, and this role has many similarities with the innovator role. The fact and nature of these similarities suggests that each analysis can lend support to the others, and that there is something in what each is telling us. Taken together, the models can be used to provide validity to an argument that, within small and less significant variations, there is some commonality in the range of roles adopted by employee development specialists.

A possible criticism of each model, though, is the time since they were formulated. In my view, this in itself is not sufficient grounds for criticism. However, as Harrison (1997) argues, there have been significant changes in the conditions within and outside organisations since the 1980s, and therefore developments in the potential and actual role of employee development are possible. Therefore we will now turn our attention to more recent research and writing. It is important to remember, however, that, as Harrison also argues, the models of the 1980s remain relevant for many practitioners.

Recent research

The American Society for Training and Development (ASTD) commissioned and published research into roles being adopted by HRD professionals in the late 1980s. To the extent that US experience is relevant to the UK, this provides a more recent empirical analysis of practice. The research classified professional practice into 11 significant roles (Harris and DeSimone, 1994) as follows:

- Executive/Manager
- Administrator
- Evaluator
- Materials Developer
- Career Development Counsellor
- Instructor/Facilitator
- Marketer
- Needs Analyst
- Organisation Change Agent
- Programme Designer
- Researcher

There are obvious similarities here with the previous models. You may wish to identify some of them. It is also the case that in the UK, large organisations employing significant numbers of development practitioners (for instance, NatWest Bank and British Telecom) use staff in very specialist roles, such as course design, evaluation and developing training/learning materials. It would seem fair to conclude, therefore, that this US-based research indicated significant similarity in professional practice between the USA and the UK, and produced no evidence to seriously question the validity or usefulness of the models discussed in the previous section.

We can compare the US evidence with that produced by major, empirical research in the UK to produce occupational standards for employee development on which NVQs for professional practitioners are based. This was carried out in the mid-1990s by the Training and Development Lead Body (TDLB), which was later incorporated into the

Employment Occupational Standards Council (EOSC). We can ignore for our purposes here any concerns about or criticisms of the research process and the methods used.

The results are instructive. NVQs in professional practice, based on the occupational standards, focus on training and development (a provider/delivery role), learning and development (which encompasses a broader range of methods than formal courses), human resource development (a managerial and organisation-focused role) and training and development strategy (encompassing HRD and a focus on culture, values and change management) (EOSC, 1996). My summaries suggest some congruence between the roles specified in NVQs and those included in the analyses of Bennett and Leduchowicz, and that of Pettigrew and his colleagues, at the level of face validity at least. While expressing some reservations about the result, Harrison (1997) is able to produce a matrix which maps the roles identified by Pettigrew *et al.* against the EOSC NVQs. It should be noted that Harrison's reservations focus more on the EOSC occupational standards and NVQs rather than on the Pettigrew typology. Therefore, it seems reasonable to conclude that the TDLB research offers no reason to seriously question earlier research.

Two further pieces of work are worthy of consideration. Moorby (1996) suggests the following nine potential roles:

- *Reception*: the first point of contact;
- *Administration*: organising events, booking facilities, etc;
- *Technical Support*: maintaining equipment, e.g. projectors, VCR, CBT;
- *Direct Trainer*: e.g. technical instructor, lecturer;
- *Tutor/Mentor*: supporter and facilitator of individual learning;
- *Training Adviser*: diagnosing needs, evaluation, programme design;
- *Consultant*: focuses on organisational problem solving;
- *Specialist*: CBT programmer, distance-learning author, for example;
- *Manager/Director*: preparing strategies, managing resources, etc.

Commonalities and similarities can again be identified between Moorby's classification and earlier research. The same seems to be true of his work and that of the ASTD in America and the TDLB in the UK. Of course, there are differences and omissions when a direct comparison between one classification and another is made, although the similarities may be of more interest and significance.

The final piece of work to be considered is that produced by Sloman (1994). This produced, or proposed, two new and emerging roles based, in part, on a rejection of the relevance of the systematic training cycle (*see* Chapter 7). The two roles are that of 'internal consultant', and 'strategic facilitator'. Harrison (1997) likens the former to that of 'provider', but with a more collaborative and customer-focused orientation. I am not certain this is entirely fair. My reading of Sloman's argument and analysis is that it has some resonance with the earlier work of Phillips and Shaw (1989), who suggested professional roles were in transition from training to consulting. They further suggested three pathways: to training consultant, to learning consultant and to organisation change consultant. The transition has congruence with Pettigrew *et al.'s* 'role in transition', and the third pathway with 'change agent'. Sloman's analysis seems to me to be concerned with a similar argument, and Harrison's comments perhaps apply only if Sloman's focus could be encapsulated exclusively within the training consultant pathway.

The second role, that of strategic facilitator, focuses on development strategies which are aligned with organisation aims and goals, and which develop and manage an appropriate learning culture. Clear objectives and accountabilities, according to Sloman, need to be built into such strategies. The role is seen as strategic in that it is associated with the long-term and organisation-wide plans of senior managers.

Discussion

We can perhaps summarise this section by re-stating the argument that recent research tends to confirm rather than seriously challenge the typologies of trainer roles produced in the early 1980s. The terminology used by Sloman, and his descriptions of the two roles he advocates, have clear resonance with earlier analyses. One element which seems to be repeated across the various classifications, and which is used as a defining variable to distinguish between specific roles, is what might be termed 'degree of proactivity' displayed by professional practitioners. Fredericks and Stewart (1996) argue that a proactive stance is essential if HRD practitioners are to contribute to developing organisation capability. Fig. 5.1 provides a representation of the range of relationships ED professionals can adopt and cultivate with their clients in terms of this variable, and thus also provides a final typology of trainer roles.

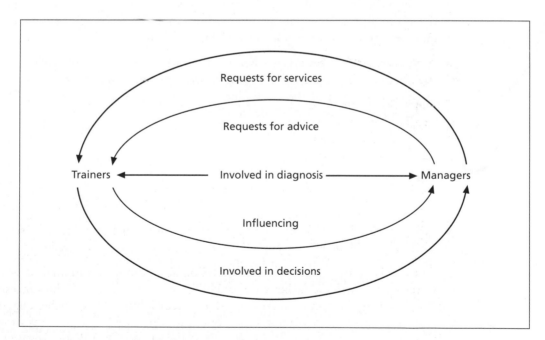

Fig. 5.1 Proactive and reactive roles

Activity 5.4

1 Produce an analysis of the critical factors which are common across all the models of trainer roles described in this chapter.

2 Identify any significant points of difference between the various models.

3 Assess the significance/importance of the similarities/differences.

4 Answer the following questions:

(a) which typology do you think has most validity and utility, and why?

(b) which role in this typology most closely corresponds to your own, and why?

(c) which role in this typology do you think will be most relevant in the next century, and why?

Applying the concept of role

Many of the activities you have undertaken in this chapter have engaged you in applying the concept of 'role'. Doing so constitutes what is referred to as *role analysis*. This is a useful method of diagnosing organisation dysfunctions and problems. Put another way, many organisation problems can arise because of, or can be analysed in terms of, confusion and other uncertainties over organisational roles. Some of the most common of these uncertainties are as follows (*see* Handy, 1976).

- *Role ambiguity.* This arises when a role-holder is uncertain of what is expected by significant others, and where those others are uncertain what they should, or are entitled to, expect of the role-holder. In other words, there is no clearly defined or specified role. There is therefore much scope for negotiation.
- *Role conflict.* Expectations here are at variance with each other. While they may be clear, those held by one, or some, significant others cannot be met while also meeting those of a different set of significant others. Jones's contract model indicates when this may be true for development specialists whose learners may have expectations at variance, or in conflict with, those of their managerial sponsors. Role negotiation is required to overcome role conflict.
- *Role overload.* In this situation, there is no conflict between different sets of significant others. However, the cumulative expectations of each set create unreasonable or impossible demands on and for the role-holder. In times of 'lean organisations' this may be an increasingly common problem. Role negotiation again provides a possible solution.
- *Role underload.* Perhaps a rare situation. The problem here is that expectations of others do not meet those of the role-holder. This may be associated with ability, and/or time, and/or other resources. In other words, the role-holder can and wishes to provide more than is expected or required to satisfy significant others.

Irrespective of applying these general categories, role analysis can be a useful approach to and method of diagnosing training and development needs (*see also* Chapter 8), especially at the occupational and individual levels. A framework for applying the process for this purpose is given in Fig. 5.2. Other approaches are possible and available (see below). Role analysis can also constitute a development method. It can be used for example, when any of the general categories listed above are indicated. The development practitioner acts as a facilitator in supporting specified role-holders, or perhaps a group of individuals fulfilling the same or similar roles, and their significant others in negotiating revised roles and boundaries which are capable of meeting the expectations of all involved. Given the fluid nature of roles, a final and lasting solution is unlikely, although role-based interventions can still prove valuable.

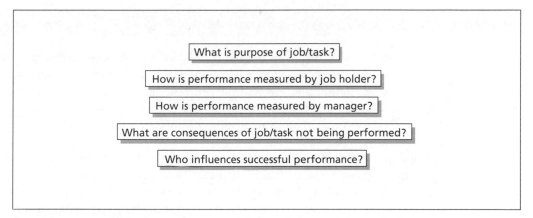

Fig. 5.2 Question framework for role analysis

Activity 5.5 provides a further framework for role analysis. It is most useful as a starting point in negotiating changes in role to meet personal expectations. Completing the activity will provide some experience in using the method, and may, in combination with the other activities and content of this chapter, suggest some other directions in which you might wish to take your own role.

Activity 5.5

1 Identify and list any expectations of generalised others in your organisation that constrain or limit individual action, e.g. policies, values or strategies.

2 Identify, name and list significant others affecting your role, e.g. your direct manager and colleagues. You may have to generalise some, e.g. senior managers.

3 Identify and list the expectations you believe each significant other has of your role. It is useful to check your understanding with the people themselves if you can.

4 Assess the degree of coherence, commonality and consistency among these sets of expectations.

5 Produce a statement describing your expectations of your current role and how you would like to see it develop in the future.

▶

6 Assess the degree of 'fit' and congruence between your expectations and those of your significant others.

7 Identify those you will need to negotiate with, and the focus of differences, in order to bring about your desired change.

Note: You can utilise any of the models (or none) in this process, especially from Step 3 onwards.

Summary and conclusion

This chapter has described the concept of role and explained its application through role analysis. In doing so, the chapter has demonstrated the influence and utility of social theory to organisation analysis and the professional practice of employee development. As part of this, the interpretive paradigm has been shown to have value and, therefore, that perspectives other than those arising from the dominant functionalist paradigm can have relevance and value.

A number of typologies of development roles have been examined and analysed. Some originate from work conducted in the early 1980s, and these have been compared with more recent research and writing. The conclusion reached is that the early models still have relevance, and that they remain useful in identifying the range of potential trainer roles. An important message of the chapter is that, perhaps within some institutionalised constraints, individuals have scope for negotiating a preferred role, based on their own criteria. The typologies of role described here, together with use of role analysis, provide frameworks for matching personal preferences and abilities with organisationally relevant and valued contributions.

The chapter closes the first part of the book and therefore ends the examination of the context within which employee development occurs. We move on in part two to examine the processes of employee development. Professional practice requires engagement in those processes, which themselves are founded on what is understood about learning. The next chapter therefore focuses on the important subject of learning theory as a basis for examining the application of ED processes.

Case study 5

The NHS has been through many changes in its relatively short history. Change has perhaps become considered the norm rather than the exception. However, this does not mean that change is any more or less welcome or any more or less easy to implement.

Heather Walton ponders these thoughts as she attempts to get to grips with the potential implications of the proposed merger of her current employer, Bainbridge NHS Trust Hospital, with another NHS Trust Hospital, known locally as the 'General'. Both hospitals provide similar services, dealing with general acute and emergency services to their local populations. Part of the rationale for the proposed merger is that there is an overlap in the populations served by the hospitals, as well as in their respective services and specialisms. Bainbridge is the larger of the two, employing 1500 people across all grades and types of staff, while the General employs 950 staff. There has in the past been an element of competition between the two hospitals as both bid for contracts and funds from the same main purchaser, the Bainbridge and District Health Authority. While Heather considers this will create its own problems in facilitating the merger, she accepts the logic of potential cost savings arising from this reduction in the need to 'compete'.

Heather is aware that impetus for a merger came about as a result of the policies of the recently elected government. These policies in turn are only part of a national scene which includes the neverending discovery and application of new treatments, the continuing emphasis on preventative medicine and community-based care, and changes in the training, development and qualifications of professional staff and associated changes to their contracts. Local pressures, including financial constraints experienced by Bainbridge and District Health Authority, as well as difficulties experienced by both hospitals in devoting enough resources to develop their services, have also been instrumental in making the case for merger.

As organisation development manager at Bainbridge, Heather is aware of current and recent research which emphasises the importance of culture and 'HR issues' in achieving successful mergers. Heather is naturally even more familiar with studies of mergers within the NHS. These tend to support the general findings on culture and HR issues as well as highlighting the support of key stakeholders and agreement on future business and direction as being critical factors influencing success or failure. While both trust boards and all directors in both hospitals have confirmed their support for a merger, Heather is unsure of the level of support among the varying staff groups. Equally, she is not at all certain that powerful groups such as consultants do, or will, agree on priorities for developing clinical services in the new trust to be created by the merger.

Actions taken so far to facilitate planning and implementation of the merger include a trust strategy group meeting held over a weekend in a local hotel. The event was organised jointly by the two chief executives and included all directors, senior managers, senior nurses and consultants from both trusts. Heather was actively involved in designing and facilitating the event, along with the director of human resources from the General and the two chief executives. A number of workshops were held with mixed groups of staff from both the hospitals to examine various questions surrounding the merger, and to produce an overall action plan to be implemented by a number of cross-functional and cross-hospital project groups, also formed at the event. However, Heather came away with a feeling that staff from the General felt they were being 'taken over' rather than merged, and that such a view was shared by some staff at Bainbridge, especially consultants. A major focus of concern, especially among staff from the General, was on the range and numbers of redundancies to arise from the merger.

Heather has personal concerns about her future. No structure has yet been proposed for the new trust. However, her work on advising the merger steering group on facilitating required changes will continue for six months at least. At the moment, Heather is faced with the task of writing a paper for the steering group to examine the training and development implications of the merger. Her brief requires a particular focus on what contribution training and development can make to ensuring the merger is a success, and what role the function should adopt in the new organisation. Heather is encouraged that the request for the paper suggests that training and development is seen by the steering group as playing an important part in the merger and the new organisation. However, she also recognises the importance of the paper, not only for her own future but for all employees of both hospitals and in establishing an appropriate training and development function in the planned new trust.

Discussion questions

1 What role and contribution can employee training and development play in managing organisation change?

2 What are the key factors influencing change in the form of the merger of the two existing NHS trusts?

3 What options might Heather consider and present to the steering group as possible roles for employee training and development?

4 Given the circumstances of the case, what contribution can you see for employee training and development in achieving a successful merger?

5 Based on your response to **4**, what role for employee training and development would you suggest is the most appropriate for Heather to recommend?

Suggested reading

Harrison, R. (1997) *Employee development.* London: IPD.

Moorby, E. (1996) *How to Succeed in Employee Development (2nd edn).* Maidenhead: McGraw-Hill.

Reid, M. and Barrington, H. (1997) *Training Interventions (5th edn).* London: IPD.

Stewart, J. (1996) *Managing Change Through Training and Development (2nd edn).* London: Kogan Page.

PART 2

The employee development process

CHAPTER 6

Individual and organisation learning

Introduction

Understanding individual learning processes is central to the practice of employee development. The model of HRD introduced in Chapter 2 includes learning as one of two critical components. Major texts on the subject of ED devote attention to theories of individual learning (Harrison, 1997, Reid and Barrington, 1997, Truelove, 1997). It is accepted as essential that specialist practitioners have a sound, working knowledge of attempts to understand and explain individual learning. In my view, such knowledge lies at the heart of professional practice.

Most writing within the HRD literature focuses on individual learning. However, there is a need to examine the notion of organisation learning. This need is associated with the growing recognition of the connections between long-term survival, corporate strategy and learning (Moingeon and Edmondson, 1996) and with ideas around the 'knowledge company' (Nonaka, 1996) and 'knowledge workers'. Organisation learning is also, of course, implicitly and explicitly bound up with the idea of the 'learning organisation' (Senge et al., 1994, Pedler et al., 1991). However, there seems to be an important distinction between these two concepts. If we conceive of organisations as learning entities, as the model of HRD in Chapter 2 suggests, then *all* organisations learn. But not all organisations are learning organisations in the sense advocated by the leading writers on that concept. Implicitly at least, it can be argued that learning organisations are efficient and effective in organisation learning, and derive strategic advantage and benefit from those processes. So, the two concepts, while related, are separate in informing the practice of ED. We will therefore examine the idea of organisation learning in this chapter and return to the concept of the learning organisation later in the book.

Attempts to explain individual learning are produced primarily within the discipline of psychology (Myers, 1995). The related discipline of social psychology is also significant, especially in terms of organisation learning. An examination of the major schools of thought within these disciplines will help to put theories of learning into context. This chapter will therefore begin with a brief overview of key concepts within psychological science.

CHAPTER OBJECTIVES

- Describe and explain individual learning from a variety of perspectives.

- Describe and explain the concept of organisational learning.

- Critically evaluate the validity of competing and complementary theories of learning.

- Articulate the connections between theories of learning and their application in the professional practice of HRD.

The science of psychology

The social sciences are concerned with understanding and explaining human experience and behaviour. Specific disciplines attempt to achieve that understanding by focusing on different levels of analysis. For example, sociology primarily, though not exclusively, examines what might be termed the macro level as expressed by its interest in the concept of 'society'. The first point to understand about psychology is that the unit of analysis is the individual. Therefore, psychological theories concerning any aspect of human experience have to be understood in the context of the focus of analysis, that is, the individual as a discrete and distinct entity. There is a minor qualification to this statement when it comes to social psychology. Here, the unit of analysis remains the individual, but the focus of attention and interest is on how individuals relate with and to other individuals. These points are reflected in the following definitions, both taken from Myers (1995).

- **Psychology** – the science of behaviour and mental processes.
- **Social psychology** – the scientific study of how we think about, influence and relate to one another.

A further important point emerges from these definitions. Both use the concept of 'science'. This is important because it reveals the value attached to application of the scientific method within psychology. The historical roots of the discipline and current practice confirm this value (Myers, 1995). If we were to categorise psychology as a discipline using the dimensions suggested by Burrell and Morgan, introduced in Chapter 2 (Morgan, 1995), we would easily place it near the objective rather than subjective end of that continuum. The continuum of radical change versus regulation would be more problematic, however. Given the attachment in psychology to emulating the physical sciences (Stewart, 1998a), including the ideal of neutral observer and researcher, we could perhaps say that the discipline does not have an agenda of radical change. We might therefore conclude that psychology, in the main, adopts a functionalist paradigm. Based on that conclusion, we need to be aware of that paradigm, together with the focus on the individual as the unit of analysis, as significant contextual features in considering the validity and usefulness of learning theories developed within psychology.

Ultimately, it is possible to argue that it is unfair or mistaken to attempt to place a whole discipline within the confines of the Burrell and Morgan typology. That is, of course, a matter for debate. What is less arguable is that there exists within psychology a number of schools of thought which vary in terms of the emphasis they place on a variety of factors. Differentiating and labelling these becomes a matter for interpretation and difference, leading to variety in classifications (Ribeaux and Poppleton, 1978, Arnold *et al.*, 1995). Here we will use part of a classification used previously in Stewart, 1998a. Three schools of thought seem to be of particular relevance when examining learning theories.

Behaviourist psychology

Behaviourist psychology is a school of thought associated with the pioneering work of J.B. Watson and B.F. Skinner. It can be argued to have two defining characteristics (Stewart, 1998a). First, in extreme form, a belief that the internal workings of the mind, or psyche, should be discounted as an area of study. Second, and relatedly, that human behaviour is the product of, and therefore explainable by, experiences within physical and social environments. This means that, again in extreme expression, biological or innate causes of behaviour are also discounted.

These two characteristics are associated in part with the early ambition of psychologists to establish their discipline as a science with the same status in academic institutions as the natural sciences such as physics and chemistry. To achieve this, it was believed that psychology needed to adopt the prevailing paradigm and research methods of the natural sciences, encapsulated in the concept of 'the scientific method'. Since the scientific method is concerned with 'proof' derived from observable 'facts', behaviourist psychology focuses only on that which is observable, i.e. behaviour. Hence the term 'behaviourist psychology'.

This provides a simplified characterisation of behaviourist psychology as established by Watson, Skinner and others. The majority of psychologists, even those committed to the behaviourist tradition, would not now hold as rigidly to the defining principles as strongly as the founders of the school of thought (Myers, 1995). However, this is a matter of degree and behaviourist psychologists still accept those principles. Of more significance here is the fact that the principles were important in developing theories of learning which we will examine later in the chapter.

Cognitive psychology

In contrast to behaviourist psychology, the cognitive school of thought emphasises the significance of internal mental processes. Indeed, the nature and operation of such processes are major areas of study for cognitive psychologists. However, in common with behaviourist psychology, this school of thought believes that experience of and within the physical and, especially, social environment is a significant factor in shaping behaviour. The connections and interactions between individual mental processes and the environment could in fact be argued to be the defining characteristic of cognitive psychology. This is illustrated by the way individual human beings are conceptualised as 'information processors' within the cognitive tradition (Ribeaux and Poppleton, 1978). There are two further concepts central to the tradition of interest here. The first is the idea of 'maturation' devised by Jean Piaget in his work on child development (Myers, 1995). The second is 'personal construct' theory developed by George Kelly (Kelly, 1955). As we shall see, both concepts have implications for and applications in individual learning.

It is important to recognise that cognitive psychology shares a concern with behaviourist psychology for the scientific method. Practitioners working in both traditions in general share a belief in the same principles governing scientific research and investigation. A possible difference is that cognitive psychologists see more potential in adapting the scientific method to allow study of internal processes. Attachment to the prevailing scientific method is of less importance in our final school of thought, however.

Humanist psychology

The last point may benefit from a little clarification. The scientific method is associated with a view of the world as having objective existence independent of the observer, and as being capable of objective investigation and explanation. However, it is possible to be scientific in the sense of being systematic and rigorous without accepting either the assumptions or techniques of the scientific method. This is an important point since our third school of thought rejects the scientific method as being appropriate to the study of human behaviour, although this does not necessarily mean it is any less scientific, in the sense of being rigorous, than either behaviourist or cognitive psychology.

Humanist psychology rests within a broad tradition of philosophical thought which accepts a phenomenological view of reality (Arnold *et al.*, 1995). A phenomenological view argues that any objective definition of reality is merely a widely agreed interpretation rather than a specification of objective facts. Such interpretations will never be universal and all experience is subject to highly individualistic and unique interpretations. A useful way of capturing this argument is the idea of 'world view' which, in effect, is an individual and unique representation of a unique reality held by each individual (Stewart, 1998a).

A central tenet of this school of thought is the belief that individual human behaviour is purposeful and goal directed. The primary goal is to fulfil potential. This is perhaps best expressed by the need, or drive, to 'self-actualise' which forms part of the seminal contribution of Abraham Maslow (1959). So, a phenomenological view of reality and a belief in self-actualisation are the two principal, defining characteristics of this school of thought. These, too, have relevance for the theories of learning to which we now turn our attention.

Activity 6.1

1 How do you think the defining characteristics of each school of thought will influence how each investigates human behaviour?

2 What might be the implications of this for the validity and reliability of their research results?

3 How and why will this affect application of theories of learning?

Individual learning

Psychological research has developed a number of theories of individual learning which, in simple terms, seek to answer questions surrounding how human beings learn. Each of the theories to be examined here have both similarities and differences, i.e. they use concepts and derive principles which in some cases support each other and which in other cases contradict each other. It is useful and instructive to be aware of this from the beginning so that these similarities and differences can be looked for as our examination of the theories unfolds. It is instructive also for two further reasons. First, the existence of theories with contradictory features suggests that no single theory has yet provided a complete or definitive description and explanation of individual learning, even though some theories claim to have done so. Second, it is likely to be the case that principles which find support in more than one theory will have more validity and usefulness than others. This is not of course necessarily the case but is a good rule of thumb.

A useful starting point is always to consider definitions. Defining learning is, as you might expect, not without problems. The word itself can be used as a verb, as in 'I am learning about employee development', or as an adjective, as in 'XYZ company is a learning organisation', or as a noun, as in 'my most important learning is achieved at work'. This latter usage refers to the outcome or product of a process which, using the word as a verb, we also refer to as learning. It is also applied in the following definition.

A relatively permanent change in an organism's behaviour due to experience.

(Myers, 1995, p. 257)

We will accept that definition for our purposes here since it is a conception widely accepted within psychology and in the theory and practice of HRD (Harrison, 1997, Reid and Barrington, 1997). It is important to note, however, the use of the word as a noun in the definition while our primary interest is in understanding the processes leading to the outcome described. You might also note the behaviourist slant to the definition.

Activity 6.2

Argyris and Schon (1978), and other writers, argue the view that we each possess our own theories about what happens in the world and our experiences of it. So, you will have your own theory of learning. This activity will help you access and articulate your personal theory.

1 (a) provide your own definition of learning

(b) list any factors that you believe help learning to occur

(c) list any factors that you believe inhibit learning

(d) identify the impact each item on your two lists has on individual learners

(e) based on the analysis you have produced through the above, answer the question 'How do people learn?'

> **2** Consider your answer to **1**(e) in relation to the schools of thought described earlier. Is your theory closest to behaviourist, cognitive or humanist psychology?
>
> **3** How do you feel about your answer to **2**?

Behaviourist learning theory

The first, specific theory of individual learning to consider is that developed within the behaviourist school of psychology. It is perhaps a little confusing to talk of *one* theory since we are concerned with the work of a number of writers, each adopting a slightly different model of learning. However, it is the case that this particular group of writers start from the same point in terms of their basic assumptions, and build on and add to the work of each other, rather than formulating brand new theory. Therefore, it is probably accurate to think of these writers as contributing to the formulation of one theory which can be labelled behaviourist.

An additional point of explanatory background will also be useful, which is that, in the case of the early behaviourists at least, the primary concern is with understanding and explaining human *behaviour*. Thus, it is not a matter of understanding learning as one aspect of human experience. Rather, it is a matter of explaining human behaviour by, or through, learning. In simple terms, we are what we are and do what we do as individuals because we have *learned* to be so and to do so. This point is illustrated by the work of B.F. Skinner, an influential behaviourist psychologist (Myers, 1995). Skinner labelled his version of the behaviourist theory 'learning theory' to reflect his argument that human behaviour is learned, and understanding that process is all we need to understand and explain human experience. As further illustration, a similar point could be made about the widely known theory of motivation devised by Maslow (1959). Maslow's theory is often mistakenly presented as an explanation of a single, unique component of human experience and behaviour, i.e. that known as 'motivation'. The theory is concerned in fact with understanding and explaining human behaviour *per se*, and therefore with addressing questions concerning who we are and what we do.

This last point is significant because behaviourists such as Skinner and Watson are often wrongly believed to reject the existence of biological or cognitive processes. In fact, they do not. Their basic argument was that such processes cannot be scientifically investigated, and indeed do not need to be because focusing only on what can be properly investigated – i.e. behaviour – provides the understanding and explanation being sought.

Within behaviourist theory, the basic building block of learning theory is the idea of *association*, or associative learning (Hilgard *et al.*, 1971, Myers, 1995). This basic idea suggests that living organisms learn to link in some form of relationship what can otherwise be two independent events. The idea of association in turn led to development of the idea of *conditioning*. This idea expresses the explanation of why and how particular events, rather than others, become linked and therefore associated. In other words, conditioning explains why an organism comes to associate event A with event B rather than with event C or D.

There are two significant models of conditioning to be considered. The first is 'classical conditioning' and refers to the work of Ivan Pavlov (Myers, 1995, Ribeaux and

Poppleton, 1978), probably best known for his experiments with salivating dogs. Pavlov provided an important distinction between *unconditioned* stimuli and responses, and *conditioned* stimuli and responses. The former are automatic, linked to biological and physiological processes and are *not learned*. As examples from Pavlov's experiments, food in the mouth is an *unconditioned stimulus* and production of saliva is an *unconditioned response*. Stimuli and responses which are learned are *conditioned*.

Associating a neutral stimulus with an unconditioned stimulus can produce the same response. Again in Pavlov's case, a particular sound tone was played to dogs at the same time as they were given food. The dogs came to associate the tone with the food. Eventually, playing the tone without providing the food produced the same response of salivating. Thus the neutral stimulus of the tone is a *conditioned stimulus* and salivating on hearing the tone is a *conditioned response*, since it is no longer automatic because food is not present in the mouth. The primary contribution of Pavlov was to confirm the existence of associative learning and to demonstrate how it works in practice through development of concepts such as acquisition and extinction which examine questions to do with initial learning and its durability (Myers, 1995).

The second model, 'operant conditioning' developed by Skinner, provides additional insights. A significant distinction between the two models is that classical conditioning focuses on responses and stimuli that the organism does not control. Thus, in Pavlov's experiments the researchers provided both the sound tone and the food. Operant conditioning, by contrast, postulates and focuses on the spontaneous and controllable behaviour of the organism. This behaviour is labelled *operant behaviour*. Relatedly, operant conditioning focuses on associations between operant behaviour and its results, what the psychologist Edward Thorndike referred to as the 'law of effect' (Myers, 1995). Thus, operant behaviour *operates* on the organism's environment and produces some effect, or result. The association in operant conditioning therefore is not between two different stimuli but between behaviour and result.

A further significant aspect of the operant conditioning formulation of learning is the role of *reinforcement*. If operant behaviour is reinforced by rewards, then the behaviour becomes associated with the positive and beneficial result, i.e. the reward, and therefore becomes more likely to recur. Conversely, behaviour which results in negative or adverse results is less likely to recur. Skinner used the concept of 'reinforcer' to refer to rewards, and defined it as any event that increases the frequency of a preceding response (Myers, 1995, p. 270). He also distinguished between two types of reinforcer. First, positive reinforcers which present positive stimuli such as food, money, attention or approval. Second, negative reinforcers which strengthen a response by removing negative or adverse stimuli such as pain, disapproval or isolation. This makes clear that negative reinforcement does not refer to the application of punishment, and indeed Skinner argued consistently that reinforcers, of both types, were much more effective than punishments in shaping behaviour.

Shaping behaviour is really what operant conditioning is all about. In application, it means providing reinforcement for operant behaviour as and when it moves towards or in the direction of the desired behaviour, and ignoring all other behaviour. The value and frequency of reinforcers can be decreased and increased depending upon how closely operant behaviour approximates the desired behaviour, culminating of course in maximum reinforcement of the actual desired behaviour.

Based on his research and analysis, Skinner believed that operant conditioning could explain all human behaviour, including his own (Myers, 1995). To support this thesis, Skinner produced refinements of his central concepts to do with, for example, reinforcement schedules. He also consistently argued that application of operant conditioning in areas such as social policy, education, employment and in child rearing practised by parents in the home could produce the kind of society most of us might wish to see. As part of this case, Skinner argued that behaviour which many individuals and societies would prefer to see eradicated, such as criminal behaviour, could be explained and accounted for by operant conditioning and, therefore, could be changed by the same process.

Activity 6.3

1 Think about Skinner's assertions and answer the following questions:

(a) what examples can you think of in current social policy in the UK which could be said to reflect the principles of operant conditioning?

(b) what examples can you think of in employment and management policies and practice in your organisation which could be said to reflect the principles of operant conditioning?

(c) how could each of the examples in (a) and (b) be improved in terms of their effectiveness by a more conscious and deliberate application of operant conditioning to produce the desired behaviour?

(d) how do you feel about the rights of the state and employers to apply operant conditioning to shape individual behaviour?

2 (a) how do the ideas of behavioural psychology discussed so far compare with your theory developed in Activity 6.2?

(b) how do you feel about any similarities/differences?

Social learning theory

Social learning theory, or 'observational learning', developed in the 1960s and 1970s by Bandura (Myers, 1995) could be placed under the heading of cognitive theories because Bandura was concerned with the implications for behaviourist learning theory of accepting a role for internal, or cognitive, processes in human learning. However, Bandura accepted the basic arguments of behaviourists such as Skinner and Watson, and incorporated the principles of operant conditioning in devising his model of observational learning. Therefore, his model can be seen as a refinement and development of Skinner's learning theory.

Bandura's contribution was to argue that learning would be both laborious and hazardous if individuals had to rely solely and exclusively on their own actions. The concept of observational learning therefore introduced notions of 'imitation' and 'modelling' into the learning process. Through behavioural experiments with children, Bandura demonstrated that human beings learn behaviour through observing and imitating the behaviour of others, both children and adults. Several factors have been found or suggested to be significant in determining which behaviour will be imitated and which not, including the perceived status of the 'model' and the consistency or otherwise of their behaviour. Bandura also argued that the principles of operant conditioning are significant in explaining which behaviour is imitated, especially in terms of the rewards and punishments experienced by both the model and imitator (Myers, 1995).

The ideas behind and within observational learning have, in part, fuelled debates on the role of television and films in creating and perpetuating violent behaviour in society. However, these ideas have also had wider influence and application in both explaining and attempting to shape human behaviour. You may like to identify and think about some of these. In summary, observational learning, as a response to pure behaviourism, allowed cognitive processes to be considered as part of human learning processes. We will now examine theories of learning which have their origins more directly in cognitive psychology.

Cognitive learning theory

We saw earlier that cognitive psychology, in simplified terms, conceives of human beings as information processors. This conception provides the basis of Gagne's (1974) theory of learning. This can be summarised as application of the following stages:

- *Motivation* – an individual experiences arousal and therefore becomes motivated to act;
- *Apprehension* – following arousal, the individual searches for, accesses and captures information;
- *Acquisition* – captured information is coded and stored in the short-term memory;
- *Retention* – coded information enters and is stored in the long-term memory;
- *Recall* – information is retrieved from the long-term memory;
- *Generalise* – information gained, coded and stored is applied in new and different situations;
- *Performance* – application of information to determine how to respond/behave/act. Differences in performance from earlier times confirms that learning has taken place;
- *Feedback* – information on the consequence and effects of performance is processed to monitor whether the motivating factor has been satisfied, e.g. objectives have been met.

The detail of this theory accommodates the application of complex processes, and their interaction, to do with factors such as perceptions, thoughts, emotions and memory. So, while the process and stages will be the same for each individual, the outcomes will vary because of individual difference in, for example, information selected (influenced by perception and motivation, for example) and how it is interpreted and coded (influenced by existing knowledge and emotional state, for example). The overall theory is a simple one, however: learning occurs through individuals accessing, processing and transforming information from their physical and social environment.

Gagne's cognitive theory of learning does not necessarily refute or contradict the validity of behaviourist learning theory. But it enables a fuller understanding by seeking to explain the role of cognition and cognitive processes which, in turn, become evident in experiments which lead to formulation of the related concepts of 'sign' and 'latent' learning (Hilgard *et al.*, 1971). These concepts, together with the distinction argued by

Tolman (Hilgard *et al.*, 1971) between learning and performance, are used to support a view that individuals formulate cognitive maps which represent the individual's understanding of their experience and environments. These maps are applied to inform and shape behaviour independently and separately from the immediate context of the behaviour itself. Thus, cognitive maps are learned, and therefore are the products of learning, and are used to decide how to perform, i.e. behave. Thus, learning and behaviour can be separate in time and place.

A concept with a related but wider meaning to cognitive map is that of 'schema' (Arnold *et al.*, 1995). The idea of schema, originally devised by Bartlett (1932), suggests that we organise information into meaningful relationships and patterns, and that we use these patterns to make sense of and respond to our experiences in and of the world. A particular form of schema is the theory of 'personal constructs' devised by George Kelly, mentioned earlier. This theory confirms the view that cognitive learning processes produce unique and individualised responses to the same stimuli. Thus, while Gagne's theory may identify and to some extent explain those processes, the work of Kelly and other cognitive psychologists suggests that we cannot predict or control the outcome for each and every individual engaging in what might appear to be the same learning experience. Personal constructs vary from individual to individual, and so what and how information is selected, coded and interpreted will also vary.

A further qualification to Gagne's theory comes from the work of Piaget. Although Piaget's ideas have been amended and refined by subsequent research (Myers, 1995), his central ideas on maturation still have wide acceptance. The basic premise of these ideas is that certain abilities have to be developed before others can be learned. The simple physical example that we cannot learn to run before we have learned to walk illustrates the argument. Therefore, Gagne's theory has to be qualified because it can only account for and explain learning processes in those who have developed the appropriate cognitive abilities. Following Piaget, this will be related to stages in child development with the stages in turn related to age. However, more recent studies have questioned the significance of age as the only or critical factor. Other factors such as cultural values, educational experiences and physical development of the brain are also now considered to be significant (Myers, 1995).

Activity 6.4

1 What are the key points of similarity and difference between behaviourist and cognitive theories of learning?

2 What are the implications for ED practice arising out of cognitive learning theories? In particular, consider the following:

(a) Gagne's theory of learning

(b) the consequences of 'personal constructs'

(c) the consequences of the idea of maturation

3 What are the similarities and differences between cognitive theories and yours developed in Activity 6.2?

4 How do you feel about what you identified in **3** above?

Experiential learning

The final theory to be considered under the umbrella of cognitive psychology deserves its own heading since it is probably the most widely known and applied, certainly in terms of adult education and development. It is the theory known as 'experiential learning', devised by David Kolb and his colleagues (Kolb, 1983). The central tenet and implication of this theory is perhaps most succinctly put in the following quote.

> Most of what we learn comes from doing . . . From infancy onwards we take actions and we learn. Throughout our lives, learning is taking place all the time as a result of our experiences.
>
> (Dennison and Kirk, 1990, p. 3)

While capturing the essential meaning of experiential learning theory, the quote is also useful in highlighting two common misconceptions. The first is that learning requires only action. The second is that experiential learning theory applies only to informal, unplanned learning that occurs outside of formal education, training and development settings. Neither of these statements is true or accurate. Experiential learning theory seeks to describe and explain human learning processes irrespective of the context in which learning occurs. And, as we shall see, the theory also postulates processes other than action as having to occur in order for successful learning to happen.

Experiential learning theory suggests that learning is continuous and cyclical. These two features are represented in the experiential learning cycle (*see* Fig. 6.1). The rationale of the theory rests on the arguments that learning is goal directed and that the process approximates that applied to solving problems (Stewart, 1996). This latter point reinforces the need for each stage of the cycle to occur for effective learning. Thus, reflection and generalising are as important as the action implicit in experiencing and experimenting. The argument on the 'goal directedness' of learning supports the idea of learning styles which is a significant feature of the theory (Stewart, 1996).

There are four broad learning styles suggested by the theory of experiential learning. The styles reflect the relevance of different stages in the cycle to different types of goals.

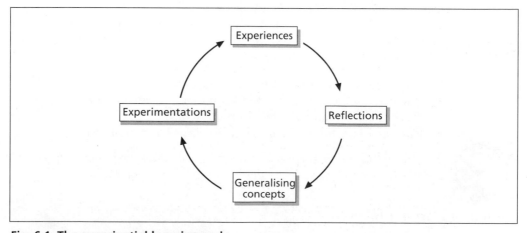

Fig. 6.1 The experiential learning cycle
Source: Based on Kolb, D.A., Rubin, I.M., and MacIntyre, J.M. (1984) *Organizational Psychology: An Experiential Approach*, 4th edn. New York: Prentice-Hall.

For example, a manager will be interested in practical application and results, and therefore will have a preference for concrete experience and active experimentation. Conversely, a research scientist will be more concerned with formulating general laws or principles, and therefore will have a preference for reflective observation and abstract conceptualisation (Stewart, 1996). The four broad styles suggested are the result of combining two stages of the cycle, and are as follows:

- *The diverger.* This style combines concrete experience with reflective observation. The style reflects a preference for engaging in tasks or activities and then analysing and thinking about the process and results achieved.
- *The assimilator.* Combining preferences for reflective observation and abstract conceptualisation results in this style. It involves using data and analysis which is the focus of reflective observation to produce generalisations which can have wider application.
- *The converger.* A style which combines abstract conceptualisation with active experimentation. The focus is on developing general principles and testing them on specific problems.
- *The accommodator.* Active experimentation is combined with concrete experiences in this style. This reflects a preference for action over cognitive processes, and for pragmatic results rather than elegant theories.

Kolb and others have produced self-analysis instruments which enable individuals to identify their preferred learning style. This is also the case with a refinement of the experiential learning cycle developed by Peter Honey and Alan Mumford (Stewart, 1996), who supply their own learning styles questionnaire (Honey and Mumford, 1986). There are two basic distinctions between these two sets of work. First, Honey and Mumford argue that learning preferences are associated with a single stage of the cycle, rather than with two in combination. Second, the Honey and Mumford instrument is based on behavioural statements, and therefore behavioural rather than cognitive preferences. The styles suggested by Honey and Mumford are described in Fig. 6.2. A useful activity at this point will be for you to access and complete one or both of these instruments to assess and identify your own preferred learning style.

The work of Kolb and others, for example the theory of individual learning labelled System Beta, devised by Reg Revans (Stewart, 1996), tends to support the following propositions about learning processes:

- learning is continuous, natural and inevitable;
- learning requires engagement in separate but related activities;
- individuals can have different learning styles;
- learning is an ability which can be developed and improved.

The first and last of these propositions would also find some support in the work of humanist psychologists. We will now turn our attention to that work.

Humanist learning theory

One theory which perhaps overlaps the cognitive and humanist perspectives is the idea of learning by and through *insight* (Hilgard *et al.*, 1971). The idea of learning through

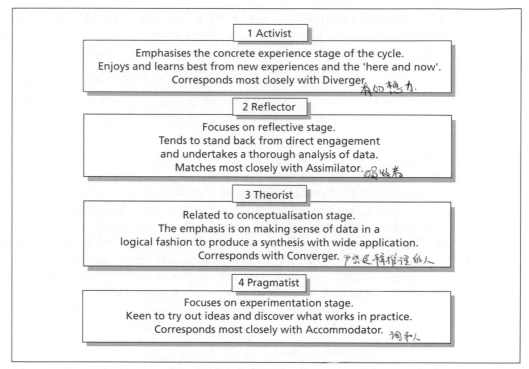

Fig. 6.2 Learning styles of Honey and Mumford
Source: Based on Honey, P. and Mumford, P. (1986) *The Manual of Learning Styles*. Maidenhead: Peter Honey.

insight was developed in part because of dissatisfaction with behaviourist studies, and a related concern to account for cognitive processes. Thus, we might include the theory under the heading of cognitive psychology. However, the theory focuses on the individual's free capacity to make sense of problems and reach their own solutions. This is consistent with the core beliefs and values of humanist psychology.

Insight occurs when new and different relationships between elements in a situation or problem are formulated. A powerful illustration of when insight occurs is provided by any time you, or someone you know, has suddenly uttered something like 'aha', having come to some answer or solution. Such illustrations are normally associated with dramatic insights, but insightful learning is more common than the dramatic examples. While little detail is provided in the theory of how insight works, the following features are argued to have been demonstrated (Hilgard, *et al.* 1971):

- *Insight depends on the arrangement of the problem situation.* The original research leading to development of the theory involved studying the behaviour of chimpanzees in their attempts to secure food under experimental conditions. This involved moving sticks of varying lengths to various positions in relation to the chimpanzee and the food. However, human beings (perhaps chimps, too?) have the capacity to mentally rearrange the elements of concrete and abstract problems and thereby potentially gain 'insight' into the true nature of the problem.

- *Once a solution occurs with insight, it can be repeated.* This feature is fairly straight-forward. It simply means that the same or similar problems will be approached in the same way, learned by insight, on future occasions.

- *Learning through insight can be applied in new or novel situations.* Again, this is self-explanatory. Connections between variables produced through insight (causal relationships, for example) are understood to be generalisable.

In summarising insight, Hilgard *et al.* (1971) make the following statement.

> An effective learner is a resourceful, adaptable person, able to use what he [*sic*] knows in new situations and to discover solutions to problems that he [*sic*] has never faced before.
>
> (p. 218)

The sentiments expressed in that quote also reflect the writing of Carl Rogers (1965, 1969), probably the leading humanist psychologist. Rogers advocated a view of learning as being in the direct and exclusive control of the individual, both in terms of process and outcomes. He also focused on, in his terms, the important distinction between learning and teaching. This is reflected in his dictum that one person cannot teach another person anything. All anyone can do, according to Rogers, is to provide an environment in which another person is free to learn. These notions concerning learning reflect Rogers's work in personal therapy. His view is captured in the two labels used to denote his approach: 'person centred' and 'non-directive' therapy. Central to this approach is the therapist adopting and exhibiting genuineness, acceptance and empathy (Myers, 1995). Translated into the learning arena, Rogers's analysis and arguments focus attention on the professional practitioner as facilitator rather than teacher or trainer, and on creating an appropriate and supportive social and emotional climate.

It is clear that humanist psychology has significance for understanding individual learning to add to that provided by the behaviourist and cognitive psychologists.

Activity 6.5 will help you review and evaluate the theories described in this section before we move on to examine organisation learning.

Activity 6.5

1 Recall a recent and successful learning experience and answer the following questions:

(a) what prompted you to learn?

(b) what do you do to prepare to learn?

(c) what happens, to and with you, as you are learning?

(d) how do you know you have been successful?

(e) how do you know if you have done a good or bad job in your learning?

2 Compare your responses to those in Activity 6.2. How do these responses modify or change your personal theory?

3 Compare your revised personal theory with those described in this section and consider the following questions:

(a) how similar or dissimilar is your theory with behaviourist and cognitive theories?

(b) how far, if at all, does your theory reflect the principles of humanist theories?

(c) how would you categorise your theory in terms of the behaviourist, cognitive and humanist typology?

▶

4 What complementary and contradictory features, or factors, can you identify between the three sets of theories?

5 Overall, based on your experience and your analyses produced in the activities so far in this chapter, which theory of learning do you consider most valid, and why?

Organisation learning

The subject of organisation learning will require less space than that of individual learning, for two reasons. First, despite a growing literature, for example Starkey (1996), Moingeon and Edmondson (1996), the idea is still a relatively new and unexplored concept in organisation theory. Second, there are methodological problems with the concept. As we saw in Chapter 2, much of organisation and management theory is built on a conceptualisation of organisations as independent, objective entities. The notion of organisation learning requires us to take that a stage further and to conceptualise organisations as *learning* entities. Doing so, I would argue, is constructive and helpful since it is useful to 'think about' organisations in those terms. An example of this usefulness is the literature on the learning organisation which would, in the main, make little sense without conceptualising organisations as learning entities. However, attempts to operationalise the abstract concept of organisation learning begin to show the difficulties of investigating and researching the concept in practice in order to build plausible theories of what it is and how it works. Therefore, there is much less theory on organisation learning than there is on individual learning.

Two related concepts that seem to be fruitful in terms of research on organisation learning are 'tacit knowledge' and 'implicit learning'. The former was developed in the 1950s and early 1960s by the philosopher Polyani (Spender, 1996). Tacit knowledge refers to that which is personal, subjective and unconscious, or non-conscious, in contrast to knowledge that is public and exists independently of individual knowing. For example, the theories of individual learning examined in the previous section constitute objective knowledge which is available to anyone and everyone. An example of tacit knowledge provided by Polyani (Spender, 1996) is that which enables an individual to ride a bicycle. Such knowledge is subjective and personal in the sense that it has not been codified and articulated in the same way as theories of learning, and therefore does not exist in the public domain. Indeed, a defining characteristic of tacit knowledge, according to Polyani, is that it is not capable of articulation or communication. It is therefore possible for many individuals to have the same tacit knowledge, but not possible to codify the knowledge in a way which enables it to be consciously learned. Individuals come to develop tacit knowledge through their subjective experience, and even in examples such as riding a bicycle, the form and nature of tacit knowledge is therefore likely to vary in unique ways.

Implicit learning is the process by which tacit knowledge is developed (Chao, 1997). Or, perhaps more accurately, the outcome of implicit learning is tacit knowledge. Implicit learning is argued to have the following six characteristics (Chao, 1997):

- *It happens at a non-conscious level.* The idea of 'non-conscious' allows for the process to happen during consciousness, as opposed to 'unconsciousness', but outside of and without conscious awareness.

- *It has primacy over conscious learning.* Implicit learning occurs without requiring conscious attention and motivation. Therefore, it can be seen as the default position that operates in the absence of explicit learning.

- *It is context bound.* Since implicit learning occurs without awareness, and its results are not capable of articulation, it is unlikely that the results can be generalised or transferred to new and different situations. An interesting example of this is given by Spender (1996) who reports research on experienced typists who were unable to correctly position key caps representing the QUERTY keyboard.

- *It is associated with incidental learning conditions.* This characteristic is associated with the fact that implicit learning occurs irrespective of there being structured and intentional learning experiences. This does not, of course, mean that implicit learning does not occur within such experiences.

- *It is associated with a sense of intuition.* When asked to explain or verbalise reasons for decisions or actions which are influenced by implicit learning, individuals use language such as 'it feels right', or expressions such as 'gut reaction' (Spender, 1996). Hence, implicit learning is not based on conscious reasoning.

- *It is robust and resilient.* Tacit knowledge, developed through implicit learning, has been found to endure long after formal knowledge, acquired through explicit learning, has been 'lost', or has ceased to be applied.

Some of these characteristics are reflected in the following definition of implicit learning.

> **The acquisition of knowledge that takes place largely independently of conscious attempts to learn, and largely in the absence of explicit knowledge about what was acquired.**
> (Reber, 1993, quoted by Chao, 1997, p. 44)

You might now be wondering what these concepts have to do with organisation learning. Your thoughts might be supported by relating the ideas on tacit knowledge and implicit learning to the theories of individual learning discussed earlier. If not, you should consider whether and how any, or all, of those theories might explain and account for tacit knowledge and implicit learning. However, the relevance of the concepts to organisation learning is demonstrated by their application in studies of organisation socialisation (Chao, 1997) and organisation strategy (Spender, 1996, Nonaka, 1996). The latter is of particular interest here.

Spender (1996) questions the individualistic and uncommunicable nature of tacit knowledge. While accepting the significance of Polyani's distinction between objective or 'scientific' knowledge – which is abstract and independent of the knower – and tacit knowledge – which is inextricably bound up with the subjective experience of the knower – Spender argues it is more accurate to view tacit knowledge as 'not yet articulated' than as inherently incapable of communication. He goes on to analyse the contextual nature of tacit knowledge, using the work of cultural anthropologists and ethnographers and, based on this, argues the importance of social knowledge as a category of tacit knowledge. Spender arrives at a four-part categorisation of types of organisation knowledge, each of which is defined as being either individual or social, and as either explicit or implicit. While the focus in Spender's work is on the strategic consequences of reliance on these different forms of tacit knowledge, the implication is that adding to and/or converting these forms of knowledge can constitute organisation learning. For example, converting what Spender calls 'automatic' knowledge, which is implicit and individual, into 'objectified', which is explicit and social, would constitute organisation learning.

A further form of knowledge in Spender's typology is 'collective knowledge'. This is both implicit and social. Collective knowledge could be used to describe the outcomes of processes of organisation socialisation (Chao, 1997). A problem with organisation socialisation is that it is a process which helps to reproduce the organisation. In other words, it results in keeping the organisation the same as it was when what is needed, as Stata (1996) argues, is management innovation in approaches to organising and managing. This relates in part to Stata's formulation of organisation learning as including 'organisation memory', constituted through institutional mechanisms such as policies, strategies and explicit mental models. These mechanisms need to be questioned and challenged in order for organisation learning to occur. The work of Nonaka (1996) suggests how this can be achieved.

Nonaka's work is focused on the creation and management of the 'knowledge creating company'. Obviously, creating knowledge requires learning and, therefore, a knowledge-creating company must facilitate organisation learning. Using empirical examples from successful Japanese companies, Nonaka argues that a number of critical organising and managing principles, such as free flow of information and use of challenging metaphors, are necessary for successful organisation learning. However, he also adapts and applies the concept of tacit knowledge to explain organisation learning. For Nonaka, organisation learning depends on what he terms 'the spiral of knowledge' (Nonaka, 1996). This requires four processes to be connected and interrelated:

- *From tacit to tacit.* This involves tacit knowledge held by an individual being shared with and passed on to other individuals. The process can be compared with organisation socialisation, but is also usefully illustrated by an apprentice working with an experienced and skilled craft worker where exposure and observation are significant.
- *From explicit to explicit.* This process involves separate and distinct components of explicit knowledge being combined to produce a new piece of explicit knowledge. The example used by Nonaka is a financial report based on data from a variety of sources.
- *From tacit to explicit.* Accepting the premise that tacit knowledge can be accessed and codified, this process involves individuals articulating tacit knowledge in a way and form that enables the knowledge to be communicated more widely.
- *From explicit to tacit.* Nonaka argues that as previously tacit knowledge becomes codified and communicated, it eventually becomes internalised by others, and therefore broadens, extends and reframes their individual tacit knowledge.

So, according to Nonaka, organisation learning occurs through the operation of these four processes, and connecting them so that each informs and influences the others to create a 'spiral' enabling the creation of knowledge. This last point suggests a weakness with the definition of implicit learning given earlier. Reber (Chao, 1997) uses the word 'acquisition'. This suggests knowledge gained through implicit learning is pre-existing, i.e. it is 'out there' waiting to be discovered and learned. The work of Spender and

Nonaka allows for the creation of knowledge, both by individuals and by collectives. Their formulation of tacit knowledge is more useful, therefore, in terms of the potential benefits of organisation learning. I am sure Reber is correct in saying that implicit learning results in the acquisition of pre-existing knowledge. Organisation socialisation would be one example of this (Chao, 1997). However, I am also sure that it is not exclusive, and that implicit learning can and does result in new knowledge.

There is one final conceptualisation of organisation learning to examine here. It comes from the work of Nancy Dixon (Dixon, 1994) and is a view of organisation learning that provides a direct link with individual learning. Dixon's definition of organisation learning is as follows.

The intentional use of learning processes at the individual, group and system level to continuously transform the organisation in a direction that is increasingly satisfying to its stakeholders.

(Dixon, 1994, p. 5)

It is clear from this definition that organisation learning requires but goes beyond individual learning. Dixon views learning as essentially concerned with creating and structuring meaning, and argues that to understand organisation learning we need to accept two propositions. First, that creation of meaning structures is both an individual and a social process. Second, and following from this, within an organisation there will be both individual and collective meaning structures. The next step in Dixon's analysis is to argue that each set of meaning structures can be accessible or inaccessible. More accurately, perhaps, some individual meaning structures will be kept private, and therefore inaccessible, and some collective meaning structures will be inaccessible because they are part of what is 'taken for granted' or because they constitute what is 'undiscussable' in the organisation. From this analysis, Dixon argues that organisation learning is facilitated and improved by increasing the accessibility of individual and collective structures of meaning, and the processes of their creation.

Increasing accessibility depends upon understanding and 'intentionally' using organisation learning process. For Dixon (1994), this process mirrors the experiential learning cycle devised by Kolb. Dixon's formulation of organisation learning is therefore the adaptation of Kolb's experiential learning cycle shown in Fig. 6.3. The description of the stages and elements in this cycle provide some indication of the kinds of policies, procedures and activities in which organisations need to engage to improve organisation learning. However, Dixon argues very strongly that universal prescriptions are neither appropriate nor possible, and that each organisation needs to develop its own approaches and methods.

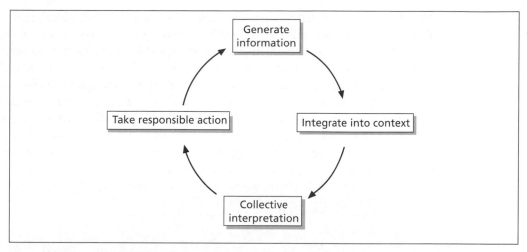

Fig. 6.3 Organisational learning cycle
Source: Based on Dixon, N. (1994) *The Organizational Learning Cycle*. Maidenhead: McGraw-Hill.

Activity 6.6

1 Review the arguments on organisation learning and consider the following questions:

   (a) what are the areas of similarity and difference between the various accounts?

   (b) how does each of them connect and relate with theories of individual learning?

   (c) which, in your view, provides most utility?

2 Using any model, assess the effectiveness of organisation learning in your organisation.

Summary and conclusion

This chapter has shown that a number of schools of thought exist within psychology. Each of these schools of thought has developed theories to describe and explain individual learning. The existence of a number of theories, and our examination of them, suggests that, as yet, we cannot claim a definitive understanding of individual learning. This seems to be true even if we limit our examination to what might be termed 'mainstream' theories of learning within an exclusively functionalist paradigm. Critical analysis of these mainstream theories from alternative perspectives would probably raise even more doubts about our understanding. However, experience suggests that the theories of individual learning examined here provide certain principles which are useful in the practice of HRD.

The model of the HRD introduced in Chapter 2 suggests learning processes constitute a significant component of practice. The model also suggests that both individual and organisation learning are significant. While research and theory on the latter is relatively undeveloped (Dixon, 1994), concepts and models relevant to organisation learning have been included in the chapter to inform thinking about interventions at that level. Connections between individual and organisation learning, and between theories and models to explain each, seem to be both apparent and important. An overall conclusion to the chapter would therefore seem to be that understanding individual and organisation learning processes is critical to the professional practice of HRD. Such a conclusion both supports and is supported by the author's model of HRD. Application of the understanding, and indeed of the model, lies in professional practice, and different theories of learning influence approaches to practice in different ways. The existence and nature of different approaches provides the focus of the next chapter in which the influence of different theories of learning will also be identified. Readers are recommended to complete the following activity before moving on.

Activity 6.7

Alvesson and Wilmott (1996) make a case for managing to serve emancipatory purposes through application and use of critical theory. I have argued elsewhere that the possibilities of serving either oppressive or emancipatory purposes in processes of organising and managing are most evident in the practices of employee development (Stewart, 1998). With these arguments in mind, consider the following questions:

1 To what extent are each of the theories of individual learning examined here inherently oppressive or emancipatory?

2 What would be the consequences for their validity and utility, of applying perspectives other than the functionalist paradigm to theories of learning?

3 What principles can be drawn from learning theory to inform the practice of employee development?

4 What are the implications and consequences for individuals and organisations arising from applying these principles?

Case study 6

Wendy Smith works as HRD manager for Oundle Brewery. Wendy began her working life with Oundle ten years ago as a commercial trainee manager, following graduation with a BA (Hons) in Business Studies. Her liking and aptitude for personnel matters and development has led to her present position, which she has had for two years. During her time with Oundle, Wendy has seen and been part of many changes. Over the past two years, she has initiated and managed a major change programme (of which more later) to support the company's intended business strategy.

Oundle is what is referred to as a 'regional brewery'. This means that the company limits its operations to particular geographic regions in the UK. While it is a publicly quoted company, Oundle is still managed by members of the founding family and the original owners. This, in Wendy's view, has both positive and negative consequences. The positive outcomes are associated with the strong backing for HRD which Wendy receives from both the chairman and the managing director. Negative outcomes arise from a long-serving and loyal workforce who still see Oundle as a family business and who therefore can be resistant to change.

The major objective for the company is to avoid takeover by one of the large, national/international brewery companies. Achieving this objective depends on the company continuing to satisfy existing shareholders which, in turn, depends on maintaining impressive business results. The company's declared and intended strategy to achieve this is to deliver first-class service and products to its customers. Standards to operationalise the strategy have been formulated in a number of 'hallmarks of service' statements for each area of the business. These statements specify and define what customers can expect to receive in terms of service from the company. Similar statements have been agreed for support functions in relation to their 'internal' customers.

Oundle employs just over 1,500 staff. The vast majority of these – more than 85 per cent – work in retail operations managing and delivering services to the 'eating and drinking public'. The remainder are concerned with 'free trade' sales and support services such as distribution, property management, finance and HR. Wendy reports through a group head of HR to the managing director and has responsibilities which cross the head office/retail divide. However, retail operations have their own training and development function which reports to the group sales director. The company has received IIP recognition and has received many awards, both national and industry specific, for its employee development activities. Comprehensive training plans and programmes exist for all categories of staff and these are fully utilised. Support is provided for professional qualifications. Every member of staff receives an annual development-based appraisal with quarterly reviews and works to an agreed individual development plan. The HRD function is well resourced with a refurbished training centre, which includes a 'training pub' complete with kitchen and cellar, and a complement of 12 staff across group and retail departments. In a recent paper for the MD, Wendy estimated that the company spends a total of £3 million on employee development (taking account of both direct and indirect expenditure) which represents more than 7 per cent of a total payroll of £40 million.

A major part of Wendy's work over the past two years has been the Hallmark Initiative. This initiative has involved all employees in Oundle Brewery attending a two-day workshop on the concept of customer service. The workshops have enabled all employees to contribute to formulation of the Hallmark statements. Follow-up activities in departments and sections have led to production of 'mini' statements for those departments and sections and, in some cases, for particular jobs. The Hallmark Initiative is central to the organisation's business strategy of delivering first-class customer service, and the relevant statements have been issued to existing customers, are displayed in all Oundle's managed and tenanted sites and are used by sales staff in negotiating new customers/business. Other development initiatives to support the business strategy have included team development events for all established teams in Oundle, a newly designed management development programme and a series of 'challenge' events designed to encourage innovation and improvements in the company's operations. The 'challenge' events involve diagonal cross-sections of staff working in teams to develop their problem-solving and creative-thinking abilities which are then applied to specific areas of the company's operations.

As Wendy reflects on the current position of the company and the role of HRD she identifies two reasons for satisfaction. First, all employees are supported in learning their jobs through well-designed training programmes. This helps to maintain the organisation's ability to continue to do its traditional business well. Second, the Hallmark Initiative and related activities help to support beneficial changes in what the company currently does. However, these initiatives and activities are beginning to bear fruit, and Wendy wonders about the future direction and contribution of HRD to individual and organisational learning.

Discussion questions

1   What development activities support individual learning in Oundle Brewery?

2   What development activities support organisational learning in Oundle Brewery?

3   What model or theory of individual learning do you think Wendy is applying in her work? Do you think this is appropriate?

4   How can HRD improve support for organisational learning in the future in Oundle Brewery?

5   What advice would you give Wendy on the future direction and contribution of HRD in Oundle Brewery?

Suggested reading

Arnold, J., Robertson, I.T. and Cooper, C.L. (1995) *Work Psychology (2nd edn)*. London: Financial Times Pitman Publishing.

Burgoyne, J. and Reynolds, M. (1997) *Management Learning:* Integrating Perspectives in Theory and Practice. London: Sage.

Dixon, N. (1994) *The Organizational Learning Cycle*. Maidenhead: McGraw-Hill.

Myers, D.G. (1995) *Psychology (4th edn)*. New York: Worth.

Starkey, K. (ed.) (1996) *How Organizations Learn*. London: International Thomson Business Press.

CHAPTER 7

Employee development: models and approaches

Introduction

Empirical research conducted over a number of years indicates that there is variety in the approaches adopted to employee development within work organisations. This chapter will examine the results of some of that research. Variety in approaches are related to models of ED in at least two ways. First, different models inform practice in ways which lead to variety in approach. Second, discovery of variety in approach leads to formulation of different, and sometimes competing, models of ED. This is a concrete example of connections between the work of academics and the work of practitioners, and illustrates how each informs and influences the other. However, we need to be clear in each particular case of the direction of the connection and influence. Clarity can be gained, in part, by answering the question: 'Does this model reflect approaches found in practice, or does it seek to inform or influence the approach to be adopted?' Answering that question will be helped by an understanding of the concept of 'model', both in the context of everyday speech and its use in academic literature. The chapter will therefore begin by exploring the meaning of the term 'model'.

There are two additional points to be made by way of introduction. Much of the content of this chapter will draw on the work of academic researchers and writers. As well as describing variety in approaches and, in some cases, formulating conceptual models, these writers also 'identify' significant factors which are argued to explain or account for a particular approach, rather than an alternative, being applied. In the main, these factors will be the same or similar to those which were examined when exploring the context of ED in Chapter 4, i.e. factors associated with external and internal contexts. For example, some analyses would suggest that rapidly changing economic conditions (an external factor), coupled with corresponding shifts in corporate strategy (an internal factor), will be significant in influencing, if not determining, the approach adopted to employee development.

We need to remember that the paradigm of organising and managing within which researchers and writers work will influence them to identify and attach weight to some factors rather than others. The same is true of professional practitioners who will be similarly influenced by their current paradigm when providing accounts and explanations of their approach to employee development practice. Perhaps the idea of 'world view' described in the previous chapter is a useful way of capturing this point. Therefore, as well as evaluating arguments for the existence and application of particular approaches *in their own terms*, we have to be aware that those terms are likely to reflect a particular paradigm, or world view, which may itself be open to question and challenge.

The final introductory point is, in part, related to the previous argument. It is simply to recognise the nature and status of the models presented in this chapter. None is a statement of 'fact' or a description of 'reality'. They are each different attempts to describe and account for a particular version of reality. For example, we will be examining various categorisations, or typologies, of approaches to employee development, and these typologies differ in the number of types identified. The existence of difference in number of types does not mean one typology is right and one is wrong. Each can be valid and useful. We should avoid thinking in terms of 'there are five approaches to ED'; all we can say is that according to the typology produced by researcher X, there are five approaches.

The previous paragraphs will, no doubt, make life more difficult since they have the effect of reducing certainty and increasing ambiguity. To alleviate this a little, this chapter intends to achieve the four objectives shown here.

CHAPTER OBJECTIVES

- Describe a number of approaches to employee development practice.

- Critically evaluate a range of models of employee development.

- Review and assess current approaches to ED within organisations.

- Formulate arguments for changes and improvements to current organisational practice.

Completing the activity which closes this introduction will help to achieve these objectives, particularly the last two. The results will also be used in activities later in the chapter, and will be helpful to bear in mind when assessing the arguments presented from academic research.

Activity 7.1

1 Produce a description of your organisation's current approach to employee development, and then consider the following questions:

(a) what factors, external and internal, seem to you significant in influencing the approach adopted?

(b) what factors do you think senior managers in your organisation would identify as significant?

(c) if there are differences (as I expect) what, in your view, are the reasons for this?

2 Provide a colleague from a different organisation with your responses to **1**, and ask them to consider the following:

   (a) does the approach adopted make sense in terms of the factors identified by the practitioner? Senior managers? Both?

   (b) would the same factors lead your colleague to a different approach/response? If so, why?

   (c) how do the significant factors and approach compare with those prevalent in your colleague's organisation?

3 Discuss with your colleague how adopting a different paradigm/perspective might shift which factors are identified as significant, and the approach applied in practice.

4 Discuss with your colleague what conclusions you each draw from the results of this activity.

The nature of a model

Mike Noon (1992), in an informative and instructive essay on the concepts of map, model, and theory, provides a persuasive argument that the concepts of model and theory are synonymous. While there are some useful elements in Noon's analysis, I am not in total agreement with his conclusion. This is because I see some differences in the association of the *functions* of description, explanation and prediction with the concepts of map, model and theory. In other words, I think it is useful to see the function of a map to be to *describe*, the function of a model to *explain* and the function of a theory to *predict*. These distinctions are, of course, matters of degree rather than absolute and unarguable categories, and therefore it can be a matter of judgement, and therefore of debate, whether a particular analysis or idea is a map, model or theory. I think, however, that the association of map with description, model with explanation and theory with prediction, even if simplistic, does have some utility. The following closer examination of the concepts will show my reasons for arguing that position.

A theory, in common with a model, provides an explanation of a particular phenomenon. However, the nature of the explanation in a theory is very specific in that theories formulate explanations of cause and effect. This requires the variables in the theory, and the propositions concerning causal relationships between the variables, to be operationalised so that they can be empirically tested. A sound theory will then allow predictions to be made about outcomes when applying or manipulating the variables. As a simplified example, the economic theory of supply and demand predicts caus   ion-ships between the variables of supply, demand and price, and predicts th   price will result in changes in both supply and demand. This example cl   the following features of a theory:

- concepts are capable of being operationalised into variables;
- explanations are based on causal relationships;
- causal relationships can be tested empirically;
- causal relationships provide the basis for predictions.

We can then argue from this example that theories are concerned with *predicting* the outcome of manipulating variables. By contrast, if we examine the concept of map, the usual and everyday use of the term would suggest the more limited function of *description*. However, as well as common examples of road or town maps which describe physical terrain, we also formulate and use maps of non-physical territory. For example, consider being asked to describe your organisation. Attempt to describe it now, and notice what happens as you do so. It is probable that you produced some kind of picture in your mind. This picture probably identified significant elements, or components, of your organisation; perhaps different departments, locations, products, customers, staff groups and/or personalities. It may also have included current objectives, issues and problems. As well as these components, your picture is likely to have contained loose representations of the connections, or relationships, between the various components. I am confident that your picture was incomplete and that the connections between the various components were not based on causal relationships. What you produced in your mind is a 'map' which helps in, though is limited to, *describing* your organisation. So, maps serve the function of description.

Models lie somewhere between theories and maps. They share a descriptive function with maps. The description contained in a model is likely to be more specific, detailed and focused than in a map. Models share a concern with theories to suggest relationships between components. The relationships, however, are not necessarily causal and the components usually stay at the conceptual level rather than being operationalised into variables, and so prediction is not possible. However, because of the specificity and focus of both the description of components and their relationship, models provide greater *explanation* than maps can achieve. Explanation here is used in the sense of aiding or supporting understanding of the phenomenon, without necessarily allowing confidence in outcomes arising from manipulation. So, models *explain* in a way which produces understanding which, in turn, can inform decisions on action without actually predicting or guaranteeing outcomes.

As was indicated earlier, these distinctions between map, model and theory are matters of degree. In that spirit, we can suggest gradations in the form models can take. The following is a useful categorisation of different types of models:

- *Abstracts*. Models can and do simply abstract 'reality' by identifying and specifying the essential components that make up that reality, and without which the reality cannot be known or understood in any useful way.
- *Represents*. A model can go further than simply 'abstracting' reality by providing more detail in terms of the number of components, their nature and how they connect and relate with each other. In this way, the model becomes more of a representation of the reality it is concerned with.
- *Idealises*. The concept of model can be used in the sense of an ideal. Such a model therefore can and often does go beyond current reality to specify some kind of ideal state that could be attained.
- *Prescribes*. Related to the above, models can and do prescribe what reality should be. Many academic models of management provide examples of prescriptive models. They specify what components should be in place and how they should connect and relate to each other.

The value and utility of this typology arises from its application in assessing and evaluating models produced by academic research and writing. Quite often, those producing such models do not make clear the nature and status of their models in the terms suggested by the typology. Making a judgement of a model in those terms is a useful starting point in assessing validity and utility. You are encouraged to do so in considering the models examined in the rest of the chapter.

Activity 7.2

1 Produce some examples to illustrate each of the categories in the typology – i.e. models which abstract, represent, idealise and prescribe – from each of the following sources:

   (a) academic models;

   (b) non-academic models.

2 Identify and consider some of the theories currently being applied in HR policy and processes in your organisation. You may want to think about selection and reward, for example, as well as development. Answer the following questions in relation to each theory:

   (a) is the theory based on academic research?

   (b) is application explicit and deliberate, or implicit?

   (c) is the theory tested by comparing predictions with empirical evidence generated by its application in the organisation?

   (d) are there alternative theories which may have more validity in explaining and predicting outcomes?

The Megginson model

We now turn our attention to models which suggest varying approaches to employee development. The first is based on work originally carried out by David Megginson more than 20 years ago (Boydell, 1983). The focus of Megginson's work was specifically approaches to training needs as opposed to employee development in general. However, his categorisation of approaches is very useful in thinking about the assumptions which can and are made about the purposes of ED, and the consequences of these assumptions for professional practice. Talking about and examining Megginson's work with practitioners confirms that his ideas are still relevant today, and more recent research which we will examine later supports this conclusion.

Megginson researched practice in a number of organisations and on the basis of his findings produced a five-category typology. We will confine our examination to four approaches from his typology at this point. Each of these is described and discussed below.

The welfare approach

As the name suggests, the welfare approach is primarily focused on the needs and aspirations of individuals. Employee development is seen as provision of a service to and for the benefit of individual employees. Provision of such a service in turn is linked to ensuring individuals gain personal satisfaction and growth from their employment. Satisfaction, though, is not exclusively, or even primarily, associated with development. It is also linked with tangible, material outcomes in terms of career progression. Therefore, in the welfare approach, training and development is most valued where it is linked to certification or qualifications which, in turn, provide clear routes for career paths and progression. There is an assumption in the welfare approach that almost any training and development is a good thing so long as it contributes to the satisfaction and happiness of individual employees.

Given these characteristics, the goals pursued by organisations and practitioners adopting this approach are associated with maximising employee satisfaction. This translates into achieving the highest amount of employee development possible and provision of development activities for all who want them. Goals will include devising and implementing structured career paths, linked to qualifications whenever possible, for all categories of roles, jobs and staff in the organisation.

There are obvious implications associated with adopting this approach to employee development. Perhaps the most obvious is that it is likely to be resource intensive. This may also suggest that it is more likely to be found in large rather than small organisations. Potential disadvantages include a lack of focus on or relevance to organisation objectives and strategy, and an associated lack of control over development activities on the part of line managers. These need to be weighed against potential advantages of employee loyalty and commitment, and associated strengthening of corporate culture. It is probably true to say that the welfare approach, while still adopted by some organisations, is less prevalent than it once was.

The administrative approach

Again, the title implies the significant characteristics of the administrative approach. The critical concern here is with design and implementation of efficient systems to plan, record and monitor development activities. This leads to a focus on information and information processing, together with formalised systems for vetting, assessing and approving expenditure on employee development. Needs or activities which do not fit the system, for instance, a development activity outside the pre-determined categories, fail to be recognised or acknowledged. Application of the administrative approach allows formulation of comprehensive, organisation-wide training and development plans which, once approved, are usually rigidly followed and therefore difficult to amend or change.

A major goal of the administrative approach is to ensure the smooth running of employee development within the organisation. Related to this, a further goal is impartial and consistent application of the rules and regulations governing approval of development expenditure and activities. A further, though associated goal, is maintenance of accurate and up-to-date records to support provision of management information on employee development.

As with the welfare approach, the significant implications of the administrative approach are fairly obvious. The concern with formalised systems and management information may again suggest an association with large rather than small organisations. It may also be associated with bureaucratic structures commonly, though not necessarily accurately or exclusively, associated with public sector organisations. Potential disadvantages include inflexibility and valuing adherence to systems or rules above relevance or benefit of outcomes. On the plus side, potential advantages include a lack of perceived or actual patronage or favouritism in resource allocation, and plans derived from and aligned with organisation objectives.

The political approach

The third approach is concerned with enhancing the power, status and influence of the employee development function. The focus therefore tends to be on what is valued, or perceived to be in favour with, significant decision makers in the organisation. Such people in most organisations are the chief executive and other senior managers. Thus, the concern of those in the ED function adopting this approach is with appealing to and satisfying the demands, preferences (perhaps prejudices) and ideas of senior managers. Development activities are confined therefore to those that have the overt approval and sanction of that group. While this condition could be said to be necessary whatever approach is adopted, the distinguishing factor in the political approach is that achieving senior manager approval is the *raison d'etre* rather than a necessary condition of development activities.

Given these characteristics, the primary goal of the political approach is in meeting the need for power, influence and resources of the employee development function. Related to this is pursuit of credibility in the eyes of senior managers through creating the right impression. The nature of the right impression will, of course, vary from organisation to organisation and over time.

We saw in an earlier chapter that organisations are usefully conceptualised as political arenas. It could be argued therefore that a political approach is, at least some of the time, essential to ensure investment in employee development. Two examples of when the approach may be most appropriate are first when the function is newly established in order to build resources and influence, and second when the organisation is seeking to cut costs and the political approach is necessary to ensure survival of the function. Interestingly, if the values and goals of other approaches such as the administrative approach are in line with those of senior managers, then applying that approach may be part of adopting a political approach.

There are pluses and minuses to the political approach. Potential advantages include clear understanding of organisation objectives and strategy through closeness to senior managers, and access to resources. Potential disadvantages include ignoring the needs and demands of other groups in the organisation, and being too closely associated with old regimes at times of change in senior personnel.

The organisation development approach

Organisation development, or OD, can be considered a separate discipline, though one which is closely associated with HR in general and HRD in particular (Stewart, 1996). Megginson, however, found evidence of development practitioners adopting and advocating the principles of OD in their work. The approach is associated with application of theory and research from the social, or behavioural, sciences to the management of work organisations. OD tends to focus attention on groups rather than on individuals, and has a major concern therefore with interpersonal relationships. This leads to a preference for work-based, or work-focused, interventions rather than prescriptive, formal courses. It also leads to 'soft' issues, such as perceptions, feelings and attitudes, being highlighted rather than the 'harder' characteristics of task-related knowledge and skills.

The primary, overall goal of the OD approach is to bring about congruence and coherence between individual and organisational needs and aspirations. Employee development policies, processes and activities serve to achieve that purpose. Related to this goal is development of humanistic values in organising and managing which will, in turn, produce greater flexibility and responsiveness on the part of both the organisation and individual employees.

Much has been and continues to be written on OD (Stewart, 1996, Stewart and McGoldrick, 1996a and 1996b, Oswick and Grant, 1996). It is therefore important to emphasise that the account given in the previous paragraphs is that provided by Megginson (Boydell, 1983) to describe OD as an approach to training and development contained within his typology. However, the focus of OD on humanist values, flexibility and congruence between individual and organisation goals would probably not be disputed as a central tenet of OD. These characteristics tend to illustrate the idealistic nature of OD, and the difficulties associated with measuring and evaluating in concrete terms the outcomes of adopting the approach. There are potential advantages, however. These include first releasing individual and collective potential and creativity through fostering and promoting productive relationships, and second increased organisation responsiveness to change. Potential disadvantages include ignoring knowledge and skill requirements at both individual and organisation levels, and the approach being seen by senior managers and others as too unstructured and unfocused.

Activity 7.3

1 What theory of individual learning would you say could be associated with, or used to support, each of these four approaches?

2 Some advantages/disadvantages have been mentioned for each approach. Of course, these depend on your viewpoint. List some additional advantages and disadvantages for each approach from the perspective of each of the following:

(a) senior managers

(b) employee development practitioners

(c) individual employees.

3 Each of Megginson's four approaches represent an ideal type which is unlikely to be found in a pure form. Accepting that is the case, recall your response to Activity 7.1 and consider the following questions:

(a) which of Megginson's approaches most closely fits your organisation's?

(b) what are the reasons for that approach being adopted?

(c) which approach, if any, do you think would be most appropriate, and why?

The Ashridge research

More recent research into approaches to employee development was carried out by the Ashridge Research Group (Barham *et al.*, 1987). The research involved a survey of a cross-section of organisations in the UK, supported by a number of in-depth case study analyses. As well as focusing on employee development, the researchers analysed the context within which HRD occurs. Based on this, they argued that significant changes in environmental conditions were and are being experienced, with related shifts in approaches in organising and managing. In summary, their conclusions suggest that environmental conditions demand more customer-orientated, internationally-focused and flexible organisations. In turn, this leads to a changing role for managers at all levels which emphasises leadership rather than control, horizontal rather than vertical relationships, and developing and nurturing the potential and contribution of employees.

Relating these arguments to employee development, the research identified three phases in the changing contribution of employee development: the *fragmented*, *formalised* and *focused* approaches. The first two are associated with organisation forms which emphasise vertical relationships, and with directive or autocratic styles of management. The focused approach is required to both support shifts to and reflect the requirements of organisation forms which emphasise horizontal relationships, and non-directive management styles. Before examining each of these approaches in more detail, it is important to stress that the Ashridge researchers found evidence of each approach being adopted at the time of their study. Their argument is that the focused approach is the most relevant to social and economic conditions prevailing at the time of the research.

The fragmented approach

As the name suggests, the fragmented approach reflects a situation where ED is *ad hoc* and unplanned. Development activities are not linked to organisation objectives and, relatedly, are perceived as at best an optional luxury or at worst a waste of resources. Training and development that does occur tends to be based on prescriptive and directive courses provided by and within the training department. The emphasis in these courses is on knowledge acquisition rather than skills or personal development. In summary, the fragmented approach is characterised by a lack of connection between ED and the business of the organisation.

The formalised approach

In the formalised approach, ED becomes more systematic and planned, commonly through explicit links with other HR functions, especially human resource planning. There are also, commonly, links with performance appraisal systems and processes. While this provides opportunities for connecting ED with organisation objectives, the tendency is to focus more on career planning and development. The link with appraisal has the effect of increasing the involvement of line managers in ED processes, and this can include contributions to pre- and post-course activities. Irrespective of those contributions, course design usually involves such activities, and also emphasises skills development as well as knowledge acquisition. In summary, the formalised approach, as the name suggests, is systems orientated.

The focused approach

The focused approach, arises when continuous learning is recognised as necessary for survival and HRD is considered to be central to formulation and implementation of organisation strategies. There are clear links between ED and organisation goals and objectives, and development activities are seen as a means of meeting individual goals. This leads to a wider range of development activities which utilise a greater variety of methods, especially those capable of application within the workplace. Individual employees have greater autonomy in managing their development, including self-nomination for a broad range of courses which emphasise values and attitudes as well as knowledge and skills. Line managers have greater responsibility for development of their staff and, relatedly, there is more concern for assessing and measuring the effectiveness and contribution of HRD. In summary, the focused approach is perhaps constituted by characteristics associated with the emerging concept of the 'learning organisation' (see Chapter 11).

Discussion

Each of the three approaches suggested by the Ashridge research can be associated with particular time periods. Generalising somewhat, the fragmented approach would typify that adopted during the 1950s and 1960s, and the formalised approach that adopted during the 1970s and 1980s. Such approaches were arguably products of, and appropriate to, conditions prevailing at the time. The focused approach is argued to be relevant to conditions in the 1990s and beyond. However, it is important to recognise that each approach, according to the Ashridge research, remains evident to some extent within the UK. The research suggests that there is a path of evolution and development from fragmented through formalised to focused which ED as an area of professional practice has followed, and perhaps through which any individual function in a specific organisation needs to progress. The idea of an evolutionary path linked to time periods is a feature to be found in the next model to be examined.

Activity 7.4

1 Consider the implications and consequences for the role of professional development practitioners within each of the three approaches. How will the role change and develop?

2 Compare the Ashridge categorisation with that produced by Megginson. What are the similarities and differences between the approaches identified?

3 What connections and influences, if any, can you identify between developments in learning theory and changes in approaches to ED suggested by the Ashridge model?

4 As with Megginson, the three approaches suggested within the Ashridge model represent ideal types. Recall your response to Activity 7.1 and consider the following questions:

(a) how accurate or otherwise do you consider the changed conditions facing organisations and managers to be?

(b) how closely does the focused approach fit that adopted in your organisation?

(c) how appropriate do you think the focused approach is or would be to your organisation?

The problem/solution model

This model of approaches to employee development conceptualises varying ED solutions to varying development-related problems experienced over the past 30 years. It is the result of work conducted by Pedler, Boydell and Burgoyne (1996) and is associated with their research into development of the 'learning company'. The time periods specified are somewhat arbitrary, although they illustrate the evolutionary nature of ED central to the analysis. It is as well to point out at this stage that while particular problems and solutions are associated with particular time periods, this should not be seen as exclusive or prescriptive. The problems highlighted as giving concern in particular time periods can and do occur at other times. Similarly, solutions applied carry over into later time periods in addition to those when the solution was first applied. The work of Pedler *et al.* is presented here in the chronology they suggest.

1950–70

The critical problem during the immediate post-Second World War period was a shortage of skilled employees. This shortage was particularly acute at craft and operative-level jobs and occupations. The problem had obvious implications and consequences for the national economy and individual employers. The solution, referred to as solution one, was 'systematic training'. We will return to this approach later in the chapter. In summary, though, the approach focuses on job analysis as a basis for producing detailed specifications of training requirements. Such specifications enable formulation of precise, behavioural objectives which support design and planning of structured training programmes, and which provide the benchmark against which programmes can be evaluated.

1970–85

Problem two, as Pedler *et al.* term it, occurred as a result of applying the solution of systematic training. An overemphasis on systematic analysis of jobs and tasks led to a narrow focus which ignored the diversity of individuals actually undertaking the work. Analytic techniques applied at craft and operator levels were inappropriate for roles and occupations providing discretion and requiring judgement, and they focused exclusively on present conditions and requirements and therefore did not support or facilitate creativity and continuous improvement in response to change. In response to these factors, between 1975 and 1985, solution two was applied. This consisted primarily of two streams: *self-development* and *action learning*. These approaches are examined in more detail in later chapters. Essentially, they both provide employees with increased levels of autonomy and control over development activities, working primarily individually in the former and in groups in the latter. Both methods illustrate an approach to ED which is as much concerned with the *person* as it is with the *job*, or organisation role. We might then characterise solution one as job orientated and solution two as person orientated.

1985–95

Solution two gave rise to two related problems between 1985 and 1990. These were first that solution two was primarily used within ED for managers and other professionals, while solution one continued to be used for other categories of employees, and second that the approaches of self-development and action learning were orientated to individual needs and aspirations at the expense of developing the organisation as a whole. A range of responses to these problems is suggested by Pedler *et al.* (1996) as constituting solution three. These include extending self-development to encompass *all* employees, an emphasis on *continuous improvement* which reflects the principles of action learning, introduction of NVQs and other competence-based approaches and pursuit of the 'ideal', of the learning organisation.

1995 onwards

At the time of writing, Pedler and his colleagues were unable to identify particular problems arising out of the application of solution three. They suggest responsibility to the environment and wider communities, ethics and cross-cultural working as possibilities. These possibilities would find support in some of the arguments presented in this book. Given the speculative nature of problem identification, the nature of solution four also cannot be analysed. Suggestions include extending the range of stakeholders involved in ED, working across existing boundaries and focusing on learning and development outside of the work context. Both sets of suggestions, on problems and solutions, find resonance and support in the analyses provided in Stewart and McGoldrick (1996a and 1996b) and therefore can be said to have merit. However, both Pedler *et al.* (1996) and Stewart and McGoldrick (1996a and 1996b) recognise a lack of empirical evidence at this stage.

Discussion

In common with the Ashridge research, Pedler and his colleagues recognise that while they associate particular solutions with particular time periods, earlier solutions can still be found being applied. It is also the case in my view that the argued connections between problems and solutions are not exclusive. Alternative solutions were and are possible to the problems identified. Similarly, solutions applied to particular problems could be relevant to different problems. There are also weaknesses in the analysis related to dating the emergence of particular solutions, for example, action learning was being applied by Revans in the 1960s. However, the work of Pedler *et al.* does provide a neat summary of the evolution of approaches to ED, and it also suggests some possible explanations for the evolutionary path followed.

Activity 7.5

1 How would you classify the overall problem/solution analysis in terms of the different types of model described earlier?

2 Think about the metaphors of organisations suggested by Morgan (1997) and described in Chapter 2. What connections and relationships can you analyse between the metaphors and the various approaches to ED detailed in the solutions of Pedler *et al.*

3 To what extent are the approaches suggested in solution three evident in your organisation? To what extent do you think they are, or could be, relevant?

4 Discuss with colleagues the validity and relevance of the problems and solutions suggested for 1995 onwards. Does your collective experience provide any evidence to support them?

Continuous development

The penultimate approach described here is very much associated with the Institute of Personnel and Development in that it arose out of the work of an IPM committee and IPM initiative called the ABCD campaign, or A Boost for Continuous Development (Reid and Barrington, 1997). The approach is labelled *continuous development* (CD). As Reid and Barrington (1997) recognise, there is little research and literature on CD, although they argue strong connections with similar and related concepts such as continuous improvement, TQM and the learning organisation, which have been subject to empirical studies.

Continuous development as an approach to ED is a little difficult to define or describe since, as Wood (1988) argues, individuals should and can create their own definitions. It is helpful in understanding the concept to see CD as representing a set of *attitudes* and *beliefs*, rather than as a set of specific methods, activities or techniques. Central to the approach is a view of the individual as an autonomous, learning entity capable of developing from any and all experiences, and of improving confidence, ability and skill in learning. The focus on 'any and all experiences' makes clear that CD is concerned with integrating work and learning. The focus on improving learning ability makes clear also that CD is concerned with what Reid and Barrington call the 'continuous development spiral' (1997, p. 93) which illustrates a process of individuals taking responsibility for and charge of their own development. In summary, CD is concerned with application of self-development, integrating learning and work and learning to learn (Reid and Barrington, 1997). These three elements are reflected in the following definitions.

> The management of learning on an ongoing basis through the promotion of learning as an integral part of work itself (definition for the organisation).

> Self-directed, lifelong learning, with a strong element of self-direction and self-management (for the individual).

> The promotion and management of learning in response to a continuous attitude in favour of improvement (general definition).

> (Reid and Barrington, 1997, p. 399)

These definitions indicate and support a view of CD as being as much about approaches to organising and managing as about ED. This is reinforced by arguments presented by Reid and Barrington (1997) and by Wood (1988) that creating and sustaining an appropriate and supportive organisation environment is critical in fostering CD as an approach to employee development. The environment argued to be necessary features characteristics in line with those suggested as necessary for the creation of a learning organisation (*see* Chapter 11). The focus on organisational and managerial approaches is also apparent in Reid and Barrington's argument that the three elements described earlier apply to work teams, units and departments as well as to individual employees.

Discussion

An understanding of CD as an approach to employee development can be further developed by referring to the IPD statement 'Continuous Development – People and Work'. It should be clear, however, that the approach has much in common with the focused approach in the Ashridge analysis, and with solution three suggested by Pedler and his colleagues. We now turn our attention to the final approach to be examined.

The systems approach

The systems approach has its antecedents in *systematic training* described as part of Pedler *et al.'s* analysis of solution one, which, according to that analysis at least, led to the creation of problem two. Systematic training was also the fifth approach suggested by Megginson in his classification, and it has similarities to the formalised approach within the Ashridge typology. These points suggest two things. First, that the systems approach is one of the older approaches described in this chapter. Second, if not simply on age grounds alone, the changed and changing conditions being experienced at the end of the twentieth century would suggest that the approach has outlived its usefulness or relevance. This would certainly seem to be a conclusion supported by the various analyses offered so far. There are a number of arguments which would question such a conclusion, however. We will return to these arguments after examining the detail of the approach.

The systems approach is also commonly referred to as formal or planned employee development, and descriptions take a number of forms. Essentially, the approach consists of applying a sequence of connected and related steps. The number and nature of these steps vary in different models of the systems approach. The model in Fig. 7.1, containing four steps, provides a typical representation. One of the key features of the model is the fact that it suggests a cyclical process. This is reflected also in the name given to the model, 'the training cycle'. As well as emphasising the interrelationship and connectedness of the four stages, the cycle emphasises a continuing and continuous process. This factor might be argued to have resonance with ideas of continuous improvement and, perhaps, the continuous development approach discussed in the previous section. It might also be argued that the training cycle operationalises the employee development function in a way which reflects the experiential learning cycle. Such an argument would find support in any similarities between systematic training and continuous development, since the latter uses experiential learning theory to support its validity and relevance, rather than any direct connections between the two cycles.

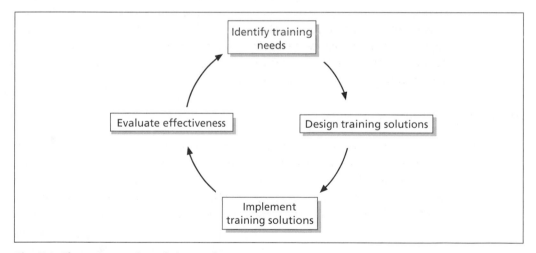

Fig. 7.1 The systematic training cycle

We will limit examination of the stages in the cycle to a brief description here as each will be the subject of later chapters. The first stage, ITN, is concerned with establishing the learning and development needs of individuals and groups in the organisation so that organisation objectives can be realised. While this assumes that such objectives can be and are articulated, it does suggest a degree of integration between employee development and the business needs of organisations. The design stage focuses on formulating employee development plans and programmes which will enable the identified needs to be met. This stage requires a sound understanding of a range of possible development methods and interventions which, in turn, relies on understanding and application of learning theories. Designing and planning development interventions also has to take account of organisational context and conditions and requires attention to issues concerning resource management. This factor is also critical during implementation. Resources allocated to employee development activities need to be controlled and accounted for during this stage. Depending on the nature of the activities, application of principles derived from learning theory can be critical. The final stage, evaluation, is primarily concerned with assessing the extent to which identified needs have been met and, relatedly, the contribution of employee development to achieving organisation objectives. Such processes are likely to reveal needs which remain unmet, and new training needs which have arisen through changed conditions. Evaluation, therefore, as well as providing an account of and for investment in development activities, will feed into the ITN process and recommence the cycle.

Discussion

The process described appears logical and rational. This is, in part, explainable by its association with the machine metaphor of organisations. According to the analysis provided by Megginson (Boydell, 1983), systematic training arose out of 'scientific management' (Mullins, 1993) and its application in work study and measurement. As indicated earlier, Pedler *et al.* argue that the resulting focus on jobs rather than people gave rise to new problems and new solutions. In my view, however, the situation is a little more complex.

Whether scientific management is good or bad, desirable or undesirable, is a question we will avoid in this discussion. Its continuing influence and application seems to be established (Ritzer, 1993). It is possible to argue that the rational approaches to strategic management described in Chapter 4 reflect similar principles. It also seems to be the case that despite persuasive arguments questioning the validity of such approaches (Stacey, 1992, Stacey, 1993, Watson, 1994), they continue to be highly influential (Cole, 1994, Johnson and Scholes, 1997), even if they are modified to incorporate more recent thinking (Mintzberg *et al*, 1998). So, we can argue that, in modified form, the principles of scientific logic and rationality are still highly influential in informing approaches to organising and managing, including the specific examples of strategic management and employee development. The relevance of this argument, and the specific example of strategic management, is illustrated in Fig. 7.2. This shows the connections between the processes involved in strategic management, according to the rational planning models, and the processes of employee development, according to the systems approach.

A further example of relationships between the training cycle and current approaches to managing will be instructive. While not without its critics, performance management continues to be widely applied in HR policy and practice (*see* Fisher, 1999). A common application is through a process referred to as the Individual Performance Review (IPR). Specific detail will vary from scheme to scheme, but the basic principles focus on linking individual performances and development to organisation requirements and objectives. The links between these principles and application of the systems approach to employee development are demonstrated in Fig. 7.3.

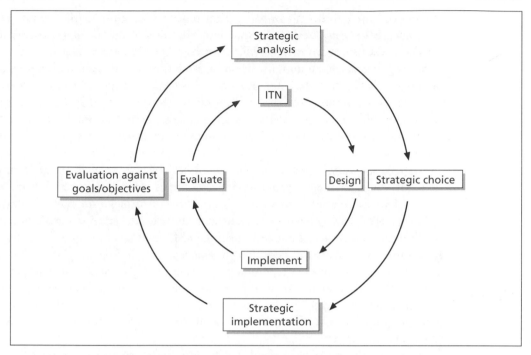

Fig. 7.2 Strategic management and the training cycle
Source: Sambrook, S. (1998) *Models and Concepts of Human Resource Development: Academic and Practitioner Perspectives,* PhD thesis (unpublished). Nottingham: Nottingham Business School.

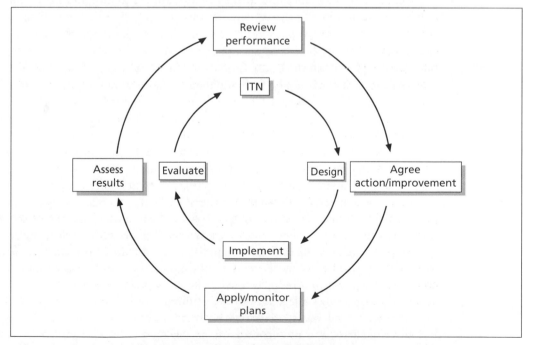

Fig. 7.3 Individual performance review and the training cycle
(with acknowledgement to Sally Sambrook)

There are three further examples of continued application of the systems approach and its associated training cycle. In the first, the four elements of the Investor in People standard can be directly related to the four stages of the training cycle. The first element requires existence and communication of some form of business plan which enables individual development to be integrated with business needs. This element provides a basis for ITN, and that stage also relates with the second element of IIP, reviewing the development needs of each employee. The third element, taking action, encompasses design and implementation within the cycle. Evaluation provides an obvious and straightforward connection between the two processes.

The second example, the development of NVQs, also arises from government policies and initiatives, and has been the subject of much controversy and debate (*see* Bates, 1995). However, what seems clear is that the principles and methods supporting the design of NVQs are entirely consistent with those espoused in scientific management (*see* Stewart and Sambrook, 1995 for a critique of functional analysis and further references). It has already been argued here that there is a connection between scientific management and the systems approach to employee development. Pedler *et al* support the point by arguing that the system of NVQs and the concept of competence retain elements of systematic training (Boydell and Leary, 1996). Therefore, we can conclude that application and take-up of NVQs provides evidence of the widespread and continued application of the systems approach.

The third example of continued application, that of the NVQs in training and development, is perhaps the most significant. As with all NVQs, these are based on and derived from occupational standards. The occupational standards in turn are derived from a 'functional map'. In developing a functional map of training and development, the lead body responsible adopted the systematic training cycle (DfEE, 1997). The resulting occupational standards are organised into five main areas of competence and these explicitly and directly relate to the four stages of the training cycle. The reason for five as opposed to four is simply that in the occupational standards the stage of evaluation is divided into two separate areas focusing on individual and organisational levels. As already indicated, there are considerable grounds for questioning NVQ's and the associated concepts of competence and occupational standards. However, to the extent that they are claimed to be based on comprehensive, empirical research, we can say that the most recent study confirms that the systems approach is the most widely recognised and applied approach to employee development in UK work organisations.

We can argue additional grounds for supporting the systems approach by examining some of the alternatives. The analysis offered by Pedler *et al.* suggests alternatives such as self-development and action learning in solution two, and variations of these in solution three. Their work on self-development, however (Pedler *et al.*, 1986), suggests the principles of the systems approach being applied by individuals for their own purposes. In other words, while there may or may not be a disconnection between individual development and organisation requirements, the *process* of self-development advocated is entirely consistent with the stages of the training cycle since it involves self-assessment to establish needs and goals, decisions on methods, formulation and implementation of development plans, and monitoring and reviewing outcomes. I fail to see any significant difference between this process and application of the systems approach. Action learning is a development method which can be and is used as an option within the second stage of the training cycle. As such, there is no inherent conflict or contradiction between action learning and the systems approach. Indeed, in that sense, action learning does not constitute an alternative. In addition, action learning as intended to be operated by its originator (Revans, 1980, 1982) reflects the rigour and principles associated with the practice of science, and so has that in common with the systems approach.

Turning to the work of the Ashridge Research Group, a similar picture emerges. Features associated with the focused approach include integration of individual and organisational goals, a wider range of methods and a concern with assessing the outcomes and contribution of development activities. The last of these is entirely consistent with the evaluation stage of the training cycle and the first feature is arguably central to the purpose of the systems approach. Use of a wider range of methods does not in itself invalidate the training cycle since, as with action learning, it simply provides more options at the design stage. Indeed, many of the methods available reflect the principles of the training cycle in their design and use. This is perhaps best illustrated in technology-based methods such as computer-based training (CBT) and interactive video (IV) which are largely based on programmes designed and developed within the spirit of the systems approach.

Finally, we have already seen some connections between the systems approach and continuous development, and the points on self-development made in a previous paragraph add to these. Perhaps the four approaches in Megginson's typology represent genuine alternatives to the systems approach. However, I would argue that the five approaches of welfare, administrative, political, OD and systems are not necessarily mutually exclusive. Megginson's research suggested that pure types did not exist and that any particular employee development function applied combinations of two, three or even four approaches. It is more likely that a particular approach gives emphasis and direction to elements of the other approaches that are applied. Overall, we can say that conceptually as well as empirically the systems approach provides a valid model of employee development.

Activity 7.6

1 What are the main points of similarity and difference between the systems approach and each of the following?

(a) the formal approach

(b) the focused approach

(c) continuous development.

2 Recall your response to previous activities and consider the following questions:

(a) how closely and in what ways does the systems approach reflect that adopted in your organisation?

(b) what are the main points of similarity and difference, and why is this the case?

(c) what advantages/disadvantages are or could be evident in your organisation from applying the systems approach?

3 (a) which paradigm of organising informs the systems approach?

(b) how would you criticise the approach from the perspective of each of the following?

- radical humanist
- interpretive

(c) considering all the arguments in this chapter, and the results of this activity so far, what approach to employee development do you consider the most useful and valid, and why?

Summary and conclusion

We have established in this chapter that a number of different categorisations of models of and approaches to employee development have been formulated by a number of different writers. Categories developed vary in the extent to which they are drawn from empirical research into practice, or are based on conceptual analysis. The work of Megginson and the Ashridge Research Group are examples of the former, and that of Pedler *et al.* and of Reid and Barrington on continuous development provide examples of the latter. Each of the works shares a questioning of, and provides a challenge to, the continued validity and relevance of the systems approach and associated training cycle model of ED. However, based on empirical research conducted for training and development NVQs, and a conceptual analysis of alternatives, this chapter has argued a position of support for the systems approach and use of the training cycle. Given that position, the following chapters will examine stages of the cycle in more detail.

Before moving on, however, it is important to acknowledge some potential weaknesses in and criticisms of the systems approach. As one of the activities in the previous chapter suggested, formalised development activities to facilitate and support learning can serve oppressive or emancipatory purposes. These competing purposes are perhaps inherent in potential and actual conflict between individual and organisation objectives and interests. The following quote is relevant to this point as it provides an example of failing to recognise, or perhaps, ignoring this issue.

> The key purpose for training and development has been defined as: 'Develop human potential to assist organisations and individuals to achieve their objectives.' This statement reflects training and development's dual role to assist both organisations and individuals.
>
> (DfEE, 1996, p. 5)

We have seen this duality of focus in earlier chapters on the organisation context and on trainer roles. The systems approach, like the above quote, assumes that both sets of objectives can be integrated, or accommodated or achieved to the mutual interest of both parties. This is not always, perhaps even rarely, the case. Dealing with potential or actual conflict of objectives and interests raises ethical issues for development practitioners (*see* Chapter 13). The existence of such conflict also provides a reason for caution in the more detailed analysis of the training cycle provided in the following chapters.

Case study 7

Paul Stacey is training and development manager of Bishopton and District Community NHS Trust (BDCT), a 'fourth wave' trust established in April 1994. The trust provides a range of services based on in-patient, out-patient and community health care through 1500 full-time equivalent staff consisting of medical, nursing, managerial, technical and PAMs (professions allied to medicine). The trust's major clients include children, elderly people, people with learning disabilities and people with mental health needs. Some specialist services, such as rehabilitation and those associated with HIV/AIDS, are also provided. Services are delivered at a wide variety of sites such as GP surgeries, clinics, schools and in patients' homes, and, in some cases, in co-operation and collaboration with other agencies such as social services and other NHS providers.

Following ten years in manufacturing industry and with only 15 months in his present post, Paul still finds the trust complex and cumbersome, especially in relation to gaining the necessary approval and resources for new initiatives in training and development. However, Paul is enjoying his job because it involves close contact with senior managers. His role is to develop the training function so that it provides clear contributions to the trust's business strategy. Since resources are limited, Paul is becoming adept at identifying and using expertise within the organisation which can be used to support and contribute to training and development initiatives. As well as Paul, the function consists of a training and development adviser, a training co-ordinator and one administrator/secretary. It has been clear to Paul from the time of his appointment that his department cannot directly provide all the training and development needed, given the size of the organisation and the complex range of roles and tasks involved in delivering the trust's services. Paul enjoys the challenge of developing new and different approaches to training and development presented by this situation.

A major current concern for Paul is to respond to recent fundamental change in the trust. A new organisation and management structure has recently been implemented. This has created two new roles, that of service manager and unit manager. Service managers are responsible for either a geographic area or a group of related services. Unit managers are, as the name implies, responsible for direct service delivery in and at specific sites. Since they report to the relevant service manager, there may be more than one unit manager in a particular site if it is concerned with multiple services and/or client groups. There are five service managers in the new structure reporting to one of two clinical general managers. All service managers and the majority of unit managers, of which there are 55, are qualified nurses. As with operational staff, these individuals have development needs associated with their continuing professional registration as well as those associated with their new roles as managers.

The chief executive of the trust, Martin Jones, has established a strategy group, which he chairs, to examine the future of the training and development function in the new structure. The group has 12 members, with representatives from across the staff groups and geographic sites of the trust. Paul and his manager, Earl Dickenson, the director of human resources, are both members. Martin Jones is quite interested in gaining IIP accreditation and in using the standard to establish the purpose and contribution of training and development. An internal survey loosely based on the standard has been carried out by Paul and reported to the strategy group. This indicates that the majority of staff continue to associate training and development with formal courses related to continuing professional development. Paul has reservations about allowing IIP to drive the approach to training and development in the trust. He believes meeting the standard will impose unnecessary and unhelpful formality in development systems. He believes that the trust needs to move away from formalised systems and to become much more flexible and innovative in development activities. Earl Dickenson has a similar view. IIP accreditation is, in his view, something worth having. However, in Earl's judgement, the trust should adopt an approach which is appropriate first to its own circumstances and needs. If this then meets IIP criteria, that will be a bonus.

The more immediate question facing the strategy group is to respond to the development needs of the newly appointed unit managers. Paul is aware that whatever is decided in relation to this group of staff will be influential in determining the future of training and development. He believes the approach adopted here will set a precedent for the approach to training and development for all staff in the trust. Paul values the support he receives from Earl, and is aware that most members of the strategy group are willing to be guided by the professional advice of who they see as the 'experts'. Martin Jones is neither dogmatic nor autocratic and is therefore open to persuasion. So, Paul knows that if he can come up with sound proposals for the development of unit managers, backed up by persuasive arguments, he can make significant progress in devising an approach to training and development he believes is right for the future of the trust.

Discussion questions

1 What model or approach to employee development would follow from seeking to satisfy the IIP standard in the trust?

2 What approach do you think has traditionally been adopted within the trust?

3 What approach to ED do you think Paul would like to see adopted?

4 What approach to ED do you think would be most appropriate for the trust, and why?

5 What principles would you suggest to Paul to incorporate into any intervention he proposes for unit managers?

Suggested reading

Boydell, T.H. (1983) *A Guide to the Identification of Training Needs*. London: BACIE.

Harrison, R. (1997) *Employee Development*. London: IPD.

Reid, M. and Barrington, H. (1997) *Training Interventions (5th edn)*. London: IPD.

Wood, S. (ed.) (1988) *Continuous Development: The path to improved performance*. London: IPD.

CHAPTER 8

Establishing training needs

Introduction

This chapter begins a more detailed examination of the systematic training cycle. It focuses on the first stage of the cycle, that of identifying training needs. This stage is significant in highlighting the importance of varying paradigms of social experience and, therefore, of competing accounts of organisations. This in turn arises for two main reasons. First, the concept of 'training need' is problematic if viewed from perspectives other than a functionalist paradigm, since orthodox treatments of the concept imply application, deliberate or otherwise, of an associated machine metaphor (Morgan, 1997) of organisations (*see* Truelove, 1997, Buckley and Caple, 1995). Attempts to overcome such associations are made by some writers by using different language, for example, the term 'learning need' used by Harrison (1997). However, the success of these attempts is debatable, and other writers who seek to question the established orthodoxy in other ways choose to retain the language of the training cycle, for example, the work of Boydell and Leary, (1996).

The second reason is that identifying, or establishing, training needs in the context of work organisations normally involves the practitioner in activities which merit being described as research. We can perhaps best justify this assertion by reference to the draft (at the time of writing) occupational standards produced by the Research Lead Body. These are based on a functional map which encompasses activities likely to be conducted by a range of professionals in organisations as part of their work and which, in terms of the functional map, can be said to constitute research. Examples include a general function of 'conduct research work, with related units covering 'carry out investigations', 'analyse data' and 'gather information from secondary sources' (Moloney and Gealy, 1997). We may, of course, question and challenge the validity and usefulness of statements derived by the process of functional analysis to produce occupational standards (Stewart and Sambrook, 1995).

However, the activities and processes to be described as the chapter unfolds seem to me to be both in line with my understanding of research and congruent with the Research Lead Body standards. So, we can argue that establishing training needs engages practitioners in the conduct and processes of research. The primary relevance of this argument at this point is that such research is, almost by definition, *social* research, and the disputes surrounding competing paradigms and accounts of organisations crystallise in debates about the nature and conduct of social research. In other words, varying perspectives on organisation are related, to some degree at least, to debates on the conduct of social research.

Given this analysis, before attempting to examine the processes involved in establishing training needs we need first to establish an understanding of the concept and, relatedly, to propose how the concept can or should be researched. Logically, perhaps, these two concerns should be dealt with in that order. However, I think the critical battle lines between competing paradigms and perspectives are more clearly drawn in debates surrounding the conduct of research. That subject will therefore receive attention first. Conclusions from that section will then inform an analysis of the concept of 'training need'. Having reached an understanding of the concept, we will move on to apply that understanding, together with insights drawn from debates on social research, to examining the processes of establishing training needs in work organisations. By the end of the chapter you can expect to have achieved the following objectives.

CHAPTER OBJECTIVES

- Compare and contrast two perspectives on social research.

- Articulate a reasoned and justified definition of the concept of 'training need'.

- Describe, compare and evaluate a range of methods and techniques for establishing training needs.

- Design and apply approaches to establish training needs in the context of work organisations.

Social and management research

We do not have the space here to address in any depth the disputes and debates surrounding social research. We can say with confidence, however, that those debates have significance for all branches and disciplines of the social sciences (May, 1997). As such, they have implications also for management research (Gill and Johnson, 1997). One critical element of the debates can be simplified into two opposing points of view (Gill and Johnson, 1997, Easterby-Smith *et al.*, 1991). These points of view can in turn be broadly related to the varying paradigms of organisations which were introduced in Chapter 2.

The varying paradigms of organisations differ in their assumption concerning the nature of the world and how it is experienced by human beings. The different assumptions can perhaps be most clearly illustrated by differentiating between *realist* and *non-realist* conceptions of the world and experience. A realist conception assumes an independent existence on the part of the world, while a non-realist conception assumes the world to be that which is created through and by human action. So, in the first case, the world is a pre-existing 'given', while in the second, to use a colloquialism, the world is what **we** make it. These different assumptions can be applied differently to different aspects of the world and experience. The most common example of this is to adopt a realist position in relation to the *physical* world, and a non-realist position to the *social* world. A simple example to illustrate this is to take a person, who can be argued to have a physical existence as a collection of organs and cells which, in turn, are collections of molecules and atoms. Viewed in this way, it is reasonable to define the person as a physical object and to adopt a realist position. However, when it comes to understanding the person as an *identity* distinct from other persons, then a realist position can become unworkable since, to take myself as the example, the person known as Jim Stewart has existence only in individual and collective social experience. I and others are continually and actively involved in creating and sustaining my identity. Jim Stewart is not an objective given, but rather a subjectively created identity.

There are schools of thought in the social sciences that would question the validity of adopting a realist position in relation to the physical world (*see* Chia, 1996). However, for our purposes we can accept the distinction described above. The adoption of a realist or non-realist position leads to different views on how we come to know about and understand the world. The processes of knowing and understanding are central to the conduct of research. But if we adopt a realist position, the processes advocated to reach knowledge and understanding will be different to those advocated by a non-realist position. This is usefully illustrated by the debates in psychology that we examined in Chapter 6. Behaviourist psychologists adopt a realist position in relation to the social world and therefore, advocate the same research processes as those applied to investigating the physical world. Humanist psychologists, by contrast, adopt a non-realist position in relation to the social world and, therefore, advocate alternative approaches to conducting research.

Activity 8.1

1 Consider the paradigms of organisations discussed in Chapter 2 and decide whether each adopts a realist or non-realist position.

2 Produce some arguments to support your conclusions on **1** and discuss their validity with a colleague.

3 Based on the results of **2**, attempt to identify some implications for the practice of HRD of adopting a realist and non-realist position.

The realist/non-realist dichotomy gives rise, broadly speaking, to two generally acknowledged traditions in social research. They are associated also with alternative analyses of the philosophy and sociology of science and knowledge (May, 1997). The two traditions are characterised in various ways by various writers (Gill and Johnson, 1997, Easterby-Smith *et al.*, 1991). We will here use the terms 'positivism' and 'naturalism'. In simple terms, positivism adopts a realist position in relation to the social world and therefore advocates adoption of the same research processes and procedures as those utilised in the physical sciences. Naturalism argues that the study of the social world should not and cannot replicate the physical sciences since the phenomenon of social action differs significantly from non-social phenomena. Thus, generalising somewhat, methods adopted within the naturalist perspective are likely to differ from those used within a positivist perspective.

Adopting one of these two broad traditions will influence to some degree research design. Decisions on research design are primarily concerned with selection of methods. In social research, we are concerned with information about and from people. Two common methods to achieve this are 'observation' and 'asking questions'. The naturalist position is more likely to favour the latter method since the concern within that tradition is to understand social action from the perspective of those engaged in the action being studied, and with establishing the meanings given to the action by the participating social actors. These concerns are unlikely to be addressed by simply observing the phenomenon. In contrast, it can be argued that researchers adopting a positivist position are more likely to favour observation as a method. One reason for this is that observation of phenomena is central to the scientific method adopted in the physical sciences. In addition, observation can cast the researcher in the role of neutral, detached scientist who merely records the behaviour of research subjects without having any impact or influence on events. This accords with a view, prevalent in the positivist tradition, of the researcher as objective scientist.

While these arguments have some validity (Easterby-Smith *et al*, 1991), it is also true that methods are not exclusive to traditions. Both methods described can be used within both traditions. While it is often argued that positivist researchers favour quantitative methods – for example, recording, counting and analysing the number and range of occurrences – and that naturalist researchers favour qualitative methods – for example, producing accounts of behaviour provided by subject participants – in practice both traditions use both quantitative and qualitative methods. The way methods are applied can and does vary in the two traditions, however. This can be illustrated by examining how the methods of observation and asking questions translate into specific techniques. We will begin with the latter.

There are many ways of asking people questions. In broad terms, the positivist tradition will have a preference for using structured questionnaires to do so. Design of questionnaires is likely to reflect a preference for closed and pre-coded responses. Attitude survey instruments using scaled responses are an example of this kind of questionnaire. If interviews are used in the positivist tradition, they are likely to be highly structured around a predetermined set of questions with forced choice responses. Market research surveys are an example of this technique. A positivist stance will also lead to application of statistical rules in determination of samples and analysis of data in both questionnaire and interview surveys. By contrast, naturalist research is likely to favour interviews over questionnaires as a technique for asking questions. The design of interviews is likely to be unstructured, leading to free response on the part of interviewees and variety in issues discussed. Where questionnaires are used, the same principles will apply, with open questions and free responses. Composition of samples will be less important because pursuit of universal and generalisable rules or laws is not considered possible or desirable.

Turning to observation, a basic decision lies in the degree of participation or otherwise by the observer/researcher. This decision is commonly characterised as either participant or non-participant observation. The dichotomy is perhaps an over-simplification (May, 1997), although it will serve our purposes here. Valuing the scientific method of the physical sciences, and pursuing the related goals of neutrality and objectivity, the positivist tradition will generally favour non-participant observation. To take a managerialist example, the image of a work study/organisation and methods analyst with clipboard and stopwatch observing, timing and recording the movements of manual operatives provides a useful illustration of applying the technique of non-participant observation. Conversely, seeking to gain understanding of the perceptions and associated meanings of the subjects being studied, the naturalist researcher is more likely to adopt participant observation. Action research as an approach within the naturalist tradition (McNiff *et al.*, 1996) is an example where participant observation is adopted. It might be argued that professional practitioners employed within HRD are always, perhaps even by definition, participant observers. It is also possible to argue that practitioners have less need than academics to be concerned about the nuances of debates over social research.

The counter to the first argument is the view that, to be effective, HRD practitioners need to be in some ways detached from their organisational environments (Fredericks and Stewart, 1996, Hamlin and Davies, 1996) and in any case are, structurally at least, perceived to be 'separate' from other departments of the organisations for which they work (Sambrook, 1998). Thus, practitioners do not have to immerse themselves in the practices of production, operations, finance, marketing, etc., and therefore can act as non-participant observers. The case against the second argument is now well established. The need for soundly researched action and decisions in HRD practice has been demonstrated both in the USA (Swanson and Holton, 1997) and in the UK (Jacobs and Vyakarnam, 1994, Hamlin and Reidy, 1997). This section has accepted that analysis as a starting point, and has sought to indicate in broad strokes the main areas of debate about conducting research in organisation contexts.

The arguments provided so far may suggest a choice between adopting a positivist or naturalist methodological position. This is not necessarily the case. The apparent choice can be rejected in favour of 'methodological pluralism' which adopts combinations of values, methods and techniques from both traditions and which has, in some interpretations, a pragmatic concern with practical application (Gill and Johnson, 1997). Such pragmatism is probably of particular relevance in organisation contexts, and to professional practitioners. The point I wish to argue here is that in planning, designing and conducting research in organisational contexts, as elsewhere, there is value in coherence and consistency. It is therefore important that consideration is given to methodological debates before decisions and choices on methods and techniques are encountered and resolved. Adopting a particular position, whether positivist, naturalist or pluralist, will both inform and legitimate decisions on methods and techniques. Since methods and techniques will influence the acceptability and perceived validity of the results they produce, it is important in reporting those results that selection of methods and techniques can be justified. This is the case whether the results are reported internally to decision makers or externally as part of academic programmes. Legitimation of decisions on methods by reference to a methodological position, and associated coherence and consistency, can therefore enhance the perceived value and status of reported results.

It is now time to examine the nature and meaning of the idea of 'training need' since this will also influence approaches to investigating the concept in organisational contexts.

Activity 8.2

1 Consider the arguments presented in this section and answer the following questions.

(a) What are the main limitations of a positivist position?

(b) What are the main limitations of a naturalist position?

(c) To what extent can methodological pluralism overcome each set of limitations?

(d) Which position is most relevant to HRD practice, and why?

2 Produce a short description of your own methodological position, giving reasons to explain and justify your position.

3 Compare and contrast your response to **2** with that of a colleague, and discuss reasons for similarity and difference.

4 Revise your response to **2** in the light of the results of **3**.

The nature of training needs

Contemporary treatments of employee development continue to relate the concept of training need to the existence and achievement of organisation objectives (Harrison, 1997, Moorby, 1996). Thus, the exact nature of organisation objectives will determine, to some extent, the nature of training needs existing in any particular organisation at any given point in time (Boydell and Leary, 1996).

The link between organisation objectives and training needs is provided by two factors. First, organisation objectives are achieved through the work and contributions of individual employees which meet personal, team and departmental, or functional, objectives derived from overall organisational objectives. However, individual employees need training in order to meet their personal objectives. So, the existence of organisational objectives both creates and, to some extent, specifies training needs. The second factor is current performance of the organisation against its stated objectives. Failure to meet objectives at the level of the organisation is likely to be associated with failure to meet personal objectives on the part of some individual employees, hence the need for and role of approaches to performance management (Harrison, 1997). The failure of individual employees to meet personal objectives can indicate the existence of a training need. Thus, training needs are associated with the level of current individual and organisational performance compared to stated and desired objectives.

These two factors, in slightly different ways, lead to the characterisation of a training need as a 'gap' (Truelove, 1997). In other words, a training need is the same as a gap between existing capability and that required to achieve performance objectives. This is not the same as a gap between current or actual, and desired or expected, performance. The latter is a performance gap which can be attributed to a variety of causes (Truelove, 1997). A performance gap indicates a training gap only if development of appropriate knowledge, skills or attitudes would help improve performance and therefore close the gap. This requires that lack of appropriate knowledge, skills or attitudes is a primary, or contributory, cause of the performance gap and, in those circumstances only, a training gap exists.

A three-level framework

Based on this way of conceptualising a training need, Boydell produced a three-level framework of training needs (Boydell, 1983). Devised nearly 30 years ago, the framework is still widely applied and advocated, either in its original form (Truelove, 1997, Reid and Barrington, 1997) or in some slightly modified versions (Boydell and Leary, 1996, Harrison, 1997), even if on occasions the application is implicit rather than explicit (*see* Moorby, 1996). The framework suggests that training needs can and do exist at three, interrelated levels: the organisation, the job or occupation, and the individual employee. To understand this framework, it is useful to begin with the middle level, i.e. the job or occupation.

Performance in any particular job or occupation depends on a complex set of factors. However, it is reasonably well recognised that one set of factors is applying a given 'body of knowledge' and a range of skills associated with the job or occupation. This is true whether the job is cleaning factory premises, selling electrical goods in a retail store, managing a clinical directorate in an NHS trust hospital or working as a chief executive of a Training and Enterprise Council. In some and perhaps all cases, adoption of certain attitudes rather than others will also be important for successful performance. Thus, it is possible to specify what any individual needs to know and understand, and to be able to do in what kind of manner, if successful performance in the job or occupation is to be possible. Such a specification constitutes training needs at the level of job or occupation. The specification is independent of any particular individual, and it identifies what all individuals need to know and to be able to do if they wish to work successfully in the job or occupation.

Identifying individual training needs follows from the job/occupation level. Any individual employee, even if newly recruited, will possess knowledge, skills and attitudes, *some* of which will be relevant to performing in the job or occupation. However, it is unlikely that any newly recruited person will possess *all* the knowledge, skills and attitudes (KSA) specified as being required at the job/occupation level. Therefore, individual training needs exist to the extent that there is a gap between the KSA currently held by a particular individual and the KSA specified at the job/occupation level. Identifying individual training needs is, in this model, constituted by establishing the extent and content of that gap. This idea is illustrated in Fig. 8.1.

Turning to the organisation level, it is useful to think of training needs at this level as being of two types. The first type follows in part from establishing needs at the level of job/occupation and at the level of individual employees. When these steps have been taken, it is possible to arrive at a summation of the total training needs of the organisation. In simple terms, the organisation needs X number of individuals trained in Y and Z, A number in C and D, B in E and F, and so on. The second type of organisation need is some KSA which all members of the organisation, irrespective of their job or occupation, will be required to develop. The KSA in question will be related to some change in policy, strategy or objective, or perhaps to some generalised performance problem which affects the whole organisation or, finally, to an external factor such as new legislation. Examples

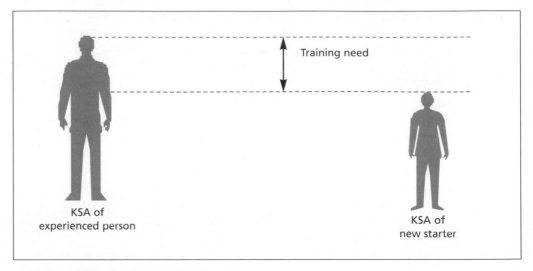

Fig. 8.1 Identifying a training gap

might include entering new markets, or rising customer complaints, or new legislative requirements related to health and safety. At the very least, all members of the organisation need to *know* of these changes and developments and, therefore, an organisation training need is created.

Activity 8.3

1 Produce a list of the second type of organisation training need experienced by your organisation over the last 1–3 years.

2 To what extent does your organisation attempt to establish training needs at each level? What methods are used?

3 Produce an analysis of the strengths and weaknesses, as you see them, of Boydell's three-level framework.

Discussion

It will be clear from this examination of the concept of training need that what might be termed conventional analyses adopt a realist position. Organisations are treated as objective entities, as are individuals. The former are assumed to possess unproblematic objectives which guide and shape the actions, behaviour and performance of all members, and the latter are assumed to possess knowledge, skills and attitudes which can be directly linked in causal relationships with performance in jobs and occupations. Thus, in conventional treatments, methods adopted to research and establish training needs are likely to be positivist in nature.

We have seen in earlier chapters that conceptualising organisations and individuals as unproblematic, objective entities is open to question and challenge. The discussion of realist and non-realist positions earlier in this chapter lends some caution in treating individuals simply in terms of 'bundles' of knowledge, skills and attitudes which they possess independently of those who surround them. If, as argued earlier, individual identity is a social construction and creation, then it is unlikely that individuals are independent repositories of KSA which have meaning and application in any and all contexts. This is clearly illustrated in the following quotation.

> The empirical self is always changing, and is never self-consistent. This means that the individual cannot be viewed as a basic unit . . . in terms of the systems of relationships investigated by sociology, the individual does not constitute a permanent uniformity.
>
> (Park, 1972 in May, 1997, p. 135)

Such an argument may be used to question the very idea and possibility of individual training needs. However, I think we can take it as support for a view that training needs are socially determined and constructed. In other words, training needs identified at any and all of the three levels are not necessarily 'objective facts'. They are unlikely to have the status of phenomena in the physical world implied by a realist position. Instead, they are social, and therefore non-realist, phenomena, subject to influences particular to specific social contexts. While it may be the case that a common influence across varying social contexts is to create the belief, and associated action, that training needs are indeed objective facts, it is advisable to bear in mind that such beliefs and actions are derived from sets of usually unstated assumptions. These common assumptions about organisations and individuals as they relate to processes of establishing training needs are usefully articulated by Boydell and Leary (1996). The point here is to recognise and accept the existence and potential value of both realist and non-realist positions in our examination of methods and techniques used in establishing training needs.

Identifying training needs

We now turn our attention to examining how to establish training needs. We will continue to apply Boydell's three-level framework, recognising that the levels are interrelated and, therefore, that methods used at one level may well produce results of relevance to other levels. One issue that occurs at all levels is that of distinguishing what is a training need and what is not (Truelove, 1997, Boydell and Leary, 1996). Before examining methods of identifying training needs in any detail, we will take a brief look at this issue.

Training and non-training problems

We have already said that, in conventional terms at least, training needs are associated with performance levels of organisations and individuals. If performance requirements are not being achieved, there can be a temptation to perceive this as indicating the existence of a training need. Current performance is defined as a problem, then associated with a training need and therefore the problem becomes identified as a training problem. The temptation to follow this line of reasoning can be quite strong for line managers, employee development specialists and other HR professionals. The political nature of organisations, in part at least, accounts for this temptation. Managers and HR professionals can avoid any involvement in or contribution to being the cause of the problem and, relatedly, avoid the risk of involvement in the solution. Employee development professionals can be flattered by demands for their services, and perceive potential opportunities for influence.

Labelling any or all performance problems as training problems can have drawbacks and negative consequences for all concerned. Factors other than lack of appropriate KSA can create or contribute to performance levels achieved by organisations and individuals. If other factors are significant, but a training solution is the only one adopted, then the following consequences are likely:

- the 'problem' remains unresolved;
- resources allocated to employee development are wasted;
- valued 'pay off' from investment in training and development is not achieved;
- opportunities to address substantive training problems are missed;
- belief in and support for training and development is diminished.

These consequences can be argued to be negative and detrimental to all concerned, but especially to the long-term interests of ED practitioners. Therefore, it is important as a starting point to conduct some initial analysis to establish the extent to which any particular performance problem is a training problem and therefore amenable to a training solution. Application of problem analysis can help with this, although to do so requires some understanding of the nature of problems, symptoms and causes.

A problem can be defined as the existence of a difference between 'actual' and 'desired'. In the context to which we are applying the concept, actual and desired will refer to performance. Thus, actual performance of X compared to desired performance of Y will be defined as a problem. Actual performance of X is not, of itself, the problem, or even *a* problem. It is the existence of a *difference* between actual X and desired Y which is the problem. An interesting feature of this way of specifying and analysing problems is the implication that the quickest and perhaps easiest way of solving problems is to modify desired to match actual. While this method of solving problems is unlikely to find much favour in work organisations, it does help to illustrate the non-realist view that problems are social and therefore human creations. Performance problems in organisations do not have the status of 'objective fact'. They are only problems because human beings, individually and collectively, define them as such because actuality does not meet their desires.

Symptoms are observable and/or measurable events or indicators which are used to identify and specify the existence and nature of a problem. So, in our context, symptoms are the full range of performance measures and indicators used to monitor organisational, functional, departmental and individual performance. To use a medical analogy, performance measures are used to monitor and assess the 'health' of an organisation, and to detect any areas of 'disease' or 'pathology'. This is the purpose of management information systems. Recall that performance level X is not a problem. It is simply a symptom which, when compared to desired level Y, indicates the existence of a problem. Causes are the explanation of the symptoms. In other words, they are the factors which produce the symptoms. In our context, causes are the reasons that the performance level is X rather than Y. To solve the problem therefore, we have to do something about the reasons that bring about performance level X so that we can change it to performance level Y. Thus, problems cannot be solved without tackling the causes, and causes cannot be established without examining and analysing symptoms.

This approach to problem specification and analysis is intended to form the basis of an initial analysis which is conducted as part of any attempt to establish training needs. In this context then, the following six-step method can usefully be applied:

- *Describe symptoms.* The critical point here is to focus on observable and measurable indicators, and not to confuse symptoms with the problem itself.
- *Estimate importance.* Does the fact that performance is X rather than Y matter much to anyone? In other words, is it worth doing anything to attempt to solve the problem? If not, amend desired to match actual as step six and miss out the other steps.
- *Analyse cause.* Examine the symptoms in more detail and seek to establish the reasons for them. In doing so, decide whether the causes are training related, or are associated with other factors. In the case of non-training causes, go to step six.
- *Generate solutions.* Decide possible training solutions. This may include more investigation to establish training needs in more detail.
- *Estimate cost/benefit.* Produce estimates of costs and benefits of each possible solution. Assess whether a worthwhile solution is available and feasible in cost/benefit terms.
- *Recommend solution.* Report to decision makers.

It can be quite difficult to distinguish between training and non-training causes in step three. The subjective rather than objective nature of problem specification in organisations, and the political pressures mentioned earlier, are two reasons why this is the case. Fig. 8.2 suggests some common training and non-training causes to help with this difficulty. We will now turn to Boydell's three levels, beginning with that of the organisation.

	Training causes	Non-training causes	
P E R F O R M A N C E	Inadequate training	Lack of feedback/motivation	**P R O B L E M S**
	Inappropriate training	Job design faults	
	Skill/knowledge gaps	Organisation structure	
	Inadequate recruitment and selection	R&S procedures	
		Poor equipment/tools, etc.	

Fig. 8.2 Training and non-training causes

Organisation level

The point was made earlier that organisation level training needs can be of two types: a summation of needs at other levels, and what might be termed 'common needs' which exist across the organisation. The processes described here can be relevant to both types. They may highlight particular areas, functions or occupations which will require further analysis and, therefore, lead to establishing needs at the job/occupation level which, when completed, will feed back into the first type of organisation level need. Similarly, the processes may identify a need for development which transcends occupational, departmental or hierarchical boundaries, and therefore contribute to the second type.

The basic activity at this level is to conduct some form of organisation analysis. The depth and detail of the analysis will vary depending upon the timing and purpose of establishing organisation needs (Reid and Barrington, 1997, Boydell and Leary, 1996). For example, Reid and Barrington (1997) suggest a number of possible reasons for carrying out an organisation-wide review, including establishing a training department, preparing a training budget and plan, or to meet the requirements of corporate planning. In all cases, there are likely to be two major focuses of analysis: current performance and future plans. The former will encompass the appropriate business indicators and measures of efficiency and effectiveness, as well as 'health' indicators such as labour turnover and absence levels, perhaps also including attitude surveys. The focus on future plans is concerned with significant changes in strategy, objectives, policies, technology and procedures. Such changes may be in response to dissatisfaction with current performance, external factors such as competitor activity or legislation, or the result of some perceived opportunity. In some ways, these two areas of focus are similar to the distinction between 'maintenance needs' (current performance) and 'development needs' (future plans) suggested by Truelove (1997) and can be considered congruent with the three-level categorisation of 'implementing', 'improving' (current performance) and 'innovating' (future plans) produced by Boydell and Leary (1996). The important point is perhaps that an organisation analysis identifies the training required to enable the organisation to keep doing what it does to an acceptable performance standard, and the training required to enable it to do new and better things (*see* Fredericks and Stewart, 1996).

Conducting an organisation level study requires the collection, analysis and interpretation of a significant amount of information. It is important to ensure that this information is relevant and appropriate. The information sought is likely to be of two types. The first type might be termed 'hard' data. This indicates data which is quantitative and, within the community which uses it, factual. Boydell and Leary (1996) refer to this as 'objective data'. Examples will include the kind of information produced by management information systems. We can label the second type 'soft'. This indicates a mixture of individual and collective opinions, beliefs, judgements, predictions and aspirations. In general terms, hard data will be available in statistical reports such as analyses of productivity, market share or labour turnover, while soft data will need to be originated through methods such as interviews, focus groups and analyses of minutes of team meetings. While the distinction between hard and soft is useful, a word of caution is necessary. Apparently hard, or objective, data can be problematic. For example, attitude surveys produce statistical analyses of satisfaction ratings which are presented as objective facts. The only fact in such reports is that X number or percentage of respondents ticked a particular box on a survey questionnaire. Perhaps it is stating the obvious to also point out that the meaning and status of hard and soft, and the allocation of any particular information to one category rather than the other, will also be influenced by adoption of a realist or non-realist position.

Information, both hard and soft, will be needed from both internal and external sources. External information is required so that training needs arising from government policy and legislation, for example, can be established. It may also be required for purposes of benchmarking (Reid and Barrington, 1997, Boydell and Leary, 1996). Government departments, employer bodies such as the CBI, trade associations, research institutes, universities, trade unions and professional/trade journals and magazines are all potential sources of relevant information on and about the external environment. Once collected, both internal and external information will require analysis and interpretation. Two broad methods are **step** analysis for external data (Stewart, 1996) and **swot** analysis for analysing internal data in a way which takes account of analyses of external data (Johnson and Scholes, 1997). (**Step** analysis factors are social, technological, economic and political; **swot** analysis factors are strengths, weaknesses, opportunities and threats.) Other methods include trends analysis, flow charts, Pareto analysis and large system interventions (Boydell and Leary, 1996). The overall process of conducting an organisational analysis, including how the main concepts and activities relate to each other, is represented in the model given in Fig. 8.3.

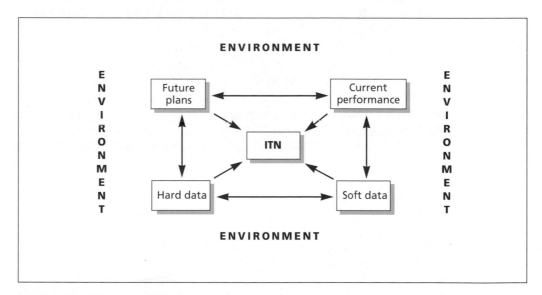

Fig. 8.3 Identifying training needs: organisational analysis

1 Identify and list internal and external sources of hard data for your organisation.

2 Decide what methods and techniques of analysis would be suitable for the information each source would provide.

3 Categorise and prioritise sources of soft data within your organisation.

4 Decide what methods and techniques would be suitable for analysing the information each category of source would provide.

Job/occupation level

Establishing training needs at this level requires a detailed examination of the selected job or occupation. The purpose of the examination is to produce a 'job training specification' (Harrison, 1997). This specification describes and details both the nature of the job, and the knowledge, skills and attitudes necessary for the effective performance at the defined standard. The use of the terms 'effective' and 'defined standard' mean that prior to examining the job, or as part of that process, measures or criteria of performance have to be agreed, for example, sales achieved, invoices processed, units produced/assembled, queries resolved or numbers of replacement staff recruited. Once criteria are in place, standards can be defined, for example, £50 000 worth of sales per month, 50 invoices per day, 200 units per shift, 75 per cent of queries resolved within one working day or 95 per cent of vacancies filled within one month. My examples are both simple and simplistic. Determining measures/criteria and standards can be fairly straightforward for assembly operators and sales staff. However, the issue can be much more complex, even in the terms of conventional theory, in other cases, for example, professional and managerial jobs. There is, however, an assumption in establishing training needs at the job/occupation level that criteria and standards can be and are agreed and defined.

A job training specification is the purpose and the result of establishing training needs at this level. The process of arriving at the specification is 'job training analysis' (Reid and Barrington, 1997). This is really the same as any other form of job analysis in terms of the process adopted. The use of the word 'training' is merely to focus on the purpose and outcome of the analysis in this context. As we have seen, the outcome is a job training specification which details required KSA. It is useful, therefore, when conducting a job training analysis to bear in mind the different forms KSA can take in relation to effective performance of jobs/occupations. These are:

Knowledge
- *technical* – specific to the job, and without which the job could not be done, e.g. range and operation of required tools and equipment;
- *context* – relates to elements to do with employment, e.g. terms and conditions; elements to do with physical environment, e.g. hazards; and role/purpose of job in function/department/organisation, e.g. contribution to final product or service;
- *background* – relates to elements such as organisation history and relationship with stakeholders.

Skills

- *intellectual* – sometimes referred to as 'mental' skills, for example, judgement, decision and creativity;
- *physical* – also known as 'manual', for example, sensory acuity, dexterity and co-ordination;
- *interpersonal* – also known as 'social', for example, verbal communication, influencing and leadership.

Attitudes

The concept of attitudes is highly complex and controversial. However, in simple terms, and in the context of jobs, attitudes held by individuals can be good/bad or positive/negative or desirable/undesirable. The distinction will depend on the nature and requirements of the job.

This categorisation is useful when analysing jobs for training purposes. A useful device in applying the knowledge categorisation is to think of the distinctions as 'must know', 'should know' and 'could know'. Any particular area of knowledge, for example, 'relationships with stakeholders', can fall into any category, depending on the nature of the job. It may form part of 'must know', for instance, in the case of senior managers.

There is a wide range of methods and techniques available for conducting a job training analysis. Pearn and Kandola (1988) discuss 18 methods of job analysis in some detail. Some of the methods described by Boydell and Leary, mentioned in relation to organisation analysis, are also relevant at this level. Truelove (1997) focuses on the specific techniques of task, skill and faults analysis. A useful categorisation of *approaches*, rather than methods and techniques, is that advocated by both Harrison (1997) and Reid and Barrington (1997). The following are the main approaches:

- *Comprehensive analysis*. As the name implies, this approach consists of a full and exhaustive analysis of all aspects of a job. It will produce a detailed specification of all tasks and associated performance requirements, together with KSA specifications for each task and activity.
- *Key task analysis*. Again, the nature of the approach is reflected in the name. The intention here is to first determine which tasks are *critical* to successful performance, and second to analyse only those and ignore others. This approach tends to be appropriate for more complex jobs with high degrees of discretion.
- *Problem-centred analysis*. A further descriptive title. The approach here is to focus exclusively on particular and specific areas of the job which job-holders themselves and/or their managers find problematic. Thus, the analysis is limited and tightly focused, and is likely to involve job-holders themselves identifying and specifying problems.

Factors such as time, resources, urgency, degree of complexity and stability in the job, level of recruitment and associated levels of familiarity with the job on the part of job-holders are argued to be relevant in deciding which approach to adopt (Harrison, 1997, Reid and Barrington, 1997). A final, and increasingly popular, approach is competency-based analysis. Reid and Barrington (1997) usefully distinguish between the 'input' and 'outcomes' versions of competence. The basic difference is that input models focus on *behaviours* displayed by individuals which result in competent performance, while outcome models focus on what is *achieved* by competent performance, i.e. the products. In the former, the focus is the person in that behaviour is associated with personal characteristics (including, but not restricted to, KSA), while in the latter the focus is the function or purpose of the job and its associated outcomes.

Individual level

We saw earlier that establishing individual training needs requires some form of comparison and assessment of current KSA against that specified as being required for successful performance in the job. The results of job training analysis in the form of job training specifications provide the benchmark against which individuals can be assessed. First, though, establishing individual needs assumes or requires that performance problems do, or will, exist. If that is the case, the question of whether training is an appropriate solution also needs to be addressed. As suggested earlier, there may be other causes of performance problems. Therefore, approaches to and methods of establishing individual training needs have to be capable of handling all these complex issues.

Perhaps the most common method of establishing individual needs is through some form of performance management system (Harrison, 1997) and/or associated appraisal scheme. Certainly, in theory at least, performance appraisal has the potential for establishing the extent to which performance problems exist, and whether some form of training will help to overcome the problem. Depending on the design, performance appraisal systems may also enable the involvement of individuals in determining their training requirements. One potential problem with appraisal is the focus on *performance* and, in some cases, allocation of reward, rather than training and development. This can create tensions and conflicts (Harrison, 1997, Boydell and Leary, 1996). Therefore, use of staff development schemes, or 'development discussions' (Harrison, 1997), either in place of or complementary to appraisal schemes, can be useful to provide a specific and exclusive focus on establishing training needs.

More sophisticated approaches which apply similar principles are the use of 360° feedback and development centres. Development centres are the same in design and operation as assessment centres used in selection and promotion decisions, but are claimed to have a different focus and purpose (Reid and Barrington, 1997). The purpose is overtly to establish individual development needs. My experience of working with three organisations directly on designing such centres, reinforced by informal discussions with students on professional and management programmes, leads me to be a little cynical about the true purpose of development centres in practice rather than intent. The use of 360° feedback involves individuals receiving information and data about themselves from a range of sources, usually including line managers, colleagues, their own staff and, perhaps, customers. Some form of rating scale, and self-assessment using the same instrument, are additional features of 360° feedback. The process can also be used as part of, or as supplementary to, performance management or appraisal schemes. A feature commonly used within both development centres and 360° feedback is some form of competency framework as the benchmark for assessment (Harrison, 1997, Boydell and Leary, 1996).

All the methods mentioned so far allow and enable some degree of self-assessment to establish training needs. Reid and Barrington (1997) identify self-assessment as a discrete approach, with some support from Harrison (1997) and, especially, Boydell and Leary (1996). In some ways, 360° feedback can be considered a *method* of self-assessment although, in practice, it is likely to inform rather than constitute self-assessment. Methods such as self-and-peer assessment (Stewart, 1996) are also relevant under this heading. Reid and Barrington advocate self-observation and self-analysis as supporting techniques for self-assessment. Questionnaire surveys, conducted by employee development departments (Truelove, 1997), can also be used as supporting mechanisms for self-assessment.

Provision for formal employee development can also be used to establish individual needs. As Harrison (1997) points out, induction and basic training programmes can help both individual employees and employee development practitioners establish further needs at the individual level. Finally, approaches and processes adopted at the organisation and job/occupation levels can and do contribute to establishing individual needs.

Activity 8.5

1 Consider current approaches to establishing job/occupation level needs in your organisation and answer the following questions:

(a) do they reflect the comprehensive, key task, problem-centred or competency approach? Or none of these?

(b) what are the reasons for the approach adopted?

(c) how do those reasons compare to those suggested earlier in the chapter?

(d) how and why might current approaches be improved?

2 Assess your approaches to establishing individual training needs and consider how they might be improved.

3 Compare and contrast your results from **1** and **2** with those of a colleague, and discuss how each might be revised and improved.

Summary and conclusion

We have in this chapter established a number of methodological positions that may be adopted in conducting research in work organisations. The concept of training need has been examined, and shown to be one which derives from and relies on a realist view of the social world, at least from the perspective of conventional treatments. Accepting that as a starting point, this chapter has described processes involved in establishing training needs at the organisation, job/occupation and individual levels. While it is true that these processes, by and large, are in the positivist tradition of research, some are more capable of accommodating naturalist or pluralist perspectives. This is perhaps best illustrated by the varying degrees of involvement, negotiation and control afforded to individual employees in the various approaches and, therefore, in establishing training needs at all three levels. It might be argued that the more training needs are seen as the outcome of socially negotiated and collectively agreed specifications, rather than as neutral facts derived from objective organisation goals, the more valid and appropriate non-realist and pluralist positions become. The final activity will support you in exploring this question.

Having examined the first stage in the training cycle, Chapter 9 moves on to stages two and three, i.e. designing and implementing training interventions.

Activity 8.6

1 Produce a list of approaches, methods and techniques discussed in this chapter which reflect each of the following perspectives:

(a) positivist

(b) naturalist

(c) pluralist.

2 Provide some reasons/argument to support your allocation.

3 Consider how each item under 'positivist, could be amended and so used and applied within a naturalist perspective.

Case study 8

The 'Excalibur Scheme' is a new employee development initiative adopted by a large, government executive agency to encourage individual employees to take more responsibility for their own development. A 360° feedback process lies at the heart of the scheme. This is intended to provide more rigorous information on the basis of which employees can formulate personal development plans. Such plans will in future, according to the rationale for the scheme, more accurately reflect actual training and development needs, rather than perceived or aspirational requirements.

The organisation is a 'next steps agency' which means it enjoys greater freedom in determining its own policy and procedures in relation to human resourcing issues. Previously, as part of a government department, the organisation was tied to central civil service conditions of employment. The new freedom has allowed the agency to implement different arrangements in relation to recruitment, promotion and grading systems over the previous five years. The same time period has seen significant 'downsizing' from more than 50 000 employees to just below 30 000. As a national agency providing services to all citizens in the UK, most staff are employed in local offices in all parts of the country. The average size of a local office numbers between 50 and 75 employees who have direct contact with members of the public on a more or less demand basis. In providing the agency's services, employees are required to 'master' and apply complex technical rules and regulations governing implementation of government policy and various pieces of legislation. These change regularly, and are usually amended and updated at least once a year. The agency nationally has agreed and contracted targets to meet with its sponsoring government department and ministers. These relate to a range of performance indicators measuring services delivered and budget allocations. Regions, areas and individual offices are measured against similar indicators and devolved targets. Although the agency claims in various mission and policy statements to 'value employees' and qualities such as 'flexibility', 'autonomy' and 'initiative', many employees feel that senior managers have an overriding aim of meeting the national targets to the exclusion and detriment of any other considerations. This aim is reflected in the emphasis given to regional, area and office targets by managers at those levels.

Support functions for the office operations, such as HRM, IT, finance and 'technical support' (a function concerned with analysing, interpreting and providing guidance on the rules and regulations governing the Agency's services) are located in a central head office and regional head offices. Ashok is employed as a development consultant in a training and development unit which is part of the personnel division headed by the director of human resources, who is a member of the executive board of the agency and who reports directly to the chief executive. Ashok's unit, called the development unit, is one of four training and development units in national personnel, which includes five other departments. Ashok has been tasked to investigate approaches to and systems of 360° feedback and prepare a discussion paper for the personnel division's management team on design principles.

Ashok has fully familiarised himself with the background of Excalibur. This scheme was initiated by the head of training and development, Shirley Smith, as a contribution to a new HR strategy intended, overtly at least, to overcome declining morale and underperformance within the local offices. Evidence from annual staff attitude surveys has revealed increasing levels of dissatisfaction on the part of employees in relation to their work, their employment conditions and the way they are managed and developed. This evidence is supported by rising labour turnover and absence levels over the previous three years. The incidence of grievance and disciplinary hearings is also on the increase, and the executive board has concluded that these symptoms indicate low levels of staff morale and commitment as a major cause of failure to meet performance targets. Excalibur is one initiative among others within a new HR strategy designed to improve levels of staff commitment. While Ashok is unclear about the purpose or meaning of the label Excalibur, he understands that Shirley Smith considers it to be a critical initiative to demonstrate the contribution of the training and development function.

Ashok will have to take into account two related and supporting pieces of work. The first is intended to devise a 'competency framework' for application within and by the field operations of the agency. The intended framework will focus on 'generic competences' expected of all staff and at all levels in the operations division of the agency, and on 'role-specific' competences which will vary according to the nature of particular jobs. Role-specific competences will, where possible and appropriate, relate to existing occupational standards such as those for customer service, administration or management and will therefore enable employees to achieve NVQs. This project is being led by Ed Stevens from the NVQ unit of training and development. Sheila Harrison, a personnel advisor who works in the personnel division but not in one of the training and development units, is leading a project to review the current performance appraisal system. Ashok will need to liaise with these projects in considering any principles he may recommend for design of a process of 360° feedback. He is clear that 360° feedback within the intentions of Excalibur will not form part of any changes to performance appraisal, will not directly relate to rewards or promotion and therefore will have an exclusively developmental purpose and focus. As Ashok sees and understands the nature of Excalibur, its major benefits will be in relation to accurate diagnosis of training and development needs.

Discussion questions

1 What evidence is there that the agency is experiencing a training and development problem?

2 What potential advantages and disadvantages exist in using 360° feedback as a means of identifying training and development needs in the context of the case?

3 What are the possible contributions and implications arising from the two related projects for Ashok's task?

4 What principles would you advise Ashok to incorporate into his recommendations at this stage? What are your reasons for this advice?

5 How should Ashok proceed with his project? What actions should he take and how should he go about them?

Suggested reading

Boydell, T. and Leary, M. (1996) *Identifying Training Needs*. London: IPD.

Buckley, R. and Caple, T. (1995) *The Theory and Practice of Training (3rd edn)*. London: Kogan Page.

Easterby-Smith, M., Thorpe, R. and Lowe, A. (1991) *Management Research: An Introduction'*. London: Sage.

May, T. (1997) *Social Research: Issues, Methods and Process (2nd edn)*. Buckingham: Open University Press.

CHAPTER 9

Design and implementation of employee development

Introduction

Chapter 9 is concerned with two stages of the training cycle: design and implementation. These two processes are closely linked and therefore best examined together rather than separately. They both also have a close connection with the previous stage of establishing training needs. As the systematic training cycle makes clear (see Fig. 7.1), decisions on design and implementation relate to and flow from the nature of training needs identified. An assumed starting point for applying the processes described in this chapter is therefore that training needs have been established.

A further set of assumptions needs to be made clear. We can think about and analyse ways of meeting training needs from various perspectives, and at what might be termed various levels. As argued in the previous two chapters, the systems approach is clearly associated with a functionalist paradigm. That paradigm therefore informs most of the content of this chapter, although we will on occasion step out of that paradigm to examine how alternative perspectives might influence decisions on design and implementation. The question of 'level' focuses on the breadth and impact of design decisions. For example, choosing whether to invest in a carefully planned and highly formalised management development programme, or whether to invest in establishing a learning resource centre or to embark on a deliberate journey towards becoming a learning organisation, are all arguably design decisions which will create particular problems of implementation. However, those decisions are clearly different in scale, if not character, to choices concerning whether to use a computer-based training package, or an external course, or to provide an internal course to meet a particular training need.

The two sets of decisions both constitute choices on what Reid and Barrington (1997) refer to as 'training interventions'. (Interestingly, Reid and Barrington also use the term 'training strategy' as a synonym for 'training intervention'.) In that sense, similar principles will be relevant in both cases. However, those principles are most easily applied, and therefore most easily explained and illustrated, in connection with the second type of decision. Following that argument, Chapter 9 will assume design decisions of the second type.

It will be helpful to note at this point that designs such as management development and pursuing learning organisation status mentioned earlier will be addressed in later chapters.

> **CHAPTER OBJECTIVES**
>
> - Articulate a case for the use of behavioural objectives.
>
> - Formulate learning objectives in behavioural and non-behavioural terms.
>
> - Compare, contrast and critically assess various training and development methods.
>
> - Specify key principles informing decisions on design and implementation.
>
> - Produce and justify designs of development activities to meet a range of identified training needs.
>
> - Formulate and justify implementation plans.

Use of objectives

A common starting point in examining design of employee development activities is the use and application of objectives (Harrison, 1997, Reid and Barrington, 1997, Truelove, 1997). Indeed, Reid and Barrington, in their version of the training process, identify the setting of objectives as a separate stage following establishing learning needs and before determining a training strategy (1997, p. 151). The use and nature of objectives is not without controversy, however (Harrison, 1997, Truelove, 1997). This in part relates to meanings and definitions attributed to various concepts by various writers, and to debates similar to those on the language of strategy which we examined in Chapter 4. There are two main areas of debate here. The first concerns the distinction between *aims* and *objectives,* and the second concerns the 'best' way to formulate and express, i.e. write, objectives. What remains constant is the direct relationship and connection between the intentions of any development activity, whether expressed as aims or objectives and in whatever form, and identified needs. Before engaging in the debate here, we can say with some confidence that there is agreement among most writers that training requirements, once established, need to be translated into development or learning *intentions* as a starting point in designing development activities.

Activity 9.1

1 Access a range of examples of literature describing development activities. These might include a course you are studying, a course you have attended recently, brochures and leaflets sent as promotional material or courses provided by your employer. Consider the following questions:

   (a) to what extent are the intentions of the activity made clear? Does this vary?

   (b) how many examples use the term 'aims' and how many the term 'objectives' to describe their intentions?

(c) to what extent does the language differ between those which use 'aims' and those which use 'objectives' in the descriptions of intentions? In what ways does the language differ?

(d) which description(s) do you prefer, and why? Is your preference related to use of 'aims' or 'objectives' and if so, in what ways?

2 Compare your preferred example(s) with the objectives given at the start of each chapter of this book. Which do you prefer, and why?

3 Compare your analysis with that of a colleague who has undertaken the same activity.

Translating established training needs into development or learning intentions requires that the question 'what needs to be learned?' is answered. Given that one view of learning focuses on changed behaviour (*see* Chapter 6), another way of phrasing this question is to ask 'what is it that learners need to be able to do?'. Expressed in this way, the question may seem primarily, if not exclusively, concerned with skills rather than knowledge or attitudes. However, this is not necessarily the case. It is true that many training needs will be concerned with 'knowing' or 'understanding' or 'awareness', for example knowing the organisational policy on recruitment and selection, or understanding the distinction between direct and non-direct discrimination, or being aware of personal prejudices or stereotypes which may influence selection decisions. However, all these examples are capable of being expressed in terms of what individuals 'can do' or, in other words, as behaviours. Thus, we can say 'apply the policy', or 'define direct and indirect discrimination', or 'articulate the possible effects of personal stereotypes'. Each of these formulations focuses on behaviour, which is externally observable, rather than internal, cognitive states which are 'knowable' only by and to individuals themselves.

The preceding analysis provides an example of focusing on the behaviour of individuals in expressing the intentions of development activities. A common argument is that this is more likely if objectives rather than aims are used (Sanderson, 1995, Reid and Barrington, 1997). This argument associates the concept of aims with broad, generalised statements of intent, and the concept of objectives with specific and measurable statements of intent. Another distinction can be made between the intentions and behaviours of the development practitioner, and those of the learners. The former are associated with aims, while the latter are associated with objectives. To continue the previous example, the statement 'to explain and examine the new recruitment and selection policy' focuses on the intention and behaviour of the practitioner, while the statement 'apply the new recruitment and selection policy' focuses on the intentions of the activity for individual learners, and their subsequent behaviour.

There are many argued benefits for using objectives which focus on behaviour, and some of these will be explored shortly. However, there are also some problems and disadvantages, which will also be examined, and it needs to be recognised that the case is not universally accepted. For example, in her authoritative and influential book, Rosemary Harrison (1997) uses what she labels 'learning objectives' at the beginning of each chapter and is happy to use concepts such as 'understand', 'know', 'appreciate' and 'be aware' in writing those objectives.

The work of R.F. Mager

The work of R.F. Mager has been highly influential in the area of expressing the intentions of development activities (Sanderson, 1995, Truelove, 1997). Mager argues the need for and benefits of 'behavioural objectives' (Mager, 1975, 1990). These are objectives which define and describe the behaviour of learners at the end of, and as a result of, the development activity. Behavioural objectives, in Mager's terms, have three components. The first specifies the actual behaviour in which learners have to engage as a result of their development, and which will demonstrate successful learning. Thus, specifying the behavioural component requires use of active verbs in phrases and sentences which describe observable behaviour. Examples of such verbs include demonstrate, select, operate, identify, construct or compare. Some of these will be more relevant to skills, e.g. operate or construct, while others translate cognitive states such as knowing or understanding into observable behaviours, e.g. identify or compare.

The second component is termed 'conditions'. The purpose of this component is to specify the circumstances and limitations within which learners will be able to meet the behavioural component. In other words, this component answers the question 'under what conditions will learners be able to identify, operate, construct, etc.?'. Sanderson (1995) provides the interesting example of a soldier dismantling a gun. The behaviour of dismantling a gun obviously provides the behavioural component. However, having an objective of 'dismantling a gun' leaves a lot of unanswered questions. Does the objective refer to a particular type of gun, or any gun? Does it matter what procedure is followed? Are we concerned about when and where dismantling occurs? For example, it could be in a warm, well-lit training room, or the cold, dark and probably frightening circumstances of a night-time battle. The purpose of the conditions component is to provide answers to these and other, similar questions. To do this, the component specifies in as much detail as is required the circumstances, or conditions, under which the behaviour will occur. As Sanderson (1995) suggests, the condition component normally specifies particular tools or equipment, methods or procedures to be adopted and the range of problems to be solved. As the example of dismantling a gun illustrates, specifications of time and place may also be required.

The third and final component is termed 'criterion'. This component is concerned with specifying *standards* of performance within behavioural objectives. Thus, the criterion component focuses on measures of speed, quality and accuracy. The latter two concepts can be difficult to apply, and can cause confusion with the 'conditions' component. For example, standards of quality may be defined in a procedural manual. If that is the case, it is sensible and legitimate to write the criterion component as something like 'as defined on page X of manual Y'. But manual Y may also feature in the conditions component in a phrase like 'referring to manual Y as necessary'. The distinction is fairly straightforward. The manual features in the conditions component as one of the circumstances under which the behaviour occurs. Learners either can or cannot refer to the manual to refresh their memory. In the criterion component, the manual specifies the acceptable, desired or required standard of performance. Whether or not learners can or do refer to the manual is irrelevant to that role for the manual.

There are, of course, more complex problems in specifying standards of performance in order to formulate a criterion component (*see* Fisher, 1999). Some of the more simple examples include phrases such as 'within X minutes/hours', 'to + or − 5 cm', 'no more than two errors per page' or 'within ± 3 per cent of budget'. One critical factor in formulating the criterion component is to be clear whether standards reached at the end of formal development are intended to be the same or less than those expected in normal work (*see* Roscoe, 1995). It is often the case that some period of supervised work experience is necessary before normal job performance is achieved. Therefore, the standard reached during formal development can be specified at a lower level.

Activity 9.2

1 Refer back to the materials used and conclusions reached in Activity 9.1 and consider the following questions:

(a) how many of the examples provide statements of objectives which include all three components?

(b) how many of the examples provide objectives which meet the requirements of Mager's 'behavioural component'?

(c) what reasons might explain the use of behavioural components in the examples that have them, and the non-use of behavioural components in those that do not?

2 Select three examples that do not use behavioural objectives. Rewrite them so that they meet the requirements of Mager's behavioural component. Attempt to add phrases and sentences that provide conditions and criterion components.

3 Compare the results of **2** with those of a colleague and discuss the potential advantages and disadvantages of using your rewritten objectives against the original.

4 How do Mager-style 'behavioural objectives' compare with your personal preference? What are your conclusions on the value or otherwise of behavioural objectives?

Discussion

Many advantages are claimed for adopting the principles advocated by Mager in formulating objectives for employee development activities. The clearest advantage, from which others follow, is probably the degree of precision and associated clarity that emerges from using behavioural objectives. As Reid and Barrington (1997) point out, this provides reasonable and realistic expectations for all concerned: specialist practitioners, learners themselves and the sponsors/purchasers of the development activity. A further significant advantage, persuasively argued by Sanderson (1995), is that objectives provide the benchmark against which the success and value of employee development activities can be assessed and evaluated. Obviously, precise and specific statements of intent will enable the success (or failure) of development to be more transparent, and therefore the benefits and value to be more clearly demonstrated. Behavioural objectives are by definition precise and specific and therefore support transparent evaluation of employee development (*but see* Chapter 10).

Two further advantages relate to the learning process. It is argued that clear objectives both motivate learners and encourage personal ownership of the process. Both these factors improve the efficiency and effectiveness of individual learning (Sanderson, 1995). Clear objectives also enable and facilitate regular or continuous assessment, by learners as well as by practitioners, which, together with associated feedback, allows progress to be monitored, reinforced and encouraged (Sanderson, 1995, Reid and Barrington, 1997). Both of these factors are more likely to be easier to achieve through the use of behavioural objectives.

There are potential and actual disadvantages, however. Perhaps the most obvious is the difficulty of precision and specificity in relation to various occupations and roles. Professional and managerial roles are probably the equally obvious examples. There are two counter arguments. First, as Mager (1975) argues, the degree of precision, especially in conditions and criterion components, can and should be variable so long as the intent is clear. Second, more generalised objectives can be formulated and then elaborated through use of 'indicative' behaviours. Achievement of any combination of specific behaviours from an indicative list can then be used as evidence of successful learning and development (Reid and Barrington, 1997). However, this alternative approach does go some way from the essential principles of behavioural objectives.

A further potential disadvantage is that behavioural objectives imply promises that may not be met. Among their other purposes, such objectives provide predictions of the outcomes of development. The vagaries of the learning process itself, and the contextual factors affecting behaviour and performance in the context of work, all lead to uncertainty about the actual outcomes of development (*see also* Chapter 10). It can therefore be both misleading and foolhardy in the political context of organisations for development practitioners to imply promises that may not be met. An additional disadvantage is that use of behavioural objectives is somehow 'de-humanising'. Truelove (1997) argues a similar point in suggesting that behavioural objectives can lead to a 'trainer-centred' rather than 'learner-centred' approach. It is possible to go further than this by suggesting that individuals are represented and constituted by their behaviour, specified in behavioural objectives, rather than as independent and unique beings.

It will be clear that use of behavioural objectives is closely associated with behaviourist learning theory (*see* Chapter 6). This leads to the focus on what is observable and measurable at the expense of internal, or cognitive, processes and states. A final potential objection to behavioural objectives, therefore, is the implicit lack of involvement of individual learners in deciding and pursuing their own goals. Associated with this is the lack of application of alternative learning theories such as experiential learning, and other approaches such as continuous development. However, the main advocates of the latter support the use of behavioural objectives where possible and appropriate, and do not present any significant objections to variants being used in particular circumstances (Reid and Barrington, 1997). It seems to me, though, that there are, potentially at least, serious philosophical, conceptual and theoretical problems with such a position. The activity which follows this section will support an exploration of what these might be.

We can summarise the arguments so far as follows. Development activities are undertaken to meet some identified need. This provides the overall purpose. However, the purpose and intentions of the activity should be expressed with as much precision and specificity as possible to inform design and evaluation, and to provide required information to learners and their sponsors. Behavioural objectives provide the greatest degree of precision and specificity, although not all training needs are capable of specification with a high degree of precision. In addition, there are potential drawbacks to using behavioural objectives, including implied promises not being kept, and ignoring the active contribution and involvement of learners. One possible response is that argued by Truelove (1997) which is to confine use of behavioural objectives to occupations and jobs such as assembly operatives, word-processor operators or photocopier repair technicians. This pragmatic approach has some value, although perhaps overlooks philosophical and theoretical problems.

Activity 9.3

1 Assess the *validity* and the *usefulness* of behavioural objectives from the perspective of each of the following:

   (a) cognitive psychology

   (b) humanist psychology.

2 Produce a critique of behavioural objectives by applying *one* of the following paradigms (*see* Chapter 2):

   (a) interpretive

   (b) radical Structuralist

   (c) radical Humanist.

3 Review the results of **1** and **2** in the light of your responses to previous activities so far in this chapter. Based on this, produce an argued and justified personal statement on the use or otherwise of behavioural objectives.

Hierarchies of objectives

Objectives, in whatever form, translate training needs into learning intentions for development activities. A useful way of doing so is to apply the principle of a hierarchy of objectives. This principle simply recognises that development activities will have a number and range of discrete yet related elements. Thus, the overall purpose will be expressed as an overall objective from which smaller, focused and more specific objectives will be derived.

There are various terms applied to these lower level objectives. Truelove (1997) uses the term 'learning unit objectives'. This clearly associates lower level objectives with particular elements of a development activity. This has the advantage of requiring each element to have, and to be associated with achievement of, an objective. An alternative is the term 'intermediate objective' used by Harrison (1997). These are related to a 'final objective'. The latter relates the overall purpose, while the former specifies the intentions of particular and specific elements of the development activity. There is, therefore, no significant difference between the terms used by Truelove and Harrison. A final term is 'enabling objectives'. While this, too, is applied to individual elements of the development activity, it has the advantage of suggesting a series of 'building blocks' with direct connections with each other. It also directly suggests that lower level objectives contribute to the achievement of the overall purpose.

The simplest way of formulating enabling objectives is to focus on the overall objective and ask 'what needs to be achieved in order to achieve this?'. It is also useful to apply the KSA distinction, contained in a training specification. Thus, learners may need to acquire some new knowledge, develop a particular skill and be encouraged to adopt a specific attitude. Each of these will lead to its own objective which will be an enabling objective in relation to the overall objective.

Designing ED activities

The distinctions between KSA are useful in designing development activities. In simple terms, learning new knowledge or skills or attitudes will require different development processes. There are two more sophisticated models which are also useful in relating different focuses of objectives to design decisions on matters such as content and methods.

Downs (1995a and 1995b) devised the mnemonic **mud** to categorise different types of learning. M stands for *memorising*, U for *understanding* and D for *doing*. Downs's argument is that all learning objectives will constitute one or more of these requirements. Categorising learning objectives as comprising one or more of these types of learning will be useful in deciding on development methods to achieve them since, according to Downs, each type of learning requires different methods. Facts need to be *memorised*, concepts need to be *understood* and skills need to be *practised* in order to achieve *doing*. But activities which aid and support memorising, understanding and doing will vary, and what might be appropriate for one will not necessarily be effective for either of the other two. So, understanding the nature of learning objectives will lead to selection of appropriate methods. Some simple examples of methods include repetition to support memorising, comparing and contrasting to support understanding and practice with observation and feedback to support doing. Additional principles can also be derived. For example, breaking up content into manageable chunks and avoiding tiredness and associated lack of concentration both support memorising. So, a design principle here is to relate selection of methods to the nature of required learning which, in turn, is derived from the objectives. Downs's taxonomy supports application of that principle.

An alternative taxonomy which supports application of the same principle is that devised by the Industrial Training Research Unit (*see* Belbin and Belbin, 1972, ITRU, 1976). This again uses a mnemonic, this time known as **cramp**. The purpose is similar to that of Downs (1995a and 1995b) although, as is evident from the mnemonic, this taxonomy suggests five different types of learning. They are:

- *Comprehending.* This is similar to understanding in Downs's taxonomy. It relates to gaining a sound understanding of basic principles so that application can occur in new ways and in new circumstances.
- *Reflex development.* Reflex actions occur as conditioned responses to particular stimuli. This often involves development of perceptual skills, physical dexterity and co-ordination. An important application therefore is in manual skills development, although this is not exclusive.

- *Attitude formation.* This type of learning is, as discussed in previous chapters, more contentious. It is clear, though, that many learning objectives more or less explicitly relate to attitudes and that particular learning methods will be required.
- *Memorising.* This is obviously the same type as in Downs's taxonomy.
- *Procedural learning.* This applies to objectives which relate to correct application of pre-determined procedures in a consistent manner.

Some examples will help to illustrate the application of **cramp**. Comprehension can be achieved through use of books, lectures and seminars. Reflex development may demand demonstrations and observation, but will certainly require intense practice with feedback on results. Attitude formation is unlikely without active involvement and therefore will require methods such as role play, games and simulations, case studies or project work. Mnemonics and jingles, as well as rehearsal and self-testing, support memorising. Finally, procedural learning will require methods such as teaching manuals, algorithms and direct instruction.

The **mud** and **cramp** taxonomies are useful in helping to select specific methods from among those which normally form part of formal, off-the-job development programmes. Such programmes are not the only possible way of achieving learning objectives, however. Reid and Barrington (1997) suggest a range of possible approaches which may form the basis of the first design decision. In other words, given a particular set of learning objectives, a judgement has to be made about which form of 'intervention' or 'strategy' (Reid and Barrington, 1997, p. 321) will be most appropriate and effective. Reid and Barrington suggest six possibilities:

- On-the-job training.
- Planned organisation experience.
- In-house courses.
- Planned experience outside the organisation.
- External courses.
- Self-managed learning.

Each of these will have its own inherent advantages and disadvantages. For example, planned organisation experience and self-managed learning have the potential for using and maximising what Marsick and Watkins (1997) term 'informal and incidental learning'. This example also suggests that the approaches are not necessarily mutually exclusive. Combinations of the approaches can form the design of an overall programme. The issue to be addressed is determining what circumstances will lead to one approach being preferred over another. As Reid and Barrington (1997) argue, there is no simple or single answer to this question, although they suggest some criteria to guide and inform decisions. These are compatibility with objectives; supporting transfer of learning to the work context; available resources; and factors to do with the learner population. We can illustrate the operation of these criteria by arguing that on-the-job training or planned organisation experience are both more likely to support and achieve learning transfer than any of the alternatives. However, given a large number of learners and a low level of resources, neither might be feasible. So, selection of overall approach as part of design is always a judgement which balances what might be ideal in learning terms, and what is possible in particular circumstances.

Activity 9.4

1 Identify the inherent advantages and disadvantages of each of Reid and Barrington's six strategies.

2 Select three examples of sets of objectives from Activity 9.1. Categorise each objective within each set using:

(a) the **mud** taxonomy of Downs

(b) the **cramp** taxonomy.

3 Select one example set of objectives. Consider the appropriateness of each of Reid and Barrington's six strategies in achieving the objectives, and decide which strategy, in your view, will be most appropriate.

The criteria suggested by Reid and Barrington (1997) find support in the work of other writers. Harrison (1997) also identifies learning objectives, resources and the learner population as critical factors influencing design decisions. In terms of the latter, numbers, location, attitudes and motivation, learning styles and skills and, importantly, current levels of KSA are argued to be significant (Harrison, 1997). Building on current ability is a useful design principle. The same three factors of objectives, resources and learners are also highlighted by Truelove (1997). He goes on to identify timings, ordering of content and duration as additional design decisions. As with all other design choices, there are no universal rules, and decisions require exercise of professional judgement. As was argued in Chapter 6, understanding learning theory is essential in informing such judgement, particularly in relation to design decisions. The following activity is intended to help reinforce your understanding of learning theories, and to provide practice of exercising your judgement.

Activity 9.5

1 Consider each of the theories of learning examined in Chapter 6 and produce a set of principles derived from each which could, or should, inform design decisions.

2 Compare and contrast the resulting principles and identify commonalities, differences and contradictions.

3 Based on the results of **1** and **2**, produce a list of design principles which you consider will be both valid and useful.

Implementing development activities

Once a development activity has been designed, arrangements need to be made to put the activity into practice. These arrangements are the concern of the implementation stage of the training cycle. However, just as there are direct connections between training needs and design, so, too, are there direct connections between design and implementation. The separation of design and implementation is a useful analytical device. There are helpful consequences in *thinking about* them as separate stages. In practice, though, they are inextricably connected. Design decisions will have direct consequences for implementation. Factors affecting implementation have to be anticipated and taken into account when reaching design decisions. Therefore, the separation implied here is for conceptual reasons rather than a reflection of what happens in practice.

An important factor which illustrates the point made in the previous paragraph is that of organisation culture and climate. This will be highly influential in decisions on implementation and will affect what is feasible and possible, and what is not (Harrison, 1997). Plans for implementing development activities, as with design decisions, have to be realistic and achievable. With this in mind, we can usefully consider the key elements of implementation under the two headings of resources and preparation.

Resources

Ideally, a development activity will have an allocated and agreed budget (Roscoe, 1995). Budgetary issues will be examined in more detail in a later chapter. The point here is that any development activity will incur some costs, and some activities will require direct expenditure on items such as training accommodation or learners' expenses. These need to be identified and planned for as part of implementation. Creation of a budget for an activity is a useful way of doing this.

As well as being paid for, training accommodation may need to be booked. Implementation requires that the location of the training activity is decided and planned for. If the 'strategy' (Reid and Barrington, 1997) adopted is off-the-job, then some form of training facility will be required. If the activity is also residential, accommodation will be required for learners. Whatever the strategy or circumstances, the place where development will take place will probably need organising as part of implementation. Related to this, equipment may need to be booked or hired (Truelove, 1997). In my own work circumstances, for example, video players and televisions need to be booked a week in advance. So, ensuring accommodation and equipment are available when and where required is a key part of implementation.

A final critical resource is that of development staff. This is concerned with ensuring that those who are to provide or support the development activity are also available when and where required (Harrison, 1997, Reid and Barrington, 1997). There is a wide range of possibilities of who might be involved: for example, you and/or your colleagues, part-time on-the-job instructors, external consultants/trainers or line managers. The actual people contributing to the activity will be determined by design decisions. Successful implementation, though, requires that their availability is secured. In summary, implementation involves planning for and organising the resources required to ensure the design works in practice.

Preparation

As well as securing necessary resources, implementation requires supporting activities which can be usefully grouped together under the heading of 'preparation'. If we carry on with the resource of people, then as well as being booked, contributors to the development activity need to be prepared through some briefing. This can take the form of written briefs and/or meetings. The key purpose is to ensure contributors understand their role in and contribution to the development activity, and how this relates to the overall objectives, and any enabling objectives which may form the focus of their contribution.

A second element under the heading of preparation is that of materials (Truelove, 1997, Reid and Barrington, 1997). The concept of learning materials can cover items as complex as an interactive video or as simple as a one-page handout. Whatever their nature, all development activities will require supporting materials of some form. These need to be available well in advance to ensure success for the activity, and therefore their preparation constitutes an essential part of implementation.

The final focus of preparation is the learners, and their sponsors or managers. Those selected for development (*see* Harrison, 1997) need to be made aware of the fact. They also need to be prepared for the development activity. At the very least, this will involve providing information on what, where, when and how. Perhaps, ideally, it will also involve individual learners engaging in some activities to prepare themselves for the development process, and to prepare for application to facilitate learning transfer. Involvement of their managers will help that process. Therefore, while managers will require, at a minimum, the same information on what, where, etc. as learners, more detailed preparation on their role in supporting learning and development and application would represent an ideal.

Implementation plans

The discussion so far suggests that implementation is primarily concerned with planning for application of the chosen design in practice. This will be helped by formulation of an implementation plan. Such a plan will make successful implementation more likely, although it will not provide a guarantee. It is also true that successful implementation can and does occur without a formal plan. However, on balance, formulating and writing an implementation plan does have merit. The content need not be too detailed, nor the process of producing a useful plan too laborious. What is needed is a simple list of what needs to be done by whom, and by when. Identifying costs associated with each 'what' element of the plan can serve the purpose of budgeting the activity, or of integrating the plan with a separate budget.

Discussion

One part of implementation not considered is actual delivery and associated skills. This is a specialist subject in its own right and, as Harrison (1997) points out, there are a number of texts which provide useful guidance (e.g. Siddons, 1997, *see also* Stewart, 1994b). In addition, applying either the **mud** or **cramp** taxonomies would suggest that it is debatable whether written texts are an appropriate medium for attempting to develop direct training skills.

Our discussion and analysis of implementation, as with the bulk of this chapter, assumes a rationalistic conception of organisations. Both organisations and individuals are assumed to be objective entities, and processes of design and implementation of development activities are assumed to be unproblematic and straightforward. The analysis of organisations as political arenas provided in Chapter 4 raises doubts about the validity and usefulness of such assumptions, and the alternative perspectives on organising and managing discussed in Chapter 2 reinforce those doubts. However, this does not necessarily mean that the content of this chapter is invalid, or that it is necessarily in conflict, or incompatible with, alternative paradigms. For example, development can be emancipatory, and self-managed learning designs may be more compatible with that purpose rather than oppressive purposes. This in turn can be compatible with a radical-humanist paradigm. It will, however, be instructive to consider the consequences for analyses of design and implementation of adopting and applying alternative paradigms, and the final activity to close this chapter will facilitate such a consideration. In carrying out the activity, the overriding principle of utility adopted as a central philosophy of this book should also be considered.

<hr />

Activity 9.6

1 Produce a critique of the analysis of design and implementation contained in this chapter from each of the following perspectives:

(a) radical humanist paradigm

(b) interpretive paradigm

(c) Radical structuralist paradigm.

2 Consider the forms of design that might be favoured by adopting each of the three paradigms.

3 What factors affecting implementation, additional to those identified in this chapter, might be emphasised within each of the three paradigms?

4 Given your responses to **1**, **2** and **3**, what do you consider to be the relative merits of adopting a functionalist paradigm?

Summary and conclusion

This chapter has examined the relative merits of behavioural objectives. Their use and purpose in linking training needs to effective design of development activities has been explored, together with some helpful principles for informing design decisions. Critical factors which need to be taken into account in design decisions, such as resources and characteristics of learners, have been identified. The important role of learning theories in informing design has also been recognised. Implementation of development activities has been examined under the headings of 'resources' and 'preparation'. The adoption of implementation plans has been suggested to be useful, though not essential.

A clear conclusion is that there are no simple or universal answers to design and implementation questions. Even within the limited perspective of a functionalist paradigm, design and implementation are seen to be complex processes which require the balancing of a range of factors, which can be, and often are, conflicting and contradictory. The example of applying learning principles within the constraints of resource availability illustrates this point. Therefore, professional judgement is called for and is the main requirement in arriving at decisions on design and implementation. This is a useful conclusion to bear in mind as we move on to examine the final stage of the training cycle, i.e. evaluation, in the next chapter.

Case study 9

Future Certain Insurance Group (FCIG) is the result of a merger of two large, well-established and household name insurance companies. The purpose of the merger included a declared intention to provide a strong basis to achieve growth in international business. The group operates in more than 60 countries, conducts business in most classes of insurance and delivers its products to individual and commercial customers through a complex set of distribution channels. The first year's operation of the new group achieved a turnover of £10 billion and the merger resulted in a market capitalisation of £8 billion. There have also been significant changes at the top of the organisation following the merger. A new chief executive has been appointed, along with a further three new directors. These appointments reflect the intention to internationalise the company as two, including the chief executive, came from a non-UK European country, one is American and the other is an Australian. The new board has introduced a matrix structure for the newly created FCIG which emphasises global, geographic regions as one of the two axes.

Alan Bryson had worked as management development manager for one of the merged companies for 12 years. In FCIG, Alan has been appointed as a management development consultant working for a group HR manager with special responsibility for 'internationalising' the HR policies and processes in the new organisation. Alan's first task in his new role is to produce a development programme for middle managers across the group which will focus on raising their awareness of the aims and ambitions of the group and enable the managers to begin to analyse the implications and opportunities for them. In particular, the intention is that the programme will result in middle managers adopting a wider vision of their role to support the international ambitions of the group.

Alan has spent six months conducting research to inform design of the programme and to help plan its implementation. The focus of his research has been internal, to identify the nature and size of the target population and to establish the expectations of key stakeholders, including middle managers, through a questionnaire survey of a representative sample; and external, to establish methods adopted by organisations of a similar size. Alan's external research has consisted of a review and analysis of published material and, where possible, visits to and discussions with relevant development staff in other, non-competitor businesses. The results of the internal research include a finding that the potential target population totalled nearly 5 000 across the world, a typical profile of a middle-aged male who is professionally qualified but with little if any experience outside the insurance industry or country of origin and who demonstrates a high level of company loyalty. External research on practices in other organisations suggests that formal development events will be insufficient by themselves to achieve the intended aims of the programme. Direct experience and exposure to different cultural influences, both national and organisational (e.g. divisional and functional), are likely to be required. Alan's research has enabled him to produce the following principles to inform design and implementation of the programme:

- use division and country/region-based HRD staff in implementation;
- involve senior managers at division/regional level in delivery of the programme;
- participant groups to represent a mix of nationality, function, age and experience;
- a varied number of methods, with a formal event forming the 'launch' and 'heart' of the programme;
- involvement of participants' line managers, especially in pre- and post-event briefings;
- an element of self-managed learning supported by appropriate materials;
- production of personal development plans by participants related to and used throughout and after the programme. PDPs to be agreed with line managers.

Alan is now in a position to produce more detailed proposals. These will be discussed with his manager before being presented to the group director of human resources. Alan has no concerns over necessary resources being allocated since internationalisation is high priority in FCIG. He is also confident that his research will support his arguments. It is now just a matter of working out the details.

Discussion questions

1 What objectives should Alan present for the programme as being relevant and achievable?

2 What methods other than a formal development event would you suggest to Alan to include in the programme, and why?

3 Given the importance of the formal development event, what design features should Alan adopt? For example, objectives, duration, content and methods?

4 What arrangements should Alan consider for implementation? What factors should he take into account in deciding these arrangements?

5 How should Alan present his proposals to his manager and what advice would you give him on handling the meeting?

Suggested reading

Buckley, R. and Caple, T. (1995) *The Theory and Practice of Training (3rd edn)*. London: Kogan Page.

Harrison, R. (1997) *Employee Development*. London: IPD.

Reid, M. and Barrington, H. (1997) *Training Interventions (5th edn)*. London: IPD.

Truelove, S. (ed.) (1995) *The Handbook of Training and Development*. Blackwell Business.

CHAPTER 10

Evaluating employee development contributions

Introduction

We have arrived at the final stage of the training cycle. Evaluation is concerned with establishing the success or otherwise of development activities, and with assessing whether the associated benefits justify the investment. The latter need not necessarily consist of direct expenditure incurred by employee development activities as there may be none involved. However, some investment will have been required, if only the time and effort of practitioners and learners (*see* Chapter 14). It is therefore a purpose of evaluation to establish the value of that investment.

As with the activities which formed the focus of the previous chapter, we can apply the concept of evaluation to various levels. The simplest way of illustrating this is to say that we can evaluate a single and discrete development activity, say an internal course on recruitment and selection for middle managers, or we can attempt to evaluate the contribution of the whole employee development function over a given time period. It is reasonable to argue that similar principles will apply whatever the level, although perhaps different methods will be used. One principle which applies at any and all levels is that evaluation requires the collection, analysis, interpretation and reporting of information. That being the case, the processes of evaluation have much in common with those involved in establishing training needs. Therefore, the arguments on the conduct of research in work organisations presented in Chapter 8 have relevance and application in this chapter. Our primary focus here will be in evaluating a single and discrete development activity. It will be useful to bear in mind, though, the possibility of evaluating at different levels, where the type and quantity of information sought is likely to be different. It is those kinds of differences which lead to application of different methods, rather than any fundamental difference of purpose or process. The use of different methods at different levels will be highlighted at various points in this chapter to illustrate and support this argument.

One final introductory point needs to be made. The fact that evaluation constitutes the final part of the training cycle suggests that it occurs after the previous stages. This also leads to a view that evaluation can be, perhaps even should be, thought about and planned separately from, and following the application of, the other stages of the cycle. Such a view misunderstands the cycle itself, and the purpose and application of evaluation (Harrison, 1997, Sanderson, 1995). All stages of the training cycle are interrelated and connected, and each has consequences for the others and therefore cannot be applied in isolation. Thus, the cycle represents an integrated and holistic approach to employee development. That being the case, evaluation can be and should be thought about, planned for and applied during the application of the other stages.

Having established these introductory points, we can proceed with the examination of evaluation, which is intended to achieve the following objectives.

CHAPTER OBJECTIVES

- Describe and explain the purposes and processes of evaluating employee development.

- Compare and contrast a range of models of evaluation.

- Critically assess the application of these models in the context of problems associated with the conduct of evaluation projects.

- Design, construct and apply evaluation studies in the context of work organisations.

- Demonstrate critical awareness of the assumptions informing conventional approaches to evaluation of employee development.

Evaluation – a central problem

This chapter will begin by addressing the final objective first. This may seem a little odd because that objective could have been listed first. The objectives, though, follow a logical progression in that one cannot criticise what one does not first understand. However, developing a critical understanding can be facilitated by being aware of potential grounds for criticism as the understanding itself is developed. So, it makes sense, in my judgement, to list the objectives in the order given but to begin to achieve the final objective first. You might wish to consider this argument in relation to the discussion of objectives in the previous chapter.

Established, influential and what might be termed conventional treatments of evaluation, for example, Jackson (1989), Hamblin (1974), or Kirkpatrick (1976), all adopt a realist position in relation to the purposes and processes of evaluation (*see* Chapter 8 on realist and non-realist positions). More recent treatments of the subject, for example, Bramley (1996) or those provided by Truelove (1997), Harrison (1997) and Reid and Barrington (1997), accept the same basic assumptions and therefore continue to apply a realist position which, in most cases, either directly applies the work of earlier writers or offers some reworked interpretation of established ideas. We can conclude, therefore, that mainstream writing on evaluation, in general, assumes that the purpose and process of establishing the success and value of employee development is unproblematic. I wish to develop a counter argument in this section by focusing on what I consider to be a central problem in these conventional approaches. Additional problems will be identified and discussed in a later section.

The *Oxford English Dictionary* defines 'evaluate' as being concerned with 'finding' or 'stating' the 'number' or 'amount'. The same dictionary defines 'assess' as 'fix amount of'. These definitions support an assertion that evaluation can be considered synonymous with assessment. A close reading of this book, and many others on employee development, would confirm that the words are used as synonyms and that, therefore, the concepts are interchangeable. Relying on this argument, and because I am drawing on a previously published analysis (Stewart, 1998b), I will focus here on use of the word 'assessment' in place of 'evaluation'.

There are many potential contexts of assessment in HR practice, for example, in recruitment and selection or performance appraisal. Many contexts (for example, development centres, award of national vocational qualifications or other qualification-based programmes) are of particular relevance to employee development. Each of these will differ in terms of the kind of information, and sources from which it is drawn, which are used to inform assessment decisions. However, if we ask the question 'where does assessment take place?', the answer in my view remains constant irrespective of the context or the information being used. The answer to the question, in all cases, is 'in the head'. In other words, an assessment decision is reached by an individual. All assessment decisions are the result of the cognitive processes of individuals, whether acting alone or collectively. If this premise is accepted, it follows that all assessment is necessarily and by definition subjective. Assessment is therefore a subjective rather than objective process.

The interpretive and radical humanist paradigms described in Chapter 2 would support such a conclusion, as would an associated non-realist position in relation to the social world, described in Chapter 8. Put a different way, viewing assessment as essentially subjective is a logical consequence of adopting an interpretive or radical humanist paradigm, and non-realist position, in relation to organisation theory and analysis. This contrasts with adoption of a functionalist paradigm, and associated realist position, which would allow for and support a view of assessment as constituting an objective process. To put this another way, conventional treatments of assessment which assume the possibility or actuality of objectivity can only be sustained within a functionalist paradigm. Even so, to be logically sustained, such treatments have to find alternative answers to the question 'where does assessment take place?'. We will move on shortly to examine some common responses to the question. First, an activity to encourage you to examine your current position.

Activity 10.1

1 Make some notes on your initial response to the proposition that all assessment is subjective. Consider to what extent your response provides support for or challenges the proposition.

2 Discuss your response with a colleague and compare and contrast similarities and differences. Attempt to identify reasons for these.

3 Produce some alternative answers to the question 'where does assessment take place?'. Analyse the implications of each of your answers for the proposition that all assessment is subjective.

4 Drawing on the results of 1 to 3, produce a personal statement on the proposition.

My view is that conventional and established thinking on assessment is firmly rooted in a functionalist paradigm. It seems to me that viewing assessment as an objective process follows from application of a machine metaphor, the reification of organisations and individuals as objective entities and associated perspectives and theories which apply rationalistic assumptions to the study of organisational behaviour. However, I cannot produce or arrive at any satisfactory answers to the crucial question of where assessment takes place other than the one already given. Therefore, my belief is that assessment is inevitably subjective. I further believe that the most common response to the subjectivity of assessment is to seek to 'objectify' the process. We try to do this in two ways (Stewart, 1998b). One of these, the construction and application of criteria, is particularly relevant here and so will be examined next. First, though, I wish to propose a more general and philosophical objection to approaches to 'objectifying' assessment.

Attempts to objectify assessment are built on a belief that it is possible to be more or less objective or subjective. In other words, it is possible to make judgements about one assessment process being more or less objective than an alternative. This belief is characterised by the idea of a continuum between objective processes and subjective processes. However, to produce a continuum requires that both 'poles' are possible since continuums are, by definition, bi-polar constructs. For example, thermometers apply a continuum between cold (say defined at 0°C) and hot (say defined as 100°C). Applying the continuum of 'cold to hot', and by using a thermometer, we are able to judge whether any given temperature is colder or hotter than another by seeing which pole it is closer to when compared with the alternative. But if assessment always occurs in the head and is, therefore, always subjective, the 'objective' pole of the continuum is not possible. Therefore, if the original premise is accepted, judgements on assessment processes being more or less subjective or objective are not possible. We simply delude ourselves that such judgements are possible by applying an assumed continuum that cannot be logically sustained.

One particular concept that we use in our delusions of objectivity is that of criteria. There are at least three problems in the application of this concept to justify 'objectivity'. The first is the extent to which any criterion is understood to have the same meaning by all those involved in an assessment process, especially those doing the assessing and those being assessed. As an example of this problem, I have not defined what I mean by criterion. I am therefore assuming that you, the reader, understand what I mean by the concept. Any differences in meaning and understanding, however, can have serious and significant implications in an assessment context.

This brings us to the second problem. The only way a shared understanding of the meaning of words can be reached is through the use of yet more words. Thus, I could attempt to define 'criteria' by writing a sentence or two about my understanding of the meaning of the concept. In doing so, I would probably introduce additional and new concepts which would provide more opportunities for misunderstanding. Language can and does confuse and obstruct communication as much as it can and does clarify and facilitate communication. We may overcome this problem by discussion and debate, although this is rarely the case in assessment processes, a fact which gives rise to the third problem. Those being assessed rarely have involvement in constructing and deciding the criteria which are to be used. They usually just have to accept them. Yet the criteria may have little meaning to those being assessed, in the sense of personal relevance, value or attachment. Their engagement with the criteria and the assessment process may therefore be limited and variable. If, as is often the case, attempts to increase objectivity through the use of overt criteria are justified on the grounds of 'fairness' and 'equity', these problems with the use of criteria make the achievement of such purposes debatable at best.

Activity 10.2

1 Select two assessment contexts within your organisation which utilise published criteria, and consider the following questions:

(a) what is the rationale for using published criteria?

(b) to what extent do the assessment processes allow the problems identified above to be overcome?

(c) how could dealing with the problems be improved?

2 Review your final response to Activity 10.1 and consider whether you wish to revise it in response to the results of this activity.

Discussion

You may be wondering what this analysis of assessment has to do with evaluation of employee development. There are at least three points of relevance and application. The first is a matter of principle. It was argued earlier that assessment and evaluation can be taken to be synonymous concepts. A case has been made that assessment is always and inevitably subjective. Therefore, and contrary to established and conventional treatments, according to this analysis, evaluation is always and inevitably subjective. This is an important principle to bear in mind as the rest of the chapter unfolds because it informs some additional arguments on evaluation. Second, the outcomes of many assessment decisions form the focus of evaluation of employee development. Two examples will suffice to illustrate this point. The number of individuals, in absolute and/or in relative terms, who achieve award of an NVQ may form part of the evaluation of the success or otherwise of employee development. We used the example earlier of a development activity on recruitment and selection for middle managers. The results of the subsequent selection decisions of those middle managers may form part of the focus of the evaluation of such an activity. It is advisable to understand the subjective nature of these kinds of outcomes if and when they provide the focus of evaluation.

Finally, the analysis of assessment provides a direct link between evaluation and the previous chapter. As we shall see, the objectives of employee development activities can provide a primary focus of evaluation. But objectives serve the same purpose in evaluation as criteria do in other assessment contexts. For example, in applying criteria in an assessment centre, the judgement being reached focuses on how well a candidate performs against those criteria. Part of evaluation of ED focuses on judging how well a development activity or process performs against the stated objectives. So, in that sense, the learning objectives of development activities serve as criteria and, therefore, the analysis of criteria given in the previous section applies equally well to the process of evaluating employee development.

We will now move on to examine ideas on evaluation in more detail. A useful structure for doing so is what I call the 'three ps of evaluation'. These are purpose, process and problems.

Purposes of evaluation

A helpful starting point in considering the purpose of evaluation is to examine the meaning of some key terms. One term which causes some confusion in relation to evaluation is 'validation'. This is often distinguished even further into 'internal validation' and 'external validation'. In simple terms, validation is concerned with assessing the degree to which the stated objectives are met. The question to be answered to establish the validity or otherwise of a development activity is 'have the objectives been achieved?'. This question also constitutes the focus of internal validation. Evaluation, as the word implies, is concerned with the 'value' or otherwise of a development activity. This raises two further questions. First, were the objectives the correct, or most appropriate, intentions? Second, and relatedly, was the achievement of the objectives worth the investment? The first of these additional two questions provides the focus of external validation. The second provides the primary focus of evaluation. However, as Sanderson (1995) argues, this final question cannot be answered with any degree of satisfaction without also answering the first two questions. We can say therefore that evaluation requires and encompasses validation, both internal and external. What follows from this is that it is possible to undertake validation of employee development without undertaking evaluation, but it is not possible to undertake evaluation without undertaking validation. So it makes sense to focus entirely on the concept of evaluation since, by definition, if employee development is evaluated, it is also validated.

This discussion of key terms suggests that the overall purpose of evaluation is to establish the value, or worth, of employee development. This overall purpose can be broken down into separate, specific purposes. Sanderson (1995) suggests eight specific purposes, including those to determine whether the objectives were met, to improve the performance of development practitioners and, interestingly, to provide marketing data. Reid and Barrington (1997) list five specific purposes which are not dissimilar to those suggested by Sanderson, while Harrison (1997) makes a generalised claim that 'there are many reasons why evaluation may be required' (p. 303). Easterby-Smith (1986), while primarily writing about evaluation of management development, provides a simple though very useful framework of purposes served by evaluation. We will apply that framework here.

Easterby-Smith (1986) suggests three primary purposes for evaluation. The first purpose is to *prove* the value of investing in employee development. The major focus here is obviously to demonstrate that the benefits gained by employee development are worth more, or have more value than, the costs associated with providing the development activity. It should be noted, however, that while costs are likely to be expressible in monetary terms, benefits do not *necessarily* have to be expressed as such since some valued benefits can be intangible, e.g. a reputation as a good employer in the labour market. The achievement of such a valued benefit may be demonstrable, for example, by number and quality of applications per vacancy. However, demonstrating achievement of a valued benefit and attaching monetary values are often two different things. This example also illustrates the significance of the term 'valued benefit'. Any particular outcome, in this case a good reputation in the labour market, is a benefit only if it is valued by those who are investing in the activity to achieve the outcome. If the outcome does not matter to them, i.e. they attach no value to the outcome, then no benefit is achieved. This point supports the view of evaluation as being a subjective process.

The second primary purpose of evaluation according to Easterby-Smith is to *improve*. The distinction here might be characterised by the difference between internal and external validation. The purpose of *improving* is primarily concerned with assessing how well learning objectives have been met. The intention therefore is to gather and process information on how the development activity might be more efficient and effective in the future. To achieve this purpose, attention is focused on design features such as content, methods, structure and pacing, and on implementation factors such as location, briefing and materials. The purpose is also likely to focus on performance of development practitioners in terms of delivery. Given that improving is associated with internal validation, attempts will have to be made to assess whether the stated objectives have been met. For this reason, the purpose of improving focuses on the performance of both learners and development practitioners. One potential weakness in pursuing this purpose is that information is in part collected from and about a particular group or collection of learners. Based on their experience, changes are sought, and perhaps implemented, for future groups or collections of learners. Given the significant individual differences that are likely to be present when comparing one group or collection of learners with another, the expected or intended improvements of any changes may not be realised. In other words, the changes would constitute improvements for the original learners but, because of individual differences, they do not for new and future learners. It is therefore often difficult to judge what changes will in fact constitute an improvement.

The final purpose is that of *learning*. Evaluation of employee development can act in support of facilitating learning. One of the key arguments here is that knowledge of results is required in order for learning to occur. This principle is supported by behaviourist learning theory. In addition, as Reid and Barrington (1997) argue, the theory of learning represented by the experiential learning cycle also suggests that reviewing and reflecting on performance is intrinsic to effective learning. Given that the achievements and performance of learners are an inherent focus and requirement of evaluation, it is therefore both legitimate and possible for evaluation to serve learning purposes. So, evaluation can be carried out explicitly to support the learning process. Doing so requires that evaluation activities and methods enable some assessment of learners' performance and associated progress and improvement. As we shall see later, this can be problematic for a number of reasons, including resistance from learners themselves. Reid and Barrington (1997) point this out in their discussion of the use of 'pre-tests' taken by learners prior to development activities, although they seem to assume that testing and other forms of assessment will not be resisted during and after development. Such testing and assessment should not be assumed to be the exclusive preserve of practitioners. Their involvement can, in fact, be minimal. Self-assessment and peer assessment are both possible approaches to evaluation which serves learning purposes (Easterby-Smith, 1986).

Discussion

These three purposes are not necessarily mutually exclusive, but it is important to be clear at the outset which or what purposes are being served by evaluation activities because different purposes will require different approaches and methods (Reid and Barrington, 1997, Harrison, 1997). If all three of Easterby-Smith's purposes are being served, this would imply an extensive range of methods. This would not be impossible, although what is possible, perhaps probable, is that some methods may create conflict, one with another, when combined. Care then is needed in designing evaluation studies which are intended to serve multiple purposes. As was argued earlier, problems with evaluation are less likely if the purpose is decided at the earliest stage of the training cycle, i.e. when establishing training needs, and appropriate methods devised for application throughout the cycle. For example, both improving and learning will require evaluation to be considered, and some methods to be applied, during both design and implementation. Focusing on the purpose of evaluation therefore emphasises and reinforces the integrated nature of the training cycle.

While Easterby-Smith (1986) fully recognises the social and political nature of organisations, and evaluation as a social and political process, I think his three purposes can be usefully extended to four. My suggested addition is that of *promoting*. This purpose is similar to that of 'providing marketing information' suggested by Sanderson (1995). If we start from the point of my earlier analysis which suggests that evaluation cannot be concerned with establishing objective truth, but instead should be viewed as an inevitably subjective process concerned with influencing the construction of social facts (*see* Giddens, 1989), then it seems entirely legitimate to me for development practitioners to engage in evaluation for the purpose of promoting the value of employee development. Given the political nature of organisations, and the associated need for development practitioners to be politically skilled (Harrison, 1997, Moorby, 1996), I would argue that practitioners would be foolish to ignore the promotional potential and possibilities of evaluation. I recognise that some readers may find this argument a little cynical, and that it does raise ethical considerations (*see* Chapter 13). However, I would further argue that promoting the value of employee development is inherent in the three purposes suggested by Easterby-Smith, and in any other purpose that has been or might be suggested. My intention in proposing a fourth purpose of *promoting* is simply to make explicit what is implicit. By doing so, I believe the purpose may be served more effectively. As a final argument, seeking to serve the purpose of promoting does not, and is not intended to, exclude any other purpose.

Activity 10.3

1 Consider evaluation activities undertaken in your organisation and answer the following questions:

(a) what purpose(s) do they serve?

(b) how explicit or otherwise are these purposes?

(c) what do you think are the reasons for particular purposes rather than others being pursued?

▶

2 Compare and contrast your responses with those of a colleague.

3 Discuss with a colleague the legitimacy or otherwise of the purpose of promoting.

The process of evaluation

Examining the purposes of evaluation has dealt with the questions of what and why. We now turn our attention to the more practical questions of how and when (Reid and Barrington, 1997, Harrison, 1997). We address these questions by considering the process of evaluation.

There are a number of different models which provide frameworks for conducting evaluation. Warr, Bird and Rackham (1970, *see also* Harrison, 1997) suggested the acronym CIRO. This stands for Context evaluation, Input evaluation, Reaction evaluation and Output evaluation. Context focuses on factors such as correct identification of needs and setting of objectives in relation to the organisational culture and climate. Inputs are concerned with the design and delivery of the development activity. Reaction is concerned with the reactions to the experience by learners, and by others such as learners' sponsors. Output focuses on the achievements gained by learners and the organisation from the activity. A similar framework is that suggested by Kirkpatrick (1976). Here, four levels of evaluation are identified: reaction, learning, behaviour and results. The common factor of reaction is more or less identical, while output in Warr, Bird and Rackham's framework encompasses learning, behaviour and results in that of Kirkpatrick. Thus the two frameworks agree on both reactions and results/outputs, although Kirkpatrick specifies different forms of output, while the framework of Warr, Bird and Rackham adds context and input to Kirkpatrick's four levels.

A third and very similar framework is that produced by Hamblin (1974). There are potential problems with these frameworks (Easterby-Smith, 1986, Bramley and Kitson, 1994, Bramley, 1996, *see also* next section). However, they are widely applied, whether implicitly or explicitly, in evaluation practice. We will focus here on the framework produced by Hamblin to examine how to evaluate. However, the points made apply to other frameworks such as those discussed so far since they are derived from similar assumptions and apply similar principles.

The Hamblin evaluation framework

Hamblin (1974) suggests a five-level framework for evaluation of employee development. The concept of 'levels' is significant. It suggests differences in value and importance in that the results of evaluation at one level will have more impact and significance than the results of another level. It also suggests movement up some form of scale in that we can and do have 'lower' and 'higher' levels of evaluation. This is related to impact and significance, but also to 'size' in the sense that we move from an individual focus to a department focus to a whole organisation focus. A final point on the concept of levels is the most significant and important. It is argued by Hamblin (1974) that the five levels constitute a 'causal chain'. To explain, evaluation is concerned with establishing the 'effects' of employee development. The potential effects occur at a number of levels. However, according to Hamblin, the 'effect' at one level 'causes', at least in part, the 'effect' at the next level. Thus, the five levels in Hamblin's framework constitute a chain of causes and effects, with effects at lower levels causing effects at higher levels (Burgoyne and Singh, 1977). The nature of this causal chain will become apparent as we examine Hamblin's five levels, which are detailed below.

Reaction level

This is level one in Hamblin's framework. In common with the other frameworks described earlier, it focuses on the experience of the development activity from the perspective of learners, and their reactions to their experience. In general terms, these reactions can be positive or negative or, perhaps more probable, variable in relation to different aspects or elements of the development experience, for instance, content, location, tutor style or pre-course briefing. Evaluation at this level requires collection of information of learners' perceptions of and feelings about these various aspects of the development activity, and analysis and interpretation of that information. Hamblin's causal chain suggests that learners' reactions will have an effect on, and thus cause, the results achieved at the next level.

Learning level

Level two, learning, also focuses on individual learners. The effect being looked for and assessed here, however, is the amount and nature of learning that has occurred as a result of the development activity. An obvious focus at this level is the learning objectives set for the development activity. This level therefore is concerned with internal validation. Evaluating at this level requires some form of assessment of individual learning. Depending on the nature of the learning objectives, methods such as multiple-choice tests, examinations, projects, phase tests, case studies or skills tests may be used (*see also* Reid and Barrington, 1997). As noted earlier, forms of self and/or peer assessment may also be appropriate. The amount of learning will cause success or otherwise at the next level.

Job behaviour level

In Hamblin's model, the focus of this level remains individual learners in that their behaviour in their jobs following development receives attention and assessment. There can be confusion here between job 'behaviour' and job 'performance' where the latter refers to results achieved in the job. For example, a salesperson's behaviour can include the frequency of use of a customer's name. If that frequency increases, we can argue that a change in job behaviour has been achieved. However, this may or may not increase sales. Sales achieved constitutes 'performance' and therefore would be the focus of assessment of changes in 'job performance'. In evaluating at this level, clarity is needed on whether behaviour, i.e. *how* the job is carried out, or performance, i.e. *results achieved*, provides the focus. Again, reference to objectives set will help clarify the situation. In most cases, though, performance provides the focus. Methods can include observation, interviews, performance appraisal, activity sampling, self-reporting using diaries and/or critical incidents and monitoring of performance data produced by management information systems. Changes in individual job behaviour/performance provide the next link in the causal chain by producing effects at the next level.

Department/organisation level

The focus changes at level four from the individual to the organisation. This change rids us of any confusion over behaviour and performance because attention is clearly on performance indicators such as quantity of output, quality measures, wastage rates, customer satisfaction and financial measures, such as reduced costs, higher turnover/profit or return on investment. Changes in these indicators can also be compared with the investment in employee development through cost/benefit analysis. However, there can be choice, and therefore potential confusion, over the specification of 'organisation' attached to this level. The argument normally applied is that it is reasonable to expect changes and improvements at level three to have impact in the immediate work context, and therefore level four should focus on the unit, department, branch, function, division or whatever unit within which learners are employed. The causal chain is quite clear here: changes in individual performance cause changes in performance of the organisation, or unit. Evaluation methods at this level use established information systems for monitoring and reporting on performance and/or data collection and analysis specifically designed and applied for evaluation purposes.

Organisation level/ultimate value

The fifth and final level is usually referred to as 'ultimate value'. The idea of ultimate value normally applies to the organisation *per se*, and therefore poses the question 'what has been the value to the organisation of employee development?'. We can apply this question to either the totality of employee development policy and practice, or to a particular and specific employee development activity. In either case, we are concerned with performance of the organisation as a whole. Therefore, evaluation at this level is concerned with achievement of organisation goals and objectives. As we saw in earlier chapters, some at least of these are likely to be expressed in economic and financial terms such as profit, return on investment, market share or shareholder value. However, the notion of ultimate value suggests wider concerns. These might include customer service levels, staff satisfaction, ethical standards and responsible environmental policies. Measures and methods such as customer and staff surveys, examination of absence, turnover and discipline/grievance statistics, environmental audits and benchmarking (Harrison, 1997) may be employed at this level. Level five represents the final link in the causal chain. Improvements in departmental performance cause improvements in organisational performance. Satisfaction on the part of individual employees with effective employee development, enabling successful job performance, produces positive results in 'health' indicators such as absence and turnover levels. Thus the chain from learner reactions to organisation success is complete.

When and how to evaluate

The issue of how to evaluate has been partly addressed in the description of Hamblin's framework. The process is simply one of collecting, analysing, interpreting and reporting information. For example, at the 'reactions level', the most common method is to issue a questionnaire to learners during and/or at the end of a development activity. A common failing is to analyse very superficially and not to complete the process by reporting. Overall, however, methods of evaluation require thought to be given to what information will be relevant and how to collect and analyse that which is required. The framework provided by Hamblin, and indeed those provided by other writers, point the direction in terms of the kind of information required.

The issue of when to evaluate is also partly answered by Hamblin's and other frameworks. The idea of a causal chain suggests time is required for each cause to work before the effects become apparent. Reactions are caused by the development experience. They will therefore be immediately apparent and can be investigated during or at the end of the experience. Learning is intended to occur during the development activity and, in most cases, to have been achieved by the end. Thus, this too can be assessed during, at the end and shortly after the development experience. Transfer of learning to the job, and consequent changes in behaviour and, especially, performance will take some time as learners apply and practise their learning. Therefore this level can be evaluated only some time after the activity. The outcomes of changes at level three will take time to work through and show effects at level four. Evaluation here then can take place only in the short to medium term following development. Similarly, changes in department performance will take more time to produce organisational level benefits. So, evaluation at level five can occur in only the medium to long term.

I have deliberately used terms such as 'short' and 'long' term since it is impossible to be precise in the abstract. The actual lengths of time will vary depending on the nature, objectives and learners involved in the development activity. For one activity, e.g. aimed at production line assembly operators with objectives related to job-related skills, medium term may be two months and long term six months. In contrast, for an activity intended to prepare rising middle managers for international assignments, short term may be six months and long term may be two to three years. Timescales are a matter of judgement based on variables surrounding a particular development activity.

What I have written so far seems, I think, reasonable, logical and practical. The situation is not quite that simple, however, especially with causal models such as Hamblin's framework. Before moving on to examine some of the problems with such models, we will look briefly at an alternative approach.

The Easterby-Smith framework

Easterby-Smith (1986) argues against the causal chain of Hamblin, and indeed the presumed causal relationships inherent in other, similar frameworks. While connections and relationships between the various elements of development activities and individual and organisation behaviour and performance are accepted, the nature of those relationships, and the isolation of causal links, are seen as complex and problematic. Hamblin (1974) also recognised this problem and complexity. As an alternative, and based on an extensive review of research and writing on evaluation, Easterby-Smith proposed the CAPIO framework, briefly described here:

- *Context*. This focuses on factors such as organisation culture and values, processes of selection and nomination and the levels of support for learners in their work context which may be associated with such factors. Context may also refer to and focus on the processes for establishing training needs and setting objectives for development.

- *Administration.* This element is concerned with factors such as publicity material, joining instructions and location. These can be significant in influencing learners' 'reactions' and responses to their learning and development experiences.

- *Process.* This focuses on what actually happens during a development activity, and how it is experienced as a learning activity by learners. Critical aspects of this element include the feelings and emotional responses of learners, as well as the nature and level of their intellectual engagement with the process. The type of relationships encouraged and experienced within learning groups, and between those groups, individual learners and development practitioners, are another critical focus. The implications of factors such as these for individual and collective learning are a key consideration here.

- *Inputs.* Context and administration *influence* learning but do not constitute learning. The same is true of inputs. These are concerned primarily with the activities and behaviour of development practitioners. We might characterise this element as focusing on content and methods, i.e. what subjects and topics are included/excluded, and how those included are dealt with, for example, through lectures, case studies, seminars or role plays. The role of learners in such decisions can also be significant.

- *Outputs.* The focus here is quite clear. Without assuming any direct causal relationships, evaluation is concerned with establishing the outputs, or outcomes, of employee development. The focus may be on individuals and changes in their KSA and behaviour, or on individual and/or organisation performance or on shifts in organisation culture and climate. Pre-set objectives may form part of the focus. However, 'goal free' evaluation (Scriven, 1972) is possible where the situation is to establish outputs without reference to, or perhaps even in ignorance of, the formal objectives. Such evaluation may be more likely to identify unintended outcomes and consequences.

Methods used in applying the CAPIO framework need not differ very much from those used in other frameworks. However, timing of application will vary according to which element in the framework is being evaluated. For example, context can be investigated before the development activity, process during the activity and outputs both during and some time after the activity. A further factor influencing timing is whether evaluation is intended to be *formative* or *summative* (Gowler and Legge, 1978). The former provides ongoing or periodic feedback as an activity unfolds, while the latter is concerned with establishing the results achieved following completion of an activity. A final factor influencing both which element is evaluated and when is the purpose of evaluation. The purpose of 'proving', for example, will probably emphasise inputs and outputs, while the purpose of learning may be more concerned with context and process. As a final point, the elements in Easterby-Smith's framework are more independent and 'free-standing' than Hamblin's five levels and, therefore, provide an initial series of choices for evaluation.

Activity 10.4

1 Assess the relative strengths and weaknesses of Hamblin's framework and the CAPIO framework.

2 Select a list of measures, and methods of assessing them, you would use in your organisation at each of Hamblin's five levels.

3 Consider current evaluation practice in your organisation and answer the following questions:

(a) which framework best represents the current approach?

(b) why, do you think, is the present approach adopted?

(c) how could current practice be improved?

(d) what problems might arise in implementing your ideas?

Problems with evaluation

I argued earlier that evaluation, conventionally at least, is associated with a functionalist paradigm and associated realist perspective in relation to the social world. We do not have to abandon that position to find some significant problems with conducting evaluation.

The first problem is that of measurement. In order to evaluate we need to assess the extent of any changes in behaviour and performance. To do that, we first need some indicators and measures. This may be simple, as some writers argue (Truelove, 1997, Reid and Barrington, 1997) for low-level, low-discretion, highly specified jobs such as typists, filing clerks or assembly operators. However, the task can be much more complex for technical, professional or managerial roles. For example, consider the role of human resources manager and attempt to produce some performance measures. A significant complicating factor is the extent to which the person in that role, and their behaviour, can be said to be the sole, or even the most influential, factor in producing the results indicated by the performance measures. This problem, in principle at least, also operates at lower levels, and therefore it may question the claimed simplicity of producing measures for those jobs. It also raises the nature of the second problem.

Isolating the impact of individual behaviour on performance achieved is a problem of establishing cause and effect. In terms of evaluation, the same problem is encountered in isolating the effects of employee development. In other words, given the myriad set of factors influencing performance, it is difficult to establish the contribution of development activities in bringing about, or causing, any measured improvements. To do so, other influencing factors have to be isolated and held constant so that the factor of employee development can be demonstrated to have produced, or caused, the effect of improved performance. There are two common ways of attempting to achieve this. The first is the use of pre- and post-tests or measures. The theory is that, since the development activity is the only changed factor, it must cause any subsequent change in performance. There are two problems here. First, application of the tests and selection for development are by definition intervening variables, the effects of which cannot be accounted for. Second, and relatedly, pre-tests may be resented and resisted (Reid and Barrington, 1997), reactions which may account for lower results than those achieved post development.

The second way of isolating other factors is use of experimental designs (Truelove, 1997, Sanderson, 1995). This requires the use of control groups who are matched with an experimental group. The former do not participate in the development activity, and the latter do. Following development, any differences and improvements in the experimental group can be attributed to the development activity. Thus, development can be claimed to have caused the improvement. Again, though, there are two methodological problems. First, it is often impossible in practice to identify all potentially significant factors which would need to be matched in the two groups and, even if this were possible, finding and assembling two groups who are perfectly matched on all the identified factors will be equally difficult. Second, given the complexity and fluidity of organisation contexts, it is highly unlikely that none of the factors would experience some change in either or both of the groups over the life of the activity or the evaluation study.

The problems described so far give rise to a further problem. This is the time, cost and effort of conducting evaluation 'properly'. Constructing and implementing studies which are intended and designed to overcome the methodological problems discussed so far can be resource intensive. It is perhaps not unrealistic to suggest that it is possible for such studies to require more investment than the development they are intended to evaluate. Part of this investment can be needed to fund the person or persons who conduct evaluation. As noted in Chapter 5, some large organisations employ development staff in specialist roles, and this includes evaluation. To avoid potential bias, neutral outsiders such as these, or external academics or consultants, may be commissioned to conduct evaluation studies. The issue of who evaluates is significant (Harrison, 1997, Reid and Barrington, 1997, Easterby-Smith, 1986). So, the question of funding evaluation arises as a potential problem and, paradoxically, deciding whether it is worth finding out if investment in employee development is worth it. If the decision is positive, the issue of where the costs of evaluation should be allocated arises, e.g. should they be counted as part of the development activity? In the case of a positive answer to this question, investment in evaluation is part of the investment which is being evaluated.

All the problems described so far can be related to a further problem, that of the politics of evaluation. It can be politically sensitive and difficult to administer pre- and post-tests, or even examinations, as part of evaluation. These political difficulties can increase when assessing behaviour and performance. In many, if not most organisations, construction and operation of experimental and control groups will not be feasible for political reasons. These points may be argued to have more relevance to professional and managerial groups, and that argument may have merit. However, if the points are conceptually sound, they have potential application in all contexts. Other political considerations apply whatever the nature of the development activity. A potential outcome of any evaluation is a conclusion that the investment was wasted since no valued benefits were achieved. Perhaps a little less dramatic example is a conclusion in a cost/benefit analysis that, while some benefits were achieved, their value is far outweighed by the costs involved in providing the development activity. A purely logical view of such conclusions would be that they are important and useful. However, organisations do not operate on pure logic.

The political question to be addressed is whose interests would be served by such conclusions? Not the person or persons who authorised the original investment, I would suggest. Nor those who sponsored the activity, nor those who identified the need or designed and implemented the activity. Given the 'shoot the messenger' syndrome that can operate in human affairs, I would suggest that the interests of those who conduct the evaluation, even if they are external consultants, are not served by such conclusions, especially if they aspire to future contracts. So, we can suggest quite powerful political reasons for evaluation studies not to reach negative conclusions. This is not to argue that evaluation studies never do, or should never reach negative conclusions. My purpose is to highlight, perhaps through exaggeration, the political context and implications of conducting evaluation.

One final set of problems deserve examination. While evaluation studies can and do use so-called 'objective data', such as measures of performance, they also usually rely on 'reported information'. This term refers to information 'told' by individuals about themselves and others. Such information is in most cases collected through techniques such as questionnaires, interviews, diaries and observation. There are two, related problems with such information. The first is one of veracity. It is possible that individuals, consciously or otherwise, do not tell the truth. We do not have to rely on, say, an interpretive paradigm here with an associated assumption of 'multiple truths'. The recent problems experienced by political opinion polls, which operate entirely within a positivist perspective, illustrate and demonstrate the problem (May, 1997). So, care has to be taken with reported information. The second and related problem is the reasons individuals may have for telling a particular version of the truth. In other words, even if we recognise that the information may be biased, we do not necessarily know why that is happening. Political considerations may point to some possible reasons, but we cannot assume that to be the case.

These problems are perhaps best illustrated by the use of end of development 'reaction' questionnaires. The feelings generated by a development experience may lead some individuals to report either more positive or more negative information, depending on their experience and feelings, than otherwise. The fact that the questionnaires will be seen and read by those delivering the activity, even if responses are anonymous (and handwriting can negate anonymity anyway), may lead some to report more or less favourable information depending on their disposition. Or not. We do not and cannot know either way. This example illustrates a final problem with reported information. Assume respondents tell the truth, so we do not have that problem. Assume further a rating scale from one to five, where one represents ineffective and five represents effective as part of the reaction questionnaire. Now, 50 per cent of respondents circle one and 50 per cent circle five and none circle any other number. What then is the truth about the effectiveness of the activity, and what is to be done with the information generated by the questionnaire? You might query the probability of such results but they are possible, and small variations raise similar questions.

Activity 10.5

1 Discuss each of these potential problems with a colleague and decide (a) how likely and (b) how significant each of them might be in practice.

2 Produce a list of problems that are both likely and significant, and answer the following questions:

(a) how might each problem be dealt with in practice?

(b) what are the implications of this for the design and conduct of evaluation studies?

(c) how will this affect the usefulness of conducting evaluation?

3 Consider evaluation practice in your organisation. How does it seek to deal with potential problems, and how could this be improved?

Discussion

This analysis of potential problems is not meant to argue against carrying out evaluation. It is rather intended to support a view that a positivist approach is unsustainable practically as well as conceptually. That being the case, recognising and acknowledging the subjective nature of evaluation will perhaps encourage us to cease pursuing an unobtainable holy grail, i.e. clear and demonstrable proof that investment in employee development brings measurable and valuable benefits. I recognise and acknowledge that this argument runs counter to recent, and increasingly influential, orthodoxies such as those associated with NVQs and, of more relevance, Investors in People. However, I would argue that a pragmatic approach to evaluation is more likely to justify the investment required than resources being wasted pursuing the unobtainable. As Burgoyne and Singh (1977) argued, the results of evaluation can provide an aid to decision making. Decisions will be better informed if the nature and status of evaluation reports are acknowledged.

Activity 10.6

1 Select an example development activity. This may be provided by your employer, an advertised 'open' course or a programme of current studies. Design an evaluation study for the example which includes a chosen framework, purpose, methods, timescales and probable costs.

2 Assess the degree to which your study will address potential problems of evaluation.

3 Produce a personal statement on your views on the pros and cons of evaluation, and discuss with a colleague.

Summary and conclusion

This chapter has described and examined the purpose and process of evaluation. It has achieved this by briefly exploring two frameworks, those suggested by Warr, Bird and Rackham and by Kirkpatrick, and by examining in more detail the models proposed by Hamblin and by Easterby-Smith. A range of problems associated with applying rationalistic and positivist frameworks has been identified and discussed. The significance and impact of these problems have been shown to be intensified if an alternative paradigm, which supports a view of evaluation as a subjective rather than an objective process, is applied. However, common practice of evaluation has been argued to apply an assumption of objectivity, with methods and timings being related to a number of factors, including the nature of the development activity and the purpose being pursued by evaluation. A pragmatic purpose of promoting has been suggested as a possible approach to reconciling the inherent contradictions and conflicts of evaluation.

A reasonable conclusion to reach, therefore, is that evaluation will continue to be a significant part of the training cycle, and will continue to be emphasised as an important activity for development practitioners. A further conclusion is that the activity and results of evaluation will be improved if their nature and status are better understood by practitioners. Given these points, a final, overall conclusion that practitioners will serve their own interests, and those of employing organisations, more effectively by adopting a pragmatic approach can be suggested.

This analysis of evaluation ends the examination of the training cycle, and closes the part of the book concerned with the process of employee development. We now turn our attention in the final part to examining issues concerned with the management of the employee development function in work organisations.

Case study 10

Vehicle Parts Limited manufactures and supplies metal-based components to leading car manufacturers in the UK and overseas. It operates in three sites, one of which is devoted to supplying a single customer. Each site operates as a separate and independent business unit required to meet agreed financial performance targets. In total, VPL has a turnover in excess of £125 million in the current year. This figure represents a significant growth since the company was established as a small factory on one site just over 30 years ago. The company employs 1 250 staff engaged primarily in engineering, manufacture and product development. Support functions such as finance and personnel are not heavily resourced and are seen by senior management and most employees as subservient to the real business of satisfying customer requirements. The company has, however, adopted 'modern' ideas such as teamwork, TQM and cellular manufacturing, as well as Japanese-inspired systems such as Just-in-Time and Total Preventative Maintenance, as deliberate strategies to maintain customer satisfaction and market share. Many of these initiatives have, in fact, been customer driven in the sense that VPL has had to adopt some of them to achieve and keep 'preferred supplier' status with some of its customers.

Steve Walsh is the recently appointed training officer for the Ashdown site of VPL.

Ashdown is production orientated, though, as with other sites, it has a small product development department. The site employs 850 people across materials handling, manufacture, quality engineering, management and general administration. The physical environment at Ashdown is variable but generally compares well with the two other sites in VPL, having recently refurbished offices and facilities such as canteens. Overall responsibility for performance at Ashdown lies with Alan Preston, the managing director. Since both are engineers, Steve relates well with Alan and expects to do well in his new role. Although Steve has made contributions to training staff in the past, the job of training officer is still very new to him. Until he was appointed three months ago, Steve had held a variety of supervisory and middle manager positions at Ashdown during his ten years with VPL.

Steve represents the sum total of a training and development function at Ashdown. He shares a secretary/administrator with the personnel manager, to whom he reports. The personnel manager in turn formally reports to Alan Preston, although in practice Steve is free to deal with the MD as and when he likes. The personnel manager is most interested in personnel matters and is happy to let Steve run his own patch, so long as she is kept informed. Training and development systems are well established in VPL and, in Steve's view, generally well applied at Ashdown. The MD takes an active interest, which probably helps explain this. New recruits are catered for through induction programmes and a system of part-time, nominated, on-the-job instructors. The company has been using NVQs for a number of years and there exists a pool of qualified assessors among supervisors and managers. Training records are computerised as part of a personnel database, and processes for identifying training needs run more or less smoothly through an annual appraisal system. New initiatives are backed by VPL headquarters staff, and training and development activities to help implement them are always supported by resources/materials produced by headquarters staff, and by the active involvement of senior managers on the site. As with Steve in the past, operational and functional managers can be called on to provide additional resources as and when required, to deliver training courses.

The major weakness in terms of training and development is in evaluation. Specific events or activities are sometimes, but not always, assessed through feedback questionnaires. Individuals receiving support for education and qualification-based courses are required to submit a 'business case' for approval by the MD. They first need the support of their manager and the training officer. They are then required to write a report on the benefits gained, using the business case as the criteria. Outside these practices, little evaluation is undertaken. Steve is concerned that the overall investment in employee development does not seem to be properly assessed. He also sees bringing about improvements in this area of the training function as a means of 'making his mark' in the job. He believes that devising and implementing processes and systems for evaluation will demonstrate an improvement over the work and contribution of his predecessor.

Steve has gained the approval of Alan Preston to submit a paper to the board of the Ashdown site on evaluation of training and development. He has also agreed with his boss, the personnel manager, that implementing an evaluation system will be his key objective for the next 12 months. While aware of some of the problems of evaluation through currently attending a Diploma in Training Management course, Steve is sure that evaluation can and must be done. Given his engineering background, and that of most of the board at Ashdown, Steve is also confident that evaluation can and should be based on quantitative analysis.

Discussion questions

1 What measures or indicators do you think Steve will and should focus on in evaluating employee development at Ashdown?

2 How do you think Steve will and should collect and analyse data on these measures/indicators?

3 What problems might Steve encounter in demonstrating the links between investment in employee development and changes/improvements in his chosen measures?

4 What advantages and disadvantages of evaluation should Steve bring to the attention of the board in his paper?

5 What are your views on whether Steve is doing the right thing in pursuing evaluation in terms of (a) his career, and (b) the future of employee development at Ashdown?

Suggested reading

Bramley, P. (1996) *Evaluating Training*. London: IPD.

Easterby-Smith, M. (1986) *Evaluation of Management Education, Training and Development*. Aldershot: Gower Publishing.

Reid, M. and Barrington, H. (1997) *Training Interventions (5th edn)*. London: IPD.

Truelove, S. (ed.) (1995) *The Handbook of Training and Development (2nd edn)*. Oxford: Blackwell Business.

PART 3

Managing employee development

CHAPTER 11

Employee development strategies

Introduction

Chapter 11 is concerned with what I have termed employee development strategies. We saw in Chapter 4 that the concept of strategy is problematic. For the purposes of this chapter, however, we will accept and apply a simple meaning that can be attached to the term. In common usage, strategy has connotations of long-term rather than short-term time orientation, effects of significant rather than marginal consequence and of an organisational rather than an individual focus. In addition, as Watson (1994) suggests, strategy is concerned with relationships external to the organisation and is therefore inextricably bound up with survival. Some of these characteristics also support the model of HRD introduced in Chapter 2 as a way of distinguishing HRD from training and development (*see also* Stewart and McGoldrick, 1996b). However, my concern here is to differentiate between various development issues and methods. Those to be described and discussed in this chapter are labelled 'strategies' since they tend towards the characteristics just described, especially if compared with methods such as those dealt with in Chapter 9. This is, of course, all a matter of degree and judgement so we need to be clear that the content of this chapter is not argued to be any more important than other chapters.

In considering what issues or methods might be considered as constituting ED strategies, a number of possibilities present themselves. One immediate and obvious candidate is development of managerial talent. Given the complexity of that issue and associated methods, Chapter 12 is devoted to the subject. Other possibilities include self-development and international employee development. One method of the former, action learning, will be examined in this chapter and a further method, open and distance learning, will form part of Chapter 14 (*see* Stewart, 1996 on approaches to and methods of self-development). International employee development is current and topical, as well as having direct links with the earlier examination of globalisation. That issue will therefore begin the substantive content of this chapter. The final part of the content will focus on the issue and concept of the learning organisation. As I have argued elsewhere (Stewart, 1994a, 1996), this concept can be seen as the latest and perhaps ultimate articulation of organisation development, which itself could constitute an employee development strategy. In addition, the learning organisation concept has direct connections with earlier analyses in this book of organisation learning and knowledge creation. The issue is therefore an appropriate inclusion in this chapter.

The chapter then examines international employee development, action learning and the learning organisation concept as three potential ED strategies. Other potential issues and methods, including self-development, are recognised and acknowledged. However, the three included here could each justify a book on their own, and so limitations of space require choices to be made. Overall, the chapter is intended to achieve the following objectives.

CHAPTER OBJECTIVES

● Explain and critically assess various meanings of and approaches to international ED.

● Describe, explain and evaluate the usefulness of action learning as a development method.

● Critically evaluate the concept of learning organisation and articulate a personal view on the validity and usefulness of attempts to apply the concept.

● Consider the potential application of the three selected ED strategies to the circumstances and contingencies of a particular organisation context.

● Construct, justify and defend a case for the application or otherwise of each of the three strategies.

Each of the strategies to be considered has received much attention in academic, professional and popular publications, including national newspapers. It is likely therefore that the terms are familiar to you, even if you have no personal or direct experience. A useful starting point will be to establish your understanding by completing the activity below. We will return to the results in later activities.

Activity 11.1

1 What do you think are the ED consequences of globalisation and, therefore, what activities/methods would constitute international ED?

2 What do you understand by the term 'action learning'? What particular design features would you expect to observe in an action-learning programme?

3 Produce a definition of 'learning organisation'. What specific characteristics follow from your definition and which might be used to distinguish a learning organisation from non-learning organisations?

Internationalisation of employee development

We begin our examination of the first issue by noting a paradox which, itself, is symptomatic of significant problems in conceptualising and practising international employee development. The paradox and related problems are best illustrated by a personal anecdote. As Lorbiecki (1997) notes, one response to the internationalisation of organisations and management has been for business schools to seek to internationalise themselves and their products, including core curriculums of business and management degree programmes. While working at Wolverhampton Business School, I was asked, along with all academic staff, to review the 'European perspective' of my teaching and materials, and to take steps to 'Europeanise' both as necessary. This 'initiative' was a response to the creation of the single European market and other developments within the EU. My response was to cite use of a Rover Cars (then British-owned) case study, among other UK case companies, as evidence of the 'Europeanised' nature of my teaching. The reaction to my response was to 'suggest' that I was both mischievous and parochial. However, my interpretation then and now is that it is in fact more parochial not to define or accept UK companies as 'European'. In insisting on non-UK cases, 'European' is being defined as 'other' and 'different', and the criteria of otherness or difference can therefore be satisfied only by non-UK examples.

The same issues and arguments will arise and be true if 'international' is substituted for 'European' in this anecdote. The paradox arises from the fact that the UK is at one and the same time a nation state, a member of the European Union and a part of the international community. Accepting this, it follows that any UK organisation is at one and the same time national, European and international, *even if* its products, operations and staff are confined within the geographic borders of the UK. However, *international* is defined in opposition to *national*, and there lies the paradox. This paradox illustrates the problem of what perspective to adopt, the problem of combining and reconciling the apparent contradictions in the admonishment 'think global, act local' (Torrington, 1994) and the problem of what Zaheer (1995) calls the 'liability of foreignness'. These problems need to be borne in mind as we move on to a more detailed analysis of international ED.

Connections with globalisation

Internationalising employee development is, in part, a response to globalisation (Iles, 1995, 1996). This response in turn can be associated with the responses of organisations to that phenomenon. Various terms are used to label and describe the various ways in which organisations can and do seek to operate globally, including 'multinational', 'transnational' and 'multi-domestic' (*see* Iles, 1995). Some writers, including Adler (1991), suggest a series of stages, or phases, through which organisations pass in internationalising their operations. These phases can include responses as simple as working through third-party agents in other countries or creating an export department, through to responses as complex as owning and operating foreign subsidiaries, or forming global strategic partnerships.

Globalisation can be argued to be both an input and an output in relation to organisations (Torrington, 1994, Iles, 1995). The phenomenon creates opportunities for organisations to operate more easily outside their country of origin. In that sense, globalisation is an input which leads to responses such as becoming a multi-national organisation, or corporation (MNC). However, as we have seen, the actions of organisation can and do provide an input to the globalisation process. This arises in part from how organisations choose to conduct their operations, through, for example, the creation of an export department or through direct investment in foreign subsidiaries. It also arises, perhaps more directly, from the perspective adopted in relation to how best to organise and manage outside the country of origin. Such perspectives have particular relevance to HR policy and practice (Iles, 1995). The work of Perlmutter (1969) is helpful here.

In an influential article, Perlmutter (1969) suggested four broad orientations to, or perspectives on, the question of how to organise and manage internationally. The first is labelled an 'ethnocentric orientation'. As the label implies, the central belief of this orientation is that the management style operated in the country of origin of the parent company will be the best and most appropriate in all other countries. This belief tends to a related view that parent country nationals (PCNs) are most suitable to managing operations in foreign countries, rather than individuals from those countries, referred to as host country nationals (HCNs). We might cite the approach adopted by Japanese manufacturers operating in Europe as an example of an ethno-centric orientation. 'Polycentric' is the name attached to the second orientation. Here, the central belief is that national differences exist and are significant, and that therefore organising and managing has to reflect local values and culture. Thus, in this orientation, operations in foreign countries are best managed by HCNs. However, this is likely to be limited to those 'foreign' operations with management in the country of origin still being dominated by PCNs. The third orientation is a variation of the second in that the existence and importance of difference remains acknowledged, but the level at which this becomes significant moves from individual countries to geographic regions. Thus, the third orientation is labelled 'regiocentric' and here Asian or European managers, for example, are preferred in those regions. Their particular nationality is, though, less important.

Finally, there is what Perlmutter terms the 'geocentric orientation'. This can be, in my judgement, a problematic and confusing term. However, Perlmutter suggests an orientation which eschews a view of management style as being necessarily associated with particular cultural or national values, but instead posits the possibility of a global approach to managing international operations. Hence, from this perspective, we have the notion of international managers who, presumably, demonstrate 'intercultural competence' (Iles, 1995) and, irrespective of their national and cultural origins, are equally able and comfortable managing operations anywhere in the world. The concept of geocentric orientation, and the notion of international managers, rely logically, in my view, on some universal, though nationality and culture-free, specification of effective processes of organising and managing. Both propositions are questionable, however.

Activity 11.2

1 Produce some examples of MNCs which, in your judgement, adopt an ethnocentric, regiocentric, polycentric and geocentric orientation.

2 Using your examples, produce a list of potential advantages and disadvantages experienced by MNCs adopting each orientation.

3 Compare your responses to 1 and 2 with those of a colleague.

Perlmutter's categorisation of orientations can be usefully compared with that produced by Calas (1992, *see* Lorbiecki, 1997). This latter classification of perspectives is directly located in the convergence/divergence debate mentioned in Chapter 4. We do not need to review the analysis in detail here as it will be sufficient for our purposes to discuss the four broad categories. The first of these is labelled 'universalistic'. Here, a view is taken that there is one best way to organise and manage, and that this way should be applied in all international activities and operations. We might relate this to an ethnocentric orientation. Paradoxically, it may also encompass a geocentric orientation. The second category is 'comparative'. This allows for some differences of significance and therefore some variation in approach. Perlmutter's regiocentric orientation may relate to this category. According to the analysis of Calas (1992), these first two categories can be associated with a 'convergence' hypothesis. The third category, 'relativistic', is associated with a 'divergence' hypothesis and therefore stands on the other side of the line in that debate. This category is, relatedly, associated with a view that difference is significant and important. We might therefore relate the category to polycentric. The fourth category, 'post-structural/ethnographic', questions the other three, and indeed would question Perlmutter's classification in total. In particular, such a perspective would challenge the possibility of a geocentric orientation which requires not only a universal approach or specification, but one which is not grounded in or derived from a particular set of cultural values. Lorbiecki (1997) adds a fifth category to those of Calas which she labels 'radical'. This, too, perhaps for additional and different reasons, would question the conceptual and practical possibility of a geocentric approach.

Development methods

Part of the critique of analyses of internationalisation provided by Calas (1992) relies on an argument that concepts such as organisation and management are essentially Western, if not exclusively European/American, and that associated theories and models are therefore the same. A similar argument is made by Stead and Lee (1996) in relation to HRD, although Lee (1996) suggests in the same volume that action learning as a development method has potential to cross cultural boundaries. It is the case in practice that action learning is commonly used in developing international managers (Iles, 1995, 1996). We will examine the method itself in the next section.

Methods adopted to develop managers and other employees to work successfully in 'global' or international organisations will in part relate to the orientation (Perlmutter, 1969) or perspective (Calas, 1992) informing and influencing decisions. Lorbiecki (1997) suggests that employers use two broad approaches: career management and training and development tactics. The use of international assignments can form part of both approaches. As Iles (1995) suggests, international assignments can also be used to 'enhance organisational learning and capability' (p. 399). While the field of international HRD has to be recognised to be relatively immature (Iles, 1996), a range of methods in addition to work assignments has been devised and applied. One method found in both business schools and other external providers, and in organisation-based programmes (Lorbiecki, 1997) is to internationalise employee development. What this means in practice is that formal courses take on an international dimension in their core content, usually in the form of teaching materials, examples and cases, with instructors and tutors drawn from an international base and, similarly, cohorts of learners composed of various nationalities (Iles, 1995, Lorbiecki, 1997). These kinds of approaches are probably more likely to be associated with a geocentric orientation. Methods such as language training and courses in cultural preparation/orientation (Iles, 1995) are most relevant when PCNs are used in foreign operations. They are, therefore, primarily associated with an ethnocentric orientation. The use of mentors and sponsors (Iles, 1996) is a method which can probably sit comfortably with any orientation.

Summary

As already noted, research and theory on the contribution of ED to international enterprises and organisational responses to globalisation is relatively under-developed and immature. If it is the case that organisations will become increasingly global in their operations and outlook, then perhaps the notion of 'inter-cultural competence' (Gertsen, 1991) will become increasingly relevant as the concept which supports development of research and theory on what constitutes international managers and how they might be developed. For now, we turn our attention to action learning, a method which has both conceptually and practically been shown to be relevant to international ED (Iles, 1995, 1996; Lee, 1996).

Activity 11.3

1 Review and revise your response to Activity 11.1(1) in the light of this section.

2 Research publications such as *People Management* to gain additional ideas on methods and techniques used by MNCs.

3 Consider the arguments for and against the possibility of a geocentric orientation and associated ideas on the international manager.

Action learning

The term 'action learning' is often misused and misunderstood. To avoid those possibilities, I wish to be clear from the start of this section that my use of the term refers exclusively to the name given by Reg Revans to a particular method of development which he devised (Revans, 1980, 1982, 1983). It is a little unfair perhaps to focus on associating action learning exclusively with a development method since the term encompasses a philosophy of management, and a theory of learning which leads to and supports the design principles on which the method is based (*see* Stewart, 1996). It is also true that refinements and revisions have been incorporated over the years which draw on additional though related philosophies and theories (e.g. McGill and Beatty, 1992). However, by focusing on action learning as a *method* of development, I hope to emphasise that the term does not mean simply learning by doing, and that it is not a sort of umbrella term which encompasses any or all methods which incorporate 'action'. So, while the philosophy and theory which gave rise to action learning will be mentioned, the primary purpose here is to describe the design principles and features which constitute action learning as intended by Revans.

Two additional introductory points will be useful. We have been concerned throughout this book with raising potential objections to conventional treatments of management and development. It is the case that action learning arose out of similar dissatisfactions, and that the method enables and supports a critical stance in relation to the established practices of both managing and developing employees (Willmott, 1997). Given that context, a critique of action learning itself will not be a high priority. Finally, it needs to be acknowledged that Revans argued the futility of writing and talking about action learning if a true understanding is to be gained (Stewart, 1996). However, he wrote and talked extensively about action learning and thereby gave permission to others to do so. The point indicates the essential meaning of the term: take the action and learn.

Philosophy of action learning

The philosophy of action learning is best described by articulating the basic assumptions made by Revans about the nature of managing and the nature of learning. There is something of a paradox in these two sets of assumptions. Revans was originally a physicist and, as such, an advocate of the scientific method. His theory of learning, labelled 'System Beta' (Stewart, 1996), approximates processes represented in that method. The reasoning in simple and simplified terms is as follows. Human knowledge is advanced through science which, in turn, derives and develops knowledge through application of the scientific method. Such advancement and application is driven by the search for answers to questions and solutions to problems. Individual learning both mirrors and is part of this process. Hence, the process of individual learning reflects the stages of the scientific method. This might be taken to indicate that Revans's work is in the tradition of realist research, reflecting a positivist perspective and functionalist paradigm. However, Revans's views on management and managing clearly reject the possibility of universal prescriptions and unproblematic specifications. Therefore, on this issue, Revans does not quite fit the previous description. This apparent paradox is probably the result, in part, of clear distinctions being drawn between the material and social worlds, and a pragmatic though principled concern to incorporate and synthesise useful and valid learning from a variety of perspectives. The nature of the possible paradox will be clear from the following description of basic assumptions:

Managing
- occurs in conditions of ignorance, confusion and uncertainty;
- is concerned with the discovery of appropriate solutions to pressing problems in those conditions through posing effective questions;
- involves personal risk on the part of individual managers and reveals personal values.

Learning
- involves the reordering and restructuring of existing knowledge, rather than acquisition of new knowledge;
- is concerned with knowing as *able to* rather than knowing *about*;
- follows action, rather than precedes it. Practices in education, training and development seem to imply dominant theories which suggest the opposite.

A comment on some of these assumptions will be appropriate. It is perhaps difficult to achieve agreement among managers on the first one, although, in my experience, most will acknowledge its truth if pressed. The other two assumptions about managing are more readily accepted. The first assumption on learning is resonant of and congruent with more recent work which conceptualises learning as creation of meaning (*see* Dixon, 1994 and Chapter 6). The final assumption relates to state education and ED practices in work organisations which both assume a model of 'first you learn and then you do'. Such a model is predicated on theories of learning which assume learning is separate from and precedes action.

Activity 11.4

1 Think about and record your response to each set of assumptions. In doing so, answer the following questions:

   (a) which do you agree with/disagree with?

   (b) what evidence do you have to support your conclusion?

   (c) how might you gather additional evidence to test the validity of each assumption?

2 Consider the implications/consequences for current approaches to managing and employee development of consciously applying Revans's assumptions.

3 Discuss your responses with a colleague and examine reasons for similarities and differences in your respective responses.

Design principles

A fundamental and important design principle which follows from these assumptions is that managers learn most effectively with and through each other by working to solve real problems in real time. I refer to managers because action learning was originally, and is still widely applied as, a method of management development, although there is no reason in principle why it cannot be used with any or all categories of staff. However, the additional design principles, detailed below, can be difficult to operationalise for non-managerial roles. These additional features follow from the first specified above and, like that one, from the basic assumptions.

Projects

Individuals participating in action-learning programmes must tackle a project. A project must also represent a live issue and problem requiring action in a real organisation. Revans distinguishes between puzzles and problems. The former are questions to which there will be only one answer, and that answer requires only application of 'programmed' (*see below*) knowledge for its discovery. An example might be to determine how much profit was generated in a given time period. In contrast, a problem is a question to which various answers are possible, and which cannot be answered by simple application of programmed knowledge. Determining an answer to a problem will also be influenced by personal and organisational values. An example would be whether to use profits to increase shareholders' dividends, invest in new technology, fund a pay rise for all or some employees, or support a charitable campaign.

Sets

Participants form small groups, usually between four and eight in number and known as sets. Each set meets regularly, say once a month, to critically review the progress of each individual member. Since projects are live issues, and should encompass implementation as well as diagnosis/recommendation, they provide a rich source of potential learning and development for individuals. The primary role of the set is to maximise that potential. This is achieved by members providing an appropriate amount and balance of support and challenge to each other and, in a way, holding each individual to account for progress in their project and development. There are no hard and fast rules for operation and conduct of set meetings, although guidelines can be and are suggested (McGill and Beatty 1992, Pedler, 1991).

Set adviser

Each set normally has a set adviser allocated to it. This person is someone experienced in the principles and operation of action learning, and who is skilled in facilitating learning and process consultation (*see* Stewart, 1996). Their role is to provide support and help to the set, especially in the early meetings when members are learning about the process. This may involve providing direct guidance. However, the role of set adviser illustrates an important part of the philosophy of action learning. Advisers are not cast in the role of experts and do not provide teaching or training. In fact, sets can operate without access to subject matter experts, although such expertise can be available in a programme and a set adviser can act as liaison to access expertise as and when a set decides it would be useful.

Syllabus

As might be clear by now, action-learning programmes do not operate to a predetermined or planned syllabus. Universal specifications of management skills or competencies are rejected on a number of grounds. First, most specifications are drawn up by subject experts. However, in the view of Revans, managers are the real experts on the demands and requirements of managing. Second, universal specifications by definition cannot accommodate the particular circumstances of specific contexts. Third, such specifications emphasise content at the expense of process, and it is the latter, according to the principles of action learning, which is of most importance in organising and managing.

Self as 'content'

This last point gives rise to the final feature of action-learning programmes. Perhaps the most critical purpose and outcome is individual learning about self, and related understanding of the role and impact of personal values. Thus, members of action-learning sets learn much about themselves as individuals and, to use Revans's phrase, as a cohort of comrades in adversity.

A final design feature concerns the nature of projects. We have already said that these must represent problems rather than puzzles. There are also four possibilities of the type of problem in relation to a particular individual. The first type was emphasised in the original and early programmes set up by Revans. This is 'different job and different organisation'. Here, participants are drawn from a number of organisations co-operating in a programme, and each individual 'swaps' both organisation and function for their project. For example, a marketing executive from a high street bank would tackle a personnel problem in an NHS trust hospital. The second possibility is 'own job and different organisation'. Here, our marketing executive would tackle a marketing problem in, for example, the same hospital as before. The third variation is 'different job and own organisation'. As the name suggests, our marketing executive would tackle, say, an HRD problem in their own bank. The final possibility is 'own job and own organisation'. This is perhaps the least satisfactory since the potential challenge and associated development is less than in the other three types. It is, though, probably the most common where action learning has been incorporated into formal education programmes for managers and other professionals.

Discussion

As well as the basic assumptions described earlier, these design principles and features derive from two simple formulae that Revans devised to represent and support the philosophy of action learning (*see* McGill and Beatty, 1992). These are:

$$L \geq C$$
$$L = P + Q.$$

The first refers to the argument that the survival of any organisation requires that the rate of learning must be at least equal to, if not greater than, the rate of change being experienced. Since this argument is now more or less conventional wisdom, both within and because of the literature on the learning organisation (*see* next section), we might argue that Revans was ahead of his time, in this respect at least. The second formula summarises the basic assumptions on learning. Here, learning is argued to be the result of, and therefore to require, the application of programmed knowledge (P) and the posing of insightful questions (Q). Programmed knowledge in this formulation refers to what already exists in terms of procedures, technologies and techniques used in management. Accounting techniques such as break-even analysis and cash-flow planning, or operational planning techniques such as critical path analysis or work-flow analysis, are examples of programmed knowledge. This type of knowledge is only appropriate for puzzles. Problem resolution requires learning, and this requires asking and seeking answers to difficult questions. The distinction perhaps has some relationship and connection with the distinction between explicit and implicit knowledge (*see* Chapter 6). For example, implementing projects requires bringing about change in organisations.

Recognising the role and significance of power, and organisations as political contexts, Revans suggests the importance of three critical questions in achieving implementation: who knows?, who cares? and who can? It might be argued that effective or successful managers implicitly understand the importance of these questions and how to go about answering them in particular contexts. Articulating implicit understanding and transforming it into explicit and public knowledge can, arguably, subject it to testing and validation, and thereby lead to both individual and organisational learning. Achieving this can be said to be a primary purpose of sets.

Action learning is not without critics and criticisms (*see* Pedler, 1997). However, its use and application continues to grow and, in my judgement, such growth reflects a recognition of its relevance and potential. The basic philosophy and related principles perhaps more accurately reflect the experience of individuals in and of work organisations. This being the case, the features applied in design and operation of action learning programmes have resonance for participants in a way which more formal or traditional programmes do not. Perhaps the practical limitations which tend to limit use of programmes to managerial staff is the most significant potential weakness. These limitations can, however, be seen as opportunities for learning and development rather than as insurmountable barriers. Recent research confirms the value of the method (Williams, 1996) and, with that support, I would argue the continued relevance of action learning as an employee development strategy.

Activity 11.5

1 Using the Burrell and Morgan framework introduced in Chapter 2, allocate the philosophy of action learning to a particular paradigm of organisation theory. Produce a justification for your response.

2 Consider the potential strengths and weaknesses of using action learning for (a) managerial employees, and (b) non-managerial employees in your organisation.

3 Focusing on either category of employee from **2**, consider how you would go about setting up and implementing an action-learning programme in your organisation.

4 Based on all the above, how appropriate or otherwise do you consider action learning as an employee development strategy?

The concept of the learning organisation

We stated earlier that arguments supporting action-learning programmes are essentially the same as those employed in support of the learning organisation. A more direct connection has been argued by Beck (1994), who suggests the method can be instrumental in the creation of learning organisations. This suggests the possibility of integration of the three topics in this chapter. Globalisation and the need for international managers is a significant change in the experience of work organisations. The ability of organisations to respond to significant change will be enhanced by moving in the direction of becoming a learning organisation (*see* Senge, 1993). Action learning supports such movement (Beck, 1994, Pedler, 1997). To finally create that possibility we need to gain some understanding of the concept of the learning organisation.

The concept of learning organisation represents an ideal type. It suggests a philosophy of and approach to organising and managing which is responsive to changed and changing conditions, and which facilitates and supports effective change management (Moss-Jones, 1994). There are many and varied definitions of the term (*see* Stewart, 1996). Most emphasise individual and collective learning to effect change in organisational behaviour and performance. A key focus of this learning is through 'learning to learn' (Swieringa and Weirdsma, 1992). This focus in turn reflects the influence of ideas about single loop, double loop and deutero-learning formulated by Argyris and Schon (1978) on developing the concept of the learning organisation. Single loop learning results in amendments, refinements and improvements in current practice. It arises from questions concerning how to do existing 'things' better. Double loop learning is more concerned with questioning existing and established practices, and with challenging the assumptions which lie behind them. The result is more likely to be innovation in processes and practices. Deutero-learning is concerned with the processes of learning which lead to single and double loop learning. The result of such learning is therefore learning about learning, with the effect of improving learning processes. Each of these forms of learning, at both individual and collective levels, is reflected in the following definition of a learning organisation as one where:

> **People continually expand their capacity to create the results they truly desire, where new and expansive patterns of thinking are nurtured, where collective aspiration is set free, and where people are continually learning to learn together.**

> (Senge, 1993, p. 3)

Senge's definition and work on the concept of learning organisation has been highly influential (*see also* Senge *et al.*, 1994). One potential criticism of his definition is that it assumes the possibility, and perhaps advocates the desirability, of a 'unitarist' frame of reference which reflects a functionalist paradigm. It is then open to criticism from the perspectives of alternative paradigms, perhaps especially those of a radical structuralist or associated critical theory analysis of organisations (*see* Chapter 2 and Alvesson and Willmott, 1996). However, in common with other definitions, Senge's articulation can be seen to be influenced by established theories in organisation studies such as socio-technical analysis and more recent arguments connecting organisational learning and strategic success (Stewart, 1996). The definition is also suggestive of the kind of features that are likely to be associated with a learning organisation.

Features of learning organisations

It needs to be recognised in any examination of the features of a learning organisation that operationalising the concept is extremely difficult and, given the state of current understanding, any attempt to do so has to be treated as provisional. As Swieringa and Weirdsma (1992) suggest, the metaphor of traveller as opposed to tourist is most appropriate in describing what might be argued to be the central feature of learning organisations. In determining their journey, in both space and time, tourists engage in detailed planning with specific points being predetermined and which can be used to plot progress. In contrast, travellers start their journey with only a broad idea of where, when and why they wish to travel. A final destination may not even be specified. The detail of the journey is decided as it progresses and adjustments made in response to unforeseen and unpredictable circumstances, for example, changes in the weather or the attractiveness or otherwise of a particular locality. This metaphor is very useful in arguing against any detailed specification of what constitutes a learning organisation. It also supports a view that becoming a learning organisation is a journey, not a destination (*see* Pedler *et* al., 1996). However, as Campbell and Cairns (1994) argue, deliberate and positive attempts to make progress in that journey implies some attempt at managing the process which, in turn, implies some planning and monitoring. The following features are therefore presented in the context of both sets of arguments.

Based on my thinking about the subject, I have previously argued four general features that can be associated with the concept of a learning organisation and which need to be nurtured and developed (Stewart, 1994a, 1996). The first is an organisation which is populated by individuals who are both committed to and skilled in managing their own development. Nurturing and developing this feature requires, among other things, promotion and support of self-development. The second feature is the existence and application of organisational processes and development methods which encourage and support mutual learning. Action learning programmes are an example of the latter. Incorporation of learning objectives and review of their achievement into business and work plans, and/or learning and development targets into performance objectives, are examples of the former. These first two features promote individual and team learning, but are not sufficient to create a learning organisation. Individual and team learning need to be shared and disseminated more widely in the organisation.

This third feature, methods and processes for disseminating and sharing learning, is emphasised by Jashpara (1993) and perhaps reflects Nonaka's arguments on converting implicit knowledge to explicit knowledge (*see* Chapter 6). Suggestions on such processes and methods are provided by Pedler *et al.* (1991) and are described later in this section. The final feature is that of organisation climate and management style. An organisation and management style which engenders control, dependence and conformity is unlikely to sustain the features described so far and is, relatedly, unlikely to make progress in becoming a learning organisation. Such an approach is not compatible with the concept of learning organisation. Instead, a style which promotes and supports experimentation, risk-taking, involvement in decisions and independence in thought and action is required. These characteristics are congruent with those which Dixon (1994) argues are required for organisational learning. They are also consistent with a philosophy of organising and managing inherent in Senge's (1993) definition.

In my view, all four features are essential to becoming a learning organisation. We will now examine the work of Pedler and his colleagues, and that of Senge, to compare their ideas on features constituting a learning organisation with each other and with mine.

Pedler (1991, 1996) and his colleagues are perhaps the leading European writers on the subject. However, they use the term 'learning company' rather than 'learning organisation'. This is not to exclude public and voluntary sector organisations. The concept of 'company' is preferred because of positive associations with similar concepts such as 'community'. According to their work, a learning company will develop and display the following 11 characteristics, or features:

- a learning approach to strategy
- participative policy making
- informating
- formative accounting and control
- internal exchange
- reward flexibility

- enabling structures
- boundary workers as environmental scanners
- inter-company learning
- learning climate
- self-development opportunities for all employees.

Some of these features, for instance the final two, are immediately resonant with my argued features on self-development and organisation style. The same is true of the first two features, which suggest an approach to organising and managing which encourages involvement and experimentation. The features of informating, formative accounting and internal exchange are specific ways in which learning can be disseminated and shared. The feature of reward flexibility can be misleadingly titled. It does not necessarily refer to rewarding flexible behaviour and attitudes. The main point is to have the capability to quickly adjust reward systems to respond to changed and changing conditions, hence 'reward flexibility'. The idea of boundary workers as environmental scanners is interesting, as is that of inter-company learning. The former refers to the fact that those in direct contact with external agents, for instance, receptionists, sales staff, customer service staff and those employed in purchasing, all have valuable data and engage in their own learning processes about the external world. Such intelligence and learning has great potential value, but is usually poorly used. Inter-company learning refers to co-operative and collaborative relationships with suppliers, competitors and other relevant organisations through networks such as trade and employer associations. Again, such networks present valuable potential for learning which is seldom fully maximised.

Peter Senge (1993) suggests a learning organisation is one where five disciplines are formally practised. In Senge's terms, a discipline is a 'body of theory and technique that must be studied and mastered to be put into practice' (p. 10). He also argues that to 'practise a discipline is to be a lifelong learner' (p. 11). Applying the five learning disciplines, which for Senge are the essential components or 'technologies', is the mark of a learning organisation. Hence we can argue that, in our terms, application of these disciplines represents the essential features of a learning organisation. The learning disciplines are:

- personal mastery
- mental models
- team learning
- building shared vision
- systems thinking.

We can elaborate on each discipline by comparing them to the features already discussed. Personal mastery has some similarity with being committed and able to manage one's own self-development. However, Senge includes a sense of and clarity about personal 'vision' in his formulation. Such clarity can be very useful in focusing and directing self-development. The discipline of mental models is concerned with surfacing, questioning and challenging basic assumptions. It recognises the powerful influence of models in shaping decisions and behaviour, and therefore the need to continually expose, test and formulate alternative perspectives. Such processes can be encouraged and informed by many of the features suggested by Pedler *et al.* (1991), perhaps especially those related to approaches to organising and managing, e.g. policy making and strategy.

Senge argues that teams rather than individuals are the basic learning unit in modern organisations. His discipline of team learning includes the practice of dialogue as well as discussion. The latter can be seen as similar to single loop learning, and the former as similar to double loop learning. The processes of dialogue and team learning are also resonant with mutual learning. The feature of shared vision emphasises the need for individuals to hold and articulate a personal vision. Senge rejects the value of organisation visions formulated on a 'top-down' basis, and argues that in a learning organisation the basic purpose represented by a genuinely shared vision will promote real commitment. This argument is implicit in his definition. Perhaps there are links here with the ideas on culture and climate contained in the earlier features.

The final discipline, systems thinking, reflects Senge's argument that the world, both material and social, consists of, and is the result of, series of complex interrelationships. This argument has some similarities with the concept of autopoiesis (*see* Chapter 4) in that both suggest a false distinction between organism, or organisation, and 'the environment' by arguing closer and more symbiotic relationships than such a distinction would normally allow. Viewing the world in terms of systems thinking would also support the argument that the process we refer to as globalisation has impact and consequences for all organisations, irrespective of their participation or otherwise in international trade. Senge's views on systems thinking emphasise the need to work hard at understanding the complex, causal relationships which provide explanations for success or failure experienced by particular organisations at particular points in time. Many of the features suggested by Pedler and his colleagues, especially those which encourage openness to learning from a variety of sources, would support the application and operation of systems thinking.

Discussion

There are philosophical and conceptual problems with the idea of a learning organisation in addition to those associated with operationalising the concept for application. The concept requires adoption of a realist position in that it not only gives entitative status to organisations, but takes this further in conceptualising organisations as learning entities. Yet many of the features suggested by both descriptive and prescriptive analyses of what might constitute such an entity seem to have a greater degree of empathy and coherence with a non-realist, interpretive understanding of organisations. This might be usefully illustrated by Senge's arguments on team learning and shared vision. It is possible, using the work of Senge and others, to build an argument that the concept is associated with postmodernist and, relatedly, anti-positivist analyses in organisation theory (*see* Franklin *et al.*, 1998). Yet Senge's views on systems thinking are clearly positivist in the value placed on the search for causal relationships. In addition and as argued earlier, the concept can be shown to be the result of influences from established theories from within mainstream thinking in organisation and management theory, for example, open systems theory and strategic management (Stewart, 1996). Perhaps these apparent philosophical and conceptual confusions can be explained by what Burrell and Morgan (1979) refer to as 'ontological oscillation'. Whatever the case may be, we can say that the concept has established an influential position in management thought, and that it presents appropriate opportunities for influence to HRD specialists.

We have not had space here to review all the literature which the influential position of the concept of learning organisation has generated. Neither have we been able to provide a full critique of the concept. I would argue, however, that anyone with a professional or academic interest in employee development in the next century needs to take the concept seriously and therefore to extend the analysis provided in this chapter.

Activity 11.6

1 Examine the features of a learning organisation suggested by Stewart, those by Senge and those by Pedler *et al.* Produce an analysis of similarities and differences in the three sets of features.

2 Compare the results of **1** with your response to **3** in Activity 11.1. Consider any changes you might want to make to your original list of characteristics, and produce a revised version of your definition.

3 Assess your own organisation against your revised definition and determine to what extent your organisation meets the definition. Use your revised list of characteristics to provide a more detailed assessment and to determine what changes would be necessary to move towards becoming a learning organisation.

4 Based on these results, discuss with a colleague the relative merits and usefulness, and otherwise, of the learning organisation concept.

Summary and conclusion

This chapter has applied a straightforward and mainstream definition of strategy in order to examine three broad-based and organisation-focused employee development methods. This has resulted in a discussion of international ED, action learning and the learning organisation concept. Each of these is argued to have particular relevance to current and future practice. We have also seen that each, perhaps especially internationalisation and the learning organisation, has conceptual problems when we attempt to translate theory into practice. We might conclude therefore that providing prescriptions for practice is not without problems. Internationalising ED and pursuing the learning organisation concept are both argued by many writers to be appropriate development responses to the changed and changing conditions of organisation contexts. Providing those responses is, however, a little more complicated than some of those writers would have us believe. Even so, a further conclusion, that the strategies examined here have potential usefulness, seems reasonable. In summary, a reasonable conclusion would seem to be that thoughtful and pragmatic application of the ED strategies discussed in this chapter can be of value in improving the contribution of the ED function.

We move on in the next chapter to examine an additional possible strategy, that of management development. This strategy will be examined in much more detail, given its prevalence and significance. It will be useful, for purposes of comparison and relative assessment, to bear in mind your conclusions on this chapter as you read my exposition in the next.

Case study 11

ABC Limited is a semi-autonomous division of a large credit card company, Creditcard, which is a wholly owned subsidiary of one of the large UK banks. ABC Limited exists to service problem accounts. These are defined as those in serious arrears and/or with balances significantly in excess of agreed limits. The ethos in the company is to move away from standard and proceduralised responses to such accounts. Indeed, staff are encouraged to continue to define account holders as customers and to deal with the circumstances being experienced by each individual. For example, unemployment and divorce are the most common reasons cited by customers as the main cause of their inability to service their debt to Creditcard. The aim of ABC Limited is to reach accommodations and agreements with customers which reflect their circumstances and satisfy the requirements of Creditcard.

Such an approach to dealing with problem accounts is not entirely altruistic. Creditcard is an established company and one of the market leaders. The industry is experiencing intensification of competition from new entrants such as supermarkets, other retailers and overseas operators, especially from the USA. Creditcard is determined to maintain and to continue to increase its market share in the face of this competition. Responses to customers experiencing problems is seen as a means of retaining potentially valuable business and building customer loyalty. The approach represents a shift from the previous work of staff which was largely determined by strict procedures. Perhaps for reasons different to those of Creditcard, the shift has the overwhelming support of employees in ABC Limited who not only value more discretion in their work but also are now more able to give expression to their personal empathy and sympathy with customers.

A number of changes have taken place in ABC Limited to support this shift in orientation. The formal hierarchy has been reduced from ten to five layers. Individualised job descriptions have been abolished and replaced by descriptions of 'job clusters' which are based on the critical processes of the organisation, e.g. customer contact, support services, technical development. A vision statement, a set of core values and a code of conduct have all been developed through organisation-wide consultation involving all 650 staff and promulgated through vision workshops. Cultural artefacts such as job titles, separate dining rooms and reserved car parking which emphasise differential status have been abolished.

Arthur Clarke is satisfied with the role of the training department in supporting these changes. Arthur was formerly training manager with ABC. However, to signal a new and changing role for the department, Arthur has, with support from the ABC board, retitled it the learning and development department. Arthur is therefore now learning and development manager. His six professional staff are called learning and development consultants to reflect their changing role. Training and development has always been valued in ABC Limited and is very well established. At any one time, more than a quarter of staff are receiving full support for qualification-based courses ranging from Level 2 NVQs in customer service to MBAs. Other staff are undertaking courses less directly relevant to their role and the organisation, with some, but not full, support. Arthur and his staff continue to play a significant role in bringing about the cultural change intended and desired within ABC. They facilitated large parts of the consultation exercises leading to the vision and values statements, and were responsible for designing and implementing the vision workshops. A management development programme intended to support adoption of a more participatory and supportive management style is nearing completion. Arthur and his staff are examining ways of introducing a process of personal development plans. Arthur believes it would be incongruous to provide employees with more discretion in their jobs while still fully controlling their development. ABC Limited has an established and well-utilised learning resource centre (LRC). In fact, according to figures Arthur has available, the LRC in ABC has the best record of all the companies in the bank and one of the best in the industry. Arthur is therefore confident that introducing a formalised approach to personal development will be well received.

Being a keen advocate and practitioner of personal development, Arthur is learning all he can about the idea of the learning organisation. This has involved attending a couple of conferences, reading three or four books on the subject and accessing numerous articles from professional journals describing the experiences of other organisations. Arthur has shared his learning and thinking with his staff and some management colleagues. Based on this, he is convinced that pursuing the concept in ABC will be an appropriate development strategy to support and consolidate the ongoing culture change programme. Arthur believes that ABC already demonstrates some of the suggested characteristics of a learning organisation. Others would need to be established or developed and improved. As a starting point, Arthur has decided that he needs to carry out an assessment of where the organisation is now. While he accepts and agrees with the argument that 'becoming a learning organisation is a journey not a destination', he also believes that some form of assessment is necessary to establish priorities for action and attention.

Discussion questions

1 What model of the learning organisation would you recommend to Arthur, and why?

2 What evidence is there that ABC Limited currently demonstrates some characteristics of a learning organisation?

3 How can and should Arthur go about his assessment? For example, what indicators or characteristics should he focus on, what data should he collect and analyse, how should he access/collect that data?

4 What are your views on the appropriateness or otherwise of pursuing learning organisation status as an employee development strategy within ABC Limited?

Suggested reading

Burgoyne, J. and Reynolds, M. (eds.) (1997) *Management Learning: Integrating Perspectives in Theory and Practice*. London: Sage.

Mabey, C. and Salaman, G. (1995) *Strategic Human Resource Management*. Oxford: Blackwell Business.

Senge, P. *et al*. (1994) *The Fifth Discipline Fieldbook*. London: Nicholas Brearly.

Stewart, J. (1996) *Managing Change Through Training and Development (2nd edn)*. London: Kogan Page.

Stewart, J. and McGoldrick, J. (eds.) (1996) *Human Resource Development: Perspectives, Strategies and Practice*. London: Financial Times Pitman Publishing.

CHAPTER 12

Management development

Introduction

The purpose of this chapter is to critically examine the concept and practice of management development. This will necessarily entail a consideration of the meaning of the terms management and development, and the results of joining them together to construct the concept of 'management development'. Expressed in this way, the task can be seen to be both ambitious and complex. Such ambition and complexity are perhaps beyond the scope of a single chapter if full justice is to be done to the task. However, there are certain important arguments that can be discerned from existing research and writing on the subject, and these arguments are critical to any serious consideration of the theory and practice of management development. The aim, therefore, is to identify and examine the important arguments and debates surrounding management development.

Management development is concerned with application. Application in turn raises questions to do with *how*. Such questions can take at least three forms. First, how *is* management development done? Second, how *could* management development be done? Third, how *should* management development be done? Answering this last question requires a prescription of what is right, or correct or best. In line with the philosophy of the book, I do not believe such prescriptions are possible, even if they might be desirable, or desired. My concern in dealing with each of the 'how' questions is to provide responses which, in my judgement, will be most useful and helpful in informing decisions on and in practice. As part of that judgement, I will be primarily, although not exclusively, concerned with the first two formulations of 'how'.

These opening points set the scope and limitations of the chapter. I will focus on examining *what* constitutes management development, and *how* it is and might be practised. In doing so, I will be necessarily selective in the material I use. My selections are guided by what I see as important and useful arguments and analyses. By the end of the chapter, you can expect to be able to achieve the objectives listed below.

> **CHAPTER OBJECTIVES**
>
> ● Articulate a range of perspectives on and definitions of management development.
>
> ● Critically evaluate varying approaches to management development.
>
> ● Formulate and argue a personal position on the value of investment in management development.
>
> ● Produce, justify and defend proposals for investment in management development.

Management development – an overview

Management development (MD) is both complex and problematic. In part, this arises from the fact that the term has no single or definitive meaning. Definitions and meanings vary according to the varying perspectives adopted by different writers (Storey, 1989, Harrison, 1997). Related to this is the fact that MD can and does pursue various agendas (Lees, 1992). In other words, investment in MD can be undertaken to serve different purposes. Mabey and Salaman (1995) suggest four possible purposes, each with distinct characteristics and problems, and derived from different assumptions. Their four purposes, or agendas, are summarised in Table 12.1.

Table 12.1 Management development agendas

Type	Description
Functional performance	Focuses on knowledge, skills and attitudes of individual managers. Assumes unproblematic link between MD and performance.
Political reinforcement	Focuses on reinforcing and propagating skills and attitude valued by top managers. Assumes top managers are correct in their diagnosis and prescription.
Compensation	MD is seen as part of the reward system for managers. Assumes development is motivational and encourages commitment.
Psychic defence	MD provides a 'safety value' for managerial anxieites. Assumes competitive careers and associated anxieties.

Source: Based on Mabey, C. and Salaman G. (1995) *Strategic Human Resource Management*. Oxford: Blackwell Business.

A second problem is that, notwithstanding variation in meaning, much research and writing, and therefore common usage of the term, assumes or implies formalised and structured systems within work organisations for the provision of MD (Mumford, 1997, Harrison, 1997). Such research and writing, more or less explicitly, further assumes medium to large-scale enterprises which can afford the investment required to operate, for example, sophisticated approaches to performance management. Indeed, each of the agendas included in Mabey and Salaman's typology in Table 12.1 seems to assume MD as a formalised and structured system, and thus the typology as a whole is limited to MD being defined and constituted by such approaches. There are two weaknesses with this perspective. First, the small firms sector is both a significant and growing feature of the UK economy (DfEE, 1995). Perspectives which assume formalised and structured MD systems will have little relevance or application in this important sector. Second, an assumption of MD as a formal system excludes, literally by definition, the role and contribution of what is variously referred to as accidental, informal or situated learning and development (*see* Fox, 1997, Mumford, 1997).

We can summarise the analysis so far by stating that disagreement exists about what constitutes MD and that, within the context of that disagreement, common usage of the term tends to exclude both important contexts of application and a range of potentially significant, if informal, learning and development opportunities. This confused and confusing situation is complicated even further by examining the concepts of 'management' and 'managing'.

The nature of managerial work

Formalised and structured approaches to MD assume, to some extent, that *managing* is a formal and structured activity. Perhaps more accurately, perspectives on MD which emphasise formalised and systemised approaches assume the possibility and actuality of clear and unambiguous specifications of management tasks and managerial behaviour. However, we have already seen in this book some reasons to doubt the possibility and actuality of such specifications. Critical and processual views of managing raise doubts about the conventional view of managing as a rational and technical activity. The processual view finds support in recent work focused directly on management learning (Chia, 1997). Doubts about conventional views on management are supported and confirmed by earlier and empirical research. The works of, for example, Stewart (1982), Mintzberg (1973), Kotter (1982) and Watson (1994) all suggest that what managers actually do is far removed from the rationalist and ordered specifications found in many textbooks. The pictures drawn by these empirical studies suggest an unstructured, unco-ordinated, unplanned and unreflective world which demands and receives, on a daily basis, short-span attention to and decisions on myriad complex issues. Such pictures stand in contrast to the logical, ordered and rational portraits contained in universalist prescriptions of management, and associated MD programmes.

Two significant implications arise from this argument. First, management as process encompasses a wider range of individuals than might be included in more conventional approaches to MD. As Watson (1994) argues, *all* managers are inextricably bound up in strategy making, and thus in contributing to managing the organisation. This argument is taken further by Chia (1997), who suggests that every individual employee is part of the process of managing. By implication, we can say that all employees are engaged in managing the organisations which employ them. Such a view finds support, from different perspectives and for different reasons, in the work of Fredericks and Stewart (1996), and that of Harrison (1997, especially Chapter 19). So, we can argue that management development could, and perhaps should, encompass wider constituencies than conventional treatments normally suggest.

The second implication concerns both the content and methods of MD. It is often argued that MD needs to be located in, and to support the achievement of, business, or organisation, imperatives (Harrison, 1997, Mumford, 1997, Jones and Woodcock, 1985). This prescription is not as simple as it may appear, for two reasons. First, it assumes those imperatives will be clear, unambiguous and predetermined. However, deciding business or organisation imperatives is part of the managing process. And selecting particular imperatives rather than others is, in part, the result of a political process, itself involving the interests, values and power bases of varying and, sometimes, competing groups (*see* Watson, 1994, Alvesson and Willmott, 1996). Second, if managing is indeed messy, confusing and uncertain, as suggested by the empirical studies referred to earlier, it is by no means clear how business imperatives can, will or should be achieved. Thus, we can argue that if MD is to truly reflect the requirements of organisation imperatives, the content cannot be universally prescribed, and methods need to recognise and work with the informal, unsystematic and political nature of managerial processes.

Activity 12.1

1 Think about the variety of potential interest groups in your organisation. What organisation imperatives might each favour and which will be in conflict with each other?

2 To what extent are management tasks and behaviour seen as being rational, ordered and predictable in your organisation? Is such a view a reasonable representation of the actuality and reality of the demands placed on managers?

3 Categorise the MD agenda in your organisation according to the types listed in Table 12.1.

4 Consider the extent to which the MD agenda reflects your answers to **1** and **2**.

The nature of development

The concept of development raises additional problems for thinking about what constitutes MD, and how it could or should be practised. One problem is to consider whether and how development is distinct from education and training; in other words, to consider again the questions raised in Chapter 2. Mumford (1997) suggests that the words education and training tend to focus attention on inputs, while the terms learning and development focus attention on results, or outputs. From that perspective, we might say that education and training are ways of achieving development and, therefore, that they contribute to, but do not constitute, management development. This can be a useful formulation since it suggests that MD does not necessarily require education or training and, relatedly, that alternative or additional approaches and methods are possible. This is similar to the case made in Chapter 2. As a reminder, Chapter 2 argued that attempts to distinguish between education and training lead to sterile debates which overlook the more important common feature that both represent deliberate interventions in learning processes. We can then dispose of this first problem by concluding that education and training programmes represent two ways of practising MD, which may or may not form part of the design of MD schemes and activities.

We have said that, in Mumford's (1997) view, development focuses on outcomes. However, this view can be problematic. It raises questions concerning the nature of those outcomes, and how and when they are, or become, known. For example, should, or even can, the outcomes of MD be specified in advance of any planned activity? The empirical analyses of the nature of managerial work would suggest that knowing what outcomes are needed or desirable in advance would be difficult, at least with any degree of specificity or confidence. The processual view of managing questions the idea, let alone the possibility, of 'fixed' or 'end' states which are capable of specification (Chia, 1996). Development is defined by some (e.g. Pedler and Boydell, 1985) as transformational change towards a different, but unknown, state of being. So, each of these varying perspectives would question the notion of specifiable outcomes. This is not to say that development is not concerned with outcomes. The point is to question conventional wisdom on MD, which would suggest that outcomes can and should be specified in advance (*see* next section).

A very useful analysis of the concept of development, especially as it applies to management learning and development, is provided by Monica Lee (Lee, 1997). Four different conceptions, or ways of understanding development, are suggested. Each conception varies in the assumptions and beliefs which are implicitly or explicitly applied to two factors. The first factor is the nature of the individual, which, according to varying perspectives, consists of either a unitary or co-regulated identity. The basic distinction here is the degree of involvement of others in creating and constructing the individual. In other words, the extent to which 'I' and who and what 'I am' exist independently of the perceptions, actions and behaviour of others and the social experience 'I' share with others (*see also* Chapter 5). The second factor is a little more straightforward and relates to the previous discussion. It concerns the 'end point' of development. This can be assumed to be either known or unknown. This now gives four broad possibilities: co-regulated identity and known end point, co-regulated identity and unknown end point, unitary identity and known end point, and unitary identity and unknown end point. These combinations are used by Lee (1997) to suggest four broad approaches to development, summarised in Table 12.2.

Lee (1997) goes on to argue that these conceptions of development can be and are applied to individuals, groups and organisations. She also attempts to highlight dilemmas associated with each approach, including those for professional developers. The value of her work here is to support the argument that the concept of development is complex and problematic. Her framework will be useful, too, in examining definitions of MD and the place of varying, and perhaps competing, methods.

To close this discussion of development, we can perhaps conclude that the concept is concerned with change and movement. These characteristics seem to be inherent in each

Table 12.2 Approaches to management development

Approach	Characteristics
Maturation	Assumes a unitary identity and known end point. Development involves passing through known and predetermined stages.
Shaping	This approach combines a co-regulated identity and known end point. The basic difference to maturation is that the end point is not determined by some inevitable process but is open to choice and decision. However, it is known.
Voyage	Assumes unknown end point and unitary identity. Development represents a journey 'into the self'.
Emergent	Combines co-regulated identity and unknown end point. This approach, in simple terms, applies the idea of 'voyage' to the social system of which the individual is a part, and development therefore becomes a joint, interactive and interdependent process.

Source: Based on Lee, M. (1997) 'The developmental approach: a critical reconsideration', in Burgoyne, J. and Reynolds, M. (eds) *Management Learning*. London: Sage Publications.

of Lee's approaches, and are in line with the arguments of Mumford (1997), Harrison (1997) and Pedler and Boydell (1985), among others. They are also, especially the notion of movement, congruent with a processual analysis of organisations (Chia, 1996). Having established the problematic status of the two central concepts of management and development, we will move on to consider how they are related in conceptions of management development.

Activity 12.2

1 Consider current approaches to MD in your organisation and answer the following questions:

    (a) what conception of development, in terms of Table 12.2, seems to be applied?

    (b) to what extent are education and training used to contribute to MD?

    (c) what are your views on the validity and usefulness of current approaches?

2 Discuss your responses with a colleague.

Management development – definitions and meanings

As was said earlier, MD can have a number of different meanings. One factor which provides a common distinction between different conceptions of MD is the focus, or emphasis, on *manager* as opposed to *management* development (Harrison, 1997). The former implies a primary concern with *individual* learning and development, and a purpose for MD associated with improving individual ability and performance. In contrast to this, the latter implies a primary concern with collective learning and development, and a purpose for MD associated with producing shared values and consistency in management style and approach. The focus in this conception of MD is then the organisation as an entity rather than the individual manager. We can therefore suggest two possible and different focuses for MD practices: the organisation or the individual.

While each of the two possible focuses suggests varying specific purposes, the broader purpose of MD programmes can also be said to vary, and there are again two broad possibilities. The first is primarily concerned with changing behaviour, either of individual managers or of the organisation as a whole, as a means of maintaining or improving performance. The second is primarily concerned with ensuring availability of skills and experience to meet future demands. This purpose can be applied to individual managers in the sense of preparing them for future promotion opportunities, or to the organisation as an entity in the sense of ensuring a supply of managerial ability to fill senior management positions as they become vacant. In both cases, the purpose represents an attempt to manage internal labour markets through interventions in career progression. Of course, more recent works might question the possibility or advisability of 'managed careers' in current and future employment contexts (*see* Handy, 1994, Hirsch and Jackson, 1995, Pemberton, 1995). Others suggest individual responses to this argued changing context (Bridges, 1995, Crainer, 1995). The argument here is that some conceptions of MD assume a purpose concerned with managed career progression.

The analysis in this section so far suggests a possible framework for categorising varying conceptions and definitions of MD. The framework categorises definitions according to whether individuals or organisations provide the primary **focus**, and according to whether changed behaviour or career progression provides the primary **purpose**. The resulting framework is given in Fig. 12.1. My suggestion is that most conceptions or definitions of MD can be accommodated by one of the four boxes in the framework. As we shall see later, the same framework can be useful in categorising varying approaches and methods since these have logical connections to varying conceptions and definitions.

The value and usefulness of the framework in Fig. 12.1 can be examined and evaluated by analysing some formal definitions of MD. One which reflects many conceptions of MD is that provided by Jones and Woodcock (1985).

> **. . . the total process which an organisation adopts in preparing its managers for the growth and change that occur in their working environment.**
>
> (Jones and Woodcock, 1985, p. 1)

This definition appears to emphasise individual managers rather than organisation entities as a focus, and future requirements rather than current behaviour as a purpose. This definition therefore appears to fit into quadrant 3 of the framework.

A more recent definition is that offered by Mumford (1997).

> **An attempt to improve managerial effectiveness through a learning process.**
>
> (Mumford, 1997, p. 6)

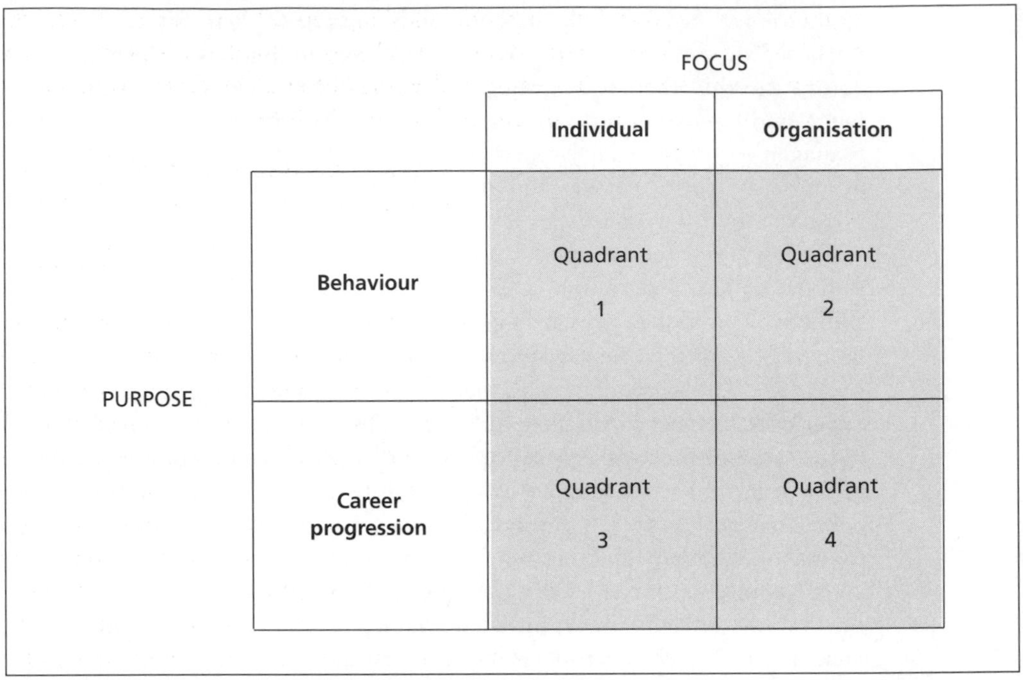

Fig. 12.1 Dimensions of management development

It seems clear from the definition that the purpose of MD in this conception is improving current performance, and therefore is associated more with behaviour than career progression. The question of focus is a little less clear. However, Mumford explains a shift in his thinking, and therefore his definition, between the second and third editions of his book (Mumford, 1993, 1997). This shift has taken out the words 'planned and deliberate' as adjectives attached to learning process to accommodate the significant contribution of accidental, incidental and informal learning. This shift and explanation makes clear a concern with the learning of individual managers. Therefore, we can with some confidence place Mumford's definition in quadrant 1 of the framework.

A further example is taken from Harrison (1997). In distinguishing between manager and management development, Harrison offers the following definition of the latter.

> **Building a shared culture across the whole management group and enhancing management capability throughout the organisation in order to improve the organisation's capability to survive and prosper.**

(Harrison, 1997, p. 356)

There is little room for doubt that Harrison, in this definition, sees MD as having a primary focus on the organisation, rather than on managers as *individuals*. The dimension of purpose is less clear or certain. However, use of the term capability suggests a future orientation, as does the concern with survival. We can therefore argue that in terms of purpose, there is greater emphasis on career progression than on current performance. This argument is strengthened if we adopt a view that ensuring a supply of appropriately developed managers to fill senior positions is significant in achieving organisation survival in the medium and long term. It seems reasonable, therefore, to say that Harrison's definition of MD can be placed in quadrant 4 of the framework.

A final definition to be considered is that offered by Chris Molander (1987), whose thinking remains influential. The definition is as follows.

> **Management development is a conscious and systematic process to control the development of managerial resources in the organisation for the achievement of the organisational goals and strategies.**

(Molander, 1987, p. 109)

There is an immediately obvious contrast here with the work of Mumford in that use of the terms conscious, systematic and control in Molander's definition would fit comfortably with the terms planned and deliberate used by Mumford in his earlier work (Mumford, 1993), but rejected by him in his more recent work (Mumford, 1997). This may suggest a shift in academic thinking about MD over recent years. We will examine in a later section whether this possible shift reflects or is translated into professional practice. We are at this point concerned with whether the suggested framework is able to accommodate Molander's definition. The concept of managerial resources suggests a concern with a collective rather than with managers as individuals, and therefore a focus on the organisation. The dimension of purpose is a little more problematic. Molander is clear that achievement of organisation goals and strategies is the purpose. This implies a concern with performance and therefore behaviour. We can therefore argue that Molander's definition complies with behaviour rather than career progression in the terms of the framework and provides an example of a conception of MD which fits into quadrant 2.

Discussion

The examination of formal definitions has demonstrated a variety of meanings attached to the concept of MD. However, the analysis suggests that this variation is neither arbitrary nor overly multifaceted. The framework in Fig. 12.1 provides two key dimensions, each with two broad possibilities, which seem capable of accommodating variation in academic conceptions of MD. We have made a case for the usefulness of the framework by examining both established and recent definitions of MD from academic research and writing. Each of the selected definitions has been shown to be capable of classification within the framework, and the definitions collectively have provided an example of each of the categories suggested by the framework. Therefore at this point we can be satisfied that the framework does and will have practical value in aiding understanding of the various meanings and purposes of MD. Such understanding will have value in informing decisions and actions in professional practice.

There are, however, a number of problems with this argument. The first and perhaps most obvious is that I have been deliberately selective in the definitions examined. It will be instructive for readers to test this by applying the framework to alternative definitions. More significant problems lie with the definitions themselves. While it can be argued that those we have included are mainstream and representative of common conceptions of MD, they do not reflect some of the points made in the previous section. None of the definitions directly or overtly acknowledges or reflects the nature of managerial work. Each seems to assume, implicitly at least, that there are unproblematic connections between managerial behaviour, performance and effectiveness. Additional connections between managerial effectiveness and organisational effectiveness are further assumed, explicitly in some cases. There is an overall sense within and across the definitions that desired, or effective, or 'best' managerial behaviour can be determined and specified. The earlier analysis of managerial work suggests otherwise, however.

The work of Lee (1997) on conceptions of development described earlier suggests additional problems. The definitions examined here all seem to assume known end points for development, represented by concepts such as 'effectiveness' or 'capability'. They perhaps vary more in terms of whether identity is unitary or co-regulated according to the emphasis they give to the individual manager or the organisation. Harrison's (1997) definition of MD, for example, with its concern with a shared culture, could arguably reflect a co-regulated perspective. However, this still limits the definitions to only two conceptions of development in Lee's analysis: either development as maturation or development as shaping. The two remaining conceptions of development, as voyage or emergent (see Table 12.2), are not therefore represented in conventional and mainstream definitions of MD.

Our chosen definitions also seem to reflect a 'unitary' conception of organisations. Such a conception assumes an unproblematic formulation of specifiable and specific organisation goals and objectives. There are, as we have seen, alternative conceptions of organisations (see Alvesson and Deetz, 1996, Morgan, 1997). In a recent application of institutional theory to the field of management learning, Burgoyne and Jackson (1997) argue what they term the 'arena thesis'. This analysis, in essence, proposes a greater validity and usefulness for pluralist conceptions of organisations, and a role for management development in providing a meeting point where 'conflicting purposes and values can meet to be reinforced, reconciled or proliferated' (ibid, p. 68). The implication here for conventional definitions of MD is that if the assumed unproblematic nature of organisations, and organisation goals, is questionable, then the conceptions of MD drawn from those assumptions are also questionable.

In defence of the originators of the definitions, and of the decision to feature them, it is fair to say that the analyses of MD provided by, for example, Mumford (1997) and Harrison (1997) do in fact reflect, take account of and apply many of the points discussed so far. Single-sentence definitions cannot accommodate every factor or detail examined in the analyses from which they are derived. Being familiar with those analyses, I can say that the potential failings and weaknesses discussed so far are much more fully recognised and acknowledged by the writers concerned than their definitions might otherwise suggest. However, there is one final problem with the definitions where this is arguably less the case.

Processual perspectives on and analyses of organising and managing both question and challenge the reification implicit in more conventional treatments. The language form of the preceding sentence makes the point. Conventional analyses treat organisations as independent, objective entities; in other words, an organisation is a 'thing', or an 'it'. They therefore suffer from what Chia (1996) refers to as 'misplaced concreteness' in their analyses. From a processual perspective, organisations do not have entitative status. They are not 'things', or 'its'. Rather, organising is a process, with more or less regularity and patterning, which produces and reproduces the shared experience which we label an, or the, 'organisation'. Organisations as entities are created by our shared experience, and the language we use to make sense of that experience, and therefore 'they' do not have independent, objective existence (*see* Chia, 1996, 1997, Watson, 1994). The same arguments can be applied to management and managing, and indeed to individuals. We merely need to rewrite the preceding sentences using words and forms to take account of the change of focus from organisation to management or individuals.

What this means for the definitions of MD examined in this section is clear. They do not, as they might claim and we might assume, provide accurate descriptions of a given reality. They represent attempts to make sense of an ongoing process of reality construction. It can be useful to conceive of organisations as objective entities, and to relate professional practices that we label management development to such conceptions, as was argued in earlier chapters. However, it is also useful and instructive to think about organising, managing and professional practice from a processual perspective. It is perhaps particularly important to emphasise this point when leading and influential writers on MD continue to apply more traditional perspectives.

We can conclude this section by stating a number of significant points. First, influential analyses of the meaning of MD continue to apply what might be labelled conventional perspectives within organisation and management theory. Second, within that context, and partly because of it, variations in meaning can be related to a small number of factors. Third, the suggested framework in Fig. 12.1 is capable of categorising varying conceptions of MD arising from conventional, though influential, analyses. Fourth, while what we are terming conventional analyses remain influential and helpful, the processual perspective is useful in providing an alternative way of thinking about MD, which both allows and encourages new insights to inform and influence professional practice. We now turn our attention to approaches and methods within MD.

Activity 12.3

1 Consider the focus and purpose of MD in your organisation and then locate the current approach in one of the quadrants in Fig. 12.1.

2 Discuss with a colleague the advantages and disadvantages that arise from adopting such a conception of MD.

3 Identify the potential advantages and disadvantages that might arise from approaches to MD that are consistent with each of the remaining quadrants.

4 Discuss the results of **3** with a colleague.

Management development – approaches and methods

It will be clear that approaches and methods adopted to MD will be influenced by and related to the conception, or definition, being applied. For example, a conception of MD fitting quadrant 1 in Fig. 12.1 is likely to lead to use of methods different from those used if a conception fitting the requirements of quadrant 4 is applied. According to some writers (e.g. Jones and Woodcock, 1985, Harrison, 1997), various other factors will also be influential in decisions on what approach and methods to adopt. These factors are associated with what Jones and Woodcock term 'organisation readiness'. This concept suggests that particular approaches will be more appropriate than others, depending on particular organisational circumstances. A different way of framing this argument is to say that particular circumstances make it more likely that one approach rather than another will be adopted. The first formulation suggests a normative theory, i.e. one in which prescriptions are provided on how to practise MD to meet the requirements of varying circumstances, while the second formulation implies a descriptive theory i.e. one which provides an analysis of how MD is practised in varying circumstances. In either case, MD is assumed to be constituted by deliberate and formalised activities. An indicative list of what circumstances, or contingencies, might be significant according to these writers is given here:

● level of top management commitment to MD
● organisation/business priorities
● intended organisation and business strategies
● the level of resources available and/or allocated to MD
● clarity and specificity of managerial roles
● size of organisation/numbers of managers.

These factors are unlikely to operate independently as they have clear connections and interrelationships. For example, resources allocated to MD will be influenced by the level of top management commitment which, in turn, is likely to be influenced by their perception of the relevance of MD to their intended business strategy. Taking potential connections and relationships further, an intended strategy of expansion may lead to increasing numbers of managers being employed. The content and objectives of MD activities for these managers will be influenced by the degree of clarity on their expected and intended roles.

A significant point arising from the indicative list needs to be made. It is simply that the factors listed do not operate independently in an additional and important sense. The factors are examples of 'organisational contingencies' (Watson, 1999). The spirit of a processual analysis suggests that such contingencies, and their consequences, are mediated by the interpretations and meanings assigned to them by decision makers (*see* Watson, 1999). We cannot, therefore, say that particular factors either should or will produce particular approaches to MD because the meaning and associated significance of each is not 'given' or 'predetermined' and will vary between managers and over time.

Approaches to MD

The argument advanced so far suggests that approaches adopted to MD will relate in some respects to variation in conceptions of MD and particular organisational contingencies, both mediated by individual and collective interpretations, and by conflicting and competing values and interests. Within that context, the available and possible approaches to MD are argued to be capable of categorisation. We saw earlier in this chapter the typology provided by Mabey and Salaman, which could be used to categorise different approaches. Two further typologies are of value and interest since, in more or less explicit ways, they can be related to the indicative organisational contingencies.

The first typology is that first suggested by John Burgoyne in 1988 (Mumford, 1997). Which approach is adopted within Burgoyne's broad categories will be a function, in part, of what Jones and Woodcock (1985) refer to as 'organisation readiness' which, in turn, will be a function, in part, of the list of organisational contingencies. Burgoyne uses the term 'organisation maturity' (Mumford, 1997) in a similar fashion to 'organisation readiness', and argues similar connections between level, or degree, of maturity and organisational contingencies. His six possible approaches to MD are distinguished and categorised according to the degree of organisation maturity. The approaches are as follows:

1　No systematic management development.
2　Isolated tactical management development.
3　Integrated and co-ordinated structural and development tactics.
4　A management development strategy to implement corporate policy.
5　Management development strategy input to corporate policy formulation.
6　Strategic development of the management of corporate policy.

Approach number 1 is, according to Burgoyne, most likely to be evident in young and small organisations. Approaches 1 and 2 are probably those most widely adopted across all organisations, and approaches 3 and 4 represent what might currently constitute 'best practice'. The final two approaches are only occasionally encountered and are rarely sustained (*see* Mumford, 1997). It seems clear from the first point, then, that size is seen by Burgoyne as a key contingency initiating formal approaches to MD. The descriptions of the remaining approaches explicitly suggest that intended business strategy is a further critical contingency in influencing the approach adopted. Finally, and related to this point, it seems reasonable to argue that the descriptions implicitly rely on top management commitment as an important contingency influencing the approach adopted.

As Mumford (1987) argues, one problem with Burgoyne's typology is that it assumes, and is therefore built on, a conception of MD as deliberate, formalised and planned programmes. While Burgoyne recognises the occurrence and potential value of informal learning and development, which accounts for the totality of MD in the first approach, his descriptions of approaches two to six rely on planned and programmed activities. This analysis is confirmed and partly explained by Burgoyne's definition of MD, which is 'the management of managerial careers in an organisational context' (Mumford, 1997, p. 47). (Readers may wish to apply the framework in Fig. 12.1 to this definition as a further test of its usefulness). A potential weakness with this typology is therefore its failure to overtly and directly accommodate informal processes of learning and development. Additional potential weaknesses will be examined later in this section.

An alternative typology is that provided by Alan Mumford (Mumford, 1993, 1997). This classification has, in my view, two particular strengths. First, it overcomes the potential weakness of not dealing directly with informal processes. This is particularly important in applying alternative perspectives to organisational analysis. Second, it is limited to only three categories, or approaches. This makes the typology less conceptually complex and therefore easier to apply to inform practice. Ease of application should not be associated with lack of rigour, however. The three approaches suggested by Mumford are described in Table 12.3.

Table 12.3 Types of management development

Type	Description
Type 1	Informal managerial – accidental process
Type 2	Integrated managerial – opportunistic process
Type 3	Formal management development – planned process

Source: Based on Mumford, A. (1997) *Management Development: Strategies for Action* (3rd edn). London: IPD.

Each of the three types has particular characteristics which, according to Mumford, will have implications and consequences for their effectiveness as approaches to MD. Type one has the strength and advantage of focusing on and occurring in 'real' work. However, learning is usually unconscious, undirected and insufficient. Type three overcomes these disadvantages by being planned and therefore directed. The disadvantages with type three are fairly obvious. The two problems of relevance and transferability are common criticism of learning and development which form the focus of formal programmes. According to Mumford, the type two approach has the potential to maximise the advantages and minimise the disadvantages of each of the other two types. This argument relies in part on Mumford's contention that the either/or choice of formal or informal approaches is in fact a false dichotomy. This view, while not directly connected, has resonance with analyses associated with a processual perspective (*see* Chia, 1996). Mumford's argument on the falseness of the dichotomy is a little weakened by his stated view that naturally occurring learning opportunities in and at work can be, and perhaps should be, planned and directed. However, his overall analysis is valuable in emphasising the actual and potential learning inherent in the everyday experience of carrying out work tasks and activities.

One further factor arising from Mumford's typology is of particular interest. Mumford suggests that a characteristic of both type one and type two approaches is that 'ownership' of MD processes and activities remains with managers themselves. Type three approaches, by contrast, imply ownership by professional practitioners. Therefore there is in Mumford's typology a clear choice to be made in terms of the relative roles and contributions of professional developers and other managers. Type three approaches provide professional practitioners with control and ownership. The other approaches do not. Control and ownership in types one and two can operate in the sense of both individual managers' control over their own development, and over the development of their employees. This issue of control and ownership is one of the main reasons, although not the only one, for Mumford advocating type two approaches as producing the most effective management development.

It was indicated earlier that Burgoyne's typology has additional potential weaknesses. These relate to applying a processual analysis. The levels of 'maturity' described in Burgoyne's six approaches explicitly rest on a notion of separation of corporate strategy and human resourcing strategy. Perhaps more implicitly, they assume that corporate strategy is associated with the plans and intentions of top and senior managers. In other words, Burgoyne's typology seems to reflect what is termed 'mainstream thinking'. An alternative view would, in fact, see Burgoyne's sixth approach as more closely reflecting the actuality of strategic processes in organisations, and therefore the remaining approaches as arguably false choices since they rely on less useful premises (*see* Watson, 1999). This is not to say that the varying degrees of formality and planning implicit in Burgoyne's typology is without value. It does have significant usefulness in making judgements concerning which approach or approaches to adopt to MD. For example, in circumstances where time, resources and attention are devoted to producing detailed strategic plans for an organisation, it would be nonsensical to refuse to undertake similar processes in relation to MD, or to not contribute the views and ambitions of MD to the corporate planning process, or indeed to not take account of formal business plans, where they exist, in formulating MD plans and programmes. However, it is arguable that more informed and, in that sense, 'better' decisions on MD approaches will arise when the actuality of organisation strategies as realised outcomes is recognised. Such a recognition is likely to lead to greater focus on and attention to the informal processes of managerial actions and behaviour and will also have implications for the content of any formal MD programmes. For these reasons, it seems that Mumford's typology offers greater usefulness in understanding and making decisions on approaches to management development, and that his type two represents a commendable overall approach. It is fair to say, too, that Burgoyne's more recent work (e.g. Burgoyne and Jackson, 1997, Pedler, Burgoyne and Boydell, 1996) would support a similar conclusion.

Activity 12.4

1 Identify the critical contingencies influencing and having impact on approaches adopted to MD in your organisation.

2 Categorise current approaches according to the typology provided by Burgoyne.

3 Consider the extent to which your allocated approach in Burgoyne's typology can be explained by organisational contingencies.

Methods

There are obvious connections between approaches to and methods of management development. A simple example would be that type three approaches in Mumford's typology are likely to be associated with programmes of management education and training, while type two approaches are likely to emphasise work and job-based methods such as action learning, coaching and mentoring (*see* Mumford, 1997). There is also a vast array of methods available and advocated for use by professional developers (Huczynski, 1983) and by managers themselves (Pedler *et al.*, 1994). We are therefore forced to be selective here. The choices are guided by the conceptual frameworks described so far in this chapter, and by some additional classifications focusing on methods.

One commonly applied method of MD is to produce frameworks of management competence (Thomson *et al.*, 1997). This concept is, as we have seen in earlier chapters, more complex than sometimes allowed, and is not without controversy or criticism (Devine, 1990, Bates, 1995, Stewart and Sambrook, 1995). It is, however, at the heart of national policy on vocational qualifications and has been applied by the Management Charter Initiative (MCI) to produce occupational standards for managers (Harrison, 1997, Reid and Barrington, 1997). These standards provide a specification of competencies, or abilities, which it is argued managers in various roles and at various levels require. They can therefore provide a starting point in determining development needs, and can be used to inform design of development programmes. The nature of assessment for MCI qualifications also provides the opportunity of applying a type two approach since award of the qualifications requires evidence of demonstrated competence in and at work. MCI specifications of competence do not have to be used, of course, and many organisations have produced their own frameworks (*see* Tate, 1995, Woodall and Winstanley, 1998). Alternative generic frameworks are available (*see* Jones and Woodcock, 1985, Boyatzis, 1982).

Mumford (1993, 1997) criticises the MCI framework and the processes which led to its production. However, he supports the value of producing some framework or model of competence. Such models, he argues, need to focus on 'effectiveness' as well as on competence, and to take account of the vagaries and ambiguities of managerial work. Using these two criteria, Mumford suggests a range of methods which, since they focus on combining learning and working and working and learning, reflect the values of a type two approach. The methods are categorised into three sets:

- *changes in the job*
  - – promotion;
  - – job rotation;
  - – secondments.
- *changes in job content*
  - – additional responsibility and tasks;
  - – specific projects;
  - – membership of committees or task groups;
  - – junior boards.
- *within the job*
  - – coaching;
  - – counselling;
  - – monitoring and feedback;
  - – mentoring.

This list of MD methods explicitly focuses on what might be described as informal methods which nevertheless are capable of, and perhaps would benefit from, some degree of formalisation and planning. It excludes off-the-job and other methods which are normally associated with more formalised and systematic approaches. Alternative classifications are offered by Reid and Barrington (1997) and by Jones and Woodcock (1985). These classifications add the following methods:

- group-based methods, e.g. managerial grid
- in-house courses
- planned experience outside the organisation
- external courses, either qualification or non-qualification based
- role analysis
- seminars
- exchange consulting

- performance review
- development centres
- career management and development.

The latter three methods have links and connections with succession planning, discussed by Harrison (1997) as a method of MD. The two lists need not be seen as mutually exclusive, nor indeed need individual methods on each list. Combinations of methods from both lists will, in fact, support and enable application of Mumford's type two approach. Expressed another way, adopting a type two approach is likely to lead to use of methods from both lists. It needs to be recognised, too, that the methods included are not exhaustive.

This discussion of methods enables us to illustrate a further application of the framework in Fig. 12.1. As well being useful for categorising and comparing meanings and definitions, the framework can be useful in categorising methods. Fig. 12.2 shows this by placing some methods in each of the quadrants. The placing of the managerial grid (*see* Stewart, 1996) in quadrant two follows the argument that MD is centrally concerned with shared values (Harrison, 1997).

		FOCUS	
		Individual	**Organisation**
PURPOSE	**Behaviour**	• Coaching • Competence specifications	• Promotion • Managerial grid
	Career progression	• Secondments • Mentoring	• Succession planning • Career management

Fig. 12.2 Classification of management development methods

In closing this section, readers will find it useful to test this application of the framework further by completing the following activity.

Activity 12.5

1 Produce a comprehensive list of MD methods by adding to those listed in this section.

2 Allocate each item on your list to one of the quadrants in Fig. 12.2, producing a justification for each allocation.

3 Produce a coherent combination of methods which could be used in a MD programme which reflects the principles of Mumford's type two approach.

Management development practice

This final substantive section is concerned with recent empirical findings on MD practice. There is some evidence for the growing prevalence of programmes of culture change being attempted and implemented in UK work organisations (IRS, 1997). It has to be recognised, though, that the IRS report on culture change suggests that 80 per cent of programmes fail to meet their intended objectives. What is of particular interest here is that development activities and a focus on management style are, according to the same report, common components of change programmes. The focus on management style is, again commonly, intended to promote 'empowerment' and devolution of authority. The IRS report notes, however, that increased levels of participation do not apply to decisions concerning culture change programmes themselves, which are often initiated and directed by senior managers. There may be possible relationships between this factor and the suggested failure rates. We might conclude from this that culture change cannot be achieved solely through MD activities aimed at promoting new or different styles of managing.

A major survey of MD practice carried out by the Institute of Management (Thomson *et al.*, 1997) suggests that the priority given to MD in UK organisations continues to grow, and is expected to increase in the future. There is, however, no expected change in approaches or methods, and therefore those described in this chapter, and in other texts, can be expected to form the basis of MD activities into the next millennium. Thomson *et al.* also suggest that there exists a balance of responsibility for MD between the individual and the employer in the majority of organisations. Taken together with the finding that most employers do not expect managers to stay for a career, there is perhaps a shift away from associating MD with career progression. These two points from the report also suggest a growing relevance and recognition of Mumford's type two approaches. This is further supported by the finding of a balance of formal and informal approaches and methods being applied in MD practice.

Two additional conclusions of this research are perhaps of particular interest. The first is that the majority of employers are satisfied with the achievements and impact of management development. We might argue that 'they would say that, wouldn't they?'(*see* Chapter 2). However, the conclusion suggests some empirical support for the value of MD. The second conclusion is that investment in MD is a matter of policy, and therefore of choice. Based on statistical analysis of the relationship between a number of variables,

Thomson *et al.* (1997) conclude that the existence or extent of investment in MD is not determined by external or structural factors, and that investment or not arises out of the choices made by decision makers. Such choices do seem to have some relationship with decision makers' views on 'strategic issues'. We can say therefore that this research supports the position taken in this chapter in that contingencies are mediated by the values and interests of managers. We might also argue that the findings on 'satisfaction' and 'impact' could have significance in influencing the perception of decision makers of the strategic importance of investment in MD. Recently published research comparing MD in the UK and Japan adds some weight to the findings of the Thomson report, although it questions the coherence of UK MD systems and processes (Storey *et al.*, 1997).

Management development can be argued to be a significant lever in achieving change in relation to issues concerning equal opportunities and managing diversity, since some models of managing and development applied to MD can propagate and legitimate, for example, stereotypical and ethnocentric conceptions of organisations and management (*see* Lee, 1996, Wilson, 1996). Leaving aside programmes specifically intended to redress the effects of such models, the empirical picture is not encouraging. Research conducted for the then Employment Department and the Commission for Racial Equality (CRE) (Cheung-Judge, 1993) found that less than 40 per cent of management programmes provided by educational institutions included equal opportunities issues in their content. The same research also found that, where employers provided development related to equal opportunities and diversity issues, such development was not, in the majority of cases, linked to or integrated with management development policy and practice. It is perhaps instructive on this point that the survey by Thomson *et al.* referred to earlier did not directly address the equal opportunities implications and applications of MD. The conclusion seems to be therefore that there remains much scope for articulating those implications and applications.

Summary and conclusion

This chapter has argued that management development can and does has multiple meanings. A range of approaches to and methods of management development has also been described. It has been further argued that conceptions and definitions of MD adopted will influence the approach and methods applied in practice. Other influencing factors will include organisation contingencies, such as size and top management commitment. In the end, though, levels of investment and approaches adopted are a matter of managerial choice rather than the result of independent forces. Some empirical evidence has been included which suggests MD is often associated with formal attempts to change organisational culture, although other research suggests this is not the case in relation to implementation of policies related to EO and managing diversity. However, a recent and major survey provides some evidence to support an argument that investment in MD produces valued outcomes. The question of what might constitute 'valued outcomes' is examined in the next chapter on policy and ethics in employee development.

Activity 12.6

1 Based on your reading of this chapter, how would you describe the perception and understanding of MD apparent in your organisation?

2 How does this compare with current practice in other organisations revealed by the empirical research described here and your knowledge from other sources?

3 What alternative conceptions of MD, in your judgement, might be more appropriate, and why?

4 How would current approaches and methods need to change to accommodate this shift in orientation?

Case study 12

Highfield College of FE is located in a medium-sized Midlands city. It has recently experienced its third reorganisation following the appointment of its third principal and chief executive since incorporation. Hilda Emanuel has retained her position as chief administrative officer for the college in the new structure. Her position is third tier, i.e. Hilda reports to the deputy principal (resources), who in turn reports to the chief executive. Hilda's responsibilities encompass finance, personnel and schools administrative support, and her level equates to the academic heads of school. Other positions at the centre of the college include a registrar and chief estates officer, both of whom report to Peter West, the deputy principal (resources). Designated managers in the college include heads of school, subject co-ordinators and course leaders among academic staff, and departmental heads, supervisors and team leaders among non-academic staff. Hilda has direct responsibility for 65 staff, including three departmental heads, one of whom is head of personnel. The new principal and chief executive is Samantha Hall, an energetic, authoritative and innovative leader who has persuaded the college board of governors that the future survival and success of the college depends on 'going for growth' which, in turn, depends on devising new products and creating new markets. Samantha's appointment was in part a response to the failure of the previous principal to address and resolve pressing financial problems, which are still there. However, Samantha believes expansion and growth cannot be achieved without some speculative expenditure. This has to be linked to securing the long-term survival and prosperity of the college.

Samantha Hall, with the support of the chair of the board of governors, Jack Golding, has instituted a strategic working group to produce new policies and working practices to support and encourage her plans for growth. Membership of this group is as follows:

- Jack Golding (chair of the board of governors)
- Samantha Hall (principal and chief executive)
- Peter West (deputy principal, resources)
- Ruth Kitchen (deputy principal, academic affairs)
- Hilda Emanuel (chief administrative officer).

Management development is currently very *ad hoc* and is primarily provided in response to individual requests and constituted by qualification-based courses such as the Diploma in Management Studies provided by a local university. Hilda has persuaded Peter West that the new organisation structure, and the intended strategy of growth, are unlikely to succeed without some improvement in managerial ability and performance. Both Peter and Hilda are aware that Mike Newell, head of finance, believes the college cannot afford to spend money it doesn't have to, or that cannot guarantee some return. They also believe that Samantha Hall, while open-minded, is not a natural supporter of MD, and that, if resources are allocated, Ruth Kitchen will argue priority be given to academic staff. They also know that Jack Golding will take a close interest in the financial implications of any proposals considered by the group. Hilda and Peter have agreed to present a joint paper to the group on the need for, and potential benefits of, investment in MD in support of the intended business strategy. They are aware that Mike Newell, as head of finance, will need to make some contribution to the paper on any financial implications. As a starting point, they have agreed to request the head of personnel, one of Hilda's staff, to prepare an initial draft.

Discussion questions

Imagine you are head of personnel for the college, and consider the following questions:

(a) What factors would you take into account in preparing your paper, and how might these influence the content?

(b) What will be the main issues you address in your paper?

(c) Which approach or approaches to MD will you advocate, and why?

(d) What preparatory steps will you take before giving your paper to Hilda, e.g. consulting on its contents with others?

(e) What advice will you give to Peter and Hilda for dealing with possible responses from members of the working group?

Suggested reading

Burgoyne, J. and Reynolds, M. (eds.) (1997) *Management Learning: Integrating Perspectives in Theory and Practice*. London: Sage.

Harrison, R. (1997) *Employee Development*. London: IPD.

Mabey, C. and Salaman, G. (1995) *Strategic Human Resource Management*. Oxford: Blackwell Business.

Mumford, A. (1997) *Management Development: Strategies for Action (3rd edn)*. London: IPD.

Watson, T.J. (1994) *In Search of Management*. London: Routledge.

Woodall, J. and Winstanley, D. (1998) *Management Development: Strategy and Practice*. Oxford: Blackwell Business.

CHAPTER 13

Policy and ethics in employee development

Introduction

Chapter 13 is concerned with two concepts which have significant impact on employee development operations and professional practice. The two concepts also have some direct connections and relationships with each other. In simple terms, we might say that *ED policy* is concerned with determining the principles which govern decisions and actions in relation to employee development activities and processes. Such principles, though, will be a matter of choice and will themselves therefore be derived from some overarching beliefs about proper conduct in human affairs. These overarching beliefs can be said to be the concern of *ethics*. As Bowie and Duska (1990) put it, 'the focus of ethics is on human actions or behaviour' (p. 3). It seems reasonable to conclude that 'ethical' principles first need to be worked out before determining the principles which are intended to guide actions and behaviour in employee development. Therefore we might suggest that the relationship between the two concepts is hierarchical in that ethical principles inform ED policy, and the latter is derived from the former.

The situation is not as clear cut as the opening paragraph might suggest. Employee development policy does not have to be, and often in practice is not, the result of deliberate analysis and choice (Reid and Barrington, 1997). Policy can and does evolve and emerge on an *ad hoc* basis. Similarly with ethical 'positions' (Bowie and Duska, 1990). An ethical position does not mean necessarily a good or right position in relation to human conduct. It simply means holding a view on what constitutes an appropriate answer to the question 'What should one do?' (Bowie and Duska, 1990). Developing such a view can equally be a matter of *ad hoc* responses to situations as and when they arise. The resulting view, or position, can remain largely unconscious and unarticulated. Therefore, connections and relationships between ethical positions and ED policies can remain unarticulated. Where there is a lack of deliberate thought and analysis informing conscious and deliberate choice, the connections between ethics and policy can be much more fluid and 'two-way' than the logical relationship suggested by an ethics-policy hierarchy.

The starting point of this chapter can be briefly stated as follows. There are connections between the concepts of ethics and policy, and these connections will be more apparent if each is subject to conscious thought and analysis. Such thought and analysis is also likely to result in a clearer understanding of current and possible ethical positions and related policies, and through this, development and implementation of a more robust and appropriate employee development policy. This in turn is likely to result in more appropriate and effective ED practices and activities. The overall purpose of the chapter is to support and enable a thorough and rigorous formulation of employee development policy. Translating this purpose into specific detail results in the following objectives.

CHAPTER OBJECTIVES

- Describe and explain two approaches to determining ethical behaviour.

- Critically assess and evaluate the relative validity of each of the approaches.

- Specify the implications for ED policy and practice arising out of the study of ethics through identifying common ethical dilemmas encountered by ED professionals.

- Articulate and apply a systematic process for formulation of ED policies.

- Provide advice and guidance on the form and content of ED policies, including production of draft policy statements.

- Apply an understanding of the study of ethics to formulation and implementation of ED policies.

As with some previous chapters, we will seek to achieve these objectives in an order different to that in which they are listed. The next section will examine the nature and meaning of the concept of policy, and its application in the context of employee development. This will include elaborating an approach to policy formulation. We will then move on to the concept of ethics, and to examine two broad philosophical positions which inform consideration of ethical questions. Each of these separate sections will seek to identify and highlight the main implications for the other, i.e. the implications for consideration of ethical questions arising from ED policy formulation and vice versa. However, the penultimate section will examine these implications in more detail through an exploration of the direct connections and relationships between policy and ethics.

Employee development policy

It will be useful to begin our examination with some definitions. The *Oxford English Dictionary* defines policy as 'a course or principle of action proposed by a government, party, business, or individual, etc.'. A number of significant points will be apparent. First, there is a clear distinction between policy and practice in the definition. This is explicit in the focus on 'proposed'. This distinction is also suggested, perhaps a little more implicitly, in the focus on 'principle of action' rather than the action itself. This distinction is in any case widely accepted (Harrison, 1997, Reid and Barrington, 1997) and so we can conclude a separation between policy and practice with the former being intended to inform and direct the latter. The association with government and party raises a second point of interest. As Reid and Barrington (1997) point out, the original Greek origins of the word policy focused on systems of order and enforcement of laws. These original meanings give rise to modern English usage in the word 'police' as both verb and collective noun. Therefore, we might argue that policies serve similar purposes in organisations as do laws in societies. They define the limits and requirements of acceptable and unacceptable behaviour. However, it could be argued that organisation policies go further in that they provide a mechanism of not only specifying behaviour, but also 'policing' behaviour to ensure compliance. A third and final point suggested by the definition is that policies are concerned with intentions. In that sense, policies are future orientated in that they define and specify what is intended to be achieved by the government, party or business. This is suggested by the association of 'course' with 'action'. A 'course of action' is carried out in future time.

This last point is central to the analysis of the learning organisation concept provided by Garratt (1988). In discussing the role of directors in creating and managing organisation learning, Garratt uses the term policy in preference to and in place of the concept of 'mission'. The concept of mission, as we saw in earlier chapters, is concerned with determining the *raison d'etre* of an organisation and, relatedly, deciding what it wishes to achieve. For Garratt (1988), the concept of policy is more appropriate for capturing such a meaning since, according to his analysis, such meaning is explicit in the original Greek from which policy is derived. We might argue from this that policy is to do with specifying what an organisation wishes or desires to achieve in and through its continued existence.

Activity 13.1

1 Access and analyse any HR-related organisation policy to determine to what extent it reflects the discussion so far. In doing so, consider the following questions:

   (a) to what extent does the policy specify action?

   (b) in what ways, if any, could the policy be said to represent an 'organisation law'?

   (c) how, if at all, does the policy operate to 'police' behaviour and ensure compliance?

   (d) what connections and relationships with organisation mission (and statement, if there is one) can you identify in the policy?

2 Think about and list some ethical considerations and implications that might arise from the dictionary definition of policy and the discussion in the previous paragraphs.

3 Discuss the results of 2 with a colleague and jointly examine the possible reasons for any similarities and differences.

We can summarise the analysis so far by arguing that a policy provides a broad framework within which decisions on practice and actions can be taken. Put another way, a policy provides a reference point against which any current or proposed action can be judged. That judgement will be the extent to which the action contributes to what the organisation wishes to achieve. These points are, generally, reflected in the following definition of a training policy.

> . . . an agreed framework within which specific actions can take place. Thus, a training policy statement is a document detailing courses of action that a company has decided to take on all matters relating to training.
>
> (Celinski, 1983, p. 1)

Two additional and significant points arise from this specific definition of employee development policy. First, the use of the words 'agreed framework'. This highlights the fact that organisations do not have independent, objective existence and therefore cannot have policies of any sort. Instead, individuals have to reach agreement about policies to adopt. This raises questions concerning who to involve in reaching agreement, and what processes to adopt in making choices about the content of policies. These questions will be examined in more detail in the next section. We can say for now that perhaps in most cases, top and senior managers are the individuals responsible for and therefore involved in making policy choices and decisions (*see* Garratt, 1988). However, this empirical exclusion of other stakeholders does not necessarily justify such a position. If we view the formulation of and agreements about policy statements as an ethical issue, there may be valid arguments against such a position, and arguments for extending involvement in reaching agreement.

Second, Celinski (1983) specifies that a training policy is a written statement. There may be advantages to having a written statement, and these will be examined later in the chapter. However, as Reid and Barrington (1997) argue, the existence of an employee development policy does not require, or necessarily imply, the existence of a written statement. As with any other policy, the nature, purpose and content of employee development policy can be inferred and analysed on the basis of precedent and established practice. So, the absence of a written statement does not necessarily imply a lack of policy in relation to employee development.

Formulating ED policy

It is important to recognise the potential and actual influence and impact of a range of factors when formulating an employee development policy (Reid and Barrington, 1997). It is also equally important to recognise that these factors do not have independent influence or impact. As with all organisational contingencies, their influence will be mediated by the significance and interpretation placed on them by decision makers (*see* Watson, 1999 and Chapter 12). The particular factors or contingencies of relevance to formulating ED policy are debatable, but they are unlikely to vary very much from those identified in earlier chapters in this book. Reid and Barrington (1997) list 14 potential factors (p. 259) and the list in Fig. 13.1 can be considered indicative. One factor which is perhaps worth emphasising is that of existing policies in related HR areas, for example, recruitment and selection, equal opportunities and succession planning. There needs to be coherence and consistency across HR policies to achieve what is referred to as 'horizontal integration' (Marchington and Wilkinson, 1996). Similar arguments are also advanced by, for example, Torrington and Hall (1998). We can conclude therefore that a particularly important first step in formulating an ED policy is to analyse existing HR policies.

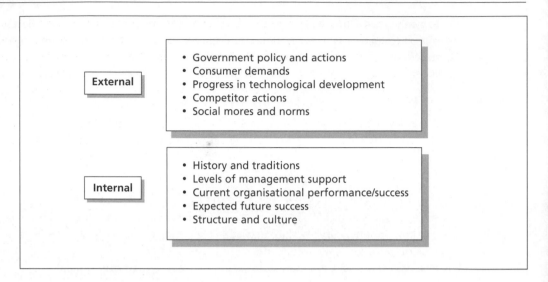

Fig. 13.1 Influencing factors

The factors suggested in Fig. 13.1 should not be taken as necessarily determining the nature, purpose and content of an ED policy. The flow of influence and impact can travel in both directions. To take the example of other HR policies, these can be as easily shaped by ED policy as vice versa. In addition, and as Fredericks and Stewart (1996) argue, there are complex relationships between ED policy and practice and organisation structure and strategy. The point then seems to be that ED policy cannot be formulated in a vacuum and in isolation. The processes adopted in policy formulation therefore must be iterative so that implications and consequences can be identified, and so that account can be taken of other aspects of organisational operations. This suggests a need for wide consultation which, in turn, again raises the question of who should be involved.

Activity 13.2

1 Consider the factors listed in Fig. 13.1. Produce an analysis of how each of them might impact on ED policy.

2 Now reverse your focus. Consider how ED policy might impact on each of the factors in Fig. 13.1.

3 Discuss your responses with a colleague.

4 Access your organisation's written statement of ED policy. Identify which of the factors in Fig. 13.1 have influenced the content of the policy, and in what ways.

5 Now reverse your focus again. Consider the implications/influences your organisation's ED policy may have for and on each of the factors in Fig. 13.1.

6 Discuss your responses with a colleague. Attempt to identify any necessary or desired changes to either the current ED policy or to other existing policies.

As indicated earlier, ethical considerations might argue against limiting decisions on ED policy exclusively to senior managers. We now have additional reasons for widening the constituency of decision makers in the form of a consultative and iterative process to take account of significant and influencing organisational contingencies. The idea of stakeholders, and that of stakeholder analysis, are perhaps relevant to meeting both requirements (*see* Bowie and Duska, 1990). This involves first specifying who the stakeholders are and then investigating their desires and interests. Stakeholders can be defined as 'those groups without whose support the organisation would cease to exist' (*ibid.*, p. 40). Such groups can include customers, employees, suppliers and local communities as well as governments, shareholders and managers. Thus, the concept of stakeholders, and the process of stakeholder analysis, enable a wide and iterative consultation in the formulation of employee development policy.

Naturally, the desires and interests of stakeholder groups are unlikely to always, if ever, coincide (Watson, 1994, 1999) and therefore there is always a potential for conflict. However, the study of business ethics can provide overarching principles to guide choices and decisions, and to help reconcile competing interests (*see* Bowie and Duska, 1990, Connock and Johns, 1995 and next section).

There is an additional argument in support of a consultative and iterative process of policy formulation. Such an approach is congruent and consistent with developing the characteristics of a learning organisation. We saw in Chapter 11 that Pedler *et al.* (1991, 1996) specify 'participative policy making' as one of their characteristics. A similar view is implicit in the analysis provided by Senge (1993), especially in relation to his arguments on shared vision as one of the five disciplines of a learning organisation. It would seem odd therefore if policy in relation to HRD and development of employees failed to adopt these principles.

The role of employee development specialists

The arguments so far on formulating ED policy raise the question of the role of the development specialist. It might have been assumed, before these arguments, that development specialists were responsible for producing policy statements. There is, though, no necessary contradiction between the two positions. A consultative process needs to be designed, implemented and managed. Draft statements need to be produced at various points for consideration and comment by stakeholders. In addition, specialist advice needs to be provided on implications, possible consequences and what might be considered good or best practice. We can argue therefore that development specialists have a critical role in managing the process of policy formulation, and in providing advice and guidance on the content of policy statements. This last point is of particular interest in suggesting that there may be specific issues to which the development practitioner will need to pay particular attention. Some examples of these need to be identified and discussed.

An obvious first example of an issue where specialist advice will be expected and required is that of government policies. One straightforward element of this is to ensure that organisation policies comply with legislative requirements. However, government policies have a wider impact than those arising simply from legislation. As well as limiting action and decisions by requiring certain things and prohibiting others, government policies create opportunities which organisations can choose to embrace or ignore. There have been many examples of these since the 1960s, especially in relation to measures taken to alleviate unemployment. Recent examples include Investors in People and the initiatives taken by government to promote lifelong learning. As well as the direct potential benefits that can be associated with engagement and participation in such initiatives, they provide opportunities for meeting 'social responsibilities' (*see* next section) and therefore operating in an ethical manner. This may also be valuable, or valued, in promoting the organisation as a responsible and caring employer.

It is arguable also that even where organisations choose to ignore the opportunities presented by government policies and initiatives, this choice is a *policy* decision and therefore should be made clear in policy statements. However, a deliberate decision to participate or not cannot be reached in ignorance of the possibilities, and it is reasonable to expect development specialists to be knowledgeable about those possibilities, and to be in a position to provide advice and guidance. Therefore, a key role for specialists is to identify and provide advice on the implications and potentialities of government policies.

A second fairly obvious example where specialist advice is required is in meeting organisational needs and requirements for employee development. It is entirely possible, in theory at least, that organisations adopt formal ED policies which are not in line with meeting their actual training and development needs. An example of this might be a contradiction between the tight controls required or imposed by a policy statement and an identified need to promote greater autonomy in work operations. Thus, any attempt to encourage and support such autonomy through employee development would be at odds with the stated policy. In addition, such a policy would create 'mixed messages' and therefore undermine the stated aims of devolving authority. A more likely example of the same issue might be where an organisation has an identified need for certain skills, but does not possess the expertise internally to develop those skills. A policy statement which prohibits expenditure on external development would, in those circumstances, be clearly inappropriate. Thus, we can say development specialists have a role in ensuring congruence between policy and identified or potential needs.

The specific point on organisation needs raises a more general issue. This is simply that any policy, whatever its purpose and content, needs to be capable of implementation, and indeed needs to be implemented if it is to have any value or meaning. Implementation will always create problems and opportunities, irrespective of the detail of the policy. So, we can say that a legitimate role for development specialists is to provide advice and guidance on those problems and opportunities so that they are fully taken into account when the policy is agreed and finalised. An additional example of a specific problem/opportunity is that of costs and income. It will be obvious that a policy on employee development, once adopted and implemented, will have cost implications. There may also be opportunities for income through, for example, government grants or through selling development facilities and products to external organisations (*see* Chapter 14). The development specialist will be expected and required to provide guidance on these implications as part of policy formulation. Policy implementation also needs to be monitored, evaluated and reviewed (*see* Harrison, 1997, Reid and Barrington, 1997). An expected contribution of development specialists will be to design mechanisms for this to happen and, probably, to apply or manage those mechanisms to ensure the policy is regularly reviewed and updated as necessary.

The preceding paragraphs have detailed a number of contributions that can be reasonably expected of development specialists in formulating ED policy, and thus have defined a role for specialist practitioners. This role is clearly supportive, and is one which facilitates rather than leads policy development. In that sense, the defined role conforms with established views which argue that ED policy, as with any other, is the responsibility of and should be owned by senior managers (*see* Harrison, 1997, Reid and Barrington, 1997). However, our earlier arguments on a wide consultative approach to policy development would question this convention. Certainly senior managers are a critical constituency, or stakeholder group, and need to endorse and support an agreed ED policy statement. My arguments in this section are, however, perhaps more sympathetic to an interpretive perspective of organisations rather than a functionalist perspective which would privilege the role and power of senior managers. My approach is perhaps also more 'developmental' in the sense argued by Lee (1996). You may therefore wish to consider your own position in relation to my perspective and associated arguments on the role of development specialists.

Content of written policy statements

We have yet to consider either the detailed content of ED policy statements or the arguments in favour of formalising policy in the form of a written statement. We will therefore now turn our attention to those questions. It is perhaps common practice to capture policy in short statements which lack detail. However, if the purpose of an ED policy is to specify intentions and to guide decisions and actions, then some level of detail is required. Indeed, as Celinski (1983) argues, policy statements of two or three paragraphs which contain nothing other than platitudes can be of little value in practice. Therefore, policy statements which are of value in practice are likely to run to a number of pages in length. The illustration provided by Celinski (1983), for example, is 18 pages long. This is in sharp contrast to the one-paragraph example provided in Reid and Barrington (1997, p. 262). The actual content of a statement will vary from organisation to organisation and over time, and will be to some extent shaped by the influencing factors identified earlier. However, it is possible to argue certain subjects or headings which need to be included (Celinski, 1983, Reid and Barrington, 1997).

Perhaps an essential item to include is that of objectives. An ED policy will be intended and designed to achieve a set of specific purposes. Among these might be to articulate the organisation's ethical stance in relation to employees and their development. In any case, the purpose or purposes of the policy need to be specified. As part of this, the relative roles and responsibilities of managers, development specialists and individual employees, for example, in implementing the policy can be defined and specified. In addition and relatedly, the policy can usefully specify how costs associated with employee development activities are to be accounted for and apportioned to various possible budgets.

One critical element to be included in a policy statement is that of record keeping. Important questions arise in terms of what information is recorded and who has access in what circumstances. The provisions of data protection legislation, for example, will be extended to manual records. There will, therefore, be legal requirements to meet in governing access. We might also argue that a particular policy adopted will be influenced by particular ethical stances. However, recording information and providing access are matters of policy, and therefore the specific policy adopted needs to be detailed in the ED policy statement.

Additional items in a policy statement arise from the choices that are open to organisations. First, ED policy can and does vary in relation to different *categories of employees*. For example, support in the form of paid leave and payment of fees may be available for qualifying courses for professional staff such as accountants, but not necessarily for other employees. Such a distinction may be particularly significant in professional partnerships. Second, policy can and does vary in relation to different *types of training*. For example, financial support may be provided for education-based external courses, but not for non-qualification related external courses. Therefore, a policy statement needs to specify the position in relation to each type of training and development. These two areas of choice provide a series of headings under which the content of a policy statement can be organised. For instance, the different categories of staff in a particular organisation can provide the focus of different sections in a policy statement, with different types of training and development providing common sub-headings in each section. What I am suggesting here is that a written statement needs to specify and detail what choices have been made, i.e. what the policy *is*, in relation to the two variables of different categories of staff and different types of development activities. The former raises ethical considerations in that different policies for different categories of staff will need to rest on some justification.

It will be clear from this discussion exactly why useful policy statements are likely to be a number of pages in length. However, this does not explain the need for a *written* policy statement. One reason is to avoid *ad hoc* development of policy which will occur in the absence of written statements (Reid and Barrington, 1997). Additional advantages include achieving consistency across the organisation and over time, the increased probability that decisions and actions on ED will support organisation objectives and that a written statement provides a basis for reviewing and evaluating current practice (*see* Harrison, 1997, Reid and Barrington, 1997). Of particular interest when linking policy and ethics is the argument of Reid and Barrington (1997) that a written statement informs employees of their rights and responsibilities in relation to employee development and that this is advantageous to both the organisation and to individual employees. We might say that overall a written statement articulates the intentions of the organisation and so provides guidance to inform and support decision making by all those involved in employee development.

These claimed advantages and overall purpose of a written policy statement raise the issue of communicating the policy. The purpose and advantages will clearly not be achieved if managers and other employees are not aware of the policy. Therefore, it is important that any policy statement is communicated effectively. This perhaps suggests a further role for development specialists. We might also argue that a consultative approach to policy development will provide a significant contribution to ensuring that all employees know and understand the purpose and content of the statement. One question that is interesting to consider is the extent to which *all* employees need to be aware of the content of *all* sections of the statement. In other words, do non-managerial employees, for example, need to be aware of the policy in relation to managerial employees? I would suggest that a common or immediate response to this question will be in the negative. However, if the example is framed in reverse, i.e. managers needing to be aware of the policy in relation to non-managerial employees, I would suggest the opposite answer would be more common. There can be legitimate and logical reasons for these different answers. However, I suggest that it is not a simple matter of human resourcing strategy (*see* Watson, 1999) that accounts for the difference. The question and the fact of different answers can raise ethical issues. We will move on in the next section to examine the ethics of employee development.

Activity 13.3

1 Consider your organisation's current policy statement on employee development and answer the following questions:

(a) what process was adopted in formulating the policy?

(b) to what extent does the statement provide guidance on the various factors such as objectives, costs and categories of employees suggested in this section?

(c) what is the role of specialist ED staff in formulating, implementing and communicating the policy?

(d) what arrangements exist to monitor, review and update the statement?

2 Consider the relative advantages and disadvantages of the suggestions in this section on formulating policies, the content of policy statements and the role of ED specialists, in the context of your organisation.

3 Using the results of **1** and **2**, discuss with a colleague what improvements could be made in the arrangements for ED policy in your organisation. Attempt to identify how these improvements could be achieved.

4 It was stated earlier that established or conventional treatments of ED policy adopt an uncritical, functionalist paradigm. Produce a critique of this view of ED policy from either a radical structuralist paradigm or a radical humanist paradigm. What would be the implications for current practice in your organisation in relation to ED policy arising from this critique?

5 Given the results of **4**, how would you seek to improve your organisation's ED policy?

6 Debate the total results of this activity with a colleague who has also completed it.

The ethics of employee development

The application of the study of ethics to business, and indeed to organisation and management theory, is relatively recent. Torrington and Hall (1998) argue that the subject has long been a concern in personnel management, but also acknowledge that there has been a resurgence of interest in the 1980s and 1990s. They also suggest that the concept can be, for many people, 'incongruous' in the context of business organisations (*ibid.*, p. 683). This implies a view that business organisations and their managers and other employees are somehow removed from ethical considerations, and that therefore the study of ethics has no relevance or application in organisation and management theory. However, as we shall see later, such a view represents an ethical position in itself. In other words, an argument against the relevance of ethical considerations in business management has to be justified on some grounds or other, and those grounds will necessarily have to draw on debates and arguments within the study of ethics. Therefore, any argument against the relevance of ethical considerations will itself represent an ethical position.

We can perhaps illustrate this point by considering the analysis of ED policy in the previous section. It was argued there that conventional treatments and analyses of policy formulation and implementation adopt a functionalist paradigm of organisations. This book, however, is premised on the existence of alternative paradigms. Each of these different paradigms suggests, more or less explicitly, varying perspectives on what constitutes an organisation, and these varying perspectives contain varying implications for how organisations should be managed. The phrase 'should be managed' provides an ethical dimension. First, it is normative in that 'should' suggests some imperatives about what is right and wrong. Second, the word 'managed' refers to decisions, actions and behaviour of managers, both individually and collectively. Thus, each paradigm implies a different view of right and wrong managerial behaviour. The functionalist paradigm associates right behaviour with serving organisation objectives to ensure continued survival. Policy formulation and implementation therefore should, within the functionalist paradigm, serve that purpose and the behaviour of managers should follow that imperative. Given the existence of alternative imperatives on what is right and wrong, the functionalist view of policy formulation and implementation represents an ethical position since it assumes its own imperatives to be right and alternatives to be wrong. Justifying such an assumption will need to draw on and apply concepts and arguments from ethical theory since, in simple terms, ethics is concerned with establishing criteria to determine what is right and wrong (Bowie and Duska, 1990).

Activity 13.4

We have yet to formally define 'ethics'. However, the opening paragraphs have provided a sense of its meaning, and you no doubt have your own understanding of the concept. It will therefore be possible to carry out the following activity which will also be useful as you go through the rest of this chapter.

1. Produce a definition of ethics in your own words, taking no more than two sentences.

2 Discuss your definition with a colleague and compare and contrast any similarities and differences. Attempt to produce an agreed definition and shared understanding.

3 Apply your agreed definition to the four paradigms within organisation theory described in Chapter 2. With your colleague, attempt to describe the ethical position of each paradigm.

Definitions and meanings

According to Bowie and Duska (1990, p. 3) the word 'ethics' can refer to many different things. Torrington and Hall (1998) suggest an important distinction between the singular and plural forms of the word. For them, the singular refers to 'moral value' and the 'principles that ought to govern ... conduct', while the plural describes ' ... codes of behaviour considered to be correct, especially that of a particular group or profession' (*ibid.*, p. 682). Connock and Johns (1995, p. 2) assert that ethics is about fairness and deciding what is 'right or wrong'. They also refer to 'practices and rules' which determine responsible conduct (*ibid.*).

We can see similarities in these two formulations. The reference to 'fairness' and 'right or wrong' by Connock and Johns could be said to express the sentiments of Torrington and Hall on 'moral value' and 'principles' in a different way. The 'codes of behaviour' of Torrington and Hall is perhaps an alternative way of expressing 'practices and rules' in Connock and Johns's formulation. There seems to be agreement here that ethics is concerned with establishing what is right or moral and with translating what is established as right or moral into a system of codes or rules which govern behaviour. The two formulations discussed accord with the analysis and arguments of Bowie and Duska (1990). Here, ethics is defined as being concerned with 'a code of rules' or 'a set of principles' or 'the study of what is right and wrong' (*ibid.*, p. 3). However, the formulation of Bowie and Duska suggests a separation which is less explicit in the other two formulations discussed so far. Thus, referring to ethics as a code of conduct or set of rules is not the same as referring to ethics as the *study* of what is right or wrong. We can perhaps argue that a code of conduct provides a system of ethics to govern behaviour, which in turn is based on a set of ethical principles which themselves are derived from a study of what is right and wrong. It is important to be clear about which meaning is being applied.

In terms of ethics as the study of what is right and wrong, Bowie and Duska (1990) argue that such study is concerned with providing guidance on the question 'What should one do?'. In other words, the focus of ethics is on human actions or behaviour. However, they go on to elaborate that the focus is not concerned with any or all human behaviour. Ethics is concerned only with actions and behaviour which are the result of free will and deliberate choice, and which have 'serious' consequences or effects for the individual concerned and/or others. To illustrate the latter condition, they give the examples of 'slurping soup' or 'not putting oil in my car' as resulting from free will but lacking serious consequences (*ibid.*, p. 3).

Ethical arguments

The discussion so far would suggest that most human behaviour or action, in theory at least, can be *claimed* to be ethical in the sense of conforming to a given set of rules or conforming to a certain code of conduct. This is particularly the case if we accept Torrington and Hall's (1998) assertion that codes of behaviour can be 'considered to be correct' by a 'particular group or profession'. This argument raises the possibility that different groups or professions can and will consider different, perhaps even conflicting or contradictory, actions and behaviour to be 'correct'. The consequence of this will be that contradictory actions and behaviour will be considered ethical in terms of the codes of behaviour of the different groups or professions. Therefore, this position adopts a view that what is considered ethical, in the sense of right or wrong, can and does vary according to the rules and standards of different groups.

Such a view is consistent with moral, or ethical, 'relativism' (Bowie and Duska, 1990). In this view, there are no absolute or universal answers to the question 'What should one do?'. Instead, answers to the question will depend on the rules and norms of behaviour determined by particular groups at particular points in time. Individuals can answer the question for themselves, and behave 'ethically', by reference to and conformance with those rules and norms. Such a position would support an analysis and argument that, in an organisation context, the question of ethical behaviour can be associated with the concept of organisation culture (*see* Connock and Johns, 1995). If we take the definition of organisation culture offered by Watson (1994, p. 21) as 'the system of meanings which are shared by members of a human grouping and which define what is *good and bad, right and wrong* and what are the *appropriate ways* for members of that group to *think and behave*' (my emphasis), we can see the connection. As Watson goes on to say, 'culture is, in part, a moral system . . .' (1994).

It is important to understand that ethical relativism is just one possible position in ethical theory, and one which is subject to debate and challenge. In a much quoted article, Albert Carr (1968) uses the existence of different groups, each with their own codes of behaviour, to defend the fact that business standards and practices may not accord with what might be considered ethical, or right, or good, in other contexts or professions. In this sense then, Carr adopts a relativist position in relation to ethics. However, as Bowie and Duska (1990) demonstrate, there are conceptual problems with this position. These include defining the boundaries of a particular group, determining who speaks for the group and how they decide codes of behaviour, and finally the fact that all individuals belong at any one time to more than one group and that any sizeable social system, e.g. a nation or society, is composed of many groups. The latter condition creates the probability of conflict between different, and perhaps competing, codes of behaviour, and ethical relativism provides little or no help in resolving those conflicts.

There are within the study of ethics alternatives to ethical relativism. We might call these, collectively, universal systems of ethics (*see* Ferrell and Fraedrich, 1997, Bowie and Duska, 1990). However, these alternatives raise additional arguments and debates. There are, broadly, two competing formulations of what constitutes right or good in universal systems. The first is referred to as 'teleological' (Ferrell and Fraedrich, 1997). This position follows the philosophy of Aristotle and Plato in applying the principle of determining whether an action or behaviour is right or good on the basis of whether it fulfils its function or purpose (Bowie and Duska, 1990). Ferrell and Fraedrich (1997) explain this principle as one which considers an act morally right if it produces some desired result. This principle then provides a universal criterion which can be used to judge and evaluate the ethicality of any given action or behaviour. An alternative principle, derived from the second formulation, provides different criteria. This second formulation is known as 'deontological'. Here, the argument is that the *intentions,* rather than the consequences of actions and behaviour, are important in determining right and wrong, and that intentions have to be judged against the *potential* effects on individual rights (Ferrell and Fraedrich, 1997). Actual effects, by definition, will provide an opportunity for *post hoc* assessment. However, the ethical standard is *intentions* in relation to individual rights. This formulation therefore has to also determine what those rights might or should be.

It will be clear that there are at least two significant differences between teleological and deontological ethics. First, one focuses on consequences or results, and the other focuses on intentions. Second, a deontological position focuses on individuals and individual rights, while a teleological position, in some versions at least (*see* below), focuses on collectivities such as society. It will also be apparent that adoption of a teleological position will produce different rules of conduct than will a deontological position, and vice versa. The following activity will help you explore what these might be before we move on to examine the implications of ethical arguments for organisation and management theory.

Activity 13.5

1 Review your definition from Activity 13.4 in the light of these ethical arguments. Consider whether your definition reflects a relativist, teleological or deontological position, and whether you wish to revise/amend it to reflect an alternative position.

2 Review your response to **3** in Activity 13.4. Decide whether the ethical position you described for each paradigm reflects a relativist, teleological or deontological position. Re-assess your conclusions to determine what ethical position is implicit in each paradigm.

3 Discuss with a colleague what ethical position is explicitly or implicitly adopted in the policies, practices and behaviour of your organisation.

4 Again with your colleague, determine what significant changes in policies, practices and behaviour would follow in your organisation from explicitly adopting an alternative ethical position.

Ethics and organisation and management theory

A teleological position can take two broad forms. The first is referred to as 'psychological egoism' (Bowie and Duska, 1990). In this view, actions and behaviour can be justified on ethical grounds if the results achieved are in line with the desires of an individual. There is therefore the teleological focus on consequences and functionality. The main criteria of 'function', though, is achievement of the purpose of a particular or given individual. Thus, in answering the question 'What should one do?', this perspective would suggest whatever achieves your purpose as an ethical response. There is an implicit assumption in this argument that satisfaction of individual desires will be enlightened, and part of this enlightenment will be an understanding that immediate and selfish gratification will not be in any individual's long-term self-interest. Thus, the ethical principle is not 'act selfishly', but rather 'act in your own long-term self-interest'.

This principle is central to the ethical justification of a free market system for the conduct of business and the management of organisations (Bowie and Duska, 1990), although whether it can ever be actually fully applied is debatable (Donaldson, 1989, 1992). An alternative principle which is applied to support what might be termed conventional business practices is that of utilitarianism. Here, the focus remains on consequences and functionality, but the principle is one of achieving the greatest good for the greatest number of people (Ferrell and Fraedrich, 1997). According to Bowie and Duska (1990), both of these principles, i.e. egoism and utilitarianism, were adopted by Adam Smith and other theorists to justify classical economics, and an associated capitalist and free market system in which business organisations were acting ethically if they pursued actions which maximised their profits.

In a widely quoted analysis (Torrington and Hall, 1998, Connock and Johns, 1995, Bowie and Duska, 1990), Milton Friedman (1963, 1970) argues from, in part, a utilitarian position that it is ethical for business organisations to pursue the maximisation of profits. The argument is slightly modified by a recognition that business organisations should operate within the 'rules of the game' and therefore, within a free market context, conduct their affairs legally and honestly. Friedman also draws on a relativist position in that he recognises that the rules of the game will reflect both the laws and 'ethical customs' prevailing in society, which can change from place to place and over time. The issue of non-profit making organisations is accommodated in this analysis through what Friedman (1970) refers to as 'eleemosynary purposes'. This means that in non-profit-making organisations, it is ethical to pursue the stated purposes or objectives through whatever means are allowable by the rules of the game. A final feature of Friedman's analysis is worth highlighting. In examining the role of managers, a distinction is drawn between that of 'principal' and 'agent'. As individuals and citizens, people are principals who are free to adopt their own system of ethics. However, as managers, individuals are employees and therefore agents of the organisation, and thus have a duty to act in accordance with the desires and interests of those who own or establish the organisation.

We can summarise so far by saying that, according to a utilitarian position, managers of work organisations act in an ethical manner if their actions and behaviour are directed at achieving organisation purposes and objectives. However, a deontological position applies different criteria. Such a position follows the work of the philosopher Immanuel Kant (1724–1804), who argued that moral behaviour can be secure only if it is built on principles which are common; in other words, universal principles that can be applied in any and all places and which endure over time. In working out such a morality, Kant formulated what he referred to as 'the categorical imperative' which encompasses the two following formulations (Bowie and Duska, 1990 p. 46):

- act only according to that maxim by which you can, at the same time, will that it should become a universal law;
- act so as never to treat another human being merely as a means to an end.

As Bowie and Duska (1990) point out, the first formulation is a version of what is known as the Golden Rule, i.e. do unto others as you would have them do unto you, and its parallel formulation, i.e. do not do unto others what you would not have them do unto you. Bowie and Duska also argue that the first principle can be described as a *principle of consistency of action*. In other words, we should not treat others in a manner different to that which we treat ourselves or wish to be treated by them. The second principle can be restated as *the principle of respect for persons* (Bowie and Duska, 1990,

p. 50). This principle provides an obvious focus on the human rights of individuals. In application to organisation and management theory, there is an immediate and obvious conflict with the teleological position. Individual human beings in a free market and capitalist economy are defined as a 'factor of production' and therefore as a means to an end. This violates both Kantian principles, but the second one in particular. However, as Bowie and Duska (1990) argue, the inclusion of the qualifier 'merely' allows some room for interpretation. The injunction means that individuals as employees, within a deontological position, cannot be defined and treated *exactly* the same as other, inanimate factors of production. Following this argument, the principle has clear implications for how employees are organised and managed.

The deontological system of ethics tends to support a focus on morality being concerned with human relationships. This perspective in turn supports the notion of organisations establishing and maintaining sets of social relationships with various groups who are referred to as stakeholders (Connock and Johns, 1995). These relationships imply responsibilities, hence the notion of 'social responsibility' as part of business ethics (Torrington and Hall, 1998). As stated earlier, Bowie and Duska (1990) suggest these stakeholders who are owed social responsibility can include shareholders, employees, customers, government, other businesses or organisations and the communities in which an organisation operates. It is the latter that is usually referenced in support of responsibility to 'the environment' since communities are affected by the physical space in which they live. Stakeholder theory has wider application than the study of ethics, and it has also been criticised as a focus for analysis (*see* Connock and Johns, 1995). However, it seems to me that it has value in pointing to issues in organising and managing that have a clear ethical dimension. Some of these, as identified by various writers (Bowie and Duska, 1990, Connock and Johns, 1995, Torrington and Hall, 1998), are listed here:

- *employees*
  - hiring and firing;
  - right to liberty, e.g. freedom of speech;
  - right to privacy;
  - right to fair wages;
  - quality of working life;
  - information/confidentiality.
- *customers*
  - product quality and safety;
  - pricing policies;
  - advertising.
- *communities*
  - pollution;
  - physical environment;
  - closure of operations.
- *government*
  - compliance with legislation;
  - implementation of regulations;
  - tax returns.
- *shareholders*
  - honesty;
  - providing a return.
- *other organisations* – act honestly and fairly;
  - honour contracts.

These issues are by no means exhaustive. Some have obvious overlap, for instance, employees are members of communities and also citizens whose interests are represented by governments. The issue of safety is another example because it also concerns employees and communities. Each of the issues raises 'ethical dilemmas' (Connock and Johns, 1995) for managers of work organisations. The overriding dilemma is in answering the question 'What should one do?', (Bowie and Duska, 1990). However, the question can have a sharper focus when alternative courses of action conflict on ethical grounds. Perhaps the best example of this is what is referred to as 'whistle blowing' (Bowie and Duska, 1990, Connock and Johns, 1995). Here, the dilemma is presented when individual employees become aware of, or perhaps are required to participate in, organisation actions and behaviour which they and others consider unethical. There is an obvious ethical dilemma in the latter case since there is a conflict between personal and organisational beliefs about what is right and wrong. However, one course of action open in both cases is to report and publicise the unethical behaviour, in other words, 'blow the whistle' on the organisation.

It is increasingly common practice for organisations to develop ethical statements, appoint senior managers to oversee social responsibility and to provide confidential telephone hotlines to help managers and other employees to deal with and resolve ethical dilemmas (*see* Connock and Johns, 1995). However, such measures, while potentially helpful, are unlikely to eradicate the existence and occurrence of individuals having to confront such dilemmas. We might argue from this that individuals as well as organisations will benefit from thinking through and working out their own ethical position to inform and guide their actions and behaviour in carrying out their role and fulfilling their duties as employees. They will then be in a more informed and enlightened position to answer the question 'What should one do?' when faced with an ethical dilemma.

Activity 13.6

1 Think of an example of an ethical dilemma that might be faced by an employee development practitioner in relation to one of the issues listed against 'employees' above. Write a description of the scenario.

2 Produce a response to the question of what the person should do from each of the following ethical positions, providing a reasoned argument in each case:

(a) relativist

(b) utilitarian

(c) deontological.

3 Discuss and debate your response with a colleague who has also completed **1** and **2**.

4 Consider each of the responses and determine which most closely reflects your own ethical position *and* that of your organisation. Examine any differences and the reasons for them, and consider the implications for your role.

Ethics and ED policy

It will, hopefully, be clear by now that the study of ethics has direct connections with and implications for employee development policy formulation and implementation. In broad terms, we can argue that a utilitarian position would support a view that senior managers are exclusively responsible for deciding policy since they are directly accountable to the 'owners' of the organisation. The same position would also lead to the policy emphasising, perhaps exclusively, employee development that supports achievement of organisation objectives. In contrast, a deontological position might arguably support a consultative approach to policy formulation. It might also produce a policy which pays more attention to individual rights and aspirations in its content. A simple example would be in relation to access to and confidentiality of employee development records.

We can frame these connections in another way. An ED policy statement sets out intentions as a guide to actions and behaviour. In a very real sense, therefore, the ED policy is a statement of ethics. It is premised on beliefs about what is right and wrong and, in broad terms at least, it represents a code of conduct or behaviour. ED policy statements are therefore capable of being subject to ethical analysis and criticism. We can develop this further with a specific example. It was argued earlier that policy statements should define and specify roles and responsibilities in relation to employee development, including those of ED practitioners. The Institute of Personnel Development adopts a Code of Professional Conduct (IPD, 1996) which sets out expected standards of professional behaviour. According to the definitions discussed earlier, such a code represents a system of ethics. This argument is supported by Torrington and Hall (1998). Any member of the IPD freely agrees, by virtue of seeking and accepting membership, to comply with the IPD code. Therefore, in providing advice on the content of ED policy statements, a member of the IPD should ensure that the role and responsibilities of ED practitioners specified in the policy are compatible with the IPD Code. If any contradiction or conflict occurs, then ED practitioners working in the organisation who are also members of the IPD will be faced with an ethical dilemma. So, we cannot consider ED policy in isolation from ethical arguments.

One final issue will be highlighted before closing the chapter. I have argued elsewhere (Stewart, 1998b) that HRD presents stark ethical questions. I use two examples to illustrate and support this argument. The first rests on the inevitable subjectivity of assessment discussed in an earlier chapter. The second follows from the conceptual model of HRD introduced in Chapter 2 (*see* Fig. 2.1). The notion of 'interventions' is central to this model. However, we can characterise 'intervening' as 'interfering' since the two concepts have similar meanings (Stewart, 1998b). Therefore, we can say that HRD involves some people (specialist practitioners) *interfering* with the natural learning processes of some other people (learners, trainees, clients or whatever). The ethical question that arises is, by what right do one group of people 'interfere' with another? The ethicality of the question is clearer, but no different, if the word interfere is used instead of intervene. I use this argument to present what I consider to be a, if not the, central ethical question in organisation and management theory. This is simply whether organisations should pursue emancipatory or oppressive purposes.

Development, and therefore the professional practice of employee development, can be liberating and therefore supportive of promoting human and individual potential. The professional practice of HRD can, however, serve the opposite purpose in promoting standardisation and conformity (*see* Fredericks and Stewart, 1996). This means, in my view, that employee development is critical in answering the central question. I believe individual practitioners need to address the question for themselves and produce their own answers. However, I also believe that, intentionally and consciously or not, statements of ED policy within organisations imply, if not contain, an answer to the question.

Summary and conclusion

This chapter has considered the two concepts of policy and ethics. It has demonstrated direct and inevitable connections and relationships between them. While it is the case that all aspects of HRD practice will have ethical dimensions, the argument here has been that ethical considerations become clearest when formulating policy statements. The analysis of the nature and purpose of policy in organisations has supported an argument that, to be of value, policy needs to be specific, detailed and issued in written form. A number of factors have been recognised and identified as shaping and influencing the content of policy statements. Ethical considerations have been highlighted as of particular importance. For that reason, this chapter has provided a brief summary of ethical theory and debates. This has shown how varying ethical positions, especially those associated with utilitarian and deontological philosophies, will lead to different actions and behaviour on the part of organisations and individuals. Competing views on what is right and wrong can and will lead to individuals facing ethical dilemmas in carrying out their professional and organisational roles.

Two significant and important conclusions are possible. First, ED policy represents a system of ethics which will have consequences and implications for all areas of ED activity. Second, ED specialists will have a critical role in formulating and implementing ED policy. For both these reasons, it is important that practitioners think through and work out their own, individual ethical position. Perhaps one area of practice which might be particularly fruitful in presenting ethical questions and dilemmas is that of securing and managing resources. This will be examined in the next chapter. Ethical considerations will not be directly identified and addressed, however. Readers are therefore advised to keep an 'ethical eye' on the content as they work through the chapter.

Case study 13

Susan Sparrow has recently been promoted to group HRD adviser in the Teesdale group of companies. The group consists primarily of engineering companies, one of which Susan previously worked for for five years as training manager. Currently, Susan is responsible for reviewing and producing recommendations on the potential of NVQs across the group, especially in relation to non-managerial and professional employees. However, as the group adviser, part of Susan's role is to provide advice and support to individual companies. She is therefore also currently active in advising Grahame Evans, chief executive of Pennycook Engineering Limited (PEL), a company within the Teesdale group.

PEL is engaged in the design and manufacture of high-precision engineering components which it supplies mainly to customers in the automotive and electronic industries. As a subsidiary of the Teesdale group, PEL is subject to financial targets which are expected to improve year on year. Results over the past five years have been more than satisfactory and PEL has experienced consistent growth. The last full year's performance showed profits in excess of £50 million on sales close to £500 million. These figures reflect PEL's history as a successful and highly regarded company. The employees of PEL, numbering just over 1000, take this success for granted and have come to expect PEL to take the lead in technical advancements and to enjoy a reputation for high quality products.

Grahame Evans, who has been in his post for just over 12 months, interprets the employees' view as complacency. He understands very clearly the demands of the board of Teesdale group for continuing success, and is fully aware of PEL's industrial customers' continuing demands for improvements in quality, cost and delivery. Grahame is under no illusions that he will have to prove his worth in the Teesdale group by increasing profits at PEL, and that this will require improvements across the company, but especially in manufacturing which employs 70 per cent of the workforce. Grahame understands, too, that this will not be an easy task. Over a decade of success has been built on an authoritarian style of management where only managers take decisions and other employees do what they are told. The manufacturing manager, Richard Slater, is used to wielding the 'big stick' and, understandably, this style is adopted by the majority of production managers and supervisors. There is therefore clear evidence of a 'them and us' atmosphere in the company and a culture of sticking rigidly to the specified requirements of the job and little or no willingness to demonstrate flexibility.

Employee development in PEL is part of the role of one of three personnel officers who report to a personnel manager. The personnel manager, Ron Edwards, considers it his role to control employee behaviour on behalf of management. Personnel services are advisory and supportive to line managers in areas such as procedural advice, recruitment and selection and technical training. Ron Edwards is proud of the fact that PEL remains non-unionised and considers it a key part of his job to maintain that situation. The success of PEL and its ability to offer high wages are important in achieving that objective. However, Grahame Evans believes the current approach to management, and especially to personnel and development, is old fashioned and outdated, hence his decision to call on the services of Susan Sparrow.

Susan has been fully briefed by Grahame Evans on his view of the future for PEL. He believes it is essential to introduce significant changes based on more 'modern' management techniques. In particular, the chief executive is committed to continuous improvement through cellular manufacturing and the process known as 'kaizen'. The former will require greater levels of autonomy on the part of shopfloor employees, while the latter demands a greater degree of involvement in and responsibility for decisions among all staff. These are very different approaches to the established autocratic management style at PEL. Grahame Evans is certain, however, that they are required to ensure continuation of PEL's success in a changing marketplace.

In her investigations to assess current practices in PEL, Susan interviewed Richard Slater. He told her that when things go wrong in PEL, managers merely 'go around the factory with a bigger piece of wood and hit them a bit harder. It usually works'. Given this attitude, Susan is unsure that Grahame Evans fully realises the size and nature of the task facing him. At the moment, Susan is working on a draft policy statement for employee development to discuss with Grahame Evans. Her immediate concern is how far it can go in the direction desired by the chief executive while still recognising and being relevant to the current situation in PEL. Susan has persuaded Grahame of the value of a written policy statement, but is unsure of his support for any content that does not fit in with his vision. The time for Susan's quarterly report to her boss, the group personnel and training director, is also fast approaching. Susan will have to report on her work and progress at PEL.

The content of that report is also taxing Susan. The demands of Grahame Evans have resulted in some slowing of progress on Susan's work on NVQs, and she is concerned that this will not be well received by her boss. Life seemed a lot simpler as training manager in a factory.

Discussion questions

1 Identify at least two decisions facing Susan that could be said to present her with an ethical dilemma.

2 How would an understanding of ethics help Susan resolve these dilemmas?

3 What are the ethical considerations of Grahame Evans's proposed changes in PEL?

4 What should be the content of an employee development policy statement for PEL which reflects the changes desired by Grahame Evans?

5 How would you recommend Susan and Grahame to set about implementing and communicating a new ED policy for PEL?

Suggested reading

Bowie, N.E. and Duska, R.F. (1990) *Business Ethics (2nd edn)*. Upper Saddle River, NJ: Prentice-Hall.

Connock, S. and Johns, T. (1995) *Ethical Leadership*. London: IPD.

Marshall, E. (1993) *Business and Society*. London: Routledge.

Reid, M. and Barrington, H. (1997) *Training Interventions (5th edn)*. London: IPD.

CHAPTER 14

Resourcing the ED function

Introduction

It is now almost axiomatic that employee development needs to be recognised as an investment rather than as a cost (e.g. Harrison, 1997). This can perhaps provide some confidence and reassurance to professional practitioners in that their work will come to be valued for its longer term returns, rather than being viewed as a short-term expediency. The latter, certainly in the past and to some extent currently, leads to a situation where expenditure on employee development becomes an initial and prime candidate for reductions when costs are being cut to meet short-term contingencies (Truelove, 1997). A perception of expenditure on employee development as an investment can perhaps provide a higher degree of protection in the circumstances of such contingencies. However, the degree of protection, and associated confidence and reassurance, should not be overstated.

In common with other functions, employee development will require resources in order to operate successfully, and securing resources requires that a sound and convincing case is made in terms that make sense to, and which are valued by, key decision makers (Moorby, 1996). Those terms are almost always likely to include financial and monetary considerations (Harrison, 1997, Reid and Barrington, 1997, Moorby, 1996). Therefore, it remains important for practitioners to be able to apply concepts from the language of finance and accounting if they are to be effective in securing necessary resources. It might be argued that success in securing resources also requires facility in the language of marketing (Harrison, 1997). This argument, I think, lends support to the purpose of 'promoting' being attached to evaluation which was suggested in Chapter 10. That suggestion focuses attention on the role of evaluation in marketing the ED function and thus contributing to securing necessary resources. We will, though, be primarily concerned in this chapter with financial considerations.

The primary focus of this chapter then is the nature of the resources required to provide effective employee development services, and the financial arguments that can be used in securing allocation of those resources to the ED function. This focus will require some examination of principles and concepts arising out of the disciplines of financial management and accounting. My examination of these principles and concepts will be conventional. That is, I will treat the concepts as unproblematic. However, such a treatment relies heavily on a functionalist paradigm and an associated 'Tayloristic' (Puxty, 1993) conception of organisation and management. Alternative and more critical treatments are possible (*see* Alvesson and Willmott, 1996). In particular, the whole subject of financial management and accounting is being increasingly subject to analysis and critical appraisal from alternative perspectives (*see,* e.g. Barber, 1997).

One of the most cogent examples of such work is the short but excellent book by Anthony Puxty (1993). As well as providing a critique of the assumptions and values which inform current practices in accounting, the book provides the clearest exposition of alternative perspectives I have read. I refer to the book here to recommend it to readers, and as support for my plea that the contents of this chapter are read in the context of the organisational paradigm that informs them.

While it is probably true that accounting practices in most if not all organisations follow the paradigm applied here, critically evaluating the results in the light of the existence of alternatives can provide valuable insight. A particular example of this is to bear in mind that organisations can be viewed as political arenas consisting of competing interests. The 'political game' or process in which these interests engage is, in part, played by the rules and through the language of accounting. Thus, accounting concepts, principles and procedures need not be seen as neutral, objective and value-free criteria by which rational decisions are reached. Rather, they can be viewed as a set of 'discursive activities' (Oswick *et al.*, 1997), which are used by both accountants and non-accountants to secure and maintain power in organisations (Barber, 1997). Similar analyses are being applied to the total field of employee development (Sambrook and Stewart, 1998a, 1998b, Sambrook, 1998) and this provides an additional reason for ensuring the critical faculties of readers are attuned to this chapter.

A range of classifications of different types of resources required for ED is presented in the specialist literature (*see* Harrison, 1997, Reid and Barrington, 1997, Moorby, 1996). We will be concerned here with three types: money, physical and human. The first of these will be dealt with through an examination of basic yet critical concepts. Physical resources will focus on the use of buildings and equipment in the form of training centres, including the topical category of 'learning resource centre'. Our concern with human resources will be focused on recruitment, selection and development of specialist ED staff. Some examples will be given to illustrate application of principles and concepts. Two caveats to this are important to state at the outset. First, actual accounting practices can and do vary from organisation to organisation and over time. These variations include differences in language and terminology. It will be necessary therefore for readers to produce their own translations. Second, I cannot predict how long this book will remain in print and therefore when it might be read. I am writing these words in the spring of 1998. They may, hopefully, be read in the next century. I can predict, though, that the price and cost of resources will be different (almost certainly greater) at the time of reading than at the time of writing. Therefore, readers will again bear the responsibility of updating any actual figures. Guidance will be given on how this might be done. With these two caveats in mind, and the context described in the previous paragraphs, this chapter is intended to achieve the objectives shown below.

CHAPTER OBJECTIVES

- Explain and apply critical concepts associated with the costing and budgeting of employee development.

- Assess and evaluate the advantages and disadvantages of dedicated physical resources in the form of training centres.

- Explain and critically assess the concept of 'learning resource centre' and its application in practical contexts.

- Articulate and apply key principles in the recruitment, selection and development of specialist ED personnel.

- Produce costed and justified proposals for investment in employee development activities.

Costing and budgeting employee development

The main content of this chapter will begin with an examination of some basic concepts and processes. These will be discussed in the context of each and all of the three types of resources identified earlier. However, their application is to some extent primarily associated with the first of these, i.e. money. As we shall see, this is because all resources, including physical and human, can be and often are constituted as and by monetary concepts.

A useful starting point is to consider why the situation implied by the last sentence is the case. This question can be answered in part by examining the purpose or purposes of costing and budgeting *per se* in work organisations. In other words, why is it that all organisation activities are expressed in and represented by financial terms? Costing and budgeting are the processes which bring this about, but why engage in costing and budgeting in the first place? There are at least three possible, related answers to this question. The first is reasonably straightforward in that there are legal requirements placed on organisations which specify the form and content of the information they publish about their activities. This is related to the second purpose, which is to both *control* and *account* for scarce resources. Organisations would wish to control use of resources so as to ensure they are not wasted and that they produce some valued outcomes, or returns. Depending on the nature and legal status of their incorporation, organisations might also wish to account for their use of scarce resources to those who provide them. However, in most cases, though subject to the same provisos of nature and status, organisations are legally required to account for their use of resources. This is achieved through publication of annual reports. Such reports give an account of the use of resources in the given period, and those who made decisions on that use can, on the basis of the reports, be held to account for their use and control of resources.

A final purpose of costing and budgeting is to assess the contribution of various activities to achieving organisation objectives. Decision makers face choices about allocating resources in the future, and information on past results and performance can provide a valuable input in making those decisions. Costing and budgeting enables assessment of contribution and thus provides that information. In summary, costing and budgeting serves the following purposes:

- to meet legal requirements;
- to control and account for scarce resources;
- to assess the varying contribution of varying activities to achievement of organisation objectives.

The final purpose is obviously related to allocation of resources. The assessment is focused on whether allocation of resources of a given amount to a particular activity, or set of activities, produced a worthwhile and valued return in terms of organisation objectives. Such assessments inform decisions on future allocations. In theory at least, it is possible for such a purpose to be achieved by means other than costing and budgeting, at least where objectives relate to non-financial criteria. This may also be true, again in theory, for other purposes, so long as legal requirements allow non-financial criteria. However, in practice, most organisations express some at least of their objectives in financial terms, even if the language used implies rather than directly states financial criteria, for example, concepts such as efficiency. This is one reason why financial criteria are used to achieve the three purposes. Other reasons include the following:

- *Measurement.* Using financial criteria creates a common and consistent yardstick against which resource allocation can be measured. In doing so, it facilitates comparison and assessment of the various activities undertaken.
- *Decision making.* This reason relates to decisions on resource allocation. The common criteria provided by the language of finance and accounting enables and supports the negotiation and agreement of budgets, for example.
- *'Bottom line'.* We might refer to financial performance representing the 'bottom line' of organisation objectives. However, we can also argue that in the context of capitalist economies, the 'bottom line' is that organisations cannot operate without resources which are expressed in and accounted for in financial terms. That being the case, it makes sense to incorporate similar terms in managing organisation activities.

Given the purposes described so far, and the reasons for using financial criteria and concepts in meeting those purposes, it is perhaps understandable that decision makers at all levels in organisations take a keen interest in money. 'How much will it cost?' or 'what will I get for my money?' are not uncommon questions to proposals submitted to decision makers for approval. Anticipating and answering such questions within proposals is therefore advisable. However, the questions also illustrate the obsessive concern with matters of finance within organisations, and the associated need for all functions, including employee development, to be able to justify their existence and activities in financial terms. The process of costing that existence and those activities is the starting point in meeting that need.

Activity 14.1

1 Imagine an organisation without an overt concern for financial criteria. What alternatives might be used to meet the purposes listed above?

2 Assess the extent to which decision makers in your organisation might be described as 'obsessed' with financial criteria. In doing so, answer the following questions:

(a) in what ways does a concern with finance express itself?

(b) what emphasis is placed on financial criteria in explicit organisation objectives?

(c) what implications can you identify for the ED function arising from the level of interest in and attention to financial criteria?

3 Consider the current level of financial sophistication displayed within the ED function in your organisation. For example:

(a) are all activities currently costed?

(b) do all proposals for approval include anticipated results/benefits expressed in financial terms?

(c) are alternative responses to ED problems assessed/evaluated in financial terms before final decisions are taken?

4 Based on the results of **3** consider whether and how the ED function could improve its facility/fluency in the language of finance.

The process of costing ED activities

Costing any activity is a necessary precursor to formulation of budgets. In that sense, it can be seen as part of any budgeting process. Two stages are involved in costing. First, the items, or 'factors', that will attract costs need to be identified and specified. Second, the actual costs associated with each of the cost factors need to be established or estimated. Establishing or estimating costs depends on the extent to which actual costs are known at the time the costing exercise is undertaken. Some will be known and therefore can be established. Some will not be known and therefore will need to be estimated.

The fact that actual costs consist of some that are known and some that are unknown suggests that costs can be categorised into different types. A conventional categorisation uses three different types. The first is known as 'fixed costs'. Other terms used for this type include 'standing charges' and 'overheads'. The former is a term more often found in public sector organisations, while the latter is a little difficult since accounting practices allow variation in what is defined as an 'overhead'. Caution is therefore advised in translating these terms to particular contexts. The key principle to apply is that fixed costs will be incurred irrespective of the level of activity. In fact, fixed costs will need to be paid even if the level of activity is zero. This principle also distinguishes the second type of cost. This is 'direct costs'. Other terms for this include 'direct expenditure', 'variable costs' and 'marginal expenditure'. Strictly speaking, the last of these is a concept from economics which is misused/misapplied in this context. The key principle is that direct costs are those which vary *according to* the level of activity. In other words, the

265

greater the level of activity, the greater the amount of direct costs incurred, and the lower the level of activity, the lower the amount of direct costs. Hence use of the term 'variable costs'.

The final cost type is more difficult to apply and more controversial in its use. It is known as 'indirect cost' or 'indirect expenditure'. An alternative term, 'hidden costs', perhaps suggests the nature of the difficulties and controversies. Two examples will illustrate the nature of this type of cost, and the associated controversies and difficulties. First, all organisations have certain costs which do not easily fall into mainstream activities. An example may be the remuneration of the board of directors. Second, when employees are undertaking formal development activities, rather than doing their jobs, an 'opportunity cost' is incurred. For example, those employees are not directly contributing to producing a return for their salaries. Difficulties and controversies surround arriving at actual costs for these factors, defining them as either indirect or fixed and in allocating them to particular mainstream activities. To take the first example, should it be an overhead or part of indirect costs? To take the second example, should the cost, however specified and defined, be considered a training cost or a cost incurred by the employing function, department or division?

The question raised by the notion of indirect costs has no simple or universal answers. Practices can and do vary across organisations. But the questions need to be answered in particular contexts in order that budgets can be formulated. Costing as a process can also serve additional purposes. It has obvious application in evaluation of employee development, especially where cost/benefit analysis is used in that process. Being able to cost development activities has potential value earlier in the training cycle. First, the process of problem analysis intended to determine which are training and non-training problems, described in Chapter 8, is also intended to establish whether corrective action will be worthwhile. Applying the notion of investment appraisal, which seeks to answer that question in financial terms, requires that potential costs are known or can be realistically estimated. Second, the same process includes the stage of estimate costs/benefits. This activity is always relevant at the design stage of the training cycle since an important factor to take into account in such decisions (for example, whether to design and provide an in-house course or to use an existing, external course) is the relative cost of available options. These two applications of existing employee development are illustrated in Fig. 14.1.

Activity 14.2

1 Identify and list the most significant cost factors involved in employee development.

2 Determine which type of cost each factor represents, and allocate each to one of three types.

3 Estimate realistic and current costs for each item. Remember that staff costs should be based on costs of employment rather than on salary (usually between 30 per cent and 50 per cent added to salary). Costs of consultants, external courses, facilities and equipment can be established through advertisements in professional journals.

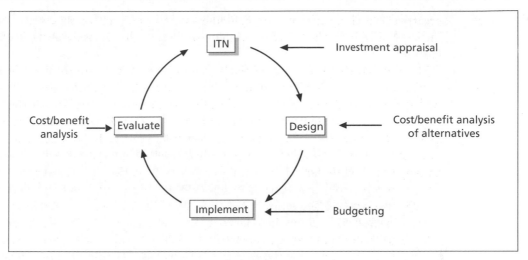

Fig. 14.1 Financial techniques and the training cycle

Formulating a budget

Once cost factors have been identified and actual costs determined, a budget can be formulated. As a reminder, budgets serve two related purposes: to justify allocation and expenditure of resources, and to provide a management control tool to ensure available resources are not exceeded and are accounted for. Critical perspectives might emphasise the control function served by 'targets', whether budgetary or otherwise (*see* Fisher, 1999). The former purpose can be very useful in marketing the employee development function. Budget proposals can highlight past successes, emphasising recent achievements in terms of valued outcomes, and can focus on the returns, in the same terms, to be achieved by future investment. Both purposes can be applied to an annual budget for the whole function, or to a particular and specific activity. We will be primarily concerned with the former.

An annual budget should provide and account for the known fixed costs and the estimated expenditure of direct costs. In most organisations, projecting costs forward for 12 months will mean that the former are known and the latter can only be estimated. The relationship between annual budgets and indirect costs very much depends on accounting practices adopted in particular organisations. A useful process to follow in constructing a budget is as follows (Kenrick, 1984):

- *Identify existing commitments.* The focus here is to establish the costs associated with running the ED function, i.e. fixed costs, and direct costs associated with continuing activities. An example of the latter might be fees for employees being sponsored on educational programmes. A significant consideration in each case is to allow for increases over the previous year in, for example, salary costs and college fees. Where these are not known, it is common practice to use an agreed percentage allowance for inflation.
- *Identify proposed actions/activities.* This stage follows from the process of identifying training needs. The purpose is to identify and specify the cost factors associated

with each new activity. This can be more difficult for some activities. It is, however, likely that most factors will be immediately obvious even if actual costs need to be estimated.

- *Cost-proposed activities*. There may be a need in a budget proposal to consider alternatives, with one option being identified as the preferred or recommended action. These options can be presented as part of this stage. However, whether options are presented or not, all proposed activities will be costed on the basis of a share of known, fixed costs and estimated direct costs.

- *Identify and specify income*. There can be many sources of income. External sources include funding from TECs or other government agencies or fees received through sale of ED products and services. The concepts of zero-budgets and service agreement contracts are being increasingly applied (Moorby, 1996) and therefore internal payments may be made to the ED function by client departments. Expected income from any source is normally included in budgets.

- *Summarise and present budget information*. The form that this final stage will take is too variable to attempt to specify here. Common practice, though, suggests that an overall total of ED costs will be broken down into specific budget headings. This can be by department, by category of employee, by type of development activity or any combination of these headings. Or indeed any heading or headings that anyone can think of. One requirement that remains constant is to allocate fixed costs proportionally across budget headings on the basis of some agreed criteria or formula.

The above process applies to an annual budget, although the same principles can be applied to constructing a budget for a particular activity. Responsibility for ED is argued to be increasingly decentralised to line departments and managers (Harrison, 1997, Reid and Barrington, 1997). This may or may not include responsibility for ED budgets. In either case, decentralised responsibility will have implications for the construction and presentation of central budgets. A final feature of the budgeting process is to use the results in identifying trends and facilitating comparisons. These may focus on internal trends/comparisons through tracking changes in allocations and expenditure over time, and on external trends/comparisons through benchmarking. A useful device for producing such analyses is the notion of ratios. Moorby (1996) suggests the following five ratios as useful for such purposes:

- cost per day of training;
- training cost as a percentage of payroll;
- budget variance;
- training days per trainer per annum;
- average training days provided per employee.

The arithmetic involved in calculating these ratios is straightforward, though defining some of the terms may not be, e.g. 'day of training'. Access to external comparative data can be through trade associations, government reports/statistics, professional journals and informal networks. The following activity closes our discussion of costing and budgeting.

Activity 14.3

Imagine you are an ED specialist who has agreed with a line manager a priority need for developing the leadership skills of 20 supervisors in the manager's department. You have also agreed that a formal programme of no more than three days would be appropriate, with no more than ten supervisors away at one time. A well respected provider, with facilities just over 50 miles from the location of your organisation, provides a suitable, 'open' course with the range of participant numbers limited to a minimum of 18 and a maximum of 25. The provider also offers an in-house course specifically tailored to organisation requirements. However, they insist on five days' consultancy in addition to the direct training time to identify specific needs, design/amend the course and prepare original materials. Consider and respond to the following questions:

(a) What options are available to you in this scenario?

(b) Which cost factors will be associated with each option?

(c) What is your estimate of the actual cost of each factor in each option?

(d) What other factors will you take into account, other than costs, in reaching a decision or recommendation?

(e) How will you proceed to arrive at a final decision?

Physical resources

Physical resources can, generally, be regarded as falling into two types: buildings and equipment. The latter will consist of items such as furniture, overhead projectors, flipchart stands and electronic equipment such as PCs and interactive video players. Buildings will include office space for staff employed in the ED function, as well as space dedicated for and to development purposes and activities. These can include training centres and training workshops which may include additional types of equipment, for example, relevant tools and machinery used in craft training. All these resources will normally form part of the fixed costs of the employee development function. However, some items, for example, video players, can be hired for use as and when necessary. The same is true of physical space, for example, using the facilities of hotels or specialist conference centres. In these circumstances, the costs become direct rather than fixed, since expenditure will vary according to the amount of development undertaken. One set of costs which are normally always direct costs are the materials used by and with items of equipment, for example, acetate sheets, flipchart pads, training videos and materials used in craft or operative training and development. The actual costs of both equipment and 'consumable materials' at any particular time are easily determined through advertisements in the professional and trade press, and through contact with established suppliers.

Establishing the fixed costs of dedicated physical space, for example, offices for specialist ED staff, will depend on varying practices adopted by particular organisations. Common practice would suggest some formula based on £X per square metre per annum, where X takes account of expenditure on rent, rates, heating, lighting, etc. The same type of formula can be used where the ED function shares space with other functions and departments and, depending on the particular arrangements for shared space, can be used to calculate either fixed or direct costs associated with physical space.

This brief overview provides an illustration of the kinds of issues and principles involved in considering physical resources from a costing and budgeting perspective. The rest of this section will be concerned with the particular resource of a training centre, and the more recent version of this resource commonly referred to as learning resource centre. We will initially be concerned with some general principles which can be applied to either or both, before separately considering specific issues to do with each.

An important point to state first is that physical space tends to be expensive, and therefore dedicating space for the exclusive purpose of employee development will, in most cases, represent a significant investment. The decision on whether or not to have such space will therefore require careful deliberation. An important factor to bear in mind in making this decision will be the notion of opportunity cost. What this means is that any expenditure on a training centre, of whatever form, cannot be used to fund alternative development activities. So, the case for such facilities in the sense of expected benefits needs to be carefully examined and thought through, especially in terms of comparing the benefits with those that might be expected from alternative activities. A key factor, as always with such decisions, will be the level of support from top managers and the relationship between expected benefits and their valued outcomes. For example, leading edge or state of the art centres may be associated with corporate image and prestige. The ED case for and against use of dedicated ED space may be secondary to the 'corporate image' case. Criteria outside a strict interpretation of advantages/disadvantages from a development perspective may therefore need to be considered.

A number of other issues need to be taken into account. First, the categories of staff and the nature of the development the physical space is intended to support. An example of each will illustrate the point. It is unlikely that a physical resource intended to support management development will be quite the same as one intended to support craft or operative level employees. Similarly, a resource capable of supporting development of social skills will probably require different facilities from one dealing with technical knowledge and skills. The second issue is, in part, related to the first since it concerns volume of use. The expected use of the facilities will depend on the size of the intended population and the need/demand for replacement, refresher and updating development. Expected volume is also a critical criterion in its own right. A third issue is that of privacy. This is also related to the intended audience, for example, in the case of sales training or senior management workshops where confidential or sensitive information may need to be disseminated or discussed. The fourth issue is the amount of flexibility that needs to be planned into the resource. For example, it may be necessary to be able to respond at short notice to the requirements of new initiatives. Finally, there is the issue of costs. An important factor here is to consider both the start-up costs, i.e. the investment required to establish the resource, and the operating costs, i.e. those arising on a continuing basis from the resource providing its intended services.

All these issues need to be considered whether the resource is a traditional training centre or a learning resource centre (LRC). Some additional issues arise more or less specifically with each of these. We will now look at some of those more likely (although not necessarily exclusively) to arise when considering a traditional training centre.

Training centres

A critical and early issue to consider is whether the centre will provide residential accommodation. Many large organisations, such as Lloyds TSB and National Westminster Bank in financial services and the John Lewis Partnership in retail, own and operate training centres with extensive and high-standard accommodation. These facilities are not essential, however, especially if arrangements can be made with local hotels for staff travelling from a distance. A related decision, assuming a centre does provide accommodation, is whether to directly operate this service, including employing the necessary staff, or whether to contract out management of these services and facilities to specialist organisations, for example, hotel or catering companies. As with any contracting-out decision, there are arguments for and against and no simple or definitive answer.

The issue of residential accommodation is related to two further questions. The first is that of location. Obviously, a training centre needs to be accessible and to have good transport links, especially if the organisation operates nationally or internationally. Other considerations might include local facilities for recreation to provide breaks from the centre, and the closeness or otherwise to the normal place of work and/or a main or head office of the organisation. Giving colleagues and/or managers easy access to learners at the centre may be disruptive. However, given the state of modern communications technology, physical access can be the least significant form of disruption. The second issue is that of teaching accommodation. As a general principle, the aim is normally to minimise a classroom or school atmosphere and to create a relaxing and supportive climate. The quality of teaching accommodation, for example, the standards of decoration and furnishing, can also signal the value attached to employee development.

Whether or not a training centre is residential, and irrespective of the intended users, a range of domestic services needs to be considered. These include reception, catering and cleaning. In the case of a non-residential centre located on the same site as a main or head office operation, the latter two can share in or be part of more general provision. However, reception services are always likely to have to be provided by the ED function. Similar considerations apply to maintenance. Physical space and equipment need to be refurbished, replaced, maintained and repaired. These services can be provided directly by the ED function, or through a contract agreement or through the general services of the organisation. These factors raise the related issue of training centre staff. This is obviously a critical question in terms of the number and nature of staff who will be dedicated to the training centre. Whatever arrangements are arrived at in relation to all these issues, the costs associated with the arrangements need to be allocated to the operating costs of the centre, and therefore to form part of the ED budget (*see* Moorby, 1996).

A final consideration is that of potential income. A number of sources are possible. Residential accommodation not being used for particular periods can be 'sold' to external users. The same is true of teaching accommodation, which can be sold independently or in combination with residential accommodation. Lloyds TSB, for example, makes its facilities available in all three ways during slack times. The service of training centres, including training and development courses, can be sold on the open market. The GEC management centre, for example, adopts this practice. Finally, the services of the centre can be charged to user departments on the basis of either full or subsidised costs (*see* Moorby, 1996). All such income will be credited to the ED budget as a contribution towards the costs of the training centre. The difficulty of these practices, however, is balancing the priorities of the organisation's own development activities against the opportunities for income generation.

Activity 14.4

1 Assuming a medium-sized organisation, what would you consider to be the minimum requirements in terms of physical resources?

2 Using your knowledge of current, actual costs, produce an estimated annual costing for these resources.

3 Consider and produce a list of advantages and disadvantages associated with ownership and operation of an 'own-use' training centre.

4 Using the results of **1** to **3**, assess the provision of physical resources in your organisation and decide whether you believe more or less investment is needed.

5 Discuss the results of **4** with a colleague from your organisation and then with a colleague from another organisation.

6 Based on the results of **5** revise, if necessary, your response to **4**.

Learning resource centres (LRCs)

The concept of learning resource centre could be said to combine that of a training centre with ideas deriving from the concept of open learning, although the latter concept has connections with alternative conceptualisations such as 'resource-based learning' and 'flexible learning' (Dorrell, 1993) which can sometimes cause confusion. This is especially the case if they are used as synonyms, or if distinctions are not directly articulated. In addition, the concept of open learning is not straightforward or unproblematic and is subject to both misuse and abuse (Stewart and Winter, 1995, Stewart, 1996). However, we do not have the space here to explore in depth what is a complex subject. Therefore, our consideration of LRCs will for the most part assume an unproblematic formulation.

Lewis and Spencer (1986, p. 9) define open learning as 'provision which tries to remove barriers that prevent attendance at more traditional courses'. We might argue then from this that open learning represents an alternative way of accessing development, rather than a replacement for more formalised approaches. In considering the nature of the barriers suggested by Lewis and Spencer, Dorrell (1993) suggests they are associated with where, when and how development opportunities are provided, and with the pace at which development occurs. To the extent that LRCs are attempts to provide open learning alternatives to formal courses they might be expected to address and overcome such barriers. This might be achieved by an LRC as a *place*, since it provides an alternative venue to a training centre or classroom and can be accessible at a wider range of *times*, and in terms of the *resources* available since they can and do provide more choices in terms of methods and media (*see* Harrison, 1997 on the latter). The combination of flexibility in terms of where and when, and greater choice in terms of how, means that individuals can also control *pace* to a greater extent. However, the control and autonomy available to individual learners remains restricted to and by the location, opening times and actual resources of an LRC.

These inherent constraints on the degree of 'openness' (*see* Stewart, 1996) provided by LRCs are apparent in the following definition.

In the physical sense . . . a room or area set apart as a quiet study centre to use and possibly store the various learning resources on offer.

(Dorrell, 1993, p. 37)

MacQueen (1996) uses the term personal development centre, although the concept is essentially the same. This is apparent from the following description.

Well stocked resource centres providing information in a variety of media, available on a drop-in basis with opening hours much longer than a public library. Whereas before employees might have been allocated a set training programme, now they have access to a wide range of development and training opportunities.

(MacQueen, 1996, p. 14)

We can, based on these definitions, summarise an LRC as a physical space equipped with learning and development materials in a variety of forms, including print, audio and electronic media, which is made available to employees at times to suit them, both within and outside the normal working pattern. We can also say that use of LRCs seems to be becoming more popular. Their use is well established in manufacturing in, for example, Jaguar Cars and the Rover Group, and is commonplace in financial services, for example, Lloyds TSB has a network of regional LRCs and Scottish Widows has been operating an LRC since the early 1990s.

Many of the issues considered in the previous section are again relevant here. Establishing and operating an LRC requires consideration of location, equipment, materials and staffing, for example. The questions of opening times and volume of usage are particularly significant. The former will have implications for staffing the LRC since, as Dorrell (1993) argues, the availability of personal support and expertise can be critical to the effectiveness of learning, and indeed to maintaining the commitment of individual learners. The latter will be affected by the intended purpose and role of an LRC in an ED strategy. If LRCs are to provide truly open learning alternatives, usage will be entirely voluntary. However, usage will then depend upon levels of support, commitment and advertising/promotion (Trassler, 1995). It will also be influenced by the learning climate in the organisation (Dorrell, 1993). Integrating LRCs as a preferred means of delivering particular development, or as the chosen method to meet a particular need, increases the predictability of and control over volume of usage. However, such an approach also decreases individual autonomy and therefore rather contradicts the central notion of open learning that is often used to both define and justify the nature and use of LRCs. Perhaps this potential contradiction represents the central paradox of LRCs which needs to be addressed in any consideration of their use.

The two previous sections have highlighted in different ways the key resource of specialist development staff. We will close this chapter with an examination of issues associated with recruiting/selecting and developing ED professionals.

Activity 14.5

1 Produce a list of the kinds of resources, e.g. equipment and materials, you might expect to be available in an LRC.

2 Consider how investment in these resources might be evaluated to determine whether they are producing a worthwhile return to the organisation.

3 Produce a list of the potential advantages and disadvantages of an LRC from each of the following perspectives:

(a) individual employees

(b) line or operational managers

(c) individual ED professionals

(d) the ED function/department as a whole

(e) top/senior managers.

4 Compare and discuss your response to **3** with a colleague.

5 Decide whether you are, in principle, in favour or against the use of LRCs. Produce a justification for your position.

Specialist ED staff

Recruiting, selecting and developing specialist ED staff is of critical importance in ensuring the function achieves and maintains the necessary credibility and status to provide a positive contribution to organisation success. For this reason, specialist staff can be argued to be the most important resource (Harrison, 1997, Reid and Barrington, 1997). However, simple rules cannot be stated. An important variable affecting recruitment, selection and development will be the intended role or roles of specialist staff. Reid and Barrington (1997) list more than 25 potential job titles, each of which implies variation in the intended role. Such variation will have impact on decisions such as where to place recruitment adverts, the content of person specifications and programmes of development for new recruits. We can therefore examine only general principles here. It is also true that recruitment and selection of specialist ED staff does not need to differ significantly from any other category of staff. Therefore, general principles which apply to recruitment and selection more widely can and should be used in the particular case of ED staff. So, the purpose and focus of this section is merely to highlight particular features of specific relevance to specialist ED staff.

A widely advocated technique in planning recruitment and selection is that of job analysis (Harrison, 1997). The technique can be useful in drawing up job descriptions or role definitions, from which person specifications can be derived. Harrison (1997) advocates three sources of information which can be useful in carrying out job analysis for ED staff. The first is the occupational standards for training and development published by the Employment Occupational Standards Council (EOSC). The standards can provide specifications of competence relevant to a wide range of specialist roles. A second source, the professional standards produced by the Institute of Personnel and

Development, can fulfil a similar purpose. These two sources can be seen as competing or complementary. Taken together, they are likely to encompass any and every generalist or specialist role within the ED function, and thereby provide a valuable starting point in producing job descriptions and person specifications. The final source suggested by Harrison (1997) is, as might be expected, the particular organisation context and a specific analysis of an intended role, especially as it will relate to achieving the intended contributions of employee development.

The outcomes, or products, of job analysis will be critical in recruitment and selection. Harrison (1997) argues that poor appointments to ED roles are, in part, the result of poorly skilled interviewers being responsible for selection decisions. It is important, therefore, that professional and experienced individuals, as well as professional processes, are used in the selection of ED staff. The former means individuals who are experienced in and knowledgeable about employee development, as well as in selection processes. The latter means processes which are capable of assessing expertise in employee development in general, and the particular abilities required in the specific organisational role. As Harrison (1997) also argues, this needs to focus on the expectations of a particular organisation culture as well as the demands of a particular professional role.

Development of specialist ED staff needs to focus on short, medium and long-term time horizons. Both Harrison (1997) and Reid and Barrington (1997) persuasively argue the need for induction and initial training and development which focuses on facilitating entry into the particular organisation context, and on the requirements of the intended professional role. Harrison (1997) also advocates the application of probationary employment periods, supported by regular appraisals, as part of induction and initial training and development. In considering the development of specialist staff more widely, Reid and Barrington (1997) argue the necessity and value of tailored programmes which focus on and reflect the requirements of particular contexts, and the needs of particular individuals.

Turning to the medium term, two broad choices are available, although they are not necessarily exclusive. These are acquisition of NVQs in training and development or membership of the IPD (*see* Reid and Barrington, 1997). The latter can be achieved through the former route. However, as indicated earlier, the IPD publishes its own professional standards which form the basis of its own qualifications and levels of membership. It is possible to argue that the IPD standards provide access to the underpinning knowledge and understanding which form part of the training and development occupational standards on which the NVQs are based (Whittaker, 1995). However, such an argument would seem to logically imply that achievement of professional competence would require *both* successful study of the IPD Professional Education Scheme *and* achievement of an NVQ. As far as I am aware, this argument is not advanced by either the IPD or the EOSC, and it is certainly not a requirement of either of those bodies. That being the case, the two routes can be considered to provide an either/or choice.

We have already seen some reasons to doubt the value of the NVQ route as a means of acquiring appropriate qualifications. In their examination of the NVQs in training and development, Reid and Barrington (1997) identify and highlight some inconsistencies and other reasons for concern with those particular awards to add to the more general concerns with NVQs. However, Reid and Barrington do not totally discount NVQs, and Harrison (1997) seems to advocate their use for and by specialist ED staff. In addition, and as already indicated, the IPD accepts competence assessment through achievement of NVQs as equivalent to its own education scheme in awarding grades of membership. We can conclude therefore that a basic decision on medium-term development of specialist ED staff will be between pursuing an award of an NVQ or studying the IPD professional education scheme. Both alternatives provide a degree of choice in the form of optional electives or units which allow for either generalist or specialist routes and qualifications. However, it should be recognised that the IPD route is more restricted in that its specialisms are focused on the wider personnel field, while the EOSC/TDLB standards (*see* Reid and Barrington, 1997) are exclusively concerned with the ED function. However, within the ED specialism, there is some choice in the IPD scheme to allow for differences in role.

The EOSC/TDLB occupational standards and associated NVQ units provide for vocational qualifications which do not meet the requirement of a full NVQ. This allows accreditation for very tightly focused and specific roles. Perhaps the best example of this is the Assessors Award for people, especially managers and supervisors, involved in assessing staff for NVQs. The IPD professional standards, arranged as they are into generalist and specialist modules (Whittaker, 1995), also allow individuals to receive development relevant to their role without pursuing a full qualification. However, such arrangements and possibilities are perhaps of more value in considering the long-term development of specialist staff. Selecting NVQ units or IPD modules can be an approach to ensuring continuous professional development. The range, in both quantity and quality, of short courses and conferences promoted in professional journals provides another way of keeping up to date and extending and developing professional expertise. Harrison (1997) emphasises the importance of self-development and varied work experience as additional approaches to achieving continuous professional development. There are increasing numbers of masters degrees in HRD and related subjects provided by universities which offer a further means of CPD. The important point here is that ED staff need to practise what they preach in terms of actively engaging in continuous learning and development (Harrison, 1997).

Two final points can be made to close this section and the chapter. First, responsibility for managing learning in organisations is, as already argued, becoming more decentralised (Harrison, 1997). Indeed, it is increasingly argued that such a role is central to the management task (e.g. Salaman, 1995). Therefore, approaches to recruitment, selection and, especially, development of specialist ED staff may have a wider relevance and application. An immediately obvious application is in terms of line and operational managers who may be increasingly involved in managing the development of their staff. Perhaps less obvious is the notion of 'non-employee development' (Walton, 1996). With ED being increasingly outsourced, potentially at least (*see* Harrison, 1997), the principles discussed here may be increasingly applied to temporary staff, consultants and sub-contractors. They may also be relevant to wider networks of non-employees (*see* Walton, 1996, Harrison, 1997). The final point is that the training cycle is a useful starting point in considering specialist roles within the ED function. Individual staff members may be required to specialise in, for example, design or delivery/implementation in their particular role, especially perhaps in large organisations. Matching the relevant stage or stages of the training cycle to specification such as the EOSC/TDLB occupational standards, or the IPD professional standards, can be a useful starting point in such cases.

Activity 14.6

1 Select one of the following job titles and produce a job description which you judge would be associated with the implied role:

(a) training officer

(b) management development adviser

(c) technical instructor

(d) open learning co-ordinator.

2 Now produce a person specification based on the job description.

3 Consider the arguments for and against using NVQs and the IPD Professional Education Scheme in developing specialist ED staff. Produce a statement of your own view, with a reasoned justification.

4 Assess the extent to which, in your judgment, line/operational managers should be involved in managing the development of their staff in your organisation. Produce some proposals on appropriate development to support them in meeting the demands of their involvement.

Summary and conclusion

This chapter has been concerned with examining three critical resources used in providing ED services in work organisations. The importance of the language of finance and accounting has been emphasised in securing and managing those resources. Key issues and principles influencing decisions on the use of physical resources have been identified and discussed, especially in relation to the operation of training centres and LRCs. Principles informing the recruitment, selection and development of specialist ED staff have been identified and examined. Processes involved in costing resources, and in formulating and managing budgets, have been described and argued to be central to securing resource allocation.

Four conclusions are possible. First, that ED professionals need to be comfortable with financial concepts, and have the ability to account for their activities using those concepts. Second, that adopting the language of finance and accounting will be important in promoting and marketing the ED function. Third, that the professionalism and credibility of ED staff will be equally important in promoting the function and securing necessary resources. Selection and development of ED specialists is therefore critical. Finally, current and future trends of learning and development in organisations suggest a wider constituency in terms of who will constitute 'ED specialists', including non-employees. Those charged with managing the function therefore will need to be familiar with a wide range of options in terms of development opportunities and approaches, to prepare a wide range of individuals to fulfil both generalist and specialist roles in employee development.

This chapter closes the substantive content of the book. We can move on in the final chapter to identify some key themes and to speculate a little about possible future directions in the professional practice of employee development.

Case study 14

Better Cover (BC) is a medium-sized insurance and pensions company. Like many others in the financial services industry, it has experienced some performance problems resulting in a reduction of employees from 4 000 to 2 800 over the past ten years. However, both performance and staff numbers have stabilised, and the past three years have even brought some improvements. The organisation is still subject to legal regulation, however, which among other things requires formal assessment and certification of the competence of some staff groups. The majority of BC's staff are employed in administrative and clerical roles related to information processing and management. More specialist and professional roles are focused on product development and marketing. These roles demand high levels of technical knowledge and professional skill.

BC is located in a large UK city, with staff spread across three office locations in the city centre. The training department, headed by Nakita Robinson as training manager, has operated a learning resource centre (LRC) for 12 years. The organisation is proud of the fact that it was one of the first in the UK, and very nearly the first in its industry, to invest in such a facility. The LRC is located in the main building of the three sites in the suite of offices and rooms allocated to the training department. The centre consists of a large room decorated in light, pastel shades which create an impression of open space. The room holds ten workstations, each of which provides comfortable seating, a spacious desk and hardware capable of running CBT and CD rom programmes as well as interactive videos. Workstations are discreetly and effectively screened from each other, and from an informal coffee area with room for about a dozen people to sit around low tables. As well as the technology-based development programmes, the centre provides a text-based library of books and journals. The range of courses available covers all the operations and functions of BC and includes subjects such as banking, finance, sales and marketing, PC skills, product knowledge and personal/interpersonal skills.

The LRC is open five days a week between 7.30am and 8.30pm. A member of LRC staff is available whenever the centre is open to provide whatever support and help users may require. Centre staff consist of Paul Jones, the centre manager, and Julie and James, two part-time open learning co-ordinators. A booking system is in operation. Any member of staff can book space in the centre outside or during working hours. However, bookings within working time have to be approved by an employee's line manager. Booking can be made by telephone, in person or through BC's intranet. The intranet is also used to advertise and promote the LRC's services, as are staff noticeboards, the employee handbook and a regular six-monthly newsletter sent to all employees.

Use of the centre is monitored and reported by Paul on a monthly basis to Nakita. They use these figures to analyse and plan development and purchase of new programmes. Nakita also uses them to target managers of particular departments who use the facility less than they could or should, and to justify continuing investment in the centre. In addition, all direct users of the centre are required to complete evaluation forms when they have completed a programme of study. Many of the technology-based programmes provide information on completion and duration rates, and this data is also used in monitoring and assessing the value of the centre. The twice-yearly newsletter always contains a feedback questionnaire to be completed and returned by previous, existing and potential users, and the annual survey of training needs conducted by Nakita collects information on actual and potential use of the LRC. All of this information is used to attempt to ensure the LRC and its services remain relevant to and valued by the organisation.

At the moment, use of the LRC is very high, as are levels of satisfaction among employees and managers within BC. There is, therefore, no immediate cause for concern about the centre's short to medium-term viability. However, its very success is beginning to create problems for the centre since waiting lists are being created for the most popular programmes. Nakita is aware that some of these at least are not directly related to individual or organisational development needs, and that some individuals wish to undertake the programmes for personal reasons. While she would wish to encourage this, Nakita is concerned that provision of the centre can be justified in relation to organisational needs as well as individual demand. To that end, she is considering proposing to the board a system of charges for the LRC which would have to be funded by the budgets of managers rather than, as now, the full costs of the LRC being allocated to the central training budget. Charging would apply only where staff were undertaking programmes in work time authorised by their managers.

Nakita believes introducing a charging system would reduce or even eliminate waiting lists, would ensure that relevant training needs gained priority and would lead to all employees of BC placing a higher value on the LRC. Before proceeding any further, though, Nakita has asked Paul to prepare a report examining the implications of such a move.

Discussion questions

Imagine you are Paul Jones, and produce responses to the following questions:

1 What cost factors would be involved in producing a charge for using the centre?

2 Based on realistic estimates, what would each of these factors cost at today's prices?

3 How should the costs be aggregated to form a reasonable basis for charging, e.g. by day, by employee, by programme?

4 What other factors should Nakita consider in making her decisions? How will each of these support a decision to institute a charging system or not?

5 As manager of the LRC, what are your views on Nakita's idea?

Suggested reading

Buckley, R. and Caple, T. (1995) *The Theory and Practice of Training (3rd edn)*. London: Kogan Page.

Harrison, R. (1997) *Employee Development*. London: IPD.

Moorby, E. (1996) *How to Succeed in Employee Development (2nd edn)*. Maidenhead: McGraw-Hill.

Puxty, A.G. (1993) *The Social and Organizational Context of Management Accounting*. London: Academic Press Ltd.

Reid, M. and Barrington, H. (1997) *Training Interventions (5th edn)*. London: IPD.

CHAPTER 15

Conclusion

Introduction

This closing chapter has three purposes. First, I will attempt to identify some significant themes that emerge from the main content of the book. Second, an attempt will be made to predict how these themes may develop in the future and to anticipate some consequences and implications for the professional practice of employee development. These first two purposes therefore have direct connections. The third and final purpose is to provide some advice and guidance to those readers preparing themselves for formal examinations as part of a course of study. Given the speculative nature of the first two purposes, and the unpredictable nature of examination success, I have not formulated or stated specific objectives for the chapter. I have also not included any reader activities. However, I hope readers will join in my speculations and that those I provide will inform and stimulate both thought and debate. In addition, I hope the advice I provide on preparing for examinations will prove useful and valuable.

A final introductory point is worth considering. The final purpose of the chapter has been presented as separate and disconnected from the first two purposes. This may be misleading. Sometimes, although by no means always, examiners pose questions which invite candidates to anticipate and speculate on future developments. As a teacher and examiner myself, I always encourage students to select such questions if they have a choice. This is based on the reasoning that there can be no right answer, since the future by definition is unknown, and therefore candidates cannot produce wrong answers. However, it is possible to produce excellent or poor answers, and every gradation in between. These will be determined by how sensible and intelligent the speculation about developing trends is judged to be by examiners, and how well or not the speculation is supported by logical argument. Both these conditions are likely to be a function, in part at least, of how well informed the speculations appear to the examiner. Therefore, there can be direct connections between the three purposes, and the first two can have potential value to examination candidates. This assumes, of course, that my speculations are sensible and intelligent. However, if they succeed in stimulating thought and debate, then the quality of my speculations will be less important than the quality of those produced by that thought and debate.

Some significant themes

The book has covered a lot of ground and drawn on writing and research from a wide range of disciplines and perspectives. This makes drawing out significant themes both a difficult and an arbitrary task. I am aware therefore that any themes I identify are likely to be different to those identified by others. However, in writing the book I have intended to produce messages on three related themes. I will consider each in turn, and in doing so I will signal possible connections and implications each may have for the others.

Understanding organisations

There are two major points to make about our understanding of organisations. The first is to do with the context in which they operate. This book started by claiming that the practice of employee development is in a state of flux and change. This claim is based on a belief that the same is true of work organisations. The established certainties, if ever they really were certainties, concerning the purpose of work organisations and how best to manage them seem to me to no longer hold true. Two examples will illustrate the argument. First, the processes of globalisation call into question the relevance and appropriateness of established approaches to managing organisations. Whether these processes spread and intensify 'Taylorist' forms of organising and managing, or demand and produce new and innovative solutions to the inherent contradictions of capitalist and market economies, is a question beyond the scope of this book. However, the fact that the question is possible and debated suggests a degree of fluidity associated with globalisation which allows and enables new organisation forms.

The second example is to do with the possibilities created by advances in information and communication technologies. We are now beyond the paperless office and into the realm of the officeless organisation. In my institution, one colleague in particular talks constantly and enthusiastically of the 'virtual university'. One of my current research projects includes a financial services company where the chief executive defines the operation as a 'virtual organisation'. The organisation directly employs, in the sense of an employer–employee relationship, only 20 people. Yet more than 2 000 people are involved in the operation and the organisation is publicly quoted. The company is the result of a strategic alliance between two established players in financial services, and is an example of what is commonly referred to as a network or third-level organisation. The point is that contextual factors such as globalisation and technological advance create a state of flux which in turn allows and enables new organisation forms to both emerge and be deliberately pursued. We therefore have different choices available to us about the nature, purpose and form of work organisations and how to go about managing them.

The second point concerns how we go about analysing and theorising the phenomenon of organisation. It would be mistaken, I think, to characterise alternative approaches to analysing organisations as advances since most of those included in this book have been available as long as the dominant functionalist paradigm. However, what is an advance is the strength of the challenge to functionalist analyses arising from application of alternative paradigms. There is something of a paradox here. In the case of critical theory, at least, the theoretical and conceptual tools used to understand social experience have their roots in Marxist analyses of society. At a time when the results produced by such tools lose favour at that level, the results produced at the level of organisation analysis are becoming increasingly significant and valued. In any case, what is most important and significant in my view is that analyses produced by paradigms and perspectives other than functionalism allow and support a questioning of the *purpose* of work organisations. This provides a useful and valuable challenge to the received or conventional wisdom that work organisations exist to serve exclusively economic ends. Such a challenge also raises important questions about the form of organisations and how they are managed. Questioning ends calls into question means. Therefore, the growing influence of alternative paradigms is likely to reinforce the attempts to find new and innovative organisation forms and approaches to management associated with a changing context.

The conclusion here seems to be that organisation forms and approaches to managing will continue to change in response to changing conditions and different ways of understanding social experience. The professional practice of HRD can expect many opportunities from this situation. A broad possibility is that serving emancipatory purposes through processes of organising becomes more and more legitimate. Development is central to emancipation and therefore the professional practice of employee development will be central to serving and achieving such purposes.

Understanding learning processes

The second significant theme is that of developments in understanding learning processes. There are two related themes here. The first is advances in understanding individual learning. The second is advances in understanding the notion of organisation learning, and how this relates to individual learning. Both of these will be important if HRD as an area of academic enquiry and a field of professional practice is to be able to respond to the opportunities suggested in the previous paragraph. A more effective contribution to achievement of individual and collective emancipation will be possible if greater understanding of individual and collective learning is achieved.

In a paper presented at a British Psychological Society conference, Professor John Burgoyne examines the case for attempting to create an overarching or 'meta' theory of learning (Burgoyne, 1997). According to my interpretation of Burgoyne's arguments, such a theory would produce a synthesis of current understandings of individual and organisational learning. In the sense of improved understanding of 'institutions of learning' and 'institutionalised learning' (*ibid.*), such a theory would go further in terms of informing concepts such as lifelong learning and the learning society. While Burgoyne remains uncommitted either way in his paper on the desirability or possibility of such a theory, my view is that an overarching theory is both necessary and feasible. I find the existence of learning theories applicable to different types of learning, for example, child and adult learning or formal and informal learning, deeply unsatisfactory. Some writers seem to be of the view that experiential learning theory applies to learning by and through 'experience' and therefore is inapplicable to formal settings such as study in a university. A similar example is a separation of work-based learning from academic courses. The logical implication of this is that study at university is neither experience nor work. While I resist both intellectually and emotionally the reductionism of behaviourist learning theory, for example, I am of the view that learning is learning wherever and to whoever it occurs.

My prediction under this heading is that the work suggested and begun by Burgoyne's paper will continue until it bears fruit in a unified theory of learning. In addition, there will be important and significant implications for the practice of employee development. I do not believe and therefore do not suggest that our understanding of learning will ever be such that professional practitioners will be totally confident of guaranteeing learning outcomes from their work. However, I do believe and suggest that the increased understanding provided by a unified theory will provide greater confidence in the design and delivery of development interventions in individual and organisational learning. This confidence will in turn provide greater insight into the form and nature of interventions of relevance to supporting the creation and development of new organisation forms discussed in the previous section.

Understanding the practice of employee development

The previous sentence leads us into discussing the final significant theme. I argued earlier in the book that understanding learning lies at the heart of professional practice. Any advances in that understanding will therefore lead to advances in professional practice. I believe also that advances in practice will occur for additional reasons, including the emergence of new organisational forms. In particular, I think the effects of different paradigms being applied to organisational analysis will lead to a greater emphasis in professional practice on facilitating *agreement* of objectives rather than their *achievement*. This means that employee development as an organisation function will become less of a management tool adopted to ensure compliance with and pursuit of objectives which serve the interests of an exclusive elite, and more of a collective resource which is used to facilitate articulation and synthesis of the objectives of a variety of stakeholders.

The argument expressed in the previous sentence may be both radical and idealistic. However, there are sound reasons for holding such a view. The idea of what we might call pathways of developments in the practice of employee development, suggested for example by the models proposed by the Ashridge Research Group and by Pedler *et al.*, described in an earlier chapter, suggests continuing threads in practice. These threads seem to include a focus on reconciling individual and organisational objectives and a concern with realisation of individual and collective potential. These threads seem to me to be apparent in current work on the concept of the learning organisation. There also seems to be a shift over time in the stages of the development pathways suggested by the models from an emphasis on the demands of organisations to the demands of individuals. This might be characterised by a shift in employee development from being concerned to 'fit' the individual to the organisation to a concern to 'fit' the organisation to the individual. If current trends continue, it therefore seems reasonable to argue that the shift in focus from organisation to individual will bring about a related shift in focus from means to ends.

My argument can be further supported by the speculations offered by Pedler and his colleagues on the next stage in their suggested path for employee development. They propose a greater concern with spirituality and ethics, and a wider constituency of stakeholders, as some of the factors influencing the practice of ED in the late 1990s and beyond. It seems to me that the messages of this book in part support these suggestions. It also seems to be the case that the factors support a greater concern with the objectives pursued by organisations than a concern with the technical means of their achievement. I do not mean to suggest by this argument that employee development will have no concern with means. Different organisation forms and approaches to management are concerned with means, and employee development practice, informed by greater understanding of learning processes, will have a significant contribution to developing new forms and approaches. It is therefore a matter of balance and emphasis. What I am suggesting is a shift in emphasis from means to ends, rather than an exclusive focus on one or the other.

Summary

To summarise, I have argued in this section particular views related to the themes of understanding organisations, learning processes and the practice of employee development. These themes in turn suggest related trends which seem to point in the direction of greater autonomy and control on the part of individuals in their experience of work organisations, and a significant contribution from employee development practitioners in supporting and facilitating movement in that direction. However, the arguments have the status of mere speculation and may prove to be wildly inaccurate. I will now move on to more certain ground to provide advice and guidance on sitting formal examinations.

Success in IPD examinations

My advice in this section is based on what I term the 'managerial approach to examinations'. I use this term because the advice is derived from applying a formal strategic planning process to the task of achieving success in a formal examination. The discussion of such processes in this and other books suggests that they involve thorough analysis before action is taken. The nature and number of steps involved in the analysis vary from model to model. For the purposes of the task in question I have applied a six-step process of analysis which I commend to you before you take the action of putting pen to paper in the examination room. The first step is that of determining your mission.

Mission statement

I cannot write a mission statement for this task because there will be many different reasons for studying and sitting examinations. I can, however, suggest two examples:

- achieve IPD membership
- secure high level/well-paid employment.

According to the theory of strategic planning, the value of mission statements lies in providing a clear and desired focus. I once heard Alan Sugar, chairman of Amstrad, speaking on the radio and declaring that the mission of his company was captured in the phrase 'we want your money!'. This seems to capture the essence of clarity and desirability recommended by the theory. I suggest you use the two examples given above, plus the one from Alan Sugar, to formulate your own statement.

Set objectives

Once a mission statement is written it is easier to set out some objectives. These need to be specific and measurable. Such characteristics will facilitate the following steps. One objective related to success in examinations, irrespective of your mission, will be:

- to achieve a minimum grade of 50 per cent.

You will need to add any other objectives of your own related to achievement of your personal mission.

Devise strategy

Strategy in this model is concerned with the means by which the objectives will be achieved. Strategies can be and often are composed of a number of elements. In the case of the objective given above, there are two elements:

- score points
- score enough points.

These elements, and the use of the words 'points', may seem a little cynical. My argument would be that managing, whether it is seen as science or art, is above all else pragmatic. Being pragmatic means recognising that examinations are conducted by certain rules, and success requires performing well in the context of those rules. Like other activities governed by rules, examinations are a form of game and, as in other forms of games, scoring points is required for success. We will return to the detail of the strategy when we examine tactics.

Assess resources

Before tactics can be planned, resources need to be identified and assessed. The resources available to a candidate in an examination are:

- time
- questions on the examination paper
- knowledge
- experience
- intelligence.

These are the resources available to implement the strategy. Each of them is finite at the point of their use and therefore they need to be used to maximum effect. The first two are common and equal, that is, they are the same for all candidates. Time will be either two or three hours. It is important to emphasise that the questions are a valuable resource. They are a friend to and ally of each candidate. Without the questions, the strategy cannot be implemented and the objective cannot be achieved. They should therefore be anticipated in a positive frame of mind because, in simple terms, the questions enable candidates to exercise their intelligence to demonstrate their knowledge and experience in the time available, and thereby score enough points to achieve the objective. The final three resources will vary from candidate to candidate and therefore each individual needs to produce their own assessment. It is imperative that this is done well before the examination since the assessment will inform and influence application of the tactics.

Plan tactics

Tactics are concerned with plans for implementing the strategy, based on an assessment of resources. Each element of a strategy requires a set of tactics which will make most effective use of available resources. Those suggested for the proposed strategy are:

- *Score points.* Points will not be scored if the wrong questions are attempted. There are two definitions of 'wrong'. First, answering a question which the candidate either thinks or wishes is being asked, rather than the question actually asked. Second, answering a question which does not allow a candidate to demonstrate knowledge and ability. In other words, attempting questions on what are for a particular candidate weak subjects or topics. This illustrates the importance of assessing personal resources. On the positive side, points will be scored for demonstrated knowledge and understanding, for demonstrated ability to apply this in practice, for independent thought and for originality. These are cumulative, i.e. for each additional feature demonstrated additional points will be scored. Answers to questions are much more likely to demonstrate these features if they are thought through and planned before being written. The tactics for this element of the strategy can be summarised as follows:

  (a) analyse and understand the questions
  (b) select 'strong' subjects in relation to knowledge and experience
  (c) demonstrate knowledge and understanding
  (d) illustrate application in practice
  (e) show independent thought and, if possible, originality
  (f) plan answers, perhaps with notes, before writing them.

- *Score enough points.* While the above tactics will score points, it is equally important to score enough points to achieve the objective. This requires two tactics. First, answering enough questions, which means the required number, and second, providing consistently good answers. This is a matter of quality and quantity. One excellent and two or three poor answers will not score enough points. It is much more effective to have, say, four answers of more or less equal length and quality than four of variable length and standard. The final point here is that an answer is more likely to be good rather than poor if it is complete, i.e. it works towards and arrives at a logical conclusion. In summary, the tactics for the element of this strategy are:

  (a) attempt/answer the required number of questions
  (b) aim for consistency in length and quality
  (c) structure each answer to a logical conclusion.

Formulate action plan

The final step in this model is to formulate an action plan. This identifies the activities that have to be undertaken to implement the strategy, and sets timescales for completion for each activity. It would not be useful for me to set out an action plan since the requirements of examinations vary. I can, however, identify the activities and suggest proportional time allocations for each. This results in the following:

Activities	Time Allocation
Reading	1/6
Thinking	1/6
Writing	2/3

Some words of explanation are necessary. The time allocation for thinking means time for doing nothing other than thinking. It may be difficult to sit in an examination room without reading or writing, especially when others around you are doing either one or both. However, I strongly recommend that you do so since it will pay off in the quality of your answers. The focus of thinking time is analysing and selecting questions and planning answers. Reading time is allocated to reading the question paper and reading your answers when they are complete. The former is in addition to any officially allocated reading time, and the latter is to ensure your hand has not lagged too far behind your brain and left incomplete sentences, or to fill the gaps if they have occurred. My final suggestion is that the time allocations and activities are translated into a specific action plan which meets the requirements of any particular examination.

Discussion

The advice and guidance provided in this section so far has general application and is not therefore specific to IPD national or associated examinations. The principles do apply to the specific case of IPD examinations, however. In addition, I recommend candidates to bear in mind two points. First, the syllabuses of the IPD modules are too large to be fully represented on a single examination paper. This is true of the employee development and other development-related modules. It is therefore useful to categorise the syllabus of any module into subject headings such as those used to structure this book, and to expect questions derived from *each* of the subjects. The whole syllabus cannot be represented on a paper, but each *part* or *subject/topic* can be included.

Second, the guiding principle informing the IPD scheme, and therefore all stages in the examination process, is that successful candidates have demonstrated their ability to perform successfully in professional personnel and development roles in work organisations. The purpose of examinations therefore is to assess and enable demonstration of this ability. This obviously, in my view at least, occurs in the context of the subjectivity of assessment that I argued in an earlier chapter. However, I can confirm from personal experience of the process that those involved work very hard to ensure consistency and fairness in the process, and start from the point of wanting to enable candidates to demonstrate their ability, rather than from the point of seeking to impose hurdles. There is no hidden agenda or any trick questions in IPD examination papers. However, the implication of the guiding principle is that, to be successful, candidates need to demonstrate more than knowledge of relevant theories or research. This is undoubtedly important. Success requires candidates to demonstrate understanding of organisation contexts and possession of the professional judgement and skills necessary for application of theory and research in practical contexts. My final piece of advice, therefore, is to ensure your preparation for IPD examinations enables you to demonstrate that judgement and those skills.

Summary and conclusion

That final advice brings the book to a close. I hope and intend that the content of the book will have made a useful contribution to preparing those readers studying formal programmes for their examinations by developing their professional judgement and skills. I hope, too, that other readers have found value in the book. Employee development is an important field of professional practice, too important in my view to be left to chance or circumstance. Serious study of relevant concepts and theories is necessary to inform practice. This book represents one of my contributions to that study. I invite readers to assess the value of the contribution by reviewing the extent to which the book has achieved its aims and objectives detailed in Chapter 1, and the extent to which their personal objectives in reading the book have been met. Reviewing aims and objectives, and their achievement or otherwise, reflects currently defined 'best practice' in employee development. It also provides a basis for planning future learning objectives and therefore, to use Kolb's theory, a future learning cycle. Inviting and encouraging such a review therefore seems an appropriate way of ending the book.

BIBLIOGRAPHY

Adler, N.J. (1986) *International Dimensions of Organizational Behaviour*. California: Wadsworth.

Adler, N.J. (1991) *International Dimensions of Organisational Behaviour*. Boston: Kent Publishers.

Alvesson, M. and Deetz, S. (1996) 'Critical theory and postmodernism approaches to organization studies', in Clegg, S.R., Hardy, C. and Nord, W.R. (eds) *Handbook of Organization Studies*. London: Sage Publications.

Alvesson, M. and Willmott, H. (1996) *Making Sense of Management: A Critical Introduction*. London: Sage Publications.

Argyris, C. and Schon, D. (1978) *Organizational Learning: A Theory of Action Perspective*. Reading, MA: Addison-Wesley.

Arnold, J., Robertson, I.T. and Cooper, C.L. (1995) *Work Psychology* (2nd edn). London: Financial Times Pitman Publishing.

Barber, P. (1997) 'Money talks: the influence of the accountant on organisational discourse', *Journal of Applied Management Studies*, Vol. 6, No. 1.

Barham, K., Fraser, J. and Heath, I. (1987) *Management for the Future*. Ashridge: Ashridge Management College/FME.

Bartlett, F.C. (1932) *Remembering: An Experimental and Social Study*. Cambridge: Cambridge University Press.

Bates, I. (1995) (ed.) 'The competence movement and the national qualification framework', *British Journal of Education and Work Special Edition*, Vol. 8, No. 2.

Beaumont, G. (1995) *Review of 100 NVQs and SVQs*. A report submitted to the Department for Education and Employment.

Beck, J.E. (1994) 'The new paradigm of management education', *Management Learning*, Vol. 25, No. 2.

Becker, G. (1975) *Human Capital: A Theoretical and Empirical Analysis with Special Reference to Education* (2nd edn). New York: Columbia University Press.

Belbin, E. and Belbin, R.M. (1972) *Problems in Adult Retraining*. Oxford: Heinemann.

Bennett, R. and Leduchowicz, T. (1983) 'What makes for an effective trainer?', *Journal of European Industrial Training*, Vol. 7, No. 2. Monograph.

Bennett-England, R. (1997) 'Urgent need for a single skills qualification', *NCJT News*, No. 19.

Blyton, P. and Turnbull, P. (eds) (1992) *Reassessing Human Resource Management*. London: Sage Publications.

Bowie, N.E. and Duska, R.F. (1990) *Business Ethics* (2nd edn). Upper Saddle River NJ: Prentice-Hall.

Boyatzis, R. (1982) *The Competent Manager*. Chichester: John Wiley.

Boydell, T.H. (1983) *A Guide to the Identification of Training Needs*. London: British Association for Commercial and Industrial Education.

Boydell, T. and Leary, M. (1996) *Identifying Training Needs*. London: Institute of Personnel and Development.

Bramley, P. (1996) *Evaluating Training*. London: Institute of Personnel and Development.

Bramley, P. and Kitson, B. (1994) 'Evaluating training against business criteria', *Journal of European Industrial Training*, Vol. 18, No. 1.

Bridges, W.I. (1995) *Jobshift: How to Prosper in a World Without Jobs*. Cambridge: Nicholas Brearley.

Brown, A. (1998) *Organisational Culture* (2nd edn). London: Financial Times Pitman Publishing.

Buckley, R. and Caple, T. (1995) *The Theory and Practice of Training* (3rd edn). London: Kogan Page.

Burgess, P. (1997) *European Management Guides: Recruitment, Training and Development.* London: IDS and IPD.

Burgoyne, J. (1990) 'Doubts about competency', in Devine, M. (ed.) *The Photo Fit Manager.* London: Unwin.

Burgoyne, J. (1997) 'Learning: conceptual, practical and theoretical issues', *British Psychological Society Annual Conference,* Heriot-Watt University, Edinburgh, April 1997.

Burgoyne, J. and Jackson, B. (1997) 'The Arena Thesis: management development as a pluralistic meeting point', in Burgoyne, J. and Reynolds, M. (eds) *Management Learning.* London: Sage Publications.

Burgoyne, J. and Reynolds, M. (eds) (1997) *Management Learning: Integrating Perspectives in Theory and Practice.* London: Sage Publications.

Burgoyne, J.G. and Singh, R. (1977) 'Evaluation of training and education: macro and micro perspectives', *Journal of European Industrial Training,* Vol. 1, No. 1.

Burnes, B. (1996) *Managing Change* (2nd edn). London: Financial Times Pitman Publishing.

Burrell, G. and Morgan, G. (1979) *Sociological Paradigms and Organizational Analysis.* Oxford: Heinemann.

Calas, M. (1992) 'Another silent voice? Representing "Hispanic Woman" in organisational texts', in Mills, A.J. and Tancred, P. (eds) *Gendering Organisational Analysis.* London: Sage Publications.

Campbell, T. and Cairns, H. (1994) 'Developing and measuring the learning organisation: from buzz words to behaviour', *Industrial and Commercial Training,* Vol. 26, No. 7.

Capey, J. (1995) *GNVQ Assessment Review: Final report of the review group chaired by Dr John Capey.* Hayes: School Curriculum Assessment Authority Publications.

Carr, A. (1968) 'Is business bluffing ethical?' *Harvard Business Review,* January/February.

Celinski, D. (1983) 'Trainers' Manual: formulating training policy statements', *Training and Development,* June.

Chao, G.T. (1997) 'Organization socialization in multinational corporations: the role of implicit learning', in Cooper, C.L. and Jackson, S.E. (eds) *Creating Tomorrow's Organizations.* Chichester: John Wiley.

Cheung-Judge, L. Mee-Yan (1983) *Equal Opportunities in Management Education and Development.* Oxford: Q & E Consultancy Services.

Chia, R. (1996) *Organizational Analysis as Deconstructive Practice.* Berlin: DeGruyter.

Chia, R. (1997) 'Process philosophy and management learning: cultivating foresight in management' in Burgoyne, J. and Reynolds, M. (eds) *Management Learning.* London: Sage Publications.

Child, J. and Kieser, A. (1979) 'Organisational and managerial roles in British and West German companies: an examination of the culture-free thesis', in Lammers, C.J. and Hickson, D.J. (eds) *Organisations Alike and Unalike.* London: Routledge and Kegan Paul.

Clare, J. (1996) 'NVQs branded a waste of £100m by watchdog', *Daily Telegraph,* 5 October.

Clegg, S.R., Hardy, C. and Nord, W.R. (eds) (1996) *Handbook of Organization Studies.* London: Sage Publications.

Cole, G.A. (1994) *Strategic Management.* London: DP Publications Ltd.

Connock, S. and Johns, T. (1995) *Ethical Leadership.* London: Institute of Personnel and Development.

Cooper, C.L. and Jackson, S.E. (eds) (1997) *Creating Tomorrow's Organizations.* Chichester: John Wiley.

Crainer, S. (1995) *How to Have A Brilliant Career Without Having A Proper Job.* London: Financial Times Pitman Publishing.

Cummings, T.G. and Huse, E.F. (1989) *Organization Development and Change* (4th edn). St Paul, MN: West Publishing Company.

Dawson, P. (1994) *Organizational Change: A Processual Approach*. London: Paul Chapman.

Dearing, R. (1996) *Review of Qualifications for 16–19-year-olds*. Hayes: School Curriculum Assessment Authority Publications.

Dennison, B. and Kirk, R. (1990) *Do, Review, Learn and Apply: A Simple Guide to Experiential Learning*. Oxford: Blackwell Education.

Department of Employment (1991a) *Setting Standards for Training: National Standards for Training and Development*. Sheffield: Employment Department.

Department of Employment (1991b) *The Development of Assessable Standards for National Certification*. Sheffield: Employment Department.

Department for Education and Employment (1995a) *Skills and Enterprise Executive – Issue 5/95*. London: Skills and Enterprise Network Publications.

Department for Education and Employment (1995b) *Employee Development Schemes: Developing a Learning Workforce*. London: DfEE.

Department for Education and Employment (1996) *Employee Development Schemes: What Impact Do They Have?*. London: DfEE.

Department for Education and Employment (1997) *Employee Development Schemes: The Benefits of Participation for Employees in Small Firms*. Research Report No. 39. Sheffield: DfEE.

Department for Education and Employment (1998) *The Learning Age: A Renaissance for a New Britain*. London: The Stationery Office.

Devine, M. (ed.) (1990) *The Photofit Manager*. London: Unwin.

Dicken, P. (1992) *Global Shift: The Internationalisation of Economic Activity*. London: Paul Chapman.

Dixon, N. (1994) *The Organizational Learning Cycle*. Maidenhead: McGraw-Hill.

Donaldson, J. (1989) *Key Issues in Business Ethics*. London: Academic Press Limited.

Donaldson, J. (1992) *Business Ethics: A European Casebook*. London: Academic Press.

Dorrell, J. (1993) *Resourced Based Learning – Using Open and Flexible Learning Resources for Continuous Development*. Maidenhead: McGraw-Hill.

Downs, S. (1995a) 'Learning to learn', in Truelove, S. (ed.) *The Handbook of Training and Development* (2nd edn). Oxford: Blackwell Business.

Downs, S. (1995b) *Learning at Work*. London: Kogan Page.

Drowley, B. (1996) *From Beaumont to Dearing*. London: Institute of Supervision and Management.

Drucker, P. (1977) *Management*. London: Pan.

Easterby-Smith, M. (1986) *Evaluation of Management Education, Training and Development*. Aldershot: Gower Publishing.

Easterby-Smith, M., Thorpe, R. and Lowe, A. (1991) *Management Research: An Introduction*. London: Sage Publications.

ED and DES (1983) *Working Together – Education and Training*. London: The Stationery Office.

Employment Committee (1996) *Report and Proceedings of the House of Commons Employment Committee on the Work of TECs*. London: The Stationery Office.

Employment Department Group (1991) *A Strategy for Skills Guidance from the Secretary of State for Employment on Training, Vocational Education and Enterprise*. Moorfoot: Sheffield Employment Department.

Employment Occupational Standards Council (EOSC) (1995) *Training and Development Standards*. London: EOSC.

Employment Occupational Standards Council (EOSC) (1996) *A Briefing Note*. Rotherham: Cambertown Ltd.

Eraut, M. (1994) *Developing Professional Knowledge and Competence*. London: The Falmer Press.

Etzioni, A. (1961) *A Comparative Analysis of Complex Organizations*. New York: Free Press.

Fairclough, N. and Hardy, G. (1997) 'Management learning as discourse', in Burgoyne, J. and

Reynolds, M. (eds) *Management Learning: Integrating Perspectives on Theory and Practice.* London: Sage Publications.

Ferrell, O.C. and Fraedrich, J. (1997) *Business Ethics: Ethical Decision Making and Cases.* Boston: Houghton Mifflin.

Finegold, D. and Crouch, C. (1994) 'A comparison of national institutions', in Layard, R. Mayhew, K. and Owen, G. (eds) *Britain's Training Deficit.* Aldershot: Avebury.

Fisher, C. (1996) 'Managerial stances: perspectives on manager development', in Stewart, J. and McGoldrick, J. (eds) *Human Resource Development: Perspectives, Strategies and Practice.* London: Financial Times Pitman Publishing.

Fisher, C. (1999) 'Judging performance', in Harris, L., Leopold, J. and Watson, T.J. (eds) *Strategic Human Resourcing: Principles, Perspectives and Practices in HRM.* London: Financial Times Pitman Publishing.

Fox, A. (1974) *Beyond Contract: Work, Power and Trust Relations.* London: Faber.

Fox, S. (1997) 'From management education and development to the study of management learning', in Burgoyne, J. and Reynolds, M. (eds) *Management Learning: Integrating Perspectives in Theory and Practice.* London: Financial Times Pitman Publishing.

Franklin, P., Hodkinson, M. and Stewart, J. (1998) 'Towards universities as learning organisations', *The Learning Organisation Journal,* Vol. 5, No. 5.

Fredericks, J. and Stewart, J. (1996) 'The strategy – HRD connection', in Stewart, J. and McGoldrick, J. (eds) *Human Resource Development: Perspectives, Strategies and Practice.* London: Financial Times Pitman Publishing.

French, J.R.P. and Raven, B.H. (1959) 'The social bases of power', in Cartwright, D. (ed.) *Studies in Social Power.* Ann Arbor: University of Michigan Press.

Friedman, M. (1963) *Capitalism and Freedom.* Chicago: University of Chicago Press.

Friedman, M. (1970) 'The social responsibility of business is to increase its profits', *New York Times Magazine,* 13 September.

Fukuyama, F. (1992) *The End of History and the Last Man.* London: Free Press.

Fukuyama, F. (1995) *Trust: The Social Virtues and the Creation of Prosperity.* London: Free Press.

Gagne, R.M. (1974) *The Essentials of Learning for Instruction.* Illinois: University of Illinois Press.

Garavan, T.N., Barnicle, B. and Heraty, N. (1993) 'The training and development function: its search for power and influence in organisations', *Journal of European Industrial Training,* Vol. 17, No. 7.

Garratt, R. (1988) *The Learning Organisation and the Need for Directors Who Think.* Aldershot: Gower Publishing.

Gertsen, M.C. (1991) 'Intercultural competence and expatriates', *International Journal of Human Resource Management,* Vol. 1, No. 3.

Giddens, A. (1989) *Sociology.* Cambridge: Polity Press.

Gill, J. and Johnson, P. (1997) *Research Methods for Managers* (2nd edn) London: Paul Chapman.

Goffman, E. (1959) *The Presentation of Self in Everyday Life.* Harmondsworth: Penguin.

Goffman, E. (1968) *Asylums.* Harmondsworth: Penguin.

Goldthorpe, J. (1985) 'The end of convergence: dualist and corporatist tendencies in modern Western societies', in Roberts, B. Finnegan, R. and Gallie, D. (eds) *New Approaches to Economic Life: Economic Restructuring, Unemployment, and the Social Divisions of Labour.* Manchester: Manchester University Press.

Gowler, D. and Legge, K. (1978) 'The evaluation of planned organisational change: the necessary art of the possible', *Journal of Enterprise Management,* Vol. 1.

Hamblin, A.C. (1974) *Evaluation and Control of Training.* Maidenhead: McGraw-Hill.

Hamel, G. and Prahalad, C.K. (1994) *Competing For The Future.* Cambridge, MA: Harvard Business School Press.

Hamlin, B. and Davies, G. (1996) 'The trainer as change agent: issues for practice', in Stewart, J.

and McGoldrick, J. (eds) *Human Resource Development: Perspectives, Strategies and Practice*. London: Financial Times Pitman Publishing.

Hamlin, B. and Reidy, M. (1997) 'Effecting change in management culture', *Strategic Change*, special edition, December.

Hamlin, R.G. (1995) 'National training policies in Britain', in Truelove, S. (ed.) *The Handbook of Training and Development* (2nd edn). Oxford: Blackwell Business.

Hamlin, R.G. and Stewart, J. (1990) 'Approaches to management development in the UK', *Leadership and Organisation Development Journal*, Vol. 11, No. 5.

Hamlin, R.G. and Stewart, J. (1994) 'Competence based qualifications: maintaining forward momentum', *Competence and Assessment*, No. 24. Employment Department.

Handy, C. (1976) *Understanding Organizations*. Harmondsworth: Penguin.

Handy, C. (1994) *The Empty Raincoat: Making Sense of the Future*. London: Hutchinson.

Harris, D.M. and DeSimone, R.L. (1994) *Human Resource Development*. Orlando: Dryden Press.

Harris, L., Leopold, J. and Watson, T.J. (eds) (1999) *Strategic Human Resourcing: Principles, Perspectives and Practices in HRM*. London: Financial Times Pitman Publishing.

Harrison, R. (1997) *Employee Development*. London: IPD.

Hilgard, E.R., Atkinson, R.C. and Atkinson, R.L. (1971) *Hilgard's Introduction to Psychology* (5th edn). New York: Harcourt Brace Jovanovich.

Hirsch, W. and Jackson, C. (1995) *Careers In Organisations: Issues for the Future*. Brighton: Institute for Employment Studies.

Hofstede, G.H. (1980) *Culture's Consequences*. California: Sage Publications.

Honey, P. and Mumford, A. (1986) *The Manual of Learning Styles*. Maidenhead: Peter Honey.

Huczynski, A. (1983) *Encyclopedia of Management Development Methods*. Aldershot: Gower.

Huczynski, A. and Buchanan, D. (1992) *Organizational Behaviour: An Introductory Text*. Hemel Hempstead: Prentice-Hall.

Iles, P.A. (1995) 'International HRM', in Mabey, C. and Salaman, G. (eds) *Strategic Human Resource Management*. Oxford: Blackwell Business.

Iles, P.A. (1996) 'International HRD', in Stewart, J. and McGoldrick, J. (eds) *Human Resource Development: Perspectives, Strategies and Practice*. London: Financial Times Pitman Publishing.

Industrial Training Research Unit (ITRU) (1976) *Choose an Effective Style: A self-instructional approach to the teaching of skills*. Cambridge: ITRU Publications.

Institute of Personnel and Development (1996) *Code of Professional Conduct*. London: IPD.

IRS (1997) 'Culture change', *IRS Management Review*, Vol. 1, No. 4.

Jackson, T. (1989) *Evaluation: Relating Training to Business Performance*. London: Kogan Page.

Jacobs, R. (1989) 'Assessing management competences', *Report of a Survey of Current Arrangements in the UK for the Assessment of Management Competences*. Berkhamsted: Ashridge Management Research Group.

Jacobs, R. and Vyakarnam, S. (1994) 'The need for a more strategically led research-based approach in management development', *BPS Occupational Psychology Conference*, Birmingham, UK.

Jagger, N., Morris, S. and Pearson, R. (1996) 'The target for higher level skills in an international context'. Brighton: Institute for Employment Studies, Report 307, University of Sussex.

Jamieson, B. (1998) 'Lagging Britain: the McKinsey view', *Sunday Telegraph* Business Comment Section, 17 May.

Jashpara, A. (1993) 'The competitive learning organisation', *Management Decision*, Vol. 13, No. 8.

Jennings, D. and Wattam, S. (1998) *Decision Making: An Integrated Approach* (2nd edn). London: Financial Times Pitman Publishing.

Jessup, G. (1991) *Outcomes: NVQs and the Emerging Model of Education and Training*. Lewis: Falmer Press.

Johnson, G. and Scholes, K. (1993) *Exploring Corporate Strategy* (3rd edn). Hemel Hempstead: Prentice-Hall.

Johnson, G. and Scholes, K. (1997) *Exploring Corporate Strategy* (4th edn). Hemel Hempstead: Prentice-Hall.

Johnston, R. (1996) 'Power and influence and the HRD function', in Stewart, J. and McGoldrick, J. (eds) *Human Resource Development Perspectives, Strategies and Practice*. London: Financial Times Pitman Publishing.

Jones, G. (1998) 'Low pay limit to be £3.60 an hour', *Daily Telegraph*, 28 May.

Jones, J.A.G. (1981) 'Figure of 8 evaluation – a fundamental change in the trainer's approach', *The Training Officer*, Vol. 17, No. 9.

Jones, J.A.G. (1986) 'The role of the management trainer', in Mumford, A. (ed.) *Handbook of Management Development*. Aldershot: Gower.

Jones, J.E. and Woodcock, M. (1985) *Manual of Management Development*. Aldershot: Gower.

Kelly, G.A. (1955) *The Psychology of Personal Constructs*. New York: Norton.

Kelly, M.R. (1989) 'Alternative forms of work organisation under programmable automation', in Wood, S. (ed) *The Transformation of Work*. London: Unwin Hyman.

Kenrick, P. (1984) *Costing, Budgeting and Evaluating Training*. Luton: Local Government Training Board.

Kerr, C. (1983) *The Future of Industrial Societies: Convergence or Continuing Diversity?* Cambridge, MA: Harvard University Press.

Kirkpatrick, D.L. (1976) 'Evaluation of training', in Craig, R.L. and Bittel, L.R. (eds) *Training and Development Handbook*. New York: ASTO/McGraw-Hill.

Kolb, D.A. (1983) *Experiential Learning: Experience as the Source of Learning and Development*. Hemel Hempstead: Prentice-Hall.

Kotter, J.P. (1982) *The General Manager*. London: Macmillan.

Lane, C. (1989) *Management and Labour in Europe*. Aldershot: Edward Elgar.

Layard, R., Mayhew, K. and Owen, B. (1994) *Britain's Training Deficit*. Aldershot: Avebury.

Lee, M. (1996) 'Action learning as a cross-cultural tool', in Stewart, J. and McGoldrick, J. (eds) *Human Resource Development: Perspectives, Strategies and Practice*. London: Financial Times Pitman Publishing.

Lee, M. (1997) 'The developmental approach: a critical reconsideration', in Burgoyne, J. and Reynolds, M. (eds) *Management Learning*. London: Sage Publications.

Lees, S. (1992) 'Ten faces of management development', *Management Education and Development*, Vol. 23, No. 2.

Legge, K. (1995) *Human Resource Management: Rhetorics and Realities*. Basingstoke: Macmillan.

Lewis, R. and Spencer, D. (1986) *What is Open Learning?*. London: CET.

Lorbiecki, A. (1997) 'The internationalization of management learning: towards a radical perspective', in Burgoyne, J. and Reynolds, M. (eds) *Management Learning: Integrating Perspectives in Theory and Practice*. London: Sage Publications.

Lundy, O. and Cowling, A. (1996) *Strategic Human Resource Management*. London: Routledge.

Mabey, C. and Salaman, G. (1995) *Strategic Human Resource Management*. Oxford: Blackwell Business.

McGill, I. and Beatty, L. (1992) *Action Learning: A Practitioners Guide*. London: Kogan Page.

McLuhan, M. (1964) *Understanding Media*. London: Routledge.

McNiff, J., Lomax, P. and Whitehead, J. (1996) *You and Your Action Research Project*. London: Routledge.

MacQueen, J. (1996) 'Personal responsibility for learning at Eastern Group', *Employee Development Bulletin No. 614*, IRS Employment Review.

Mager, R.F. (1975) *Preparing Instructional Objectives*. Belmont, CA: Fearn.

Mager, R.F. (1990) *Measuring Instruction Results* (2nd edn). London: Kogan Page.

Mansfield, B. (1989) 'Functional analysis – a personal approach', *Competence and Assessment. The Analysis of Competence: Current Thoughts and Practice*, Special Issue No. l, December.

Mansfield, B. and Mitchell, L. (1996) *Towards a Competent Workforce*. Aldershot: Gower.

Marceau, J. (1992) *Reworking the World*. Berlin: De Gruyter.

Marchington, M. and Wilkinson, A. (1996) *Core Personnel and Development*. London: Institute of Personnel and Development.

Marshall, E. (1993) *Business and Society*. London: Routledge.

Marsick, V.J. and Watkins, K.E. (1997) 'Lessons from informal and incidental learning', in Burgoyne, J. and Reynolds, M. (eds) *Management Learning: Integrating Perspectives in Theory and Practice*. London: Sage Publications.

Maslow, A.H. (1959) *Motivation and Personality*. New York: Harper & Rowe.

May, T. (1997) *Social Research: Issues, Methods and Process* (2nd edn). Buckingham: Open University Press.

Mead, G.H. (1934) *Mind, Self and Society*. Chicago: University of Chicago Press.

Megginson, D. and Whitaker, V. (1996) *Cultivating Self-Development*. London: Institute of Personnel and Development.

Mintzberg, H. (1973) *The Nature of Managerial Work*. Hemel Hempstead: Prentice-Hall.

Mintzberg, H. (1990) 'Strategy formation: schools of thought', in Frederickson, J.W. (ed.) *Perspectives on Strategic Management*. New York: Harper & Rowe.

Mintzberg, H., Quinn, J.B. and Ghosal, S. (1998) *The Strategy Process*. Hemel Hempstead: Prentice-Hall.

Moingeon, B. and Edmondson, A. (eds) (1996) *Organizational Learning and Competitive Advantage*. London: Sage Publications.

Molander, C. (1987) 'Management development', in Molander, C. (ed.) *Personnel Management: A Practical Introduction*. London: Chartwell Bratt.

Moloney and Gealy (1997) *Draft Occupational Standards in Research*. London: Moloney and Gealy, and Researchers' Lead Body.

Moorby, E. (1996) *How to Succeed in Employee Development* (2nd edn). Maidenhead: McGraw-Hill.

Morgan, G. (1990) 'Paradigm diversity in organisational research', in Hassard, J. and Pym, D. (eds) *The Theory and Philosophy of Organisations*. London: Routledge.

Morgan, G. (1995) 'Paradigms, metaphors, and puzzle solving in organization theory', in Smircich, L. and Calas, M.B. (eds) *Critical Perspectives on Organization and Management Theory*. Aldershot: Dartmouth.

Morgan, G. (1997) *Images of Organization*. London: Sage Publications.

Moss-Jones, J. (1994) *Learning Organisation: Concepts, Practices and Relevance*. Bristol: NHSTD.

Mullins, L.J. (1999) *Management and Organisational Behaviour* (4th edn). London: Financial Times Pitman Publishing

Mumford, A. (ed.) (1986) *Handbook of Management Development*. Aldershot: Gower.

Mumford, A. (1993) *Management Development: Strategies for Action* (2nd edn). London: Institute of Personnel Management.

Mumford, A. (1997) *Management Development: Strategies for Action,* (3rd edn). London: IPD.

Myers, D.G. (1995) *Psychology* (4th edn). New York: Worth.

National Commission on Education (1993) *Learning to Succeed: A Radical Look at Education Today and a Strategy for the Future*. Oxford: Heinemann.

Nonaka, I. (1996) 'The knowledge-creating company', in Starkey, K. (ed.) *How Organizations Learn*. London: International Thomson Business Press.

Noon, M. (1992) 'HRM: A map, model or theory', in Blyton, P. and Turnbull, P. (eds) *Reassessing Human Resource Management*. London: Sage Publications.

O'Dwyer, T. (1995) *Structures of the Education and Initial Training Systems in the European Union: A Joint Publication,* based on EURYDICE and CEDEFOP Information. Luxembourg: European Commission.

Oswick, C. and Grant, D. (eds) (1996) *Organization Development: Metaphorical Explorations.* London: Financial Times Pitman Publishing.

Oswick, C., Keenoy, T. and Grant, D. (1997) 'Managerial discourses: words speak louder than actions?', *Journal of Applied Management Studies,* Vol. 6, No. 1.

Pearn, M. and Kandola, R. (1988) *Job Analysis: A Practical Guide for Managers.* London: Institute of Personnel Management.

Pedler, M. (ed.) (1991) *Action Learning in Practice* (2nd edn). Aldershot: Gower.

Pedler, M. (1997) 'Interpreting action learning', in Burgoyne, J. and Reynolds, M. (eds) *Management Learning: Integrating Perspectives in Theory and Practice.* London: Sage Publications.

Pedler, M. and Boydell, T. (1985) *Managing Yourself.* London: Fontana.

Pedler, M., Burgoyne, J. and Boydell, T. (1986) *A Manager's Guide to Self-Development* (2nd edn). Maidenhead: McGraw-Hill.

Pedler, M., Boydell, T. and Burgoyne, J. (1991) *The Learning Company: A Strategy for Sustainable Development.* Maidenhead: McGraw-Hill.

Pedler, M., Burgoyne, J. and Boydell, T. (1994) *A Manager's Guide to Self-Development* (3rd edn). London: McGraw-Hill.

Pedler, M., Boydell, T. and Burgoyne, J. (1996) *The Learning Company* (2nd edn). Maidenhead: McGraw-Hill.

Pemberton, C. (1995) *A New Career Deal.* London: Financial Times Pitman Publishing.

Perlmutter, H.V. (1969) 'The tortuous evolution of the multinational corporation', *Columbia Journal of World Business,* Vol. 4, No. 1.

Pettigrew, A., Jones, E. and Reason, P. (1982) *Training and Development Roles in their Organisational Setting.* Sheffield: Manpower Services Commission.

Phillips, K. and Shaw, P. (1989) *A Consultancy Approach for Trainers.* Aldershot: Gower.

Porter, M.E. (1980) *Competitive Strategy: Techniques for Analysing Industries and Competitors.* New York: Free Press.

Porter, M.E. (1985) *Competitive Advantage.* New York: Free Press.

Prahalad, C.K. and Hamel, G. (1990) 'The core competence of the corporation', *Harvard Business Review,* May–June.

Puxty, A.G. (1993) *The Social and Organizational Context of Management Accounting.* London: Academic Press.

Reid, M. and Barrington, H. (1994) *Training Interventions* (4th edn). London: Institute of Personnel and Development.

Reid, M. and Barrington, H. (1997) *Training Interventions* (5th edn). London: IPD.

Revans, R.W. (1980) *Action Learning.* London: Blond and Briggs.

Revans, R.W. (1982) *Origins and Growth of Action Learning.* Bromley: Chartwell Bratt.

Revans, R.W. (1983) *The ABC of Action Learning.* Bromley: Chartwell-Bratt.

Ribeaux, P. and Poppleton, S.E. (1978) *Psychology and Work.* London: Macmillan Education.

Ritzer, G. (1993) *The McDonaldization of Society.* California: Sage Publications.

Robertson, R. (1992) *Globalisation.* London: Sage Publications.

Rogers, C. (1965) *Client-centred Therapy.* Boston: Houghton Mifflin.

Rogers, C. (1969) *Freedom to Learn.* Ohio: Merrill.

Roscoe, J. (1995) 'Learning and training design', in Truelove, S. (ed.) *The Handbook of Training and Development* (2nd edn). Oxford: Blackwell.

Royle, T. (1997) *Globalisation, Convergence and the McDonald's Corporation.* PhD thesis (unpublished). Nottingham: Nottingham Business School.

Salaman, G. (1995) *Managing.* Buckingham: Open University Press.

Sambrook, S. (1998) *Models and Concepts of Human Resource Development: Academic and Practitioner Perspectives.* PhD thesis (unpublished). Nottingham: Nottingham Business School.

Sambrook, S. and Stewart, J. (1998) 'HRD as a discursive construction?', *Leeds–Lancaster*

Conference on Emergent Fields in Management: Connecting Learning and Critique. Leeds University, July.

Sanderson, G. (1995) 'Objectives and evaluation', in Truelove, S. (ed.) *The Handbook of Training and Development* (2nd edn). Oxford: Blackwell.

Scriven, M. (1972) 'Pros and cons about goal-free evaluation', *Evaluation Comment*, Vol. 3, No. 4.

Senge, P.M. (1990) *The Fifth Discipline: The Art and Practice of the Learning Organization.* London: Doubleday.

Senge, P.M. (1993) *The Fifth Discipline: The Art and Practice of the Learning Organisation* (2nd edn). London: Century Business.

Senge, P., Kleiner, A., Roberts, C., Ross, R. and Smith, B. (1994) *The Fifth Discipline Fieldbook.* London: Nicholas Brearly.

Senker, P. (1996) 'The development and implementation of National Vocational Qualifications: an engineering case study', *New Technology, Work and Employment*, Vol. 11, No. 2.

Shackleton, J.R., Clarke, L., Lange, T. and Walsh, S. (1995) *Training for Employment in Western Europe and the United States.* Aldershot: Edward Elgar Publishing.

Sheldrake, J. and Vickerstaff, S. (1987) *The History of Industrial Training in Britain.* Aldershot: Avebury.

Siddons, S. (1997) *Delivering Training.* London: Institute of Personnel and Development.

Simon, H.A. (1960) *The New Science of Management Decision.* New York: Harper & Rowe.

Sloman, M. (1994) 'Coming in from the cold: a new role for trainers', *Personnel Management*, Vol. 26, No. 1.

Smircich, L. and Calas, M.B. (eds) (1995) *Critical Perspectives on Organization and Management Theory.* Aldershot: Dartmouth.

Smithers, A. (1993) *All Our Futures: Britain's Education Revolution*, Channel 4 Television Dispatches Report on Education. London: Channel 4 TV.

Snell, R. (1997), 'Management learning perspectives on business ethics', in Burgoyne, J. and Reynolds, M. (eds) *Management Learning: Integrating Perspectives in Theory and Practice.* London: Sage Publications.

Soskice, D.W. (1994) 'Social skills from mass higher education: lessons from the US', in Layard, R., Mayher, K. and Owen, G. (eds) *Britain's Training Deficit.* Aldershot: Avebury.

Spender, J.-C. (1996) 'Competitive advantage from tacit knowledge? Unpacking the concept and its strategic implications', in Moingeon, B. and Edmondson, A. (eds) *Organizational Learning and Competitive Advantage.* London: Sage Publications.

Stacey, R.D. (1992) *Managing Chaos: Dynamic Business Strategies in an Unpredictable World.* London: Kogan Page.

Stacey, R.D. (1997) *Strategic Management and Organisation Dynamics* (2nd edn). London: Financial Times Pitman Publishing.

Starkey, K. (ed.) (1996) *How Organizations Learn.* London: International Thomson Business Press.

Stata, R. (1996) 'Organizational learning: the key to management innovation', in Starkey, K. (ed.) *How Organizations Learn.* London: International Thomson Business Press.

Stead, V. and Lee, M. (1996) 'Inter-cultural perspectives on HRD', in Stewart, J. and McGoldrick, J. (eds) *Human Resource Development: Perspectives, Strategies and Practice.* London: Financial Times Pitman Publishing.

Stewart, J. (1992) 'Towards a model of HRD', *Training and Development*, Vol. 10, No. 10.

Stewart, J. (1994a) *Organisation Development: History, Perspectives and Relevance to NHS Organisations.* Bristol: NHSTD.

Stewart, J. (1994b) *Speed Training: Systems for Learning in Times of Rapid Change.* London: Kogan Page.

Stewart, J. (1996) *Managing Change Through Training and Development* (2nd edn). London: Kogan Page.

Stewart, J. (1998a) 'The psychology of decision making', in Jennings, D. and Wattam, S. (eds) *Decision Making: An Integrated Approach* (2nd edn). London: Financial Times Pitman Publishing.

Stewart, J. (1998b) 'Intervention and assessment: the ethics of HRD', *Human Resource Development International,* Vol. 1, No. 1.

Stewart, J. and Hamlin, R.G. (1992) 'Competence based qualifications: the case against change', *Journal of European Industrial Training,* Vol. 16, No. 7.

Stewart, J. and Hamlin, R.G. (1993) 'Competence based qualifications: a way forward', *Journal of European Industrial Training,* Vol. 17, No. 6.

Stewart, J. and McGoldrick, J. (eds) (1996a) *Human Resource Development: Perspectives, Strategies and Practice.* London: Financial Times Pitman Publishing.

Stewart, J. and McGoldrick, J. (1996b) 'Editors' Introduction', in Stewart, J. and McGoldrick, J. (eds) *Human Resource Development: Perspectives, Strategies, and Practice.* London: Financial Times Pitman Publishing.

Stewart, J. and Sambrook, S. (1995) 'The role of functional analysis in National Vocational Qualifications: a critical appraisal', in Bates, I. (ed.) *British Journal of Education and Work,* Special Edition, Vol. 8, No. 2.

Stewart, J. and Winter, R. (1995) 'Open and distance learning', in Truelove, S. (ed) *The Handbook of Training and Development* (2nd edn). Oxford: Blackwell Business.

Stewart, R. (1982) *Choices for the Manager.* Maidenhead: McGraw-Hill.

Storey, J. (1989) 'Management development: a literature review', *Personnel Review,* Vol. 18, No. 6.

Storey, J., Edwards, P. and Sisson, K. (1997) *Managers in the Making: Careers, Development and Control in Corporate Britain and Japan.* London: Sage Publications.

Strauss, A., Schatzman, L., Ehrlich, D., Bucher, R. and Sabshin, M. (1963) 'The hospital and its negotiated order', in Friedson, E. (ed.) *The Hospital in Modern Society.* New York: Macmillan.

Swanson, R. and Holton, E. (eds) (1997) *Human Resource Development Handbook: Linking Research and Practice.* San Francisco: Berrett-Hoehler.

Swieringa, J. and Weirdsma, A. (1992) *Becoming a Learning Organisation: Beyond the Learning Curve.* New York: Addison-Wesley.

Tate, W. (1995) *Developing Managerial Competence: A Critical Guide to Methods and Materials.* Aldershot: Gower.

Taylor, P., Richardson, J., Yeo, A., Marsh, I., Trobe, K. and Pilkington, A. (1995) *Sociology in Focus,* Ormskirk: Causeway Press.

Thomson, A., Storey, J., Mabey, C., Grey, C., Farmer, E. and Thomson, R. (1997) *A Portrait of Management Development.* Leamington Spa: Institute of Management.

Torrington, D. (1994) *International Human Resource Management: Think Globally, Act Locally.* Hemel Hempstead: Prentice-Hall.

Torrington, D. and Hall, L. (1998) *Human Resource Management* (4th edn). Hemel Hempstead: Prentice-Hall Europe.

Trassler, J. (1995) 'Open learning: abdication or opportunity?', *Management Training,* Vol. 4, No. 5.

Truelove, S. (ed) (1995) *The Handbook of Training and Development* (2nd edn). Oxford: Blackwell Business.

Truelove, S. (1997) *Training in Practice.* Oxford: Blackwell Business.

van der Klink, M. and Mulder, M. (1995) 'Human resource development and staff flow policy in Europe', in Harzing, A.W. and van Ruysseveldt, J. (eds) *International Human Resource Management.* London: Sage.

Walton, J. (1996) 'The provision of learning support for non-employees', in Stewart, J. and McGoldrick, J. (eds) *Human Resource Development: Perspectives, Strategies and Practice.* London: Financial Times Pitman Publishing.

Warr, P., Bird, P. and Rackham, N. (1970) *Evaluation of Management Training.* Aldershot: Gower.

Waters, M. (1995) *Globalisation.* London: Routledge.

Watson, T.J. (1994) *In Search of Management*. London: Routledge.

Watson, T.J. (1995) *Sociology, Work and Industry* (3rd edn). London: Routledge.

Watson, T.J. (1999) 'Human resourcing strategies: choice, chance and circumstance', in Harris. L., Leopold, J. and Watson, T.J. (eds) *Strategic Human Resourcing: Principles, Perspectives and Practices in HRM*. London: Financial Times Pitman Publishing.

Weick, K.E. (1979) *The Social Psychology of Organising*. Reading, MA: Addison-Wesley.

Whittaker, J. (1995) 'Three challenges for IPD standards', *People Management,* 16 November.

Williams, S. (1996) 'The role of the Action Learning Set', in Stewart, J. and McGoldrick, J. (eds) *Human Resource Development: Perspectives, Strategies and Practice*. London: Financial Times Pitman Publishing.

Willmott, H. (1997) 'Critical management learning', in Burgoyne, J. and Reynolds, M. (eds) *Management Learning: Integrating Perspectives in Theory and Practice*. London: Sage Publications.

Wilson, E. (1996) 'Managing diversity in HRD', in Stewart, J. and McGoldrick, J. (eds) *Human Resources Development: Perspectives, Strategies and Practice*. London: Financial Times Pitman Publishing.

Wood, S. (ed.) (1988) *Continuous Development: The Path to Improved Performance*. London: Institute of Personnel Development.

Woodall, J. and Winstanley, D. (1998) *Management Development: Strategy and Practice*. Oxford: Blackwell Business.

Woodward, J. and Winstanley, D. (1998) *Management Development: Strategy and Practice*. Oxford: Blackwell.

Zaheer, S. (1995) 'Overcoming the liability of foreignness', *Academy of Management Journal,* Vol. 38, No. 2.

INDEX

ABCD campaign   133
Abitur qualification   29
Accreditation of Prior Learning or Achievement
   (APL/APA)   55
accommodator, the   110–11
acquisition of learning   107, 115
action learning   132–3, 138–9, 201, 205, 206–7,
   216
  design and operation   211, 213
  design principles
    projects   208, 211
    self as 'content'   209–10
    set adviser   209
    sets   209–10
    syllabus   209
  philosophy of   207–8
activities, discussion of   5–6
actual behaviour   166
Adler, N.J.   67, 203
advanced industrial countries (AICs)   22–3,
   26–8, 37–8, 58
Alvesson, M.
  management   15, 20, 118, 222, 228
  paradigms   13
  resourcing ED function   261
American Society for Training and Development
   (ASTD)   89
anti-positivist analyses   215
Apprentice Training Centre   32
Apprenticeship Training Tax (France)   31
apprenticeships   29, 38
arena thesis   228
Argyris, C.   103, 212
Arnold, J.   101–2, 108
Ashridge research   129, 130, 133–4
  focused approach   130, 139
  formalised approach   130
  fragmented approach   129, 130
Ashridge Research Group   129–30, 139–40, 283
assessment centres   158
assessment, evaluation and   180–2
Assessors' Award   276
Association of Greek Industries (SEU)   35
associative learning   104–5
assimilator, the   110–11
Australia   22, 26–7
'automatic' knowledge   115
autopoiesis   62, 64, 215

baccalaureat   31
Barber, P.   261–2
Barrington, H.
  continuous development   133–4, 140
  ED activities   171–4
  ED function   82–4, 86
  ED policy   240, 243, 246–8
  education and training   16, 19
  evaluation and   179, 183–7, 191–2
  individual learning and   99, 103
  management and development
    classifications   234–5
  objectives   165, 167–8
  resourcing the ED function   261–2, 268
  specialist ED staff   274–6
  training interventions   163
  training needs   149, 154–8
  VET and   48
Bates, I.   50, 138, 234
Beatty, L.   206, 209–10
Beaumont Report   52–3, 56–7
behavioural objectives   166–9, 173
behaviourist learning theory   104–6, 168, 184,
   283
behaviourist psychology   101
Belgium   25, 27
benchmarking   44, 155, 158, 167, 188, 268
Bennett, R.   87–8, 90
best practice   231
body of knowledge   149
'bottom line', finance and   264
boundary workers as environmental scanners
   11, 214
bounded rationality   11, 63
Bowie, N.E.   240, 245, 250–6
Boydell, T.
  'boundary workers'   11
  'learning company'   131, 136
  management development   223–4
  organisational development   125, 128
  systematic training   136, 138
  training needs   143, 148–9, 151, 154–5,
    157–9
Bramley, P.   179, 186
brevet de technicien (BT)   31–2
brevet d'études professionnelles (BEP)   31–3
British Psychological Society conference   282
British Telecom   89

BTEC National Certificate and National Diploma 31, 42, 48
Burgoyne, J.
  boundary workers   11
  evaluation   187, 194
  learning company   131
  management development   228, 231–3
  paper on learning   282–3
  UK VET system and   50
Burnes, B.   15, 65, 69
Burrell, G.   11–14, 21, 68, 100, 215
business brain   11
business contract   86, 88
Business Growth through Training (BGT)   44

Calas, M.   204–5
Capey Report   52–3, 57
CAPIO framework   189–90
caretaker role   88
case studies,
  1   20–1, 59–61, 76–7, 94–6
  2   118–120, 141–2, 160–2, 176–7, 195–7
  3   156–60, 217–18, 238–9, 258–60, 278–9
categories of employees   246
CBI (Confederation of British Industry)   155
Celinski, D.   243, 247
Centre for Economic Performance   51
certificat d'aptitude professionnelle (CAP)   31–3
Certificate of Vocational Training (Vevaiosi epagelmatikis katartisis)   36
certificated vocational education   55
Chao, G.T.   113–15
change agent role, the   85–6, 88, 90
Chia, R.   13, 221, 223–4, 228–9, 232
CIRO   186
City and Guilds   42, 48
Code of Professional Conduct (1996)   257
coercive power   72–3
cognitive learning theory   106, 107–8
cognitive psychology   101–2, 169
collective knowledge   115
collective learning   225
Commission for Racial Equality (CRE)   237
communication technologies   281
community colleges   34
'comparative' category   205
compensation   220, 235
competence, concept of   54
competitive advantage   22
computer-based training (CBT)   139, 163
conditioning   104–5
conditions component   166, 168
Connock, S.   245, 251–2, 254–6
converger, the   110–11

continuous assessment   168
continuous development   133–4, 139–40, 168
Continuous Development – People and Work   134
continuous development spiral   134
continuous improvement   132–3
continuous professional development (CPD)   74, 276
contribution of ED   78
convergence thesis   65, 67, 205
corporate image   270
cost leadership   72–3
Cowling, A.   22, 42
craft apprenticeship system   33
cramp mnemonic   170–1, 174
criteria concept   181–2
criterion component   166–8
cultural goals, normative power   72

Dearing Report   52–3, 56–7
Dearing, Sir Ron   47
decision making, resource allocation and   264
Deetz, S.   13, 228
deontological ethics   252–5, 257
Department for Education and Employment (DfEE)   6, 46, 140
descriptive theory   230
deutero-learning   212
development   17–19
development activities   168
  implementing   172–3, 175
    plans for   174
    preparation   173–4, 175
    resources   173, 175
differentiation   73, 76
Diploma in Management Studies   3
divergence   205
the diverger   110–11
Dixon, N.   116, 118, 213
Dorrell, J.   272–3
double loop learning   212, 215
Duska, R.F.   240, 245, 250–6

Easterby-Smith evaluation framework   189–90, 192, 195
Easterby-Smith, M.   144–5, 183–6
economic goals, remunerative power   72–3
ED   4–5, 17, 281, 283
  costing and budgeting   263–5
    formulating a budget   267–9
    process of costing activities   265–7
  design and implementation   163
  designing activities   170–1
  evaluation of   182

ED (*continued*)
  function   82–4
  influences on   9–10
  models and approaches   121–2, 140
  organisations and   62, 75
  'people focus'   82
  policy and ethics in   240–1
  role and contribution of   78–9
  understanding the practice of   283–4
ED policy   241–3
  content of written statements   247–9
  ethics and   257–8
  formulating   243–5
  role of ED specialists   245–7
ED roles   84–5
  applying the concept   92–4
  Bennett and Leduchowicz   87–8
  contract model   86–7
  Pettigrew *et al.*   85–6
  recent research   89–91
ED staff
  recruitment   262, 277
  specialist   274–7
ED strategies   201–2
Edmondson, A.   99, 113
education   16–17, 27, 223
Education Reform Act (1988)   46
educational or basic contract   86
educational orientation   87
educator role   88
eleemosynary purposes   254
emergent approach to MD   224, 228, 235
employee development, *see* ED
employer associations   38
employers, VET and   24
Employment for the 1990s   42
Employment Act (1987)   42
Employment Act (1988)   42
Employment Department   23, 237
Employment Occupational Standards Council
  (EOSC)   90, 274–6
Employment and Training Act (1973)   40–1
Employment and Training Act (1981)   41
Employment Training (ET)   42, 44
empowerment   236
enabling objectives   169
enacted environment   11, 63–5
engineering craft apprenticeship, NVQs and   50
equal opportunities   237, 243
Eraut, M.   49, 51
ethics   240–1, 247, 251, 257–8
  ED   249–50
    arguments   251–53
    definitions and meanings   251

organisation and management theory and
  253–6
ethnocentric orientation   204–6
Etzioni, A.   72, 74
European perspective   203
European Union (EU)   53, 66, 203
evaluation   135–6, 138, 176, 178–9, 185
  a central problem   179–82
  ED contributions   178–9, 182
  problems with   191–3, 194
  process of   186–91, 195
  purposes of   183–4, 185, 195
evangelist role   88
experiential learning   109–10, 116, 135, 168,
  184, 282
expert power   73
explicit knowledge   115, 210, 213
external aspect of market labour   22
external courses   171
external processes   62–3, 75, 121
external validation   183

famine   66
Federal Institute of Vocational Education   25,
  28
Federal Vocational Training Act (1969)   28–9
feedback   107, 158–9, 168, 170
Ferrell, O.C.   252, 254
Fisher, C.   21, 136, 166, 267
flexible learning   272
focus   73, 225–6, 235
formal learning   282
formal management development   232
Fraedrich, J.   252, 254
France   25, 28, 34, 37, 45, 267
  VET   47–8, 51, 58
    continuing training for adults   32–3
    initial vocational training system for young
      people   31–2
    some concerns   33
    State Training Fund   27, 57
    state-interventionist approach   38
Fredericks, J.   69, 91, 147, 154, 222, 258
free market in training   51
functional map   138, 143
functional performance   220, 230, 235
functionalist paradigm   12, 19, 68
  action learning and   207, 212
  ED function and   82
  evaluation and   180–1, 191
  policy and   247, 250
  psychology and   100
  resourcing ED function and   261
  systems approach to ED and   163, 175

functionalist paradigm (*continued*)
  training need and   143
  understanding organisations and   281–2
future learning cycle   288

Gagne, R.M.   107–8
Garratt, R.   11, 242–3
GCSE A-levels   46
GEC management centre   271
General Confederation of Workers of Greece
  (GSEE)   35
General National Vocational Qualification
  (GNVQ)   46, 50, 52–3
generalised others   80, 82
geocentric orientation   204–6
Germany
  quality route to competitiveness   22
  VET   34, 37, 45, 47–9, 51, 57–8
    continuing training for adults   30
    dual systems   25, 28
    employer-led corporatism   27, 38
    initial vocational training for young people
      29–30
    some concerns   30–1
  workforce education and   27–8
Giddens, A.   65–6, 79, 81, 185
Gill, J.   144–5
globalisation   63, 65–6, 201, 203–4, 211, 215,
  281
goal directness   109
goals and objectives   70
Golden Rule   254
government policies, ED and   245–6
Government Training Centres (GTCs)   39
Greece   26, 57
  continuing training for adults   35–6
  VET (initial vocational training system for
    young people)   35
Gymnasio (lower secondary level school)   35

Hall, L.   243, 249, 251, 254–5, 257
Hamblin, A.C.   179, 186–7, 189
Hamblin evaluation framework   186–7, 188–9,
  195
  department/organisation level   188
  job behaviour level   187–8, 189
  learning level   187, 189
  organisation level/ultimate value   188
  reaction level   187, 189
  when and how to evaluate   188–9
Hamel, G.   65, 82
Hamlin, R.G.   24, 49–50, 54–6, 59
Handy, C.   16, 92, 225
hard data   154–5

Harrison, R.
  ED   82, 84–6, 90
  ED policy   246–8
  evaluation   178–9, 183, 185–6, 188, 192
  globalisation and   65
  HRD   17–19
  individual learning   99, 103
  learning need   143
  learning objectives   165, 169, 172–4
  MD   220–2, 224, 226–8, 230, 234–5
  power in organisations   73–4, 78
  resourcing the ED function   261–2, 268, 272
  specialist ED staff and   274–6
  training needs   148–9, 156–9
  VET systems and   22, 30–1, 51–2
  vision and   69
Helping Businesses to Win (1994)   45
Higher Education: a new framework   46
Higher Education Funding Councils   46
higher education (HE) institutions   46, 55
Hilgard, E.R.   104, 107–8, 110–12
Holland   25, 49
Honey, P.   110–11
host country nationals (HCNs)   204
House of Commons Employment Committee on
  the Work of TECs   51
Huczynski, A.   69, 233
human resource development (HRD)   1, 4,
  17–19, 73, 82, 136, 201
  assessment and   180
  model of   18, 99, 117–18, 257
  specialists   74–5, 86, 91, 147, 152, 257–8,
    276
humanist psychology   102, 169
Humanistic learning theory   110–12

'I'   80, 223
identifying training needs (ITN)   135–6, 137–8,
  151–9
Iles, P.A.   203–6
Images of Organization   10
impact in MD   237
implicit knowledge   210, 213
implicit learning   113–16, 210
in-house training   32, 171
indicative behaviours   168
individual employees' training needs   149
individual learning   18, 99, 103–4, 117, 225,
  282
individual learning accounts   47, 58
individual level training needs   149, 158–9
Individual Performance Review (IPR)   136–7
individual training leave (France)   32
individuals, VET and   24

Industrial Training: Government Proposal (1962) 39

Industrial Training Act (1964)   39–40, 43

Industrial Training Boards (ITBs)   39–41

Industrial Training Research Unit   170

Industry Training Organisations (ITOs)   41–3, 51

inferred competence   55

informal and incidental learning   171, 282

informal managerial development   232

information processors   101

information technologies   22, 281

innovator role   88–9

insight   110–12

Institute of Management   236

Institute of Personnel and Development (IPD)   1–2, 4, 133–4, 257, 274–6

Institutes of Vocational Training (IEK)   35–6

institutionalised and generalised limitations   81

institutions of learning
  institutionalised learning   282

integrated managerial development   232

intentions, ethical standard and   253

inter-cultural competence   206

interactive video (IV)   139, 174, 269

intermediate objective   169

internal aspect of market labour   22

internal consultant   90

internal processes   82, 88–9, 73, 121

internal validation   183

International Monetary Fund   66

internationalisation of ED   201, 202–3, 216
  connections with globalisation   203–5
  development methods   205–6

interpretive paradigm   12, 81, 169, 175, 180, 193, 215, 247

interrupted apprenticeship scheme   39

intervention orientation   87

interventions   18, 257

interviews   193

Investors in People (IIP)   44–5, 138, 194, 246

Italy   27, 51

Jackson, B.   228, 233

Jacobs, R.   50, 147

Jagger, N.   23, 28

Jaguar Cars   273

Japan   68, 115, 204
  management development   237
  VET   22, 28, 34, 45
    general education system   25–6
    State-led employer co-operation   27

job/occupation training needs   149, 154, 156–9

John Lewis Partnership   271

Johns, T.   245, 251–2, 254–6

Johnson, G.   70, 136, 155

Johnson, P.   144–5

Johnston, R.   73–4

Jones, J.A.G.   86–8

Jones, J.E.   222, 225, 230–1, 234

Kant, Immanuel   254–5

Kelly, G.A.   102, 108

Kirkpatrick, D.L.   179, 186, 195

knowledge company   99

knowledge creation   201

knowledge, skills and attitudes, *see* KSA

knowledge workers   99

Kolb, D.A.   109–10, 116, 288

KSA   149–52, 158, 170, 172
  attitudes   18, 157–8
  knowledge   18, 156
  skills   18, 157

Labour Code (France)   32

latent learning   107

Law 2009 (1992, Greece)   35

Layard, R.   28, 36, 51, 58

Lead Bodies (LBs)   42–3, 51

Learning Age (1998)   37, 46, 47, 57, 59

learning company   131, 213

learning organisations   11, 99, 103, 113, 132–4, 183
  concept   201, 211–12, 215–16, 283
  features of   212–15
  Senge on   245

learning processes, understanding   282–3

learning resource centre   262, 270, 272–4

learning to learn   212

learning unit objectives   169

Leary, M.   138, 143, 148–9, 151, 154–5, 157–9

Leduchowicz, T.   87–8, 90

Lee, M.   205–6, 223–4, 228, 247

Legge, K.   13, 190

legitimate power   73

Liberal Democratic Party   57

lifelong learning   246

line managers   83, 276

Lloyds TSB   271, 273

Local Enterprise Companies (LECs)   43, 47, 51–2

Local Government Training Board   39

Lorbiecki, A.   202, 204–5

Low Pay Commission   58

Lundy, O.   22, 42

Lykeia (upper secondary level education colleges)   35–6

McDonaldization 67
McGill, I. 206, 209–10
McGoldrick, J. 17, 19, 71, 82, 128, 132, 201
McKinsey management consultants 58
Mabey, C. 220–1, 230
Mager, R.F. 166–8
management 15–16, 19
Management Charter Initiative (MCI) 43, 50, 54, 234
management development 219–20
  see also MD
Manpower Services Commission (MSC) 16–17, 40–2, 82
map, concept of 123–4
market labour matrix 22
Marxist analyses of society 282
Maslow, A.H. 102, 104
mastery learning 50, 54
maturation approach to MD 224, 228, 235
maturity 231–2
May, T. 144–5, 151, 193
MBA programmes 3
MD (management development)
  approaches and methods 229–30
    approaches 230–3
    methods 233–6
  definitions and meanings 224–7, 237
  overview 220–1, 227, 229, 231, 235
    nature of development 222–4, 228, 235
    nature of managerial work 221–2
  practice 236–7
'me' 80
measurement, finance and 264
Megginson, D. 17, 125, 128, 134, 136, 139
Megginson model 125, 140
  the administrative approach 126–7, 139
  the organisation development approach 128, 139
  the political approach 127, 139
  the welfare approach 126, 139
methodological pluralism 147, 159
Ministry of National Education and Religious Affairs (MNERA) 35
Mintzberg, H. 70, 136, 221
mission 69, 71, 242
model, nature of 123–5
Modern Apprenticeships 47, 49, 53, 57
Moingeon, B. 99, 113
Moorby, E.
  ED 78, 90
  evaluation and 185
  globalisation and 65
  organisation objectives and 19
  organisation purpose 69–70, 73–4

resourcing the ED function 261–2, 268, 271–2
training needs and 148–9
Morgan, G. 10–11
  autopoiesis 62, 64
  MD 228
  ontological oscillation and 143
  paradigms and 12–14, 21, 68, 81, 143
  psychology and 100
motivation 104, 107
mud mnemonic 170–1, 174
Mullins, L.J. 69, 83, 136
multinational corporation (MNC) 203
Mumford, A. 50, 110–11, 221–8, 231–6
Myers, D.G. 79, 99–101, 103–8, 112

National Advisory Council on Education and Training Targets (NACETT) 44–5
National Council for the Training of Journalists (NCTJ) 49
National Council for Vocational Qualifications (NCVQ 1986) 41–2, 46, 48, 50–2, 54
National Curriculum 46
National Education and Training Targets (1993) 44
National Skills Task Force 47
National targets 44–6
National Traineeships 47, 52
National Training Initiative (NTI) 41–2
National Vocational Qualifications, see NVQs
National Westminster Bank 271
natural disasters 66
naturalism 145–7, 159
New Adult Training Programme 42
New Training Initiative – A Programme for Action 41
non-employee development 276–7
non-participant observation 146–7
non-realist conception of world 144–5, 155, 179–80, 215
Nonaka, I. 99, 114–16, 213
normative theory 230, 250
NVQs 26, 28, 41, 43–5, 47, 132
  criticism of 48–51, 58–9, 138
  ED and 180
  evaluation and 182, 194
  observation and comments 53–7
  research findings on 89–90, 140
  specialist ED staff and 275–6

objective data 154, 193
objective knowledge 114
objectives 15, 164–5, 167
  hierarchies of 169–70
  work of R.F. Mager 166–7

observation   146, 170, 193
observational learning   106–7
Occupational Standards Councils (OSCs)   51
off-the-job training   28–9, 33–4, 35, 171, 173, 234
on-the-job training   28–9, 32–3, 171, 173
ontological oscillation   215
OPEC   66
operant conditioning   105–6
opportunity cost   266, 270
order, coercive power   72
organisation learning   18, 99, 113–17, 201
organisation and management theory   4, 62
Organisation for Manpower Employment (OAED Greece)   35
organisation maturity   231
organisation memory   115
organisation readiness   230–1
organisation structure   69
organisation training needs   149, 154–5
Organisation for Vocational Education and Training (OEEK)   35
organisational contingencies   230–1
organisational learning cycle   117
organisations   10–15, 19, 62, 68
  external context   62, 63, 75, 121
    globalisation   65–6
    limiting factors   63–5
    other arguments   67–8
  internal context   68–9, 75, 121
    implications for practice   74–5
    political dimension   72–3, 175, 210
    purpose   69–71
  negotiated orders and   79
  understanding   281–2
  unitary conception of   228
Oswick, C.   128, 262
'ownership' of MD processes   232
Oxford English Dictionary definitions
  evaluate   179–80
  policy   241

paradigms   6, 11–13, 143–4, 250
  alternative   19, 68, 75, 175, 195, 212, 250, 281–3
parent country nationals (PCNs)   204, 206
Pareto analysis   155
participant observation   146–7
the passive provider role   85, 88
Pavlov, Ivan   104–5
Pedler, M.   11, 99
  boundary workers   11
  ED and   131–4, 136, 138, 140, 209, 283
  learning organisation   99, 211–15

MD   223–4, 233
  policy in ED   245
peer assessment   159, 184
performance appraisal   158, 180
performance gap   148–9
Perlmutter, H.V.   204–5
person-centred and non-directive therapy   112
personal constructs schema   108
Pettigrew, A.   85, 88, 90
phenomenological view of reality   102
Piaget, Jean   101, 108
planned organisation experience   171
policy   240–1, 258
policy and ethics, ED   240–1
political reinforcement   220, 235
polycentric orientation   204–5
polytechnics, universities and   46
Poppleton, S.E.   101, 105
Porter, M.E.   72–3, 76
positivism   145–7, 159, 194–5, 207
post-structural/ethnographic category   205
postmodernism   13, 215
power   72–4, 210
Prahalad, C.K.   65, 82
Private Industry Councils (PICs)   43
problem, definition   152–3
problem/solution model of ED   131
  1950–70   131–2
  1970–85   132
  1985–95   132
Professional Education Scheme   1
programmed knowledge   210
the provider role   85, 88, 90
providers of VET   24
psychic defence, MD and   220
psychological egoism   253
psychology   100–2, 117
Puxty, A.G.   261–2

Qualifications and Curriculum Authority (QCA)   46, 52, 54
questionnaires   146, 159, 189, 193

radical humanist paradigm   12–13, 169, 175, 180
radical structuralist paradigm   13, 169, 175, 212
realist conception of world   144–5, 155, 159, 179, 191, 207
record keeping   247
recruitment and selection   180, 243, 262, 274, 276
referent power   73
regiocentric orientation   204–5

Reid, M.
  continuous development   133–4, 140
  ED activities   171–4
  ED function   82–4, 86
  ED policy   240, 243, 246–8
  education and training   16, 19
  evaluation and   179, 183–7, 191–2
  individual learning and   99, 103
  MD classifications   234–5
  objectives   165, 167–8
  resourcing the ED function   261–2, 268
  specialist ED staff and   274–6
  training interventions   163
  training needs   149, 154–8
  VET and   48
reinforcement of learning   105
relativistic   205, 252, 254
replacement training and development   87
reported information   193
Research Lead Body   143
resource-based learning   272
resourcing the ED function   261–3
  physical   269–70, 277
    learning resource centres (LRCs)   272–4
    training centres   271–2
Revans, R.W.   110, 133, 139, 206–10
Review of Vocational Qualifications   49
reward, power and   73
Ribeaux, P.   101, 104–5
Ritzer, G.   65, 67–8, 136
Robertson, R.   65–6
role in transition   85, 90
roles   78–81, 84–6, 88, 90–4
Roscoe, J.   167, 173
Rover Group   273
RSA awards   42

Salaman, G.   220–1, 230
Sambrook, S.   49, 137–8, 143, 147, 234, 262
Sanderson, G.   165–8, 183, 185, 192
schema   108
Scholes, K.   70, 136, 155
Schon, D.   103, 212
Schools Curriculum Assessment Authority (SCAA)   46, 52
science concept   100
scientific knowledge   114
scientific management   101, 136, 138, 207
Scotland   41, 43
Scottish Affairs Committee of Inquiry into the Work of LECs   52
Scottish Vocational Qualifications (SVQs)   26, 41, 43
Scottish Widows   273

secondary contract   86
'self'   80
self-assessment   158–9, 184
self-development   17, 132, 134, 138–9, 201, 213, 276
self-managed learning   171
self-observation   159
Senge, P.   99, 211–15, 245
Senker, P.   49–51, 53
Shackelton, J.R.   27–8
shaping approach to MD   224, 228, 235
Sheldrake, J.   40–1
sign learning   107
significant others   80, 82, 88
Simon, H.A.   11, 63
Singh, R.   187, 194
single loop learning   212, 215
Skinner, B.F.   101, 104–6
Sloman, M.   90–1
small and medium-sized enterprises (SMEs)   58
Smith, Adam   254
Smithers, A.   48–50, 53
Smithers Report   48
SNVQs   41–2, 52
social learning theory   106–7
social and management research   144–8
social psychology   100
social responsibilities   246, 255–6
soft data   154–5
Soskice, D.W.   30, 34, 58
special measures scheme   40
Spender, J.C.   113–14
spiral of knowledge   115
staff   83
stakeholders   24, 132, 245, 255, 283–4
start-up costs   270
state-interventionist approach   38, 40, 57
State, The   24
step analysis   155
Stewart, J.
  assessment   180–1
  criticism of NVQs   49–50, 54–6
  ED   82, 174
  ED models   128, 132, 138
  ED strategies   201, 206–7, 209, 211–13, 215
  experiential learning and   109–10
  globalisation and   65
  HRD   17–19, 91, 257–8
  management   15
  MD   221–2, 234–5
  organisation and   62, 69, 71
  psychology   100–2
  resourcing ED   262, 272–3
  training needs   143, 147, 154–5

Storey, J. 220, 237
strategic facilitator 90–1
strategy 70–1
subjective assessment 181–2, 194
success in IPD examinations 284
  assess resources 285–6
  devise strategy 285
  formulate action plan 287
  mission statement 284–5
  plan tactics 286
  set objectives 285
successional planning 243
Sugar, Alan 284–5
sunrise industries 34
Sweden 25, 27
swot analysis 155
symbolic interactionism 81
System Beta 110, 207
systematic training 131–2, 134, 136
systematic training cycle 135, 143, 163
systems approach 134–6, 138–40, 163

tacit knowledge 113–14
'taken for granted' structures 116
Tate, W. 50, 234
Taylor, P. 79, 81
Tayloristic conception 261, 281
team learning 214–15
Technical Instruction Act (1889) 38
Technical and Vocational Education Initiative
  (TVEI) 45
Technical-Vocational School (TES) 35–6
techniques (means) 15
teleological ethics 252–3, 255
televisions 173
a theory 123–4
Thomson, A. 17, 233, 236–7
threshold competence or potential competence
  54–5
Torrington, D. 65, 203, 243, 249, 251, 254–5,
  257
Total Quality Management (TQM) 20, 44, 133
trade unions 24, 27, 32, 38, 40, 47, 155
Trades Union Council 42
Trading Standards Council 47
trainer roles 88, 91, 94
training, definition 16, 223
Training Agency 42
Training and Enterprise Councils (TECs) 43, 47,
  51–2
  and local enterprise companies 43–4
Training Commission 42
Training Credit (TC) scheme 44
training cycle 137–40, 276

design stage 135–6, 139
evaluation and 176, 178, 185, 195
financial techniques and 267
Training and Development Lead Body (TDLB)
  43, 89–90, 276
Training for Employment (1986) 42
training gap 148–50
training levy scheme 27, 31
training manager role 85
training needs 143–4, 147, 159, 165
  identifying 151, 155
    individual level 158–9
    job/occupation level 149, 154, 156–8, 159
    organisation level 154–5
    training and non-training problems 151–3
  nature of 148–9
    three-level framework 149–50
training policy 242–3
Training Standards Council 47
training strategy 163
transnational 203
the training manager role 85
Truelove, S.
  ED 166, 168–9, 172–4
  evaluation 179, 191–2
  individual learning 99
  resourcing ED function 261
  training needs 143, 148–9, 151, 154, 157, 159
Types of training, policy and 248

UK 24, 28, 34, 36–7, 66, 130
  educated workforce and 27
  European companies and 203
  HRD practice and 147
  MD in 236–7
  short-termism 38, 58
  systems approach in work organisations 138
  VET 22–3, 28, 36–7, 57
    historical perspective 37–8
    market-based systems 27
    mixed system 26
    national system (1889–1979) 38–40
    national system (1980–1998) 41–3
    observations and comments 53–4
    review of current system 47–53
    way forward 54–7
  voluntarism 27, 38, 40–1, 43, 57–8
unconditioned stimuli 105
United Nations 66
universal systems of ethics 252
universalistic 205
University of Industry (Ufi) 47
USA 22, 25, 28, 47, 58–9
  HRD practice and 147

USA (*continued*)
  market-based systems of VET   27
  Private Industry Councils (PICs)   43
  VET
    continuing training for adults   34
    initial vocational training system for young
      people   33–4
    some concerns about   34
utilitarianism   254

validation   183
VE-certificated evidence   55
VET   4, 22, 23–4
  adults
    employer-led corporatism   27
    market-based systems   27
    State intervention   26–7
    State-led employer co-operation   27
  an initial comparison of   27–8
  international comparison of national   28–53
  young people   24–5
    broad occupational system   25
    dual system   25
    general education system   25–6
    mixed system   26
    State-led system   25
    see also France, Germany, Greece, UK and
      USA
Vickerstaff, S.   40–1
video players   173, 269
virtual university   281
vision   69, 71, 215
vocational education and training, *see* VET

voluntarism   27, 38, 40–1, 43, 57–8
voyage approach to MD   224, 228, 235

Walton, J.   18, 276
Warr, P.   186, 195
Waters, M.   65–6
Watson, J.B.   101, 104, 106
Watson, T.J.
  ED models   136
  ED policy and ethics   243, 245, 249
  ED strategies   201
  MD   221–2, 229–30, 233
  organisations and   68–70, 72
  postmodernist ideas   13, 15
Weick, K.E.   11, 64
whistle blowing   256
Willmott, H.
  action learning   207
  management   15, 20, 118, 222
  paradigms   13, 212
  resourcing ED function   261
Wolverhampton Business School   59, 203
Wood, S.   133–4
Woodcock, M.   222, 225, 230–1, 234
Working Together – Education and Training   41
works councils (Germany)   30
world view of reality   102, 121–2
world-class education and training   58–9

Youth Credit (YC) scheme   44
Youth Opportunities Programme (YOP)   40
Youth Training Scheme (YTS)   41–2, 44
Youth Training (YT)   44, 52